Crypto Anarchy, Cyberstates, and Pirate Utopias

DATE DUE

Digital Communication
Edward Barrett, editor

Crypto Anarchy, Cyberstates, and Pirate Utopias

edited by
Peter Ludlow

The MIT Press
Cambridge, Massachusetts
London, England

This book was set in Adobe Sabon in QuarkXPress by Asco Typesetters, Hong Kong. Printed and bound in the United States of America.

Library of Congress Cataloging-in-Publication Data

Crypto anarchy, cyberstates, and pirate utopias / edited by Peter Ludlow.
    p.   cm. — (Digital communication)
  Includes bibliographical references and index.
  ISBN 0-262-12238-3 (hc: alk. paper)—ISBN 0-262-62151-7 (pbk: alk. paper)
  1. Cyberspace—Social aspects. 2. Cyberspace—Political aspects. 3. Internet—Social aspects. 4. Internet—Political aspects. 5. Anarchy. 6. State, The.
I. Ludlow, Peter. II. Series.
HM851 .C78 2001

                                                                    00-064597

per i nipoti
Jay, Eliza, Robert, Stefanie, Giuliana, Daniela

and in memory of John Calvin Robertson,
who visited many Temporary Autonomous Zones in his 43 years

Let us admit that we have attended parties where for one brief night a republic of gratified desires was attained. Shall we not confess that the politics of that night have more reality and force for us than those of, say, the entire U.S. Government?

—Hakim Bey

Contents

Series Foreword

Digital communication is one of the most exciting, rapidly expanding fields of study and practice throughout the world, as witnessed by the increasing number of Web sites and users of the Internet, as well as publication and use of multimedia CD-ROM titles in schools, homes, and corporate environments. In addition, Web and multimedia publications have created a vast secondary literature of scholarly analysis in a range of subject areas. Professional societies and degree-granting programs devoted to digital communication have steadily increased. And the language and concepts of digital life have become central in popular culture. In cyberspace the roles of writer and audience are no longer static but dynamic; the concept of text is no longer fixed but fluid. Computational technology has delivered us a powerful tool for the creation, presentation, exchange, and annotation of a text (in words, images, video, and audio)—so powerful that we speak in terms of transparent and seamless information environments that integrate all media.

We are witnessing a profound revolution in communication and learning in a post-Gutenberg world. The MIT Press series on digital communication will present advanced research into all aspects of this revolutionary change in our forms of expression, thought, and being. This research will be published in traditional book format or as Web sites or multimedia CD-ROM titles as demanded by content. As this series finds its expression in hard-copy or in digital format, it will seek to explore and define new genres of thought and expression offered by digital media.

Edward Barrett

Preface

When I edited *High Noon on the Electronic Frontier* (MIT Press, 1996), my principal strategy was to include a number of nonacademic "rants and manifestos" that would raise philosophical issues in an interesting and provocative way. I explained the genesis of the strategy as follows (pp. xvii–xviii):

In the fall of 1994 I taught an undergraduate course entitled "Philosophical Issues on the Electronic Frontier." My plan was to lead with Julian Dibbell's *Village Voice* article "A Rape in Cyberspace" and then move to more standard readings that might typically be taught in a course on computer ethics. Things began well enough, but the class slipped into a collective coma when we moved on to the standard academic readings in this area. Accordingly, I did what any reasonable person would do under the same circumstances—I sold out. I went back to assigning the more "in your face" rants and manifestos that are easy enough to find in cyberspace but virtually impossible to find in textbooks.

When I turned to the more gonzo readings, the class woke up (which always helps when you are trying to teach something) and it actually began to think seriously about some of the deeper issues underlying these assigned electronic rants. This shouldn't be surprising, really. Most of the academic writing on cyberspace is just awful. It either reeks of half-learned post-modern cant, or is a dense thicket of bad sociology. It puts me to sleep, so why shouldn't it put my students to sleep? Besides, even for students, it is sometimes more fun to actually do the thinking part yourself. Sometimes we academics can analyze things to death, when maybe it would be better to set up the problem in an interesting way, and then just leave the room.

At the time I wondered if readers would get it. Would they be angry that I had validated these rough and, at times, shrill essays by juxtaposing them with serious academic work, or would they understand that the essays were there to initiate discussion and have some fun with rather than give the final word about the nature of cyberspace?

What I discovered was that not only did most readers get it but that they resonated to the idea very strongly. I was surprised by the number of reviewers who commented favorably on this strategy. The sympathetic comments came from quarters like *Internet Underground*, but they also came from unlikely sources like the *Times Higher Education Supplement*. Meanwhile, the *Chronicle of Higher Education* reprinted the above *High Noon* passage in its Melange column.

Naturally I began to wonder about this strong reaction. On the one hand, it seemed to me that there was a great deal of pent-up hostility toward academic discourse. Too many intelligent laypersons have been frozen out of a conversation that would otherwise interest them and to which they probably have much to contribute. But on the academic side, it seemed to me that scholars were feeling constrained by the rules that govern proper academic discourse. Perhaps that frustration was already evinced by the post-Derridian word salad currently popular in certain academic circles. In any case, I concluded that many academics, like myself, were wondering if there might not be some way to loosen up the language of the academy—to make it less dry, more accessible, and at the same time more reflective of the energy and excitement that many of us experience in our research (excitement that is almost never reflected in the pages of our journal articles).

On this score, *High Noon* had been successful, but I began to wonder if the general strategy could be extended from trendy topics like the nature of the self in cyberspace to topics that fall within the purview of political philosophy (albeit with a cyberspace angle). Would it be possible to construct a collection, using nonstandard contributions from intelligent laypersons, that could inform readers about key conceptual issues surrounding the emergence of governance structures within online communities or even about the visions of political sovereignty shaping some of those communities? I hoped so.

Take the issue of anarchy. For whatever reason, most of us suppose that anarchists are long-haired freaks who throw Molotov cocktails through bank windows. In point of fact, anarchy is nothing of the kind. As the interview with Noam Chomsky in the appendix makes clear, it is rather a thesis that hierarchical authority must be justified (often it can) and that when institutions of authority cannot be justified, they should be dismantled. It is not a thesis about the blanket rejection of authority or morality (to the contrary, autonomy places a great moral burden on each of us).

The reason that anarchy becomes a topic of interest in cyberspace is simply that with the widespread availability of various technologies (such as public key cryptography) it now appears that certain anarchist ideals may be possible, if not inevitable. That is, cryptography and related technologies like anonymous remailers and electronic cash may undermine the concentrations of power that we are currently familiar with (nation states, for example), thus allowing us to take on substantially more individual responsibility.

Anarchy is not the only possible outcome as we begin to colonize cyberspace. I expect that there will be a great deal of experimentation with various legal systems in different virtual communities. Indeed, we have already seen some evidence of this. One marvelous example is the experimentation with governance structure on LambdaMOO, from aristocracy (in this case rule by "wizards") to the "New Direction" (LambdaMOO's grand experiment in democracy) and back to the aristocracy. The best part is that all of these changes and the debates surrounding them have been archived. What a fantastic resource for studying the emergence and development of political structures in virtual communities. Indeed, I think that MOOs and other virtual communities can be seen as laboratories for the governance structures that will emerge in the new millennium. Many of these experiments will fail, but given the sheer number and variation in the possible experimental settings, new and superior governance structures are bound to emerge.

Are genuine utopias also in the works? Well, we've heard a lot about possible utopias since Thomas More (indeed, since Plato's *Republic*), but so far we haven't seen anything remotely utopian in the real world. But perhaps that is because we are looking for a grand, even global, utopia. Genuine utopias are more likely to be small, community-based, and fleeting. And perhaps the Internet provides the opportunity for utopias to emerge in various remote corners of cyberspace—in various "islands in the Net," to borrow a phrase from Bruce Sterling.

These are just some of the general themes that I wanted to touch on, but there are also possible themes that are conspicuously absent here.

For example, I have studiously avoided important issues of cyberspace law such as government censorship of the Net, the right to Internet access, and so on. These are important issues, but they are issues about the relation between current governance structures and the Net. Here I am more concerned about the emergence of new governance structures *within* the Net than with efforts to establish legal sovereignty over the Net. To me, these are the conceptually interesting issues, and if they seem relatively unimportant or otherworldly now, in the fullness of time I think they will become central to our understanding of the complex worlds that we inhabit.

While some cyberspace collections tend to be unstructured, it seems to me that this material suggests a certain linear logic of exposition. In section I, we take up the issue of the sovereignty of the Internet, beginning with John Perry Barlow's "Declaration of the Independence of cyberspace." This essay offers the provocative claim that the traditional nation states have no legitimate authority over cyberspace. Not surprisingly, Barlow's piece has generated a fair bit of criticism, most of it concluding that Barlow is offering a kind of escape from reality. Others have held that this criticism may be hasty.

Whatever the merits of political independence for cyberspace, it would be a mistake to conclude that it is unfeasible on technological grounds. In section 2 we take up the question of how widespread access to resources like Pretty Good Privacy and anonymous remailers allow the possibility of crypto anarchy—in effect, carving out space for activities that lie outside of the purview of nation states and other traditional powers.

As we will see, crypto anarchy may not be necessary to carve out spaces that are autonomous from the nation states: to a large degree this is already taking place without the help of encryption technologies. The readings in section 3 show that the growth of commerce on the Internet is generating questions of legal jurisdiction and taxation for which the geographic boundaries of nation states seem obsolete. It appears ever more likely that independent online legal jurisdictions will be established and that they will remain largely independent of standard terrestrial legal authorities.

If politically autonomous islands in the Net do become possible, then what sort of governance structures will arise? As we see in section 4, there is plenty of room for experimentation. Indeed, experimentation is already under way. A number of online communities, including MUDs and MOOs, have evolved from experiments that move from lawlessness to democracies, from virtual aristocracies to democracies, and in at least one case, from aristocracy to democracy and back to a form of limited aristocracy. There have been experiments with virtual lawmaking, with virtual magistrates, and with forms of virtual punishment. What can we learn from these experiments? What can they tell us about the future governance structures of the islands in the Net? Will they give rise to just and equitable governance institutions that respect individual moral autonomy? Or will they go the way of real-world (RW) governments?

Many have argued that the emerging governance structures need not go the way of the RW governments. Indeed, some writers have advanced a utopian vision of the sort of future that will be ushered in by these islands in the Net. Others argue that this is sheer turn-of-the-millennium escapism. But again, perhaps that criticism is driven by a misunderstanding of the kinds of utopias expected—not grand permanent governance structures but rather fleeting, isolated "pirate utopias."

Who's right about the outcome of all this? In a certain sense it doesn't matter. If the birth of the Internet and the emergence of crypto anarchy at the dawn of a new millennium in the West bring us utopian visions, perhaps that is all for the best, even if those visions never come to fruition. It is so rare that we sit back and reflect in a deep way on our existing political structures. If it takes a new technology and a new millennium to get us to reflect, then let us be thankful that a new millennium and a new technology are upon us. For surely, in the grand scheme of things, the political options currently available to us in the real world are negligible. Nowhere is this more true than in the United States, where the differences between the Republican and Democrat Parties are played up as being monumental, and shifts in power are characterized as revolutions, but in reality the differences are vanishingly small. Perhaps that becomes clear only if we gaze on the political landscape of the last ten centuries rather than the last ten days. Perhaps it takes utopian visions—

in this case, visions grounded in the emerging information technologies of our age—to give us the inspiration to reflect on how things *could* be, and, more important, how they *should* be.

But ultimately my principle goal with this book is not to inspire new utopias or even deeper thought about possible governance structures: it is first and foremost to have some fun while entertaining these possibilities. Thus, the heroes of this work include Haakon the wizard, a couple of cypherpunks, an assortment of science fiction writers, journalists, cattle ranchers, college professors, and whatever it is that Hakim Bey is. They are an eclectic assortment, to be sure, but no more eclectic than the online world itself. My hope is that this collection reflects some of the diversity of views in the online world today and that it shows the tremendous creativity and energy of the current denizens of that world. In my opinion, this is where the *real* end-of-the-millennium party is taking place. In the years to come, the suits may colonize cyberspace and turn it into a vast suburban shopping mall, and the current party may be forced to dissolve, but the lesson of this collection is that it cannot be dissolved forever and that the party will start up again on some island in the Net. And here's the best part: If you can find us, you are welcome to join in. See you there.

Peter Ludlow
ludlow@well.com

About the Contributors

John Perry Barlow is a retired Wyoming cattle rancher, a former lyricist for the Grateful Dead, and cofounder of the Electronic Frontier Foundation. Since May 1998, he has been a fellow at Harvard Law School's Berkman Center for Internet and Society.

Richard Barbrook is cofounder of the Hypermedia Research Center.

William E. Baugh Jr. is Vice President, Information and Technology Systems Sector, Science Applications International Corporation. He is former assistant director Federal Bureau of Investigation.

David S. Bennahum is a contributing editor at *Wired, Spin, Lingua Franca*, and *I.D.* His articles have appeared in the *New York Times, Harper's Bazaar, New York, The Economist, Marketing Computers, Slate, Feed*, and *NetGuide*.

Hakim Bey (a.k.a. Peter Lamborn Wilson) has been described as "the Marco Polo of the subunderground." Apart from his underground classic *Temporary Autonomous Zones* (part of which is reprinted in this volume), he has written essays on topics ranging from neopaganism to simian aesthetics.

David Brin is a scientist and best-selling novelist. His 1989 thriller *Earth* foresaw both global warming and the World Wide Web. A movie with Kevin Costner was loosely based on his book *The Postman*, and another movie based on his book *Startide Rising* is in preproduction at Paramount Pictures. Brin's nonfiction book—*The Transparent Society: Will Technology Make Us Choose between Freedom and Privacy?*—deals with threats to openness and liberty in the new wired age. His latest novel, *Foundation's Triumph*, brings to a grand finale Isaac Asimov's famed Foundation Universe.

Andy Cameron is cofounder of the Hypermedia Research Center.

Dorothy E. Denning is Professor, Department of Computer Science, Georgetown University and is author of *Information Warfare and Security*.

Mark Dery is a cultural critic. His writings on fringe culture, technology, mass media, and the arts have appeared in the *New York Times, Rolling Stone, Wired, 21.C, Mondo 2000, Elle, Interview, New York*, and the *Village Voice*. He is a regular contributor to *Virtual City*, for which he writes a column of pop cyber-crit called Uplist. He is the author of *Culture Jamming* and *Escape Velocity* and is the editor of *Flame Wars: The Discourse of Cyberculture*.

Duncan Frissell is an attorney and privacy consultant. He writes and speaks about the political and social effects of communications technology.

Eric Hughes is cofounder of the Cypherpunks.

Karrie Jacobs is an architecture and design critic and is the editor-in-chief of *Dwell*, a new, San Francisco–based magazine of residential design that depicts home as a laboratory for both aesthetic and cultural innovation.

David R. Johnson is chair of Connsel Connect and codirector of the Cyberspace Law Institute.

Timothy C. May is a former Intel physicist who retired at the age of thirty-four and has since devoted his energies to crypto rights. He is a cofounder of the Cypherpunks.

Jennifer Mnookin is associate professor of law at the University of Virginia Law School.

Nathan Newman is a Ph.D. student at the University of California at Berkeley.

David G. Post is visiting associate professor at Georgetown University Law Center, codirector of the Cyberspace Law Institute, and policy fellow for the Electronic Frontier Foundation.

Jedediah S. Purdy is a senior correspondent of the *American Prospect* and a student at Yale Law School. He is author of *For Common Things: Irony, Trust, and Commitment in America Today*. In 1999 he was a faculty member at the Century Institute Summer Program on America's liberal and progressive political traditions.

Charles J. Stivale is professor at and chair of the department of French at Wayne State University.

Crypto Anarchy, Cyberstates, and Pirate Utopias

1

New Foundations: On the Emergence of Sovereign Cyberstates and Their Governance Structures

Peter Ludlow

The Sovereignty of Cyberspace

On February 8, 1996, shortly after the Telecommunications Act of 1996 (which contained the Communications Decency Act) was signed into law by President Bill Clinton, John Perry Barlow uploaded his "Declaration of the Independence of Cyberspace." His declaration (see chapter 2 in this volume) began as follows:

A Declaration of the Independence of Cyberspace
Governments of the Industrial World, you weary giants of flesh and steel, I come from Cyberspace, the new home of Mind. On behalf of the future, I ask you of the past to leave us alone. You are not welcome among us. You have no sovereignty where we gather.

We have no elected government, nor are we likely to have one, so I address you with no greater authority than that with which liberty itself always speaks. I declare the global social space we are building to be naturally independent of the tyrannies you seek to impose on us. You have no moral right to rule us, nor do you possess any methods of enforcement we have true reason to fear.

Governments derive their just powers from the consent of the governed. You have neither solicited nor received ours. We did not invite you. You do not know us, nor do you know our world. Cyberspace does not lie within your borders. Do not think that you can build it, as though it were a public construction project. You cannot. It is an act of nature, and it grows itself through our collective actions.

You have not engaged in our great and gathering conversation, nor did you create the wealth of our marketplaces. You do not know our culture, our ethics, or the unwritten codes that already provide our society more order than could be obtained by any of your impositions.

You claim there are problems among us that you need to solve. You use this claim as an excuse to invade our precincts. Many of these problems don't exist.

Where there are real conflicts, where there are wrongs, we will identify them and address them by our means. We are forming our own Social Contract. This governance will arise according to the conditions of our world, not yours. Our world is different.

Great reading, but isn't it just plain crazy? I mean, how can we possibly think of cyberspace as a real place with its own real governance structures? More to the point, why is Barlow wasting time with these crazy out-of-touch rants when there are serious political problems to be dealt with? Problems like fighting Internet censorship in court and in Congress. Problems like fighting restrictions on cryptography. Problems like providing Internet access to the poor and disenfranchised—real problems of every make and stripe. So many real problems to worry about that one has to wonder what could be less productive than Barlow's declaration. Doesn't it just amount to a call for a retreat from reality?

That is certainly how a number of commentators have viewed Barlow's essay. For example, David S. Bennahum (chapter 4) argues that we don't actually inhabit cyberspace and that it is not even clear what it would mean to do so:

I'm wondering what it means to form a social contract in cyberspace, one with the kind of authenticity and authority of a constitution. It sounds great in theory, but I don't actually live in cyberspace: I live in New York City, in the state of New York, in the United States of America. I guess I'm taking things too literally. Apparently my mind lives in cyberspace, and that's what counts. It's my vestigial meat package, also known as my body, that lives in New York. Government, geography, my body: all are obsolete now thanks to "cyberspace, that new home of mind."

David Brin (chapter 3) contends that whatever cyberspace might mean, it is clearly a distraction. Brin notes that about the same time Barlow published his "Declaration," the government of China was calling for all Internet users to register with the police and that this is the sort of thing we should be concerned about:

Witness a news item that lay buried deep below lurid stories about the Telecommunications Act of 1996 (which despite its flaws will increase competition and routing diversity, the core of Net independence):

***ORDERS NET USERS TO REGISTER WITH POLICE.

Which government? What's hidden in the asterisks? Where did the story originate? Here's a clue: the policy affects over a billion people, far across the ocean.

Brin closes his essay with the following tag, one expressing views that are no doubt widely shared:

IAAMOAC!

I am a member of a civilization. Try saying it aloud sometime. It is a mantra against the modern self-doped drug of self-righteousness. Compared to anything else human beings have done, it is the best civilization ever. It's fun. It created the Net. It's earned your loyalty a thousand times over.

Richard Barbrook (chapter 5) is no more sympathetic when he argues that Barlow's rant is simply the product of a kind of disillusionment that comes when libertarian ideology collides with the reality of capitalism:

[Barlow's essay] is a symptom of the intense ideological crisis now facing the advocates of free-market libertarianism within the online community. At the very moment that cyberspace is about to become opened up to the general public, the individual freedom that they prized in the Net seems about to be legislated out of existence with little or no political opposition. Crucially, the lifting of restrictions on market competition hasn't advanced the cause of freedom of expression at all. On the contrary, the privatization of cyberspace seems to be taking place alongside the introduction of heavy censorship. Unable to explain this phenomenon within the confines of the Californian Ideology, Barlow has decided to escape into neoliberal hyperreality rather than face the contradictions of really existing capitalism.

The critiques by Brin, Bennahum, and Barbrook are precisely the ones we expect to be raised. They reflect the obvious worries about Barlow's manifesto. The only problem is that the obvious worries are not always the correct ones.

In the first place, how fair is it to accuse Barlow of escapism? He is certainly better known than most for concrete work in fighting for online rights. He did, after all, cofound the Electronic Frontier Foundation in response to overly zealous hacker crackdowns by the U.S. Secret Service. And he has taken the lead in fighting for crypto rights. Perhaps one can both advance a radical thesis *and* fight in everyday causes.

But what about the claim that we don't *really* inhabit cyberspace—that, in fact, we are inhabitants of Plovdiv, Bulgaria, or Des Moines, Iowa, or Milton Keynes, England. Surely *that* observation is unassailable. Or is it? In fact, matters are not so simple.

This is actually a point that I've tried to explore elsewhere. In the introduction to section 5 of *High Noon on the Electronic Frontier*, I held that maybe the identities we construct online (our virtual reality or VR identities) may be just as important—indeed, just as real—as the ones that we have constructed in the so-called real world (hereafter RW). I tried to illustrate that via the example of gender (p. 315):

If the bulk of my social contacts are in VR rather than the RW, then why wouldn't VR have greater claim to the construction of my gender? That is, if social institutions determine gender and if the bulk of the social institutions in which I participate are VR institutions, then why isn't my VR gender my "real" gender?

Of course, my claim in that piece wasn't that you swap your gender simply by logging on as a member of the opposite sex. Time has to be spent in the new world, and a lot depends on how you are viewed by the other inhabitants of that world. The key idea here is not so much that VR worlds have the final claim on reality as that the RW has overstated its claim on reality. Maybe RW isn't the final arbiter of what's real after all.

If the social construction of reality has some plausibility for the construction of the self, it has even more plausibility for the construction of political institutions like governments. In the case of persons we can point to a physical body and make some sort of claim that the self is to be identified with that physical organism, but in the case of governments there is no genuine physical body that we can identify as the thing we are talking about. Governments and governmental institutions and laws *have* a kind of reality, but it is pretty clearly a socially constructed reality. It seems to me that this point has been lost on some of the contributors to the debate over the sovereignty of cyberspace. As we will see, attention to this point can have consequences for discussions of the sovereignty of online communities and for the emergence of online governance structures for those communities.

Crypto Anarchy

Crypto anarchy is a phrase initially coined by Timothy C. May (chapters 6 and 7) to describe a possible (inevitable?) political outcome from the widespread use of encryption technologies like Pretty Good Privacy. The leading idea is that as more and more of our transactions take place behind the veil of encryption, it becomes easier and easier for persons to undertake business relations that escape the purview of traditional nation states. For example, not only will certain "illegal" transactions become more widespread (or at least easier to carry out), but nation states will find it increasingly difficult to enforce their taxation laws. Indeed, full-fledged black-market economies may emerge that will eventually become larger and more vibrant than the legitimate economies that are controlled by the nation states.

That is a pretty contentious position—in effect, it amounts to a claim that the nation states as we know them are doomed—but it is not a priori false. One argument in support of the position goes like this: not only is the Internet undermining the traditional media, but it is also reshaping the nature of our commercial infrastructure. Strictly speaking, it just *is* our new commercial infrastructure. Whereas in past ages goods were transported by ship or rail or truck, increasingly products of value can be delivered via the Internet. Notice also that the Internet does not respect international borders. Information and software can be transferred to Bulgaria almost as easily as to Boston: on the Internet your business partners can be scattered about the globe. If identity remains hitched to regular trade and commerce (as it has for at least three thousand years), then it is clear that our sense of identity is about to be unhitched from our national borders.

A great example of this phenomenon was reported in the EFF's *EFFector Online* (volume 9, number 3, March 6, 1996): "A 'virtual' software corporation, ACD, with software engineers in both California and Hungary but no real physical business infrastructure, was recently slapped with an $85 fine by U.S. Customs." ACD's product, EPublisher for the Web, was developed over the Internet with no physical meetings or other contact between the developers. When Hungarian developers sent versions of the software on diskette to their U.S. counterparts, the shipment was stopped by U.S. Customs at Los Angeles International Airport for "mark violation." The Hungarians had marked "Country of Origin" on the forms as "Internet" because the product was not decidably made in Hungary or the United States and the owners of the intellectual property rights to the product were in no single physical location. In the words of ACD's Laslo Chaki, "We had to pay an $85 fine for mark violation. Virtual company, in virtual city with $85 real fine!"

The employees for ACD correctly saw that they did not have a home in any real nation but rather that their base of operations was simply the Internet. Global boundaries meant nothing in this case.

Also possible is the emergence of different currencies for different trading partnerships. These new currencies, however, would not be confined to specific geographical regions but would depend rather on networks of business relationships. In a sense, they would be similar to the time-honored practice of barter within industry groups or to payment with credits for use in company stores.

Much has been made of the fact that cash will be digital in nature and that with current encryption technology it may be possible for underground economies to escape detection by established nation states altogether. The cypherpunks argue that the emergence of such underground economies is not just possible but inevitable.

If my business is information intensive, there is no reason I cannot conduct my business from an account offshore, trade with offshore partners, and bank offshore as well. It is inevitable that there will be future Ross Perots and Bill Gateses who amass billion-dollar fortunes, spend little of it, and conduct their business using offshore banks on the Internet. This does not make for a mere billion-dollar underground economy, however. The underground electronic bank will invest in other ventures, thus expanding the monetary supply in the underground economy. At a certain crucial threshold, enough money will escape the taxation net of the nation state so that its abilities to operate effectively will erode. If the nation state chooses to raise taxes, more businesses will slip into the electronic underground, further eroding the viability of the national government. Or so the argument goes.

The cypherpunk claims about crypto anarchy can be challenged on two fronts—whether crypto anarchy really is inevitable or even likely and, if it is, whether it is at all desirable. On this latter question, Dorothy E. Denning (chapter 9) argues that Timothy May's phrase "crypto anarchy" is simply a way of sugar coating an undesirable state of lawlessness:

Although May limply asserts that anarchy does not mean lawlessness and social disorder, the absence of government would lead to exactly these states of chaos. I do not want to live in an anarchistic society—if such could be called a society at all—and I doubt many would. A growing number of people are attracted to the market liberalism envisioned by Jefferson, Hayek, and many others but not to anarchy. Thus, the crypto anarchists' claims come close to asserting that the technology will take us to an outcome that most of us would not choose.

Crypto anarchy would not be desirable in Denning's view, but this point is academic, since, according to her, crypto anarchy is not going to come about in any case—although her views about *why* it won't come about have shifted over the last few years. Initially, Denning (chapter 9) held that crypto anarchy would not come to pass thanks to "key escrow" encryption technology:

I do not accept crypto anarchy as the inevitable outcome. A new paradigm of cryptography—key escrow—is emerging and gaining acceptance in industry. Key escrow is a technology that offers tools that would ensure no individual absolute privacy or untraceable anonymity in all transactions. I argue that this feature of the technology is what will allow individuals to choose a civil society over an anarchistic one.

Key escrow encryption technology involves the introduction of encryption strategies that allow government authorities back-door access to all encrypted communications. Of course, such technology would be an anathema to cypherpunks like Eric Hughes (chapter 8), since it would effectively undermine his concerns about trusting large "faceless" organizations to respect our privacy:

We cannot expect governments, corporations, or other large, faceless organizations to grant us privacy out of their beneficence. It is to their advantage to speak of us, and we should expect that they will speak.

To see the concern, simply consider the trustworthiness of the government officials who would handle the key escrow. Can underpaid government bureaucrats be trusted with keys to all of our encrypted messages—particularly if those messages involve information of extreme financial value or of great political sensitivity?

In recent years, as attempts to introduce key escrow encryption have foundered, Denning's studies have shown that even without key escrow, law-enforcement agencies have, on balance, been capable of thwarting crime and underground activities. For examples, see the essay by Denning and William Baugh Jr. (chapter 12). Denning (chapter 10) concludes that crypto anarchy is not in the cards:

Whereas encryption has posed significant problems for law enforcement, even derailing some investigations, the situation in no way resembles anarchy. In most of the cases with which I am familiar, law enforcement succeeded in obtaining the evidence they needed for conviction.

Still, there are those who hold that law-enforcement agencies are fighting a losing battle and that crypto anarchy remains inevitable—and even desirable. On the latter point, Duncan Frissell (chapter 11) responds to Denning's claim that she wouldn't want to live in a state of crypto anarchy, suggesting that if persons like her prefer to live under strong government control, that will remain an option for those who choose it:

> Whatever happens, there will always be plenty of cults around (perhaps even one called the Government of the United States of America) to which anyone will be free to belong and at the altars of which one will be free to worship. In fact, the deregulation of human interaction will make it easier for more oppressive cults to exist than is possible today as long as they keep to themselves. There will be no shortage of people willing to tell their followers what to do. Nothing will stop anyone from joining such a society.

Of course, as Denning would doubtless observe, the point is not really about worshiping oppressive states but rather about having strong states that provide security from crime. On this point too, however, Frissell is skeptical. For him, the "security" they can provide is all too often chimerical.

Shifting Borders

Arguably we don't need to wait for crypto anarchy to see the erosion of power of RW governmental and legal institutions. Quite independently of encryption technology it is happening already, and it is being driven by the very real loss of revenue being felt by state and local governments. In the words of Nathan Newman (chapter 15), state and local governments are rapidly becoming "road kill on the information superhighway." This is a byproduct of recent moves in which taxation authority is taken from the federal government and states and handed over to the localities. The problem with the current situation is that the localities are utterly helpless in the face of the multinational corporations currently engaged in e-commerce. Tax collection has been handed to the localities, and they simply can't collect taxes in an information economy.

Taxation and loss of revenue are not the only relevant factors, however. A number of legal questions no longer make sense when viewed from within the framework of territorial boundaries. David Johnson and David Post observe (chapter 13) that it is becoming increasingly clear that an independent legal jurisdiction is emerging for cyberspace. Disputes can emerge in cyberspace that cross all existing legal authority. For example, what happens when a dispute arises between business partners who live in the same neighborhood in cyberspace but who live in different parts of the world with radically different legal institutions? Is the dispute to be settled by the RW laws of one of the physical locations? Or is it best resolved by new institutions with new jurisdictions as determined by their virtual "location" in cyberspace? Some of the thorny issues that will create conundrums for traditional territory-based law include issues about trademark law (which is traditionally territory-based), defamation law, the regulation of Net-based professional activities, and copyright law. Johnson and Post conclude that new online legal jurisdictions will emerge:

> Global computer-based communications cut across territorial borders, creating a new realm of human activity and undermining the feasibility—and legitimacy—of applying laws based on geographic boundaries. While these electronic communications play havoc with geographic boundaries, a new boundary—made up of the screens and passwords that separate the virtual world from the "real world" of atoms—emerges. This new boundary defines a distinct cyberspace that needs and can create new law and legal institutions of its own.

David Post (chapter 14) goes further and suggests that a plurality of online rule systems may emerge and that a kind of free market in these rule sets might develop—with online networks competing for competing for citizens by optimizing their rule sets:

> Although each individual network can be constrained from "above" in regard to the rule sets it can, or cannot, adopt, the aggregate range of such rule sets in cyberspace will be far less susceptible to such control. A kind of competition between individual networks to design and implement rule sets compatible with the preferences of individual internetwork users will thus materialize in a new and largely unregulated, because largely unregulatable, market for rules. The outcome of the individual decisions within this market—the aggregated choices of individual users seeking particular network rule sets most to their liking—will therefore, to a significant extent, determine the contours of the "law of cyberspace."

The Emergence of Law in Cyberspace

So far we have discussed the possibility that new online legal jurisdictions may emerge, but we have said little about what the character of the laws and institutions themselves might be. While we are largely limited to speculation, it is possible to gain some insight into this question by studying the legal institutions that have emerged to date. For the most part these emerging new systems of laws have appeared in whimsical settings like MUDS (multiuser dimensions or domains) and MOOs (MUDs–object oriented), which are essentially text-based virtual-reality environments. For some people MUDs and MOOs are nothing more than elaborate Dungeons and Dragons games, but others have maintained that these environments foster very real virtual cultures and governance institutions and that we can learn much by studying them.

One famous example is LamdaMOO, which was initially started by Pavel Curtis at Xerox's Palo Alto Research Center (PARC). LamdaMOO's fame is due in large measure to a famous *Village Voice* article ("A Rape in Cyberspace") by Julien Dibbell (reprinted as chapter 29 in *High Noon on the Electronic Frontier*). As with many MUDs and MOOs, LambdaMOO began as an aristocracy (or wizardocracy) in which the programmers held absolute power and were responsible for resolving virtually all social conflicts. Then, in a famous posting to a LambdaMOO bulletin board, the head wizard Haakon (a.k.a. Pavel Curtis), announced a new direction for LamdaMOO:

Message 537 on *social-issues (#7233):
Date: Wed Dec 9 23:32:29 1992 PST
From: Haakon (#2)
To: *social-issues (#7233)
Subject: On to the next stage ...

[snip]

I realize now that the LambdaMOO community has attained a level of complexity and diversity that I've actually been waiting and hoping for since four hackers and I first set out to build this place: this society has left the nest.

I believe that there is no longer a place here for wizard-mothers, guarding the nest and trying to discipline the chicks for their own good. It is time for the wizards to give up on the "mother" role and to begin relating to this society as a group of adults with independent motivations and goals.

So as the last social decision we make for you and whether or not you independent adults wish it, the wizards are pulling out of the discipline/manners/

arbitration business; we're handing the burden and freedom of that role to the society at large. We will no longer be the right people to run to with complaints about one another's behavior, etc. The wings of this community are still wet (as anyone can tell from reading *social-issues), but I think they're strong enough to fly with.

[snip]

My personal model is that the wizards should move into the role of systems programmers: our job is to keep the MOO running well and getting better in a purely technical sense.

Haakon's new direction was soon tested when a dispute arose involving the virtual sexual assault perpetrated by a LamdaMOO denizen named Mr. Bungle. Bungle used a "voodoo doll"—a software subroutine that allows one to temporarily control the actions of other characters—to seize control of a number of characters and force them into a number of outrageous (virtual) sexual acts. For the victims—or rather their RW counterparts—there was nothing to do but watch their characters be violated (or, of course, stop watching what was happening to their characters).

Of course, in the real world all that was happening was a number of people were typing on their keyboards over the Internet, but the way the participants experienced the episode was quite another matter. A number of them felt violated by the incident and demanded immediate action. One such individual was Legba, who posted the following on a LambdaMOO discussion group that was discussing the event (*High Noon*, p. 380):

Mostly voodoo dolls are amusing.... And mostly I tend to think that restrictive measures around here cause more trouble than they prevent. But I also think that Mr. Bungle was being a vicious, vile fuckhead, and I ... want his sorry ass scattered from #17 to the Cinder Pile. I'm not calling for policies, trials, or better jails. I'm not sure what I'm calling for. Virtual castration, if I could manage it. Mostly, [this type of thing] doesn't happen here. Mostly, perhaps I thought it wouldn't happen to me. Mostly, I trust people to conduct themselves with some veneer of civility. Mostly, I want his ass.

Dibbell later interviewed Legba's "typist" and reported the following (*High Noon*, p. 380):

Months later, the woman in Seattle would confide to me that as she wrote those words posttraumatic tears were streaming down her face—a real-life fact that should suffice to prove that the words' emotional content was no mere playacting.

Ultimately, Legba proposed that Mr. Bungle be toaded—that is, that his character be terminated and that Mr. Bungle's typist should lose his/her/their account. The ensuing discussion saw positions that covered the political spectrum. Dibbell catalogued the positions as including the following (*High Noon*, pp. 384–386):

Parliamentarian legalist types: "Unfortunately Bungle could not legitimately be toaded at all, since there were no explicit MOO rules against rape, or against just about anything else—and the sooner such rules were established, they added, and maybe even a full-blown judiciary system complete with elected officials and prisons to enforce those rules, the better."

Royalists: "Bungle's as-yet-unpunished outrage only proved this New Direction silliness had gone on long enough, and that it was high time the wizardocracy returned to the position of swift and decisive leadership their player class was born to."

Technolibertarians: "MUD rapists were of course assholes, but the presence of assholes on the system was a technical inevitability, like noise on a phone line, and best dealt with not through repressive social disciplinary mechanisms but through the timely deployment of defensive software tools. Some asshole blasting violent, graphic language at you? Don't whine to the authorities about it—hit the @gag command and the asshole's statements will be blocked from your screen (and only yours). It's simple, it's effective, and it censors no one."

Anarchists: "Like the technolibbers, the anarchists didn't care much for punishments or policies or power elites. Like them, they hoped the MOO could be a place where people interacted fulfillingly without the need for such things. But their high hopes were complicated, in general, by a somewhat less thoroughgoing faith in technology ('Even if you can't tear down the master's house with the master's tools'—read a slogan written into one anarchist player's self-description—'it is a damned good place to start')."

The consensus that emerged was that Mr. Bungle should be toaded. Shortly thereafter, Haakon terminated the Bungle account. What makes the episode particularly interesting, however, was that it led to the introduction of a system of petitions and ballot initiatives, the ultimate goal of which was to complete the transition from wizardocracy to democracy.

As Jennifer Mnookin relates (chapter 16), there was subsequently a debate on LambdaMOO between the "formalizers" and the "resisters," where the formalizers were inclined to codify the laws for LambdaMOO, and the resisters hesitated, arguing that LambdaMOO is supposed to be a game and therefore shouldn't be taken too seriously. As Mnookin notes, however, the point of view of the formalizers generally held sway, and a number of ballot initiatives were offered (some enacted) that indentified specific MOO crimes. One example that ultimately did not pass (it did not receive a two-thirds majority), was the following initiative, which attempted to define "MOOrape" and to distinguish it from "speech":

A virtual "rape," also known as "MOOrape," is defined within LambdaMOO as a sexually related act of a violent or acutely debasing or profoundly humiliating nature against a character who has not explicitly consented to the interaction. Any act which explicitly references the nonconsensual, involuntary exposure, manipulation, or touching of sexual organs of or by a character is considered an act of this nature.

An "act" is considered, for the purposes of this petition, to be a use of "emote" (locally or remotely), a spoof, or a use of another verb performing the equivalent presentation, whether by a character or by an object controlled by a character.

The use of "say," "page," and "whisper" … and other functionality creating an equivalent sense of quotation generally are not considered "acts" under this petition; they are considered "speech." Notes, mail messages, descriptions, and other public media of communication within LambdaMOO that provide a sense of quotation or written expression rather than conveying action are also forms of "speech." This petition should not be interpreted to abridge freedom of speech within LambdaMOO community standards. Communications in the form of speech might still be considered offensive and harassing but generally are not considered virtual rape unless they explicitly and provokingly reference a character performing the actions associated with rape.

In addition, as Mnookin notes, a number of proposals for legal oversight and mediation were debated and in some instances introduced.

An interesting question arises when we begin to consider whether MOO crimes in a particular vitual environment should carry over to another virtual environment or indeed to real life (RL). One very interesting instance of this question came about in the "SamIAm" incident, in which a judicial decision made on LambdaMOO was carried over to another virtual community—MIT's MediaMOO, which was run by Amy Bruckman. What makes the episode particularly remarkable is that MediaMOO was a rather different environment from LambdaMOO. It did not have its roots in Dungeons and Dragons gaming but rather was a text-based environment where individuals engaged in media research could meet, socialize, and discuss their work. The administrators of MediaMOO were not wizards but rather were called "janitors." Like LambdaMOO, however, dispute resolution had been passed from the administrators (in this case to an elected advisory council).

As discussed by Charles Stivale (chapter 17), a dispute between two LambdaMOO denizens—SamIAm and gru—took place on LambdaMOO in 1994. Because of the delicacy of the charges, the normal dispute-resolution procedures were suspended, and the net result of the deliberation was that SamIAm was "newted," or suspended, for six months. Shortly thereafter, the advisory council on MediaMOO met and suspended SamIAm on the basis of charges "imported from" LambdaMOO. For Stivale one of the key concerns about the SamIAm case was that it showed how easy it is for established online judicial procedures to be abrogated:

> While these tales may strike some as an insider's view of *As the MOO Turns*, the aftermath of these allegations is quite instructive about the delicate balance between laws that regulate site administration, interstate, and, indeed, international communication and the freedom of expression that sustains the very dynamic of these sites, asynchronous and synchronous alike. These tales stand, I would argue, as a sobering lesson of just how limited are the current efforts, however well intentioned, to develop online cyberdemocracy due to concomitant practices of distortion and infringement on rights, practices imported piecemeal from real-time personal and political processes.

Perhaps most interesting, for our purposes, are the questions that arise concerning the interlinking of legal jurisdictions in cyberspace. Despite being decidedly distinct virtual worlds, there was at least some de facto legal-political linkage between them, whether justified or not.

By way of epilogue it is worth noting that after these events took place the advisory council on MediaMOO disbanded, and a few years after that the return of wizardly fiat on LambdaMOO was announced:

Message 300 from *News (#123):
Date: Thu May 16 11:00:54 1996 PDT
From: Haakon (#2)
To: *News (#123)
Subject: LambdaMOO Takes Another Direction

On December 9, 1992, Haakon posted "LambdaMOO Takes a New Direction" (LTAND). Its intent was to relieve the wizards of the responsiblity for making social decisions and to shift that burden onto the players themselves. It indicated that the wizards would thenceforth refrain from making social decisions and serve the MOO only as technicians. Over the course of the past three and a half years, it has become obvious that this was an impossible ideal: the line between "technical" and "social" is not a clear one and never can be. The harassment that ensues each time we fail to achieve the impossible is more than we are now willing to bear.

So we now acknowledge and accept that we have unavoidably made some social decisions over the past three years and inform you that we hold ourselves free to do so henceforth.

1. *We Are Reintroducing Wizardly Fiat.*   In particular, we henceforth explicitly reserve the right to make decisions that will unquestionably have social impact. We also now acknowledge that any technical decision may have social implications; we will no longer attempt to justify every action we take.

No doubt there is good reason to draw pessimistic conclusions from these events, but Stivale for one does not appear ready give up *trying* to build online communities—although he also anticipates much disappointment and a very steep learning curve:

For those of us committed to participating in and developing online "microworlds" and to contributing to the concomitant community building, however fluid and even ephemeral this conception of "community" may be, the "evidence" of cyberpolitical indifference, gridlock, and lack of appropriate models should not deter us from attempting to pursue modes of governance that fall prey neither to the pitfalls of democracy nor to the traps of democracy's "alternative," particularly of the dictatorial form. This experimentation with the medium at our disposal is but one phase in a learning process that is far from complete and that might yield some unforeseen results, in some flickering virtual space-time.

I don't mean to give the impression that all of the interesting developments in cyberlaw have revolved around dispute resolution in MUDs and MOOs. In section 3 of this collection we see that very real jurisdictional issues are emerging and that kinds cyberlaw may emerge to cover certain domains of online commerce. As David R. Johnson observes (chapter 18), we are already into interesting questions of cyberlaw when we consider the issue of the system operator's power to ban someone from an online domain. This might involve a case like SamIam, discussed above, or it may involve removing someone's Web site from a certain location, or it may involve banning someone from a particular chatroom. Of course, users can move to a new virtual community much more easily than they can move to another geographic territory. But as Johnson notes, when individuals have invested considerable time in building reputations on a particular site, an arbitrary decision by a system administrator to terminate an account cannot simply be shrugged off.

Cyberlaw ultimately will emerge in response to conflicts between system administrators and users rather than between RW governments and their citizens, and there is a corresponding different fabric to the nature of the laws that will emerge. Johnson catalogs some of the new legal strategies that will emerge, including online forms of dispute resolution. Some attempts at online dispute resolution (beyond those in communities like LambdaMOO) have already been put into effect, including the online Virtual Magistrate (chapters 19 and 20).

The scope of all of these efforts is certainly narrow, but it would be a mistake to conclude from this that they will not evolve into full-blown legal systems with profound impact on future legal theory worldwide. It is important to remember that our current systems of law have humble and in some cases whimsical beginnings (in the English-speaking world we can look to the laws of the Anglo-Saxon kingdoms or to the laws of feudalism after the Norman conquest). Rather than be dismissive, perhaps we should consider the possibility that we are witnessing the birth of the juridical systems and practices of the new millennium.

Even if the outcome is less grandiose, there is certainly much to be learned from the experimentation—a point summed up aptly by Mnookin:

In an often quoted dissenting opinion, Justice Louis Brandeis wrote: "It is one of the happy incidents of the federal system that a single courageous State may, if its citizens choose, serve as a laboratory; and try novel social and economic experiments without risk to the rest of the country." Sixty years later, it may be virtual spaces that can best serve as laboratories for experimentation, places in which participants can test creative social, political, and legal arrangements.

Utopia, Dystopia, and Pirate Utopias

If we really are constructing new legal systems and institutions (or at least experimenting with them), is it also possible to speculate that we are in a unique position to optimize these institutions—to actually improve them to the point where genuine utopias might emerge? Here it is easy to get caught up in some of the utopian fervor that is gripping a number of commentators on the digital revolution, from Kevin Kelly, to Douglas Rushkoff, Lou Rossetto, and John Perry Barlow. Karrie Jacobs (chapter 21) catalogues some of the utopian claims made by these individuals and notes that all the above authors have ignored the fact that "the electronic culture in which they operate is still largely run by white men (and written about by them; see 'Scenarios: the Future of the Future,' published by *Wired* in October 1995) and still dominated by big corporations such as ATT, Microsoft, and Sony." Things might appear less utopian to critics like Kelly et al. if they were not affluent white males. But referring specifically to Thomas More's *Utopia*, Jacobs also offers that utopian visions in and of themselves are not always so attractive:

What strikes me as the most oppressive—and familiar—quality of More's island state is the fact that Utopians couldn't escape the confines of their own lives because every place on the island was the same as every other place: "There are 54 cities on the island, all spacious and magnificent, identical in language, customs, institutions, and laws," More wrote. "So far as the location permits, all of them are built on the same plan and have the same appearance."

More might have been writing about America's shopping malls or Holiday Inns. Or his description could apply to the cities built by Soviet architects 450 years after his death, with their identical apartment blocks punctuated every mile or so by a grim public square, a token shopping area, a pub, and a drab community center.

Reflections of the original Utopia—a word, by the way, that literally means "no place"—can also be seen in the way software designers have repackaged the world. You can go anywhere on the Web with Netscape, and you will still be within the familiar confines of your "navigator." Like More's Utopia, the Net is a place where "if you know one of their cities, you know them all." Whether hopping from Web site to Web site or getting money from an ATM, the electronic world is a place with a limited range of gestures.

Of course, there is room to take issue with Jacobs on this latter point. While browser interfaces are more or less standardized, the locations that we visit with those browsers are fairly diverse. For example, a big difference exists between the text-based virtual environments of LambdaMOO and MediaMOO, and those two MOOs are in turn quite different from virtual communities like the WELL. The question is not whether the Net will be a utopia but whether there will be utopias on the Net—and what varieties they will come in.

Still, there is conceit in thinking that we can make better worlds simply by emigrating to the online world and starting over. This is one of the points that is made by Jedediah S. Purdy (chapter 22) when he takes aim at Kevin Kelly et al. and in particular at the general moral perspective of the prophets of *Wired* magazine. About the flight by some to virtual communities, Purdy is hardly charitable:

A few people, mostly college students, have largely withdrawn from their embodied lives to participate in virtual communities. Kelly wants this practice to go much further, to see more people inhabiting specialized online communities, sometimes of their own making. Creating these worlds extends "life," and "every creative act is no more or less than the reenactment of the creation." By entering these realms, their programmers reproduce the "old theme" of "the god who lowered himself into his own world." Kelly identifies this theme with Jesus, but one wonders if Narcissus is not a more appropriate touchstone for his ambition.

But more generally, Purdy sees the *Wired* philosophy as being "contemptuous of all limits—of law, community, morality, place, even embodiment." He writes,

The magazine's ideal is the unbounded individual who, when something looks good to him, will do it, buy it, invent it, or become it without delay. This temperament seeks comradeship only among its perceived equals in self-invention and world making; rather than scorn the less exalted, it is likely to forget their existence altogether. Boundless individualism, in which law, community, and every activity are radically voluntary, is an adolescent doctrine, a fantasy shopping trip without end.

This criticism is obviously aimed at *Wired* magazine and its techno-libertarian ideals, but it also has lessons for online communities. Are they exclusively going to be retreats where libidos can run wild, or are some of them going to become real communities where persons depend on each other? In section 4 we see a number of examples where virtual communities like LambdaMOO evolved away from adolescent fantasy worlds into real communities with (in my opinion) real laws. One hopes that many of those who opt for virtual communities will reject the *Wired* ideology and proceed to build viable communities. In building such communities they need not buy into Kelly's hubris that they are thereby "reenacting the Creation."

While it is certainly important to identify the *Wired* ideology and warn of its corrosive nature, it is also valuable to try to understand its origins and see how it fits into the broader context of American political life. Richard Barbrook and Andy Cameron (chapter 23) address this question by examining what they call the "Californian Ideology" underlying much of the thinking exhibited by Kelly, Rossetto, and others. In their view, the ideology is the result of a tension faced by "hi-tech artisans"—

the information technology professionals who are well paid but are under contract and hence face uncertain futures:

Living within a contract culture, the hi-tech artisans lead a schizophrenic exis- tence. On the one hand, they cannot challenge the primacy of the marketplace over their lives. On the other hand, they resent attempts by those in authority to encroach on their individual autonomy. By mixing New Left and New Right, the Californian Ideology provides a mystical resolution of the contradictory attitudes held by members of the 'virtual class'. Crucially, antistatism provides the means to reconcile radical and reactionary ideas about technological progress. While the New Left resents the government for funding the military-industrial complex, the New Right attacks the state for interfering with the spontaneous dissemina- tion of new technologies by market competition. Despite the central role played by public intervention in developing hypermedia, the Californian ideologues preach an antistatist gospel of hi-tech libertarianism: a bizarre mish-mash of hippie anarchism and economic liberalism beefed up with lots of technological determinism.

Mark Dery (chapter 24) takes aim at another of the digerati— Nicholas Negroponte, the director of the MIT Media Lab and former essayist for *Wired* magazine. In Dery's view, Negroponte's utopian visions of the future are striking for the way in which they consistently leave out the social dimension of life:

Troubling thoughts of social ills such as crime and unemployment and home- lessness rarely crease the Negroponte brow. In fact, he's strangely uninterested in social *anything*, from neighborhood life to national politics. Despite his in- sistence that the Digital Revolution™ is about communication, not computers, there's no real civic life or public sphere to speak of in his future.

There, most of the communicating takes place between you and talkative doorknobs or "interface agents" such as the "eight-inch-high holographic assis- tants walking across your desk."[1] In the next millennium, predicts Negroponte, "we will find that we are talking as much or more with machines than we are with humans."[2] Thus, the Information Age autism of his wistful "dream for the interface"—that "computers will be more like people."[3] Appliances and house- hold fixtures enjoy a rich social life in Negroponte's future, exchanging elec- tronic "handshakes" and "mating calls." "If your refrigerator notices that you are out of milk," he writes, "it can 'ask' your car to remind you to pick some up on your way home."[4] Human community, meanwhile, consists of "digital neighborhoods in which physical space will be irrelevant"—knowledge workers dialing in from their electronic cocoons, squeezing their social lives through phonelines.[5]

As Dery also notes, Negroponte's utopia is often "Jetsonian" in its fetish for gadgets like holographic assistants and talking appliances:

there is something quaint and old fashioned about it. But the old-fashioned nature of Negroponte's utopia is not restricted to the technology. It also robustly manifests itself in the elitism of the digerati—the very same elitism that Jacobs, Purdy, Barbrook, and Cameron took exception to. Dery sums this point up nicely:

[The digerati] and the world they inhabit is a memory of futures past—the top-down technocracies of the 1939 World's Fair or Disney's Tomorrowland, socially engineered utopias presumably overseen by the visionary elites who "basically drive civilization," as Stewart Brand famously informed the *Los Angeles Times*.[6]

Sometimes we celebrate individuals as being cutting-edge thinkers, when in reality they are nothing more than old-time hucksters, repackaging tired ideas (perhaps calling them "wired" ideas) but breaking no new ground where it matters. No doubt the media will continue to fete these individuals and their "vision." That does not mean that we must do so as well. The digerati of the utopian visions of *Wired* are nothing more than repackaged versions of the Guardians of Plato's *Republic* and the Samurai caste of H. G. Wells's *A Modern Utopia*. To suppose that the digerati are capable of driving civilization anywhere interesting is a mistake born of an old idea adopted without reflection and no doubt fueled by the boundless narcissism of this new class of elite. George Orwell once remarked that H. G. Wells's *A Modern Utopia* was "the paradise of little fat men." We might add that the utopian visions of the digerati are the paradise of self-absorbed white guys.

So where are we? Are utopian visions passé? Are online encounters really just exercises in alienating ourselves from embodiment and community? I wish to close on an optimistic note, and I think that properly informed by the above critiques we *can* navigate a path in which life online can be edifying and in which utopian thinking can make sense.

Clearly, we don't want the kind of utopia that Thomas More offered —the kind from which Karrie Jacobs so understandably recoils. There is nothing attractive about a world without diversity. Likewise, the adolescent male fantasy worlds envisioned by Kelly and Negroponte hold no genuine appeal. There is certainly nothing worthwhile in a world where community withers to the point that household appliances have better social lives than we do. Just as clearly, online communities have only limited appeal if we take them as being hermetically sealed off from the rest of our lives or if they can never evolve beyond Dungeons and Dragons role playing.

But we know for a fact that online environments can foster genuine personal relationships and genuine communities and that these online friendships often spill over into face-to-face meetings and RW friendships (see section 5 of *High Noon on the Electronic Frontier* for numerous examples). We also know that great variations evolve in the fabric and structure of online meeting places and that participants can take active roles in improving these meeting places. As we see in section 4, significant experimentation has occurred in law making and conflict resolution. Moreover, I think that it is in this variation and experimentation that we can seriously talk about utopias.

As Dery rightly points out, the utopias envisioned by the digerati are painfully old-fashioned—"driven" by elites and engineered around Jetsonian technofetish gadgetry. The kinds of utopias that we should rather aspire to may be community-based, experimental, dynamic (in the sense that they constantly change), and perhaps short-lived. They may be places carved out of cyberspace and protected by encryption technology, and they may nonetheless be squashed out of existence by government action or by economic reality. But this makes them no less utopian.

The final reading (chapter 25) is part of Hakim Bey's fringe culture classic, *Temporary Autonomous Zones*—a book that illustrates some examples of the kinds of utopias I think possible. For Bey, temporary autonomous zones (TAZs) represent an alternative to head-on encounters with entrenched powers—encounters that lead to martyrdom at best:

The TAZ is like an uprising which does not engage directly with the State, a guerilla operation which liberates an area (of land, of time, of imagination) and then dissolves itself to re-form elsewhere/elsewhen, before the State can crush it. Because the State is concerned primarily with Simulation rather than substance, the TAZ can "occupy" these areas clandestinely and carry on its festal purposes for quite a while in relative peace. Perhaps certain small TAZs have lasted whole lifetimes because they went unnoticed, like hillbilly enclaves—because they never intersected with the Spectacle, never appeared outside that real life which is invisible to the agents of Simulation.

Bey draws an analogy to what he calls the "pirate utopias" of the eighteenth century:

The sea-rovers and corsairs of the 18th century created an "information net-work" that spanned the globe: primitive and devoted primarily to grim business, the net nevertheless functioned admirably. Scattered throughout the net were islands, remote hideouts where ships could be watered and provisioned, booty traded for luxuries and necessities. Some of these islands supported "intentional communities," whole mini-societies living consciously outside the law and determined to keep it up, even if only for a short but merry life.

Perhaps there are creases—"islands in the Net," to borrow a phrase from Bruce Sterling—in which we can form better worlds, if only for brief periods. Perhaps these islands will be made possible by encryption technology, or perhaps they will simply be out-of-the-way MOOs or TAZs that the state does not concern itself with. Within these spaces experimentation with governance structures will be possible, and some of them may lead to communities that seem utopian to their denizens. These episodes will doubtless be temporary and may well dissolve from within, but that ephemeral quality does not diminish their value, for some of them will provide alternatives to the top-down, elitist, would-be utopias led by the Guardians, the Samurai, or the digerati. Indeed, their transience and permeability is ultimately important, for they should not be locations for escape from the world but rather places where we can rest, have fun, educate ourselves, and yet never lose sight of the business of helping each other (on this last point there is an apparent departure from the original pirate utopias).

The part about having fun should not be overlooked. It is, I think, one of the root concerns of Hakim Bey, and why shouldn't it be? Bey's language is audacious, of course; some would say it's over the top. But his talk of insurrection and hillbillies and pirate enclaves is at bottom designed to free the imagination and to allow us to have some fun—to perhaps escape from the boardroom tech-speak of Nicholas Negroponte and infuse our thoughts with images of islands and pirates rather than intelligent toasters. This collection of essays is, by intent, an attempt to do something in that same spirit.

Am I serious when I talk about crypto anarchy and the death of the nation state? Do I seriously think it is plausible to talk about the sover-eignty of cyberspace? Do I really think the wizardocracy of LambdaMOO is a serious government? Am I serious about MOO denizens creating laws? The answer to all these questions is both yes and no because of an ambiguity in the meaning of *serious*: these are all fundamentally serious questions, but we can have lots of fun while we entertain them.

But, some might ask, are these online institutions "really real"? Questions like this strike me as poorly motivated. Why do we suppose that because there is play and fun involved that reality cannot be part of the equation? On this point, the concluding paragraph from Hakim Bey is apt:

Let us admit that we have attended parties where for one brief night a republic of gratified desires was attained. Shall we not confess that the politics of that night have more reality and force for us than those of, say, the entire U.S. Government? Some of the "parties" we've mentioned lasted for two or three years. Is this something worth imagining, worth fighting for? Let us study invisibility, webworking, psychic nomadism—and who knows what we might attain?

Indeed. Who knows?

Notes

1. Nicholas Negroponte, *Being Digital* (New York: Knopf, 1995), p. 148.

2. Ibid., p. 145.

3. Ibid., p. 101.

4. Ibid., p. 213.

5. Ibid., p. 7.

6. Paul Keegan, "The Digerati," *New York Times Magazine*, May 21, 1995, p. 42.

I

The Sovereignty of Cyberspace?

2

A Declaration of the Independence of Cyberspace

John Perry Barlow

Yesterday, that great invertebrate in the White House signed into the law the Telecommunications Act of 1996—which contains the Communications Decency Act—while Tipper Gore took digital photographs of the proceedings to be included in a book called *Twenty-four Hours in Cyberspace*.

I had also been asked to participate in the creation of this book by writing something appropriate to the moment. Given the atrocity that this legislation would seek to inflict on the Net, I decided it was as good a time as any to dump some tea in the virtual harbor.

After all, the Act, passed in the Senate with only five dissenting votes, makes it unlawful and punishable by a $250,000 to say *shit* online. Or for that matter, to say any of the other seven dirty words prohibited in broadcast media. Or to discuss abortion openly. Or to talk about any bodily function in any but the most clinical terms.

It attempts to place more restrictive constraints on the conversation in cyberspace than presently exist in the Senate cafeteria, where I have dined and heard colorful indecencies spoken by United States senators on every occasion I did.

This bill was enacted on us by people who haven't the slightest idea who we are or where our conversation is being conducted. It is, as my good friend and *Wired* editor Louis Rossetto put it, as though "the illiterate could tell you what to read."

Well, fuck them.

Or more to the point, let us now take our leave of them. They have declared war on cyberspace. Let us show them how cunning, baffling, and powerful we can be in our own defense.

I have written something (with characteristic grandiosity) that I hope will become one of many means to this end. If you find it useful, I hope you will pass it on as widely as possible. You can leave my name off it if you like because I don't care about the credit. I really don't.

This chapter originally appeared as an e-mail message from Barlow, distributed widely on the Internet. Reprinted by permission of the author. © John Perry Barlow, 1996.

But I do hope this cry will echo across cyberspace, changing and growing and self-replicating, until it becomes a great shout equal to the idiocy they have just inflicted on us.

I give you ...

A Declaration of the Independence of Cyberspace

Governments of the Industrial World, you weary giants of flesh and steel, I come from Cyberspace, the new home of Mind. On behalf of the future, I ask you of the past to leave us alone. You are not welcome among us. You have no sovereignty where we gather.

We have no elected government, nor are we likely to have one, so I address you with no greater authority than that with which liberty itself always speaks. I declare the global social space we are building to be naturally independent of the tyrannies you seek to impose on us. You have no moral right to rule us, nor do you possess any methods of enforcement we have true reason to fear.

Governments derive their just powers from the consent of the governed. You have neither solicited nor received ours. We did not invite you. You do not know us, nor do you know our world. Cyberspace does not lie within your borders. Do not think that you can build it, as though it were a public construction project. You cannot. It is an act of nature, and it grows itself through our collective actions.

You have not engaged in our great and gathering conversation, nor did you create the wealth of our marketplaces. You do not know our culture, our ethics, or the unwritten codes that already provide our society more order than could be obtained by any of your impositions.

You claim there are problems among us that you need to solve. You use this claim as an excuse to invade our precincts. Many of these problems don't exist. Where there are real conflicts, where there are wrongs, we will identify them and address them by our means. We are forming our own Social Contract. This governance will arise according to the conditions of our world, not yours. Our world is different.

Cyberspace consists of transactions, relationships, and thought itself, arrayed like a standing wave in the web of our communications. Ours is a world that is both everywhere and nowhere, but it is not where bodies live.

We are creating a world that all may enter without privilege or prejudice accorded by race, economic power, military force, or station of
birth.

We are creating a world where anyone, anywhere may express his or
her beliefs, no matter how singular, without fear of being coerced into
silence or conformity.

Your legal concepts of property, expression, identity, movement, and
context do not apply to us. They are based on matter. There is no matter here.

Our identities have no bodies, so, unlike you, we cannot obtain order
by physical coercion. We believe that from ethics, enlightened self-interest,
and the commonweal, our governance will emerge. Our identities may be
distributed across many of your jurisdictions. The only law that all our
constituent cultures would generally recognize is the Golden Rule. We
hope we will be able to build our particular solutions on that basis. But
we cannot accept the solutions you are attempting to impose.

In the United States, you have today created a law, the Telecommunications [Act of 1996], which repudiates your own Constitution and
insults the dreams of Jefferson, Washington, Mill, Madison, Tocqueville,
and Brandeis.

These dreams must now be born anew in us.

You are terrified of your own children, since they are natives in a
world where you will always be immigrants. Because you fear them, you
entrust your bureaucracies with the parental responsibilities you are too
cowardly to confront yourselves. In our world, all the sentiments and
expressions of humanity, from the debasing to the angelic, are parts of a
seamless whole, the global conversation of bits. We cannot separate the
air that chokes from the air on which wings beat.

In China, Germany, France, Russia, Singapore, Italy, and the United
States, you are trying to ward off the virus of liberty by erecting guard
posts at the frontiers of Cyberspace. These may keep out the contagion
for a small time, but they will not work in a world that will soon be
blanketed in bit-bearing media.

Your increasingly obsolete information industries would perpetuate
themselves by proposing laws, in America and elsewhere, that claim to
own speech itself throughout the world. These laws would declare ideas

to be another industrial product, no more noble than pig iron. In our world, whatever the human mind may create can be reproduced and distributed infinitely at no cost. The global conveyance of thought no longer requires your factories to accomplish.

These increasingly hostile and colonial measures place us in the same position as those previous lovers of freedom and self-determination who had to reject the authorities of distant, uninformed powers. We must declare our virtual selves immune to your sovereignty, even as we continue to consent to your rule over our bodies. We will spread ourselves across the Planet so that no one can arrest our thoughts.

We will create a civilization of the Mind in Cyberspace. May it be more humane and fair than the world your governments have made before.

3

Getting Our Priorities Straight

David Brin

A few days ago John Perry Barlow, a cofounder of the Electronic Frontier Foundation published across the Internet a torrid manifesto called "A Declaration of the Independence Cyberspace"—his response to the passage of the Telecommunications Act of 1996. With typically entertaining flair, he portrayed the issue in melodramatic terms, calling on all liberty-loving netizens to man the ramparts against dinosaurian governments preparing to trample electronic freedom. Among the Orwellian threats he decried was the V-chip, which enables parents to program their TVs, setting maximum acceptable thresholds to sexual or violent program content.

Getting past the theater and drama, isn't it silly to see the V-chip as anything more than a convenient mechanism for TV owners to exercise market decisions? To portray it as Big Brother mind control patronizes the American public—and especially the countless kids who will inevitably use great skill to bypass the V-chip, anyway.

Other offensive aspects to the Telecommunications Act were as perniciously ominous as its opponents claimed. And yet the Act faded from our agenda as courts overruled parts of it, other portions were superseded in legislation, and large fractions proved impotent or unenforceable in the face of ever-changing technology. In retrospect, it's hard to recall what all the fuss was about. The sole moment truly worth remembering was the wonderfully vivid "A Declaration of the Independence of Cyberspace," which retains a certain timelessness as art.

This chapter originally appeared in the electronic newsletter *Meme*. Reprinted by permission of the author. © David Brin, 1997.

Elsewhere I proclaim my respectful affection for Barlow and his peers, who are among the most creative, eccentric, and dynamic members of this civilization, both wired and unwired. Indeed, their basic instincts are correct—that the Net represents a fundamental enhancement of human freedom, with a transforming potential that is worth defending. Alas, I would find their righteous oratory more convincing if they began by accepting a couple of basic facts—that the United States and Western civilization in general are right now pretty damn free, at least compared to any human society ever known, and that our institutions seem favorably disposed to the growth and promulgation of this new commons called the Net. Indeed, this new tool for independence by sovereign individuals is as emblematic of our new culture as Barlow himself, proudly rambunctious and almost completely out of control. Understanding why the Net came about and fit so well into our already existing culture is an essential prerequisite to defending it.

Of course, Barlow and others (such as the so-called cypherpunks) are behaving as they were trained to do by several generations of American propaganda. Go through nearly all of the most popular films and novels produced in the last forty years. You'll find one unifying theme, one common message, pervading nearly every medium: that theme is suspicion of authority. In fact, you'd be hard pressed to find more than half a dozen first-rank films in which even one large corporate or government entity is depicted doing its job honestly or well. More generally, public institutions are portrayed as flat-out evil, since this makes it easier for Hollywood directors to keep their protagonists in jeopardy for ninety minutes.

Make no mistake, I generally approve of this mythos (suspicion of authority), in contrast to the We're-Great/Don't-Question-the-Elders message preached by past cultures. In *The Transparent Society* (1998), I discuss how a special confluence of factors—antiauthority indoctrination, copious education, and the delightful endorphin high of self-righteousness—combine to foster the world's first effective social immune system against tyranny and error. This new system, unleashing millions of bright and suspicious young minds to aim eager criticism at any elite, may be our one hope to thrive in the long term.

Nevertheless, it can grow a bit tedious when so few of these irate immune "cells" pause to notice or acknowledge how they suckled their attitudes toward authority from an early age. The ultimate irony of having been trained to be rebels and having their denunciations help prove the health of the overall system they denounce seems to escape them. This failure of perspective is especially telling in the way so many cypherpunks focus their ire at only one dangerous center of authority—government—while excusing or ignoring other ominous concentrations of power. True, any elite that has such a fantastic array of guns and prisons has to merit especially close scrutiny. (Even more would be better!) Still, in the West it is not government but megacommercial interests that presently threaten to fence off vast realms of cyberspace. I'd feel better if the Internet's self-appointed defenders felt obliged to guard *all* sections of the frontier and not just those facing their favorite and obvious foe.

Elsewhere, things are different. Witness a news item that lay buried deep below lurid stories about the Telecommunications Act of 1996 and Barlow's riveting manifesto for Net independence:

*** GOVERNMENT ORDERS NET USERS TO REGISTER WITH POLICE.

Which government? What's hidden in the asterisks? Where did the story originate? Here's a clue: the policy affects over a billion people, far across the ocean. Nor will those people be the only losers if this policy is effectively carried out. It could manifest danger to our very lives.

In the West we have learned the hard way that criticism is the only known antidote to error (and the Net provides criticism a-plenty!). But throughout human history, nearly all ruling cliques cared much more about their own power than about the error-detecting benefits of free speech. Let's put it in terms of memes. Our upstart meme of openness will win if it is allowed to infect the world's populace. So the leaders of closed societies rationalize that they must "protect" their people against this infection. In contrast, we fully-infected carriers of the openness meme are driven to push it into closed societies, whatever their self-declared guardians say about it.

But there is a more powerful reason to oppose this knee-jerk, predictable measure on the part of an archaic old guard. That reason is the growing danger of war—yes, old-fashioned physical war. Dictatorships are notorious for making fantastic miscalculations and strategic blunders (witness the days leading to World War I or the German-Soviet non-aggression treaty). This is because ruling cliques like to operate in near isolation, quashing any voice that might point out flaws in their enthusiastic plans. In other words, suppression of criticism has always been a principal condition leading to armed conflict.

This will be much less a danger when all countries are fully enmeshed in the Net. Whether the resulting system resembles what we call "democracy" or has other, more Eastern flavors, a fully and openly wired society will acquire the sort of transparency that makes sudden, impulsive aggression much less likely and far more accountable.

Nor will the CIA be able to talk *us* into unneeded defense buildups, as they did during much of the cold war, if they lack a monopoly on information about foreign military capabilities. Rather, we'd all have access to the data on which to base informed, self-interested decisions.

The important thing is to get our priorities right. Let's worry about getting the world wired first, preventing war, and promulgating the cantankerous habits of mutual accountability so that they spread throughout a maturing Terran Civilization.

In contrast, it's really rather tedious to hear all this moaning and complaining that the sky is falling because (for instance) parents may get to program filters on their home televisions instead of having to monitor the damned things in person, day and night.

How to Preserve Freedom in an Uncertain World

Let me conclude with a little parable, borrowed from *The Transparent Society*. This ancient Greek myth tells of a farmer, Akademos, who once did a favor for the sun god. In return, the mortal was granted a garden wherein he could say anything he wished—even criticism of the mighty Olympians—without fear of retribution.

I have often mulled over that little story, wondering how Akademos could ever really trust Apollo's promise. After all, the storied Greek deities were notoriously mercurial, petty, and vengeful. They could never be relied on to keep their word, especially if provoked by censuring mortals. In other words, they were a lot like human leaders.

I concluded there were only two ways Akademos could truly be protected. First, Apollo might set up impenetrable walls around the glade, so dense that even keen-eyed Hermes could not peer through or listen. Alas, the garden wouldn't be very pleasant after that, and Akademos would have few visitors to talk to.

The alternative was to empower Akademos so that somehow he could enforce the gods' promise. Some equalizing factor must make them keep their word, even when the mortal and his friends started telling bad Zeus jokes.

That equalizing factor could only be knowledge.

The roots of this particular legend permeate Western thought. In the days of Pericles, free citizens of Athens used to gather at the garden of Akademos, where individuals would freely debate issues of the day. That liberty lasted while Pericles was around to remind them of the contract they had made—a pact of openness.

Alas, it was a new and difficult concept. This miracle did not long outlive the great democrat. Outspoken Socrates paid a stiff price for practicing candor in the Akademos, whereon his student, Plato, took paradoxical revenge by writing stern denunciations of openness, calling instead for strict government by an "enlightened" elite. Plato's advice served to justify countless tyrants during the following two and a half millennia, remaining influential almost to this generation.

But now, at last, the vision of Pericles is getting another trial run. Today's "academy" extends far beyond the sacred confines of earth's thousand major universities. Throughout the neo-West—and to some extent the rest of the world—people have begun to accept the daring notion that ideas are not in themselves toxic, at least not to those (from all social classes) who cultivate brave minds. Free speech is increasingly seen as the best font of criticism—the only practical and effective antidote to error. Moreover, it goes both ways. Most honorable people have little to fear if others know things about them.

Let there be no mistake: this is a hard lesson to swallow, especially since each of us (some with the best of intentions) would be a tyrant, if we could. Very little in our history has prepared us for the task ahead of living in a tribe of more than six billion equal citizens, each guided by his or her own sovereign will, loosely administered by chiefs we elect and by just rules that we made through hard negotiation among ourselves. Any other generation would have thought it an impossible ambition—though countless ancestors sweated and strove to get us to the point where we can try.

Even among those who profess allegiance to this new hope, there is a bitter struggle over how best to protect it from the old gods of wrath, bigotry, conspiracy, and oppression—spirits who reside not on some mountain peak but in the hearts of each man or woman who tries to expand a little secular power or profit by suppressing others. Perhaps someday our descendants will be mature enough to curb these impulses by themselves. But meanwhile, a way is needed to foil the self-justified ambitions of those who would rationalize robbing freedom from the rest of us by saying that it is their right—or that it is for our own good.

According to some vigorous champions of liberty, the best means to protect our worldwide "academy" is obvious. Many "privacy champions" want to erect shields to put people on even ground with the mighty. According to this view, we must build walls to safeguard every private garden, so that freedom may thrive in each secure sanctum of the mind.

To this I can only reply that *it's been tried*. And there is not a single example where a commonwealth based on that principle thrived.

There is a better way—a method that is primarily responsible for this renaissance we're living in. Accountability is a light that can shine even on the gods of authority. Whether they gather in the Olympian heights of government, amid the spuming currents of commerce, or in the Hadean shadows of criminality, they cannot harm us while pinned by its glare.

Accountability is the only defense that ever adequately protected free speech, in a garden that stands proudly with no walls.

I'm not the first to say this. Pericles, Bruno, Spinoza, Sequoia, and countless others gave openness a voice during their own dark epochs. Nor can I pretend to have offered anywhere near the scholarly eloquence that Karl Popper poured into *The Open Society and Its Enemies* (1950) during a period when it seemed all-too likely that our grand experiment would be destroyed, either from outside or within. During the dark early days of the cold war, Popper movingly praised those common folk who manage to transform themselves into *citizens*—independent, cooperative, and indomitable.

Writing about the "longing of uncounted unknown men to free themselves and their minds from the tutelage of authority and prejudice," he posited hope in "their unwillingness to leave the entire responsibility for ruling the world to human or superhuman authority, and their willingness to share the burden of responsibility for avoidable suffering, and to work for its avoidance."

Even when it comes to a more down-to-earth or popularized version of the same message, I am far from alone. Take for example the following extract from an article that appeared before my book went to press:

With the coming of a wired, global society, the concept of openness has never been more important. It's the linchpin that will make the new world work. In a nutshell, the key formula for the coming age is this: Open, good. Closed, bad. Tattoo it on your forehead. Apply it to technology standards, to business strategies, to philosophies of life. It's the winning concept for individuals, for nations, for the global community in the years ahead.[1]

In their *Wired* magazine commentary, Peter Schwartz and Peter Leyden went on to contrast what the world may look like if it takes either the "closed" route or an "open" one. In the former case, nations turn inward, fragmenting into blocs. This strengthens rigidity of thought, stagnates the economy, and increases poverty and intolerance, leading to the vicious cycle of an even more closed and fragmented world. If, on the other hand, society adopts the open model, then a *virtuous* circle turns cultures outward, receptive to innovation and new ideas. Rising affluence leads to growing tolerance, smaller economic units, a more open society, and a more integrated world.

Synergies like this underlie the movement for openness, in stark contrast to the zero-sum approaches offered by the devil's dichotomies that call for wretched tradeoffs between pairs of things we cannot endure without. Those who favor an open society believe we can have both liberty and efficient government, both freedom and safety. In fact, we know that those pairs will thrive or fail in unison.

This confidence extends to the way we would envision developing the character and institutions of the information age, which until now have been "deposited like sediment" rather than sapiently planned. Making an analogy to the framing of the U.S. Constitution, Jaron Lanier called for a pragmatic mutualism of competition and cooperation as we design—and then redesign—the Internet to come:

Well-meaning and brilliant people with nasty, conflicting interests somehow created a collective product that was better than any of them could have understood at the time.... As in Philadelphia two hundred years ago, a collective product (the Internet) has to emerge that is better than any of them, or any of us, could achieve singly.[2]

In such negotiations it is perfectly reasonable to "trade off" particular interests, negotiating a give and take of concessions from one group to the next. That is adversarial pragmatism, a form of accountability. But it does not have to entail accepting dour dichotomies about matters of fundamental importance.

If we are all doomed to be either courteous slaves or liberated barbarians, what's the point?

In the long run, what use is a civilization unless it gently helps us become so smart, diverse, creative, and confident that we choose—of our own free will—to be decent people?

That is the point that I wish those irate heroes, those genuine Palladins of Western freedom—John Perry Barlow and his comrades—would try to remember. In the long run, independence and interdependence come down to the same thing. Only sovereign grownups can help each other grow and stay free.

IAAMOAC!*

*I am a member of a civilization. Try saying it aloud sometime. It is a mantra against the modern self-doped drug of self-righteousness. Compared to anything else human beings have done, it is the best civilization ever. It's fun. It created the Net. It's earned your loyalty a thousand times over.

Notes

1. Peter Schwartz and Peter Leyden, "The Long Boom: A History of the Future, 1980–2020," *Wired* (July 1997).

2. Jaron Lanier, "Karma Vertigo: Or Considering the Excessive Responsibilities Placed on Us by the Dawn of the Information Infrastructure" (1994), accessed at ⟨http://www.advanced.org/Jaron/essay.html⟩.

4

United Nodes of Internet: Are We Forming a Digital Nation?

David S. Bennahum

If you're like me in just two ways—you live in the United States and subscribe to a lot of electronic discussion groups—chances are your e-mail box is brimming with alerts, updates, and invective about the "end of the Internet."

The Internet—or cyberspace—reached one of those rare and crucial junctures in its history in February 1996. As you probably know, the Congress of the United States passed a law called the Communications Decency Act (CDA) (part of the Telecommunications Act of 1996), making it a felony to transmit "indecent" or "patently offensive" material online. This law, signed by President Clinton, is now in quasi-limbo, awaiting a final verdict from the U.S. judiciary on its constitutionality. I will not tire you with the logistical details of this process, other than to invite you to visit Voters Telecommunications Watch (http://www.vtw. org), which contains plenty of information on the timetable and the bill's history. You can also read my editorial opposing the bill, printed in the *New York Times* in May 1995 (http://www.reach.com/matrix/nyt-gettingcybersmart.html).

But why is this a critical juncture? No, it is not because the Internet will be "shut down," as some argue. It is not because the CDA passed. This is a critical juncture because the CDA is pushing avid users of the Internet toward a self-defining decision, a decision with long-term consequences. At the heart of this decision is a basic question: will we deal with the real world or retreat into our own private delusion—one that places cyberspace above and beyond the realities of the physical world?

This chapter originally appeared in the author's electronic newsletter, *Meme*. Reprinted by permission of the author. © David S. Bennahum, 1996.

The Myth of Digital Nirvana

Some people believe cyberspace is separate from the realities of the physical world. They argue that cyberspace, because it is "not where bodies live," is the inevitable catalyst that will usher in a new, better world. The CDA is then just another example of foolish, ham-fisted government. Government, according to these prophets, a vestige of primitive society, will soon become obsolete and be replaced by a society of mind. So who cares what governments think? Why not just wait out these times of troubles until the new world is unveiled? Don't roll your eyes yet. Serious people—at least serious in the sense that they get media attention and the public sees them as representatives of cyberspace—argue that

> This bill was enacted upon us by people who haven't the slightest idea who we are or where our conversation is being conducted. It is, as my good friend and *Wired* editor Louis Rossetto put it, as though "the illiterate could tell you what to read."
> Well, fuck them.
> Or, more to the point, let us now take our leave of them. They have declared war on Cyberspace. Let us show them how cunning, baffling, and powerful we can be in our own defense.

The quote comes from "A Declaration of the Independence of Cyberspace" by John Perry Barlow (http://www.eff.org/homes/barlow.html). Barlow, a cofounder of the Electronic Frontier Foundation (www.eff.org), former Grateful Dead (an American rock'n roll band) tunemaster and cattle rancher, is perceived by the public and the media as a messenger representing the views of a new wired culture. So his opinions do matter. This declaration of independence, written the week after the CDA became law, is the best encapsulation to date of all that is wrong with seeing cyberspace as separate from the rest of the world. (See chapter 2 of this collection.) It is wrong because it invites people to ignore reality and sit with their thumbs in their eyes while the real world passes them by.

Reality Check

The Internet received direct U.S. federal funding until April 1995, through the National Science Foundation (NSF), which managed the high-capacity fiber backbone (in April, management was turned over to private industry). Today the Internet receives indirect federal funding through government agencies that use the Internet to distribute information to the public and from federal research grants to universities conducting research that the U.S. government wants to promote. The National Air and Space Administration (NASA) is one such institution; the Massachusetts Institute of Technology is another. All the protocols governing the exchange of information through the Internet—things like FTP, TCP/IP, HTTP, SMTP—were set by standards bodies, a de facto kind of government.

The Internet is a wonderful product, the beneficiary of a rare kind of international cooperation. In a world where the dynamics of the free market are hailed as the best way to manage systems, the Internet is a great and fascinating example of a successful collective. Too easily we dismiss this phenomenon, but the development of the Internet is remarkable. It flies in the face of those who argue government is inherently inefficient and tyrannical—a vestige of some primitive cycle in human evolution. I cannot fathom how Internet users like Barlow can dismiss the importance or role of government in shaping this medium and claim that it can have no positive influence from now on. Was the U.S. government not a primary influence behind the development of the Internet—from 1969 (the year the Pentagon started funding research on packet networks) to 1995?

In the world of polemic, invective, and hyperbole, history is nothing more than fiction to be manipulated to suit the appropriate end. So when Barlow trashes government—by claiming "Cyberspace does not lie within your borders. Do not think that you can build it, as though it were a public construction project. You cannot. It is an act of nature, and it grows itself through our collective actions"—I look back at the Pentagon, the Defense Department, and American universities with federal funds paying AT&T, Sun Microsystems, and others to build a network of cables and computers and telephone lines, and I think, "What is he talking about?" Government built the heart of this thing with real money—the kind you get by collecting taxes. An "act of nature" is a rain storm or the moon rising; it is not the spontaneous birthing of packet network spanning the globe.

Anyway, having ditched history, Barlow presents a simple solution to problems that might interest governments, like phone sex companies advertising their services through Web pages featuring nude women and orgasmic audio tracks (http://www.cyberslut.com/cyber.html):

You claim there are problems among us that you need to solve. You use this claim as an excuse to invade our precincts. Many of these problems don't exist. Where there are real conflicts, where there are wrongs, we will identify them and address them by our means. We are forming our own Social Contract.

I'm wondering what it means to form a social contract in cyberspace, one with the kind of authenticity and authority of a constitution. It sounds great in theory, but I don't actually live in cyberspace: I live in New York City, in the state of New York, in the United States of America. I guess I'm taking things too literally. Apparently my "mind" lives in cyberspace, and that's what counts. It's my vestigial meat package, also known as my body, that lives in New York. Government, geography, my body: all are obsolete now, thanks to "cyberspace, that new home of mind," Barlow explains. That's why, speaking to government, Barlow argues: "Your legal concepts of property, expression, identity, movement, and context do not apply to us. They are based on matter. There is no matter here."

This philosophy is a Potemkin village, a sham of language that serves to create its own self-contained universe of logic where the real world is always wrong and the cyber world is always right. It is not a universe I want to live in.

This is the cyberspace I know—and there are lots of them.

The essay you are now reading is being disseminated, initially, to the readers of *MEME*—a biweekly newsletter I author. At last check, *MEME* had twenty-five hundred subscribers in fifty-four different nations, including Iran, Pakistan, Singapore, Turkey, Chile, India, Saudi Arabia, New Zealand, Japan, England, the United States, and Ukraine. This is the world into which this essay goes. What, might I ask, are the binding values among the nations I mention above—Muslim, Christian, Hindu, secular, democracy, monarchy, theocracy? How do we "form our own Social Contract," as Barlow proposes? Is it realistically possible? Each and every reader of *MEME* is participating in the creation of cyberspace. How, cutting through the digital polemic, do we then, as supposed cybercitizens or netizens, act in consort to form a community with the depth of complexity equivalent to a geographic nation? The last time I checked, some of these countries on my subscription list were in state of near war, yet we are all expected to form some autonomous, self-governing community online, bypassing the very real history of *Homo sapiens*? Unless the last thirty thousand years of recorded human history are suddenly null and void, I think the odds of pulling that off in the near future are pretty low.

So this ostensible solution of creating a parallel government in cyberspace will not work anytime soon. Why is this then a centerpiece of debate over establishing standards for cyberspace?

What Will Work?

Computer networks and the communications they carry are products of people, and people live by geography, in physical space, under the rule of law. Cyberspace then will be governed by people in the context of their culture. The great challenge is to create a set of standards that somehow bridges this incredible range of cultures, while allowing people the freedom to communicate. Part of what makes this difficult to solve is the mystique surrounding cyberspace, as if the whole thing were one monolithic environment. It is not. Cyberspace is actually a set of different communications tools, each of which should be treated differently. One end can be marked "private," and the other end "public." The more "public" a forum, the greater the rights of society; the more "private," the greater the rights of the individual. In the real world, life is a constant balancing act, a perpetual negotiation. Cyberspace is part of the real world. By forcing this debate into a "winner takes all" do or die struggle, we get to avoid the tedium of negotiating, arguing, and trading to reach a consensus. But that, in the end, is the tried and true way of succeeding. So to start with, here are examples of what I mean by different communications tools, ranging from the private to the public:

Private
Electronic mail, one-to-one
Internet Relay Chat (IRC) (by invitation only)
File Transfer Protocol (FTP) (password protected)

CU-SeeMe video conferencing (point-to-point, by invitation only)
Internet audio telephone (point-to-point, by invitation only)
World Wide Web (WWW) (password protected sites)

Public
Electronic mail–based distribution lists (like *MEME*)
File Transfer Protocol (FTP) (anonymous, no password required)
Usenet news
Internet relay chat (IRC) (open, no invitation needed)
World Wide Web (WWW) (no password required)
CU-SeeMe video conferencing (open reflector site, no password required)

There is a precedent for seeing media this way (in the United States). The content of telephone conversations is seen as private, and moving through the spectrum of media the other extreme is broadcast television. Broadcast television is the ultimate public medium (and hence faces the most public restrictions on content). In between the telephone and television you get a series of media, moving from private to public, with print, videocassettes, and film falling in the middle. The tricky thing with cyberspace is that it is all these mediums rolled into one. When Yahoo!, a popular Web site, gets fourteen million hits a day, that starts to look a lot like television. This newsletter, sent to several thousand people who subscribe, looks a lot like print—a bit more regulated than a phone call but a lot less regulated than a television show. Yet the technology behind *MEME* and Yahoo! is the same.

I don't think a lot of lawmakers really understand this. That's one good reason that we must work to demystify cyberspace. Prose that keeps this medium mysterious serves only to increase confusion and does more harm than good. Legislators, unfamiliar with this medium, look askance to rhetoric that simply tells them they are dinosaurs trudging toward the dust bin of history. Their response is to listen to the stimulus they do understand—politics. What we—as people who cherish this medium—can do is work to get it in the hands of those who set our laws. Unfamiliarity with the medium is cyberspace's worst enemy.

Lost in the shuffle may be the important fact of why cyberspace is worth nurturing: it is a medium that, for the first time in the history of the world, gives one person the power to reach another person or a million people equally easily. Never before has such power rested in hands of nonelites, such as television companies and governments. Wider access to power is the essence of what is great about the Internet, acting like vaccine for a world where information is consolidating into the hands of a few media monoliths. But this power is also the source of the Internet's own potential undoing. Greater power for each of us requires greater responsibility. That's the flip side of the equation: are we up to that challenge?

5

HyperMedia Freedom

Richard Barbrook

Neoliberal Fantasies

Introduction

By passing the Telecommunications Act of 1996 (which includes the Communications Decency Act), the two dominant political parties in the United States have jointly agreed that the convergence of media, telecommunications, and computing should be driven by market competition between large corporations. Recognizing that massive economies of scale are needed for the construction of a national broadband network, the Democratic president and the Republican legislature have lifted most restrictions on the cross-ownership of media and telecommunications systems. In addition, further legislation is pending that will propose a dramatic extension of the rights of copyright owners to provide the legal structure for an electronic marketplace in information commodities. Quietly forgetting its New Deal aspirations for an information superhighway construction program, the U.S. government has now abdicated its strategic responsibilities to the private sector. But this faith in market competition entails risks. In the near future, no nation will be able to compete within the global marketplace without a fiber-optic grid. Just as the building of railway, road, electricity, gas, telephone, and water networks in the past laid the basis for modern urban living, the infobahn will provide the basic infrastructure for the next stage of capitalism. The fiber-optic grid

This chapter originally appeared on the HyperMedia Research Centre's Web site, and, in modified form, in the e-journal *C-Theory*. Reprinted by permission of the author. © Richard Barbrook, 1996.

will not only distribute entertainment and information but also enable people to work collaboratively in almost every sector of production. Encouraged by funding from high-tech corporations, the American political establishment is gambling that the construction of the National Information Infrastructure can be successfully carried out through the neoliberal panaceas of deregulation and privatization.

Given the history of the development of the personal computer and the Internet, it seems more likely that the infobahn will emerge from the miscegenation of the public, private, and community sectors. Yet, ironically, debate in the United States over the Telecommunications Act of 1996 hasn't been centered on whether unrestrained market competition between private companies is the only way to develop cyberspace. Instead, a fierce controversy has raged around an attempt to impose broadcasting-style content controls on the Net. Under the terms of the Act, online services cannot allow access to "pornography" or the use of the "seven dirty words" in any form. From being a largely unregulated form of communications, the Net has now suddenly come under the most restrictive form of censorship applied in the United States. Not surprisingly, there has been a storm of protest from the online community. Net sites were turned black, and blue ribbons have been attached to Web pages in protest against these restrictions on the freedom of speech. Legal actions are underway to test whether the regulations contravene the right of freedom of expression guaranteed by the First Amendment of the Constitution. There are important issues at stake in this controversy. Parents are justified to be concerned about pedophiles using the Net to contact minors or distribute pornography. Children should be allowed to grow into puberty at their own pace and free from sexual violence. Yet the restrictions in the Telecommunications Act aren't simply concerned with clamping down on a small minority of child abusers. Under pressure from Christian fundamentalists, the two main political parties have passed a law that could potentially prevent the distribution of any form of sexual material—even among consenting adults. If this attempt at censorship succeeds, online services in the United States would only be able to provide content that conformed to the repressive mores of the American Puritan tradition.

Turn On, Log In, and Drop Out!

As with any other law, the Telecommunications Act of 1996 will face the problem of enforcement. The "War on Drugs" hasn't stopped Americans from voraciously consuming billions of dollars of illegal chemicals every year. There must be similar doubts about the practicality of the censorship measures in the new Act. Is the American state really going to be able to prevent its citizens saying *fuck* to each other in their private e-mails? How will it prevent people logging on to Web sites in other countries with a less hypocritical attitude toward adult sexuality? The development of hypermedia is the result of the convergence not only of radio and television broadcasting but also of other types of less censored media, such as printing and music. Why should the Net be subject to broadcasting-style restrictions rather than those applied to printed material? A long political battle is now beginning to find an acceptable level of legal controls over the new forms of social communications.

Yet at this crucial moment, one of the leaders of the principal cyber-rights lobbying group—the Electronic Frontier Foundation (EFF)—has been gripped by an attack of ideological hysteria. In a bizarre act of presumption, John Perry Barlow, the EFF's cofounder, has issued "A Declaration of the Independence of Cyberspace." In this manifesto, he casts himself as the new Thomas Jefferson calling the people to arms against the tyranny of Bill Clinton—"the great invertebrate in Washington." Claiming to speak "on behalf of the future," he declares that the elected government of the United States has no right to legislate over "Cyberspace, the new home of the Mind." Because "we are creating a world that is both everywhere and nowhere, but it is not where bodies live," Barlow asserts that cyberspace exists outside the jurisdication of the U.S. or any other existing state. In cyberspace, only Net users have the right to decide the rules. According to Barlow, the inhabitants of this virtual space already police themselves without any interference from federal legislators: "you do not know our culture, our ethics, or the unwritten codes that already provide our society with more order than could be obtained by any of your impositions." Users of the Net should therefore "reject the authorities of distant, uninformed powers" and ignore the censorship imposed by the Telecommunications Act.

It is too easy to laugh at this "Declaration" as a high-tech version of the old hippie fantasy of dropping out of straight society into a psychedelic dreamworld. In sci-fi novels, cyberspace has been often poetically described as a "consensual hallucination." Yet in reality, the construction of the infobahn is an intensely physical act. It is flesh and blood workers who spend many hours of their lives developing hardware, assembling PCs, laying cables, installing router systems, writing software programs, designing Web pages, and so on. It is obviously a fantasy to believe that cyberspace can be ever be separated from the societies—and states—within which these people spend their lives. Barlow's "Declaration of the Independence of Cyberspace" therefore cannot be treated as a serious response to the threat to civil liberties on the Net posed by the Christian fundamentalists and other bigots. Instead, it is a symptom of the intense ideological crisis now facing the advocates of free-market libertarianism within the online community. At the very moment that cyberspace is about to become opened up to the general public, the individual freedom that they prized in the Net seems about to be legislated out of existence with little or no political opposition. Crucially, the lifting of restrictions on market competition hasn't advanced the cause of freedom of expression at all. On the contrary, the privatization of cyberspace seems to be taking place alongside the introduction of heavy censorship. Unable to explain this phenomenon within the confines of the Californian Ideology, Barlow has decided to escape into neoliberal hyperreality rather than face the contradictions of really existing capitalism.

Cyberspace: The Final Frontier
The ideological bankruptcy of the West Coast libertarians derives from their historically inaccurate belief that cyberspace has been developed by the "left-right fusion of free minds with free markets" (Louis Rossetto, editor-in-chief of *Wired* magazine). As Andy Cameron and I showed in our article, "The Californian Ideology," neoliberalism has been embraced by the West Coast version of Kroker and Weinstein's "virtual class" as a way of reconciling the anarchism of the New Left with the entrepreneurial zeal of the New Right. Above all, this weird hybrid has relied on projecting old myths about the American revolution onto the

process of digital convergence. According to *Wired* magazine, the development of hypermedia would create a high-tech "Jeffersonian democracy": the eighteenth century will be reborn in the twenty-first century.

In his "Declaration," John Perry Barlow consciously mimics the rhetoric of the founding fathers' Declaration of Independence of the United States. Once again, free-spirited individuals are standing up to an oppressive and corrupt government. Yet these revolutionary phrases from the past contain within them many reactionary aspirations. Back in 1776, Jefferson expressed the national dream of building a rural utopia in the wilderness of America. The winning of independence from Britain was necessary so that Americans could live as independent, self-sufficent farmers in small villages. Jefferson's pastoral vision rejected city life as the source of corruption—which he saw in the rapidly expanding conurbations of contemporary Europe. But as America itself began to industrialize, the pastoral dream had to be displaced westward toward the frontier. Even after the Indian wars had ended, the Wild West remained a place of individual freedom and self-discovery in American mythology. Jefferson had become a cowboy.

By its name, the Electronic Frontier Foundation is therefore invoking not just the cowboy myths of the last century but also the pastoral fantasies of the writer of the original Declaration of Independence. When U.S. government agencies first decided to crack down on hackers, a group of old radicals decided to defend the new generation of cyberpunks. Out of this act of solidarity, the EFF emerged as the political lobby group of the West Coast cybercommunity. Using libertarian arguments, it campaigned for minimal censorship and regulation over the new information technologies. But the EFF was never just a campaign for cyberrights. It was also a leading cheerleader for the individualist fantasies of the Californian ideology. According to the tenets of this confused doctrine, hippie antiauthoritianism is being finally realized through the fusion of digital technologies with free-market liberalism. Yet the inevitable rebirth of Jeffersonian democracy now seems to have been postponed. Above all, the lobbying work of the EFF appears to have been in vain: the repressive measures in the Telecommunications Act passed with almost no opposition in the legislature or from the executive. At this moment of crisis, Barlow has embraced the wildest fantasies of the West Coast anarchocapitalists. Once encryption is widely available, they believe that free-spirited individuals will be able to live within a virtual world free from censorship, taxes, and all the other evils of big government. Unable to face the social contradictions of living within the digital city, Barlow has decided to join the virtual cowboys living on the electronic frontier.

If This Is the Electronic Frontier, Who Are the Indians?
It is no accident that Barlow mimics Jefferson for this retrofuturist program. Unlike Europeans who fantasied about rural utopias, Jefferson never rejected technology along with the city. On the contrary, the "sage of Monticello" was an enthusiastic proponent of technological innovation. Crucially, he believed that it was possible to freeze the social development of the United States while simultaneously modernizing its methods of production. The proponents of the Californian Ideology follow a similar logic. They wish to preserve cyberspace as the home of rugged individuals and innovative entrepreneurs while at the same time supporting the commercial expansion of the Net. For them, the development of the new information society can take place only through the realization of the eternal principles of liberalism revealed by the founding fathers. Yet like all other countries, the United States exists within profane history. Its political and economic structures are the result of centuries of contradictory social processes and are not the expression of sacred truths. Its leaders were complex human beings, not one-sided "men of marble."

This dialectical reality can be most easily seen by looking at the lives of those founding fathers—Thomas Jefferson, George Washington, and James Madison—invoked by Barlow in his Declaration. On the one hand, they were great revolutionaries who successfully won national independence and established constitutional government in America. Yet at the same time, they were vicious plantation owners who lived off the forced labor of their slaves. In other countries, people have come to terms with the contradictory nature of their modernizing revolutionaries. Even Chinese Communists now admit that Mao Zedong's legacy contains both positive elements, such as the liberation of the country from colonialism, and negative features, such as the massacres of the Cultural Revolution. In contrast, Barlow—and many other Americans—can never acknowledge that their beloved republic wasn't just created by hard-working, freedom-loving farmers but also through the slavery of black people and the "ethnic cleansing" of Indians. The plantation economy of the Old South and the extermination of the First Nations are the equivalents of the Irish famine, the Holocaust, and the gulag archipelago in American history. But these contradictions of the real history of the United States are too painful to contemplate for Barlow and other believers in the ahistorical truths of liberal individualism. Jefferson must remain as an unsullied portrait chiseled into the face of Mount Rushmore.

Yet in understanding contemporary debates over the future of the Net, it is important to remember the contradictory nature of historical precedents glibly invoked by the Californian Ideology. Back in the early nineteenth century, the spread of the new industrial technologies freed no slaves. On the contrary, the invention of the cotton gin and mechanical spinning machines actually reinforced the archaic and brutal institutions of slavery in the Old South. Nowadays, the libertarian rhetoric of individual empowerment through new information technologies is similarly used to hide the reality of the growing polarization between the largely white virtual class and the mainly black underclass. If interpreted with a European sense of irony, Jeffersonian democracy can be an appropriate metaphor for the dystopian present found in the inner cities of the United States.

Social Democratic Solutions

The First Electronic Frontier

Because the liberal principles of Jeffersonian democracy exist outside real history, Barlow and other Californian ideologues cannot recognize the temporal dynamics of really existing capitalism. Although new frontiers may be opened up by enterprising individuals, the original pioneers are quickly replaced by more collective forms of organization, such as joint-stock companies. For instance, the free-spirited cowboys of the Wild West soon ended up as employees of agribusinesses financed by the industrialized East. A similar process occured in the first electronic frontier in U.S. history—radio broadcasting. Back in the early 1920s, radio was initially developed by an enthusiastic minority of amateurs and entrepreneurs. With few restrictions over broadcasting, almost anyone could either set up their own station or rent airtime on somebody else's. Yet once cheap radio receivers became widely available, the airwaves were rapidly taken over by the corporate networks provided by NBC and CBS. This process of monopolization was consolidated by the federal government through the Radio Act of 1927, which restricted broadcasting to the holders of licenses granted by a state-appointed regulatory body. Not surprisingly, conservative politicians seized the opportunity to silence political and cultural radicals, especially from the left. However, this imposition of censorship encountered little popular disapproval. On the contrary, most voters supported the Radio Act because the licensing system ensured that the popular programs of the national networks could be heard clearly without interference from other stations. The democratization of the availability of radio broadcasting had ironically removed most opportunities for participation within the new media.

The key question now is whether the new electronic frontier of cyberspace is condemned to follow the same path of development. Contrary to Barlow's assertion that cyberspace is not a "public construction project," the principal obstacle to the expansion of the Net in the United States is the problem of who pays for the building of the fiber-optic grid. Given that they refuse to provide state investment, the Democrats and Republicans have had to use the Telecommunications Act of 1996 to create a regulatory framework friendly to the large corporations that possess the capital needed for the construction of the infobahn. Above all, both parties have given their blessing to the growing number of mergers between companies operating within the converging sectors of the media, computing, and telecommunications. Because it has lost its competitive edge in its traditional Fordist industries, the American economy now relies heavily on companies at the center of the process of digital convergence, such as the Hollywood studios, Microsoft, and AT&T. Far from encouraging a Jeffersonian democracy composed of small businesses, the Telecommunications Act has cleared the way for the emergence of American "national champions" that have sufficent size both to build the infobahn at home and to compete successfully abroad against their European and Asian rivals.

For many on the left, these multimedia corporations are the greatest threat to free speech on the Net. As happened in radio—and later television—broadcasting, the desire to attract a mass audience can be a far more effective method of inhibiting political radicalism and cultural experimentation than any half-baked censorship provisions tacked onto the end of a Telecommunications Act. The neo-Luddite pessimists have their worst fears confirmed when corporate leaders openly proclaim their aim to transform the Net into "interactive television." In this scenario, the new forms of sociability existing within contemporary cyberspace would be replaced by the passive consumption of pop entertainment and biased information provided by multimedia corporations. Despite their disingenuous protests against the antipornography provisions in the new Act, these corporations cannot be too sad to see the introduction of regulations that would turn the Net into a safe—and therefore profitable—form of family fun.

In this vision of the future, Jeffersonian democracy is simply neoliberal propaganda designed to win support for the privatization of cyberspace from the members of the "virtual class." By promiscuously mixing New Left and New Right together, the Californian ideology attracts those individuals who hope that they're smart—or lucky—enough to seize the opportunities presented by the rapid changes in the technological basis of social production. But while they're being sold the dream of making it big as cyberentrepreneurs, most digital artisans are, in reality, denied the employment security previously enjoyed by workers in Fordist industries. Far from being self-sufficent pioneers on the electronic frontier, many end up living hand-to-mouth from one short-term corporate contract to another. Similarly, the privatization of cyberspace also threatens community uses of cyberspace. As more commercial money is spent on providing online services, it becomes increasingly difficult for amateurs to create Web sites of sufficent quality to attract large number of users. Yet as happened in 1920s radio broadcasting, many people will happily accept corporate control over cyberspace if they are provided with well-produced online services. According to the neo-Luddites, the democratization of the availability of the Net is removing most opportunities for meaningful participation within cyberspace.

Cyberspace Is Social

The current controversy in the United States over the Telecommunications Act of 1996 has cruelly exposed the limitations of the Californian ideology. Barlow may dream of escaping into the hyperreality of cyber-space, but he is simply trying to avoid facing the political and economic contradictions of really existing capitalism. Far from producing an electronic frontier composed of many small businesses, the commercialization of cyberspace is creating the conditions for the concentration of capital on a global scale. Given the huge costs of building a national broadband network, only very large corporations can mobilize enough investment to carry out this infrastructure project. Within this emerging oligopoly, innovative entrepreneurs will still achieve public prominance as either leaders of big businesses or as subcontractors of the multimedia corporations. But their individual success will be made possible only through the huge collective effort to build the infobahn. The dynamics of digital convergence within really existing capitalism are pushing toward the ever-increasing socialization of production and communications and not the realization of eighteenth-century fantasies of individual self-sufficency.

It is therefore rather one-sided for the EFF to direct its criticisms solely against the antipornography regulations contained within the Telecommunications Act. Freedom of expression on the Net is threatened not only by the state but also by the market. As shown by the history of radio broadcasting in the United States, these two forms of censorship have often been imposed in parallel. Both politicians and corporations have a common interest in ensuring that middle America is not disturbed by any radical political and cultural ideas emanating from new forms of mass communications. Therefore, any meaningful campaign for cyber-rights has to fight for freedom of expression against both state and market forms of censorship. The development of the Net offers a way of overcoming the political and economic restrictions on free speech within the existing media. Everyone could have the opportunity not only to receive information and entertainment but also to transmit their own productions. The problem is how this potentiality will be realized.

A campaign for hypermedia freedom can be successful only if it recognizes the inherent contradictions within this fundamental right of citizens. The political rights of each individual are circumscribed by the rights of other citizens. For instance, to protect children, the state has a duty to restrict the freedom of speech of pedophiles on the Net. Because ethnic minorities have the right to live in peace, the democratic republic should try to prevent fascists from organizing online. But apart from these minimal restrictions, citizens do have the right to say what they like to each other. A democratic state certainly has no mandate to impose a narrow religious morality on all its citizens regardless of their own beliefs.

Similarly, a campaign for cyberrights must also recognize the economic contradictions within hypermedia freedom. Because they use amateur labor, community hypermedia projects can happily exist within the high-tech gift economy. But if digital artisans are to be paid for their work, some form of commodity exchange will have to be created within the Net. However, the dominance of the free market will inhibit the free circulation of ideas. Therefore, campaigns for cyberrights have to engage with the economic contradictions of hypermedia freedom. Above all, they cannot take absolutist positions over the shape of the digital economy. On the contrary, the development of cyberspace has so far been carried out through a hybrid of public, private, and community initiatives. All sectors have played an important role in the construction of the infobahn. But in the Telecommunications Act, Americans now face the problem of the wrong type of government action rather than too much state intervention. While it seems all too eager to impose moral censorship on Net users, the federal government has simultaneously shirked its duty to ensure that all citizens can have access to online services. While the corporations may possess the resources to build the broadband network, the state should use its powers to prevent any section of society being excluded from cyberspace for lack of resources.

Contrary to the predictions of the pessimists, it is possible to win the struggle against both the political and economic censorship of cyberspace. Although the state can—and should—prosecute the small minority of pedophiles and fascists, the resources needed to spy on everyone's e-mail and Web sites will make the imposition of moral puritanism very difficult to enforce. Even with sophisticated censorship programs, the sheer volume of Net traffic should eventually overwhelm even a well-funded surveillance body. While it might just about be possible to regulate the output of thousands of radio and television stations, the sheer cost of vetting many millions of users logging onto a global network of online services would be prohibitive. The social nature of hypermedia is the best defense of the individual's right of freedom of expression.

Similarly, the corporation's ambition to buy up the whole of cyberspace will also be checked by the social basis of the process of convergence. For instance, the recent trials of interactive television have been commercial failures. As Andy Cameron points out in *Dissimulations*, the corporate cheerleaders are trapped within a category mistake: they're trying to impose the form of earlier media onto the new hypermedia. Above all, interactivity can't be restricted to clicking through a series of menu options. Many people want to meet other people within cyberspace. Unlike the existing electronic media, the Net is not centered on the one-way flow of communications from a limited number of transmitters. On the contrary, hypermedia is a two-way form of communications where everybody is both a receiver and a transmitter. The multimedia corporations will undoubtedly play a leading role in building the infrastructure of the infobahn and selling information commodities over the Net, but they will find it impossible to monopolize the social potential of cyberspace.

Over recent years, the advocates of the Californian Ideology have been claiming that eighteenth-century liberal individualism would be miraculously reborn through the process of digital convergence. Yet now that online services are becoming available to the mass of the population, the collective nature of the new information society is becoming increasingly obvious. Within politics, electronic democracy will be at the center of the relationship between representatives and their voters. Within all sectors of the economy, the infobahn will soon become the basic infrastructure for collaborative work across time and space. Crucially, this socialization of politics and economics will be the best protection for individual freedom within cyberspace. Far from having to escape into a neoliberal hyperreality, people can utilize the new digital technologies to enhance their lives both inside and outside cyberspace. The electronic agora is yet to be built.

II

Crypto Anarchy

6

The Crypto Anarchist Manifesto

Timothy C. May

Cypherpunks of the World,
Several of you at the "physical Cypherpunks" gathering yesterday in Silicon Valley requested that more of the material passed out in meetings be available electronically to the entire readership of the Cypherpunks list, spooks, eavesdroppers, and all.

Here's "The Crypto Anarchist Manifesto" I read at the September 1992 founding meeting. It dates back to mid-1988 and was distributed to some like-minded technoanarchists at the Crypto '88 conference and then again at the Hackers Conference that year. I later gave talks at Hackers on this in 1989 and 1990.

There are a few things I'd change, but for historical reasons I'll just leave it as is. Some of the terms may be unfamiliar to you.... I hope the Crypto Glossary I just distributed will help.

—Tim May

The Crypto Anarchist Manifesto

A specter is haunting the modern world, the specter of crypto anarchy. Computer technology is on the verge of providing the ability for individuals and groups to communicate and interact with each other in a totally anonymous manner. Two persons may exchange messages, conduct business, and negotiate electronic contracts without ever knowing the True Name, or legal identity, of the other. Interactions over networks will be untraceable, via extensive rerouting of encrypted packets and tamper-proof boxes which implement cryptographic protocols with nearly perfect assurance against any tampering. Reputations will be of central importance, far more important in dealings than even the credit ratings of today. These developments will alter completely the nature of government regulation, the ability to tax and control economic interactions, the ability to keep information secret, and will even alter the nature of trust and reputation.

The technology for this revolution—and it surely will be both a social and economic revolution—has existed in theory for the past decade. The methods are based upon public-key encryption, zero-knowledge interactive proof systems, and various software protocols for interaction, authentication, and verification. The focus has until now been on academic conferences in Europe and the U.S., conferences monitored closely by the National Security Agency. But only recently have computer networks and personal computers attained sufficient speed to make the ideas practically realizable. And the next ten years will bring enough additional speed to make the ideas economically feasible and essentially unstoppable. High-speed networks, ISDN, tamper-proof boxes, smart cards, satellites, Ku-band transmitters, multi-MIPS personal computers, and encryption chips now under development will be some of the enabling technologies.

The State will of course try to slow or halt the spread of this technology, citing national security concerns, use of the technology by drug dealers and tax evaders, and fears of societal disintegration. Any of these concerns will be valid; crypto anarchy will allow national secrets to be trade freely and will allow illicit and stolen materials to be traded. An anonymous computerized market will even make possible abhorrent markets for assassinations and extortion. Various criminal and foreign elements will be active users of CryptoNet. But this will not halt the spread of crypto anarchy.

Just as the technology of printing altered and reduced the power of medieval guilds and the social power structure, so too will cryptologic methods fundamentally alter the nature of corporations and of government interference in economic transactions. Combined with emerging information markets, crypto anarchy will create a liquid market for any and all material which can be put into words and pictures. And just as a seemingly minor invention like barbed wire made possible the fencing-off of vast ranches and farms, thus altering forever the concepts of land and property rights in the frontier West, so too will the seemingly minor discovery out of an arcane branch of mathematics come to be the wire clippers which dismantle the barbed wire around intellectual property.

Arise, you have nothing to lose but your barbed wire fences!

7

Crypto Anarchy and Virtual Communities

Timothy C. May

Modern Cryptography

The past two decades have produced a revolution in cryptography (crypto, for short)—the science of the making of ciphers and codes. Beyond just simple ciphers, useful mainly for keeping communications secret, modern crypto includes diverse tools for authentication of messages, for digital time stamping of documents, for hiding messages in other documents (steganography), and even for schemes for digital cash.

Public key cryptography, the creation of Diffie and Hellman, has dramatically altered the role of crypto. Coming at the same time as the wholesale conversion to computer networks and worldwide communications, it has been a key element of security, confidence, and success. The role of crypto will only become more important over the coming decades. Pretty Good Privacy (PGP) is a popular version of the algorithm developed by Rivest, Shamir, and Adleman (known, of course, as RSA). The RSA algorithm was given a patent in the United States, though not in any European countries, and is licensed commercially.[1]

These tools are described in detail in various texts and conference proceedings and are not the subject of this chapter.[2] The focus here is on the implications of strong crypto for cyberspace, especially on virtual communities. Mention should be made of the role of David Chaum in

---

defining the key concepts here. In several seminal papers,[3] Chaum introduced the ideas of using public key cryptography methods for anonymous, untraceable electronic mail, for digital money systems in which spender identity is not revealed, and in schemes related to these. (I make no claims that Chaum agrees with my conclusions about the political and socioeconomic implications of these results.)

Virtual Communities

Notes: cyberspace, Habitat, VR, Vinge, etc. Crypto holds up the "walls" of these cyberspatial realities. Access control, access rights, modification privileges.

Virtual communities are the networks of individuals or groups that are not necessarily closely connected geographically. The "virtual" is meant to imply a nonphysical linking but should not be taken to mean that these are any less communitylike than are conventional physical communities.

Examples include churches, service organizations, clubs, criminal gangs, cartels, fan groups, etc. The Catholic Church and the Boy Scouts are both examples of virtual communities that span the globe, transcend national borders, and create a sense of allegiance, of belonging, and a sense of community. Likewise, the Mafia is a virtual community (with its enforcement mechanisms, its own extralegal rules, etc.) Lots of other examples: Masons, Triads, the Red Cross, Interpol, Islam, Judaism, Mormons, Sindero Luminoso, the IRA, drug cartels, terrorist groups, Aryan Nation, Greenpeace, the Animal Liberation Front, and so on. There are undoubtedly many more such virtual communities than there are nation-states, and the ties that bind them are for the most part much stronger than are chauvinist nationalist emotions. Any group in which the common interests of the group, be it a shared ideology or a particular interest is enough to create a cohesive community.

Corporations are another prime example of a virtual community, having scattered sites, private communication channels (generally inaccessible to the outside world, including the authorities), and their own goals and methods. In fact, many "cyberpunk" (not cypherpunk) fiction authors make a mistake, I think, in assuming the future world will be dominated by transnational megacorporate "states." In fact, corporations are just one example of many of such virtual communities that will be effectively on a par with nation states. (Note especially that any laws designed to limit use of crypto cause immediate and profound problems for corporations and that countries like France and the Philippines, which have attempted to limit the use of crypto, have mostly been ignored by corporations. Any attempts to outlaw crypto will produce a surge of sudden "incorporations," thus gaining for the new corporate members the aegis of corporate privacy.) In an academic setting, "invisible colleges" are the communities of researchers.

These virtual communities typically are "opaque" to outsiders. Attempts to gain access to the internals of these communities are rarely successful. Law-enforcement and intelligence agencies (such as the National Security Agency in the United States, Chobetsu in Japan, SDECE in France, and so on) may infiltrate such groups and use electronic surveillance (ELINT) to monitor these virtual communities. Not surprisingly, these communities have been early adopters of encryption technology, ranging from scrambled cellphones to full-blown PGP encryption.[4]

The use of encryption by "evil" groups—such as child pornographers, terrorists, abortionists, and abortion protesters—is cited by those who wish to limit civilian access to crypto tools. We call these groups the "Four Horsemen of the Infocalypse," as they are so often cited as the reason that ordinary citizen units of the nation state should not have access to crypto.

This is clearly a dangerous argument to make, for various good reasons. The basic right of free speech is the right to speak in a language one's neighbors or governing leaders may not find comprehensible—encrypted speech. There's not enough space here to go into the many good arguments against a limit on access to privacy, communications tools, and crypto.

The advent of full-featured communications systems for computer-mediated virtual communities will have even more profound implications. MUDs and MOOs (multi-user domains, etc.) and 3D virtual realities are one avenue, and text-centric Net communications are another. (Someday, soon, they'll merge, as described in Vernor Vinge's prophetic 1980 novella, *True Names*.)

Observability and Surveillance

An interesting way to view issues of network visibility is in terms of the transparency of nodes and links between nodes. *Transparent* means visible to outsiders, perhaps those in law enforcement or the intelligence community. *Opaque* means not transparent, not visible. A postcard is transparent; a sealed letter is opaque. PGP inventor Phil Zimmermann has likened the requirement for transparency to being ordered to use postcards for all correspondence, with encryption the equivalent of an opaque envelope (envelopes can be opened, of course, and long have been).

Transparent links and nodes are the norm in a police state, such as the former Soviet Union, Iraq, China, and so forth. Communications channels are tapped, and private use of computers is restricted. (This is becoming increasingly hard to do, even for police states; many cite the spread of communications options as a proximate cause of the collapse of communism in recent years.)

There are interesting "chemistries" or "algebras" of transparent versus opaque links and nodes. What happens if links must be transparent but nodes are allowed to be opaque? (The answer: the result is the same as if opaque links and nodes were allowed—that is, the full implications of strong crypto. Hence, any attempt to ban communications crypto while still allowing private CPUs to exist....)

If Alice and Bob are free to communicate, and to choose routing paths, then Alice can use "crypto arbitrage" (a variation on the term, "regulatory arbitrage," the term Eric Hughes uses to capture this idea of moving transactions to other jurisdictions) to communicate with sites—perhaps in other countries—that will perform as she wishes. This can mean remailing, mixing, etc. As an example, Canadian citizens who are told they cannot access information on the Homolka-Teale murder case (a controversial case in which the judge has ordered the media in Canada and entering Canada not to discuss the gory details) nevertheless have a vast array of options, including using telnet, gopher, ftp, the Web, etc., to access sites in many other countries or even in no country in particular.

Most of the consequences described here arise from this chemistry of links and nodes: unless nearly all node and links are forced to be transparent, including links to other nations and the nodes in those nations, then private communication can still occur. Crypto anarchy results.

Crypto Anarchy

"The Net is an anarchy." This truism is the core of crypto anarchy—no central control, no ruler, no leader (except by example or reputation), no "laws." No single nation controls the Net, no administrative body sets policy. The Ayatollah in Iran is as powerless to stop a newsgroup—alt.wanted.moslem.women or alt.wanted.moslem.gay come to mind—he doesn't like as the president of France is as powerless to stop, say, the abuse of the French language in soc.culture.french. Likewise, the CIA can't stop newsgroups, sites, or Web pages that give away its secrets. At least not in terms of the Net itself. What non-Net steps might be taken are left as an exercise for the paranoid and the cautious.

This essential anarchy is much more common than many think. Anarchy (the absence of a ruler telling another person what to do) is common in many walks of life—choosing books to read, movies to see, friends to socialize with, and so on. Anarchy does not mean complete freedom (we can, after all, read only the books that someone has written and had published), but it does mean freedom from external coercion. Anarchy as a concept, though, has been tainted by other associations.

First, the anarchy here is not the anarchy of popular conception—lawlessness, disorder, and chaos. Nor is it the bomb-throwing anarchy of the nineteenth century "black" anarchists, usually associated with Russia and labor movements. Nor is it the "black flag" anarchy of anarcho-syndicalism and writers such as Proudhon. Rather, the anarchy being spoken of here is the anarchy of "absence of government" (literally, "an arch," without a chief or head).

This is the same sense of anarchy used in anarchocapitalism, the libertarian free-market ideology that promotes voluntary, uncoerced economic transactions.[5] I devised the term *crypto anarchy* as a pun on crypto, meaning "hidden," on the use of "crypto" in combination with political views (as in Gore Vidal's famous charge to William F. Buckley: "You're crypto fascist!") and of course because the technology of crypto makes this form of anarchy possible. The first presentation of this term was in a 1988 "Manifesto," whimsically patterned after another famous manifesto.⁶ Perhaps a more popularly understandable term, such as "cyber liberty," might have some advantages, but crypto anarchy has its own charm, I think.

And *anarchy* in this sense does not mean that local hierarchies don't exist or that no rulers exist. Groups outside the direct control of local governmental authorities may still have leaders, rulers, club presidents, elected bodies, etc. Many will not, though.

Politically, virtual communities outside the scope of local governmental control may present problems of law enforcement and tax collection. (Some of us like this aspect.) Avoidance of coerced transactions can mean avoidance of taxes, avoidance of laws saying who one can sell to and who one can't, and so forth. It is likely that many will be unhappy that some are using cryptography to avoid laws designed to control behavior.

National borders are becoming more transparent than ever to data. A flood of bits crosses the borders of most developed countries' phone lines, cables, fibers, satellite up/downlinks, and millions of diskettes, tapes, CDs, etc. Stopping data at the borders is less than hopeless.

Finally, the ability to move data around the world at will, the ability to communicate to remote sites at will, means that a kind of "regulatory arbitrage" can be used to avoid legal roadblocks. For example, when remailing into the United States from a site in the Netherlands, whose laws apply? (If one thinks that U.S. laws should apply to sites in the Netherlands, then does Iraqi law apply in the United States? And so on.)

This regulatory arbitrage is also useful for avoiding the welter of laws and regulations that operations in one country may face, including the "deep pockets" lawsuits so many in the United States face. Moving operations on the Net outside a litigious jurisdiction is one step to reduce this business liability. Like Swiss banks, but different.

True Names and Anonymous Systems

Something needs to be said about the role of anonymity and digital pseudonyms. This is a topic for an essay unto itself, of course.

Are true names really needed? Why are they asked for? Does the nation state have any valid reason to demand they be used?

People want to know who they are dealing with, for psychological/ evolutionary reasons and to better ensure traceability should they need to locate a person to enforce the terms of a transaction. The purely anonymous person is perhaps justifiably viewed with suspicion.

And yet pseudonyms are successful in many cases. We rarely know whether someone who presents himself by some name is "actually" that person. Authors, artists, performers, etc., often use pseudonyms. What matters is persistence and nonforgeability. Crypto provides this.

On the Cypherpunks[7] mailing list, well-respected digital pseudonyms have appeared and are thought of no less highly than their "real" colleagues are.

The whole area of digitally authenticated reputations, and the "reputation capital" that accumulates or is affected by the opinions of others, is an area that combines economics, game theory, psychology, and expectations. A lot more study is needed. It is unclear if governments will move to a system of demanding "Information Highway Driver's Licenses," figuratively speaking, or how systems like this could ever be enforced. (The chemistry of opaque nodes and links, again.)

Examples and Uses

It surprises many people that some of these uses are already being intensively explored. Anonymous remailers are used by tens of thousands of persons—and perhaps abused.[8] And of course encryption, via RSA, PGP, etc., is very common in some communities (hackers, Net users, freedom fighters, white separatists, etc.... I make no moral judgments here about people who use these methods).

Remailers are a good example to look at in more detail. There are two current main flavors of remailers:

• Cypherpunk-style remailers process text messages to redirect mail to other sites, using a command syntax that allows arbitrary nesting of remailing (as many sites as one wishes) with PGP encryption at each level of nesting.

• Julf-style remailers are based on the original work of Karl Kleinpaste and are operated/maintained by Julf Helsingius in Finland. No encryption, and only one such site at present. (This system has been used extensively for messages posted to the Usenet and is basically successful.

The model is based on operator trustworthiness and his location in Finland, beyond the reach of court orders and subpoenas from most countries.)

The Cypherpunks remailers currently number about twenty, with more being added every month. There is no reason not to expect hundreds of such remailers in a few years. One experimental "information market" is BlackNet, a system that appeared in 1993 and that allows fully anonymous, two-way exchanges of information of all sorts. There are reports that U.S. authorities have investigated BlackNet because of its presence on networks at Defense Department research labs. Not much they can do about it, of course, and more such entities are expected.

The implications for espionage are profound and largely unstoppable. Anyone with a home computer and access to the Net or Web, in various forms, can use these methods to communicate securely, anonymously, or pseudonymously and with little fear of detection. "Digital dead drops" can be used to post information obtained, far more securely than the old physical dead drops (no more messages left in Coke cans at the bases of trees on remote roads).

Whistleblowing is another growing use of anonymous remailers, with folks fearing retaliation using remailers to publicly post information. (Of course, there's a fine line between whistle blowing, revenge, and espionage.)

Data havens for the storage and marketing of controversial information is another area of likely future growth. Nearly any kind of information—medical, religious, chemical, etc., is illegal or proscribed in one or more countries, so those seeking this illegal information will turn to anonymous messaging systems to access and perhaps purchase this information with anonymous digital cash. This might include credit databases, deadbeat renter files, organ bank markets, etc. (These are all things which have various restrictions on them in the United States. For example, one cannot compile credit databases or lists of deadbeat renters without meeting various restrictions—a good reason to move them into cyberspace or at least outside the United States and then sell access through remailers.) Matching buyers and sellers of organs is another such market with a huge demand (life and death) but various laws tightly controlling such markets.

Digital cash efforts. A lot has been written about digital cash.[9] David Chaum's company, DigiCash, has the most interesting technology and has recently begun market testing. Stefan Brands may or may not have a competing system that gets around some of Chaum's patents. (The attitude crypto anarchists might take about patents is another topic for discussion. Suffice it to say that patents and other intellectual property issues continue to have relevance in the practical world, despite erosion by technological trends.) Credit card–based systems, such as the First Virtual system, are not exactly digital cash, in the Chaumian sense of blinded notes, but they offer some advantages the market may find useful until more advanced systems are available. I expect to see many more such experiments over the next several years, and some of them will likely be market successes.

Commerce and Colonization of Cyberspace

How will these ideas affect the development of cyberspace? "You can't eat cyberspace" is a criticism often leveled at argument about the role of cyberspace in everyday life. The argument made is that money and resources "accumulated" in some future (or near future) cyberspatial system will not be able to be "laundered" into the real world. Even such a prescient thinker as Neal Stephenson, in *Snow Crash*,[10] had his protagonist a vastly wealthy man in "the Multiverse" but a near pauper in the physical world.

This is implausible for several reasons. First, we routinely see transfers of wealth from the abstract world of stock tips, arcane consulting knowledge, etc., to the real world. "Consulting" is the operative word. Second, a variety of means of laundering money, via phony invoices, uncollected loans, art objects, etc., are well-known to those who launder money.... These methods, and more advanced ones to come, are likely to be used by those who wish their cyberspace profits moved into the real world. (Doing this anonymously and untraceably is another complication. There may be methods of doing this. Proposals have looked pretty solid, but more work is needed.)

The World Wide Web is growing at an explosive pace. Combined with cryptographically protected communication and digital cash of some form (and there are several being tried), this should produce the long-awaited colonization of cyberspace. Most Net and Web users already pay little attention to the putative laws of their local regions or nations, apparently seeing themselves more as members of various virtual communities than as members of locally governed entities.

This trend is accelerating.

Most important, information can be bought and sold (anonymously, too) and then used in the real world. There is no reason to expect that this won't be a major reason to move into cyberspace.

Implications

I've touched on the implications in several places. Many thoughtful people are worried about some of the possibilities made apparent by strong crypto and anonymous communication systems. Some are proposing restrictions on access to crypto tools. The recent debate in the United States over Clipper and other key escrow systems shows the strength of emotions generated by this issue.

Abhorrent markets may arise. For example, anonymous systems and untraceable digital cash have some obvious implications for the arranging of contract killings and such. (The greatest risk in arranging such hits is that physical meetings expose the buyers and sellers of such services to stings. Crypto-anarchy lessens, or even eliminates, this risk, thus lowering transaction costs. The risks to the actual triggermen are not lessened, but this is a risk the buyers need not worry about. Think of anonymous escrow services which hold the digital money until the deed is done. Lots of issues here. It is unfortunate that this area is so little-discussed.... People seem to have an aversion for exploring the logical consequences in such areas.) The implications for corporate and national espionage have already been touched upon. Combined with liquid markets in information, this may make secrets much harder to keep. (Imagine a "Digital Jane's," after the military weapons handbooks, anonymously compiled and sold for digital money, beyond the reach of various governments which don't want their secrets told.)

New money-laundering approaches are another area to explore.

Something that is inevitable is the increased role of individuals, leading to a new kind of elitism. Those who are comfortable with the tools described here can avoid the restrictions and taxes that others cannot. If local laws can be bypassed technologically, the implications are pretty clear.

The implications for personal liberty are of course profound. No longer can nation-states tell their citizen-units what they can have access to, not if these citizens can access the cyberspace world through anonymous systems.

How Likely?

I am making no bold predictions that these changes will sweep the world anytime soon. Most people are ignorant of these methods, and the methods themselves are still under development. A wholesale conversion to "living in cyberspace" is just not in the cards, at least not in the next few decades. But to an increasingly large group, the Net is reality. It is where friends are made, where business is negotiated, where intellectual stimulation is found. And many of these people are using crypto-anarchy tools. Anonymous remailers, message pools, information markets. Consulting via pseudonyms has begun to appear and should grow. (As usual, the lack of a robust digital cash system is slowing things down.)

Can crypto-anarchy be stopped? Although the future evolution in unclear, as the future almost always is, it seems unlikely that present trends can be reversed:

• Dramatic increases in bandwidth and local, privately owned computer power,
• Exponential increase in the number of Net users,
• Explosion in degrees of freedom in personal choices, tastes, wishes, and goals, and
• Inability of central governments to control economies, cultural trends, and so on.[11]

The Net is integrally tied to economic transactions, and no country can afford to "disconnect" itself from it. (The U.S.S.R. couldn't do it, and they were light-years behind the U.S., European, and Asian countries.) And in a few more years, no hope of limiting these tools at all, something the U.S. F.B.I. has acknowledged.[12]

3 s

Technological Inevitability: These tools are already in widespread use, and only draconian steps to limit access to computers and communications channels could significantly impact further use. (Scenarios for restrictions on private use of crypto.)

As John Gilmore has noted, "The Net tends to interpret censorship as damage, and routes around it." This applies as well to attempts to legislate behavior on the Net. (The utter impossibility of regulating the worldwide Net—with entry points in more than a hundred nations, with million of machines—is not yet fully recognized by most national governments. They still speak in terms of "controlling" the Net, when in fact the laws of one nation generally have little use in other countries.)

Digital money in its various forms is probably the weakest link at this point. Most of the other pieces are operational, at least in basic forms, but digital cash is (understandably) harder to deploy. Hobbyist or "toy" experiments have been cumbersome, and the "toy" nature is painfully obvious. It is not easy to use digital cash systems at this time ("To use Magic Money, first create a client ..."), especially as compared to the easily understood alternatives.[13] People are understandably reluctant to entrust actual money to such systems. And it's not yet clear what can be bought with digital cash (a chicken or egg dilemma that is likely to be resolved in the next several years). Digital cash, digital banks, etc., are a likely target for legislative moves to limit the deployment of crypto anarchy and digital economies. Whether through banking regulation or tax laws, it is not likely that digital money will be deployed easily ("Kids, don't try this at home!").

Some of the current schemes may also incorporate methods for reporting transactions to the tax authorities and may include "software key escrow" features that make transactions fully or partly visible to authorities.

Conclusions

Strong crypto provides new levels of personal privacy, all the more important in an era of increased surveillance, monitoring, and the temptation to demand proofs of identity and permission slips. Some of the "credentials without identity" work of Chaum and others may lessen this move toward a surveillance society.

The implications are, as I see it, are that the power of nation states will be lessened, tax collection policies will have to be changed, and economic interactions will be based more on personal calculations of value than on societal mandates.

Is this a Good Thing? Mostly yes. Crypto anarchy has some messy aspects, of this there can be little doubt. From relatively unimportant things like price fixing and insider trading to more serious things like economic espionage, the undermining of corporate knowledge ownership, to extremely dark things like anonymous markets for killings.

But let's not forget that nation states have, under the guise of protecting us from others, killed more than 100 million people in this century alone. Mao, Stalin, Hitler, and Pol Pot, just to name the most extreme examples. It is hard to imagine any level of digital contract killings ever coming close to nationstate barbarism. (But I agree that this is something we cannot accurately speak about; I don't think we have much of a choice in embracing crypto anarchy or not, so I choose to focus on the bright side.) It is hard to argue that the risks of anonymous markets and tax evasion justify worldwide suppression of communications and encryption tools. People have always killed each other, and governments have not stopped this (arguably, they make the problem much worse, as the wars of this century have shown).

Also, there are various steps that can be taken to lessen the risks of crypto-anarchy impinging on personal safety.[14]

Strong crypto provides a technological means of ensuring the practical freedom to read and write what one wishes to. (Albeit perhaps not in one's true name, as the nation-state-democracy will likely still try to control behavior through majority votes on what can be said, not said, read, not read, etc.) And of course if speech is free, so are many classes of economic interaction that are essentially tied to free speech.

A phase change is coming. Virtual communities are in their ascendancy, displacing conventional notions of nationhood. Geographic proximity is no longer as important as it once was.

A lot of work remains. Technical cryptography still hasn't solved all problems, the role of reputations (both positive and negative) needs further study, and the practical issues surrounding many of these areas have barely been explored. We will be the colonizers of cyberspace.

Notes

My thanks to my colleagues in the Cypherpunks group, all seven hundred of them, past or present. Well over 100 megabytes of list traffic has passed through the Cypherpunks mailing list, so there have been a lot of stimulating ideas. But especially my appreciation goes to Eric Hughes, Sandy Sandfort, Duncan Frissell, Hal Finney, Perry Metzger, Nick Szabo, John Gilmore, Whit Diffie, Carl Ellison, Bill Stewart, and Harry Bartholomew. Thanks as well to Robin Hanson, Ted Kaehler, Keith Henson, Chip Morningstar, Eric Dean Tribble, Mark Miller, Bob Fleming, Cherie Kushner, Michael Korns, George Gottlieb, Jim Bennett, Dave Ross, Gayle Pergamit, and especially the late Phil Salin. Finally, thanks for valuable discussions—sometimes brief, sometimes long—with Vernor Vinge, David Friedman, Rudy Rucker, David Chaum, Kevin Kelly, and Steven Levy.

1. RSA Data Security Inc., Redwood Shores, California, is the license administrator. Contact them for details.

2. Many cryptography texts exist. A good introduction is Bruce Schneier's *Applied Cryptography* (2nd ed.) (New York: Wiley, 1996). This text includes pointers to many other sources. The annual Crypto Proceedings (*Advances in Cryptology*) (Berlin: Springer-Verlag) are essential references. The annual crypto conference in Santa Barbara and the Eurocrypt and Auscrypt conferences are where most crypto results are presented.

3. David Chaum, "Untraceable Electronic Mail, Return Addresses, and Digital Pseudonyms," Communications of the Association for Computing Machinery 24 (February 2, 1981): 84–88 (cypherpunk-style remailers are a form of Chaum's "digital mixes," albeit far from ideal); David Chaum, "Security without Identification: Transaction Systems to Make Big Brother Obsolete," Communications of the Association for Computing Machinery 28 (October 10, 1985) (this early paper is on digital cash; be sure to consult more recent papers).

4. The political opposition in Myan Mar—formerly Burma—is using Pretty Good Privacy running on DOS laptops in the jungles for communications among the rebels, according to Phil Zimmermann, author of PGP. This life-and-death usage underscores the role of crypto.

5. David Friedman, *The Machinery of Freedom: Guide to a Radical Capitalism* (2nd ed.) (Ashland, Olt: Open Court, 1989), is leading theoretician of anarchocapitalism. Friedrich Hayek was another.

6. Timothy C. May, "The Crypto Anarchist Manifesto," July 1988, distributed on the Usenet and on various mailing lists. Also included in this book as chapter 6.

7. The Cypherpunks group was mainly formed by Eric Hughes, John Gilmore, and me. It began with physical meetings in the Bay Area and elsewhere and with virtual meetings on an unmoderated mailing list. The name was provided by Judith Milhon as a play on the cyberpunk fiction genre and the British spelling of *cipher*. The mailing list can be subscribed to by sending the single message,

subscribe cypherpunks, in the body of a message to majordomo@toad.com. Expect at least fifty messages a day. About six hundred subscribers in many countries are presently on the list. Some are pseudonyms.

8. Abuse, according to some views, of remailers is already occurring. A Cypherpunks-style remailer was used to post a proprietary hash function of RSA Data Security, Inc. to the Usenet. Let me hasten to add that it was not a remailer I operate or have control over.

9. Article on digital cash, *The Economist*, 26 November 1994, pp. 21–23. Article on digital cash, Steven Levy, *Wired* (December 1994).

10. Neal Stephenson, *Snow Crash* (New York: Bantam, 1995).

11. See Kevin Kelly's *Out of Control: The Rise of Neo-Biological Civilization* (Reading, MA: Addison Wesley, 1994) for a discussion of how central control is failing and how the modern paradigm is one of market mechanisms, personal choice, and technological empowerment.

12. During the debate on the digital telephony bill, an FBI official said that failure to mandate wiretap capabilities within eighteen months would make the bill moot as the cost would rise beyond any reasonable budget (currently $500 million for retrofit costs).

13. "Magic Money" was an experimental implementation of Chaum's digital cash system. It was coded by "Pr0duct Cypher," a pseudonymous member of the Cypherpunks list. None of us knows his real identity, as he used remailers to communicate with the list, and digitally signed his posts. Many of us found it too difficult to use, which is more a measure of the deep issues involved in using digital analogs (no pun intended) to real, physical money.

14. Robin Hanson and David Friedman have written extensively about scenarios for dealing with the threats of extortionists, would-be assassins, and so on. Much of their discussion took place in 1992 and 1993, on the Extropians mailing list.

8

A Cypherpunk's Manifesto

Eric Hughes

Privacy is necessary for an open society in the electronic age. Privacy is not secrecy. A private matter is something one doesn't want the whole world to know, but a secret matter is something one doesn't want anybody to know. Privacy is the power to selectively reveal oneself to the world.

If two parties have some sort of dealings, then each has a memory of the interaction. Each party can speak about its own memory of the encounter. How could anyone prevent this? One could pass laws against it, but the freedom of speech, even more than privacy, is fundamental to an open society. We seek not to restrict any speech at all. If many parties speak together in the same forum, each can speak to all the others and aggregate together knowledge about individuals and other parties. The power of electronic communications has enabled such group speech, and it will not go away merely because we might want it to.

Since we desire privacy, we must ensure that each party to a transaction can have knowledge only of what is directly necessary for that transaction. Since any information can be spoken of, we must ensure that we reveal as little as possible. In most cases personal identity is not salient. When I purchase a magazine at a store and hand cash to the clerk, there is no need to know who I am. When I ask my electronic mail provider to send and receive messages, my provider does not need to know to whom I am speaking or what I am saying or what others are saying to me. My provider needs only know how to get the message there and how much

I owe them in fees. When my identity is revealed by the underlying mechanism of the transaction, I have no privacy. I cannot here selectively reveal myself; I must always reveal myself.

Therefore, privacy in an open society requires anonymous transaction systems. Until now, cash has been the primary such system. An anonymous transaction system is not a secret transaction system. An anonymous system empowers individuals to reveal their identity when desired and only when desired; this is the essence of privacy.

Privacy in an open society also requires cryptography. If I say something, I want it heard only by those for whom I intend it. If the content of my speech is available to the world, I have no privacy. To encrypt is to indicate the desire for privacy, and to encrypt with weak cryptography is to indicate not too much desire for privacy. Furthermore, to reveal one's identity with assurance when the default is anonymity requires the cryptographic signature.

We cannot expect governments, corporations, or other large, faceless organizations to grant us privacy out of their beneficence. It is to their advantage to speak of us, and we should expect that they will speak. To try to prevent their speech is to fight against the realities of information. Information does not just want to be free; it longs to be free. Information expands to fill the available storage space. Information is Rumor's younger, stronger cousin: Information is fleeter of foot, has more eyes, knows more, and understands less than Rumor.

We must defend our own privacy if we expect to have any. We must come together and create systems that allow anonymous transactions to take place. People have been defending their own privacy for centuries with whispers, darkness, envelopes, closed doors, secret handshakes, and couriers. The technologies of the past did not allow for strong privacy, but electronic technologies do.

We the Cypherpunks are dedicated to building anonymous systems. We are defending our privacy with cryptography, with anonymous mail forwarding systems, with digital signatures, and with electronic money.

Cypherpunks write code. We know that someone has to write software to defend privacy, and since we can't get privacy unless we all do, we're going to write it. We publish our code so that our fellow Cypherpunks may practice and play with it. Our code is free for all to use, worldwide. We don't much care if you don't approve of the software we write. We know that software can't be destroyed and that a widely dispersed system can't be shut down.

Cypherpunks deplore regulations on cryptography, for encryption is fundamentally a private act. The act of encryption, in fact, removes information from the public realm. Even laws against cryptography reach only so far as a nation's border and the arm of its violence. Cryptography will ineluctably spread over the whole globe and with it the anonymous transactions systems that it makes possible.

For privacy to be widespread it must be part of a social contract. People must come and together deploy these systems for the common good. Privacy extends only so far as the cooperation of one's fellows in society. We the Cypherpunks seek your questions and your concerns and hope we may engage you so that we do not deceive ourselves. We will not, however, be moved out of our course because some may disagree with our goals.

The Cypherpunks are actively engaged in making the networks safer for privacy. Let us proceed together apace.

Onward.

9

The Future of Cryptography

Dorothy E. Denning

A few years ago, the phrase *crypto anarchy* was coined to suggest the impending arrival of a Brave New World in which governments, as we know them, have crumbled, disappeared, and been replaced by virtual communities of individuals doing as they wish without interference. Proponents argue that crypto anarchy is the inevitable—and highly desirable—outcome of the release of public key cryptography into the world. With this technology, they say, it will be impossible for governments to control information, compile dossiers, conduct wiretaps, regulate economic arrangements, and even collect taxes. Individuals will be liberated from coercion by their physical neighbors and by governments. This view has been argued recently by Tim May.[1]

Behind the anarchists' vision is a belief that a guarantee of absolute privacy and anonymous transactions would make for a civil society based on a libertarian free market. They ally themselves with Thomas Jefferson and Friedrich Hayek, who would be horrified at the suggestion that a society with no government control would be either civil or free. Adam Ferguson once said "Liberty or Freedom is not, as the origin of the name may seem to imply, an exemption from all restraints, but rather the most effectual applications of every just restraint to all members of a free society whether they be magistrates or subjects." Hayek opens *The Fatal Conceit: The Errors of Socialism* with Ferguson's quote.[2]

This chapter was originally given as a talk to the Joint Australian/OECD Conference on Security, Privacy and Intellectual Property Protection in the Global Information Infrastructure in 1996. Reprinted by permission of the author. © Dorothy E. Denning, 1996.

Although May limply asserts that anarchy does not mean lawlessness and social disorder, the absence of government would lead to exactly these states of chaos. I do not want to live in an anarchistic society—if such could be called a society at all—and I doubt many would. A growing number of people are attracted to the market liberalism envisioned by Jefferson, Hayek, and many others but not to anarchy. Thus, the crypto anarchists' claims come close to asserting that the technology will take us to an outcome that most of us would not choose.

This is the claim that I want to address here. I do not accept crypto anarchy as the inevitable outcome. A new paradigm of cryptography— key escrow—is emerging and gaining acceptance in industry. Key escrow is a technology that offers tools that would assure no individual absolute privacy or untraceable anonymity in all transactions. I argue that this feature of the technology is what will allow individuals to choose a civil society over an anarchistic one. I will review this technology as well as what it will take to avoid crypto anarchy. First, however, I review the benefits, limitations, and drawbacks of cryptography and current trends leading toward crypto anarchy.

Cryptography's Benefits, Limitations, and Drawbacks

The benefits of cryptography are well recognized. Encryption can protect communications and stored information from unauthorized access and disclosure. Other cryptographic techniques, including methods of authentication and digital signatures, can protect against spoofing and message forgeries. Practically everyone agrees that cryptography is an essential information security tool and that it should be readily available to users. I take this as a starting assumption and, in this respect, have no disagreement with the crypto anarchists.

Less recognized are cryptography's limitations. Encryption is often oversold as the solution to all security problems or to threats that it does not address. For example, the headline of Jim Warren's op-ed piece in the *San Jose Mercury News* reads "Encryption could stop computer crackers."[3] Unfortunately, encryption offers no such aegis. Encryption does nothing to protect against many common methods of attack, including those that exploit bad default settings or vulnerabilities in network protocols or software—even encryption software. In general, methods other than encryption are needed to keep out intruders. Secure Computing Corporation's Sidewinder™ system defuses the forty-two "bombs" (security vulnerabilities) in William R. Cheswick and Stephen M. Bellovin's book, *Firewalls and Internet Security*, without making use of any encryption.[4]

Moreover, the protection provided by encryption can be illusory. If the system where the encryption is performed can be penetrated, then the intruder may be able to access plaintext directly from stored files or the contents of memory or modify network protocols, application software, or encryption programs to gain access to keys or plaintext data or to subvert the encryption process. For example, Pretty Good Privacy (PGP) could be replaced with a Trojan horse that appears to behave like PGP but creates a secret file of the user's keys for later transmission to the program's owner, much like a Trojan horse login program collects passwords. A recent penetration study of 8,932 computers by the Defense Information Systems Agency showed 88 percent of the computers could be successfully attacked. Using PGP to encrypt data transmitted from or stored on the average system could be like putting the strongest possible lock on the back door of a building while leaving the front door wide open. Information security requires much more than just encryption: authentication, configuration management, good design, access controls, firewalls, auditing, security practices, and security awareness training are a few of the other techniques needed.

The drawbacks of cryptography are frequently overlooked as well. The widespread availability of unbreakable encryption coupled with anonymous services could lead to a situation where practically all communications are immune from lawful interception (wiretaps) and documents from lawful search and seizure, and where all electronic transactions are beyond the reach of any government regulation or oversight. The consequences of this to public safety and social and economic stability could be devastating. With the government essentially locked out, computers and telecommunications systems would become safe havens for criminal activity. Even May himself acknowledges that crypto anarchy provides a means for tax evasion, money laundering, espionage (with digital dead drops), contract killings, and implementation of data havens for storing and marketing illegal or controversial material. Encryption also threatens national security by interfering with foreign intelligence operations. The United States, along with many other countries, imposes export controls on encryption technology to lessen this threat.

Cryptography poses a threat to organizations and individuals too. With encryption, an employee of a company can sell proprietary electronic information to a competitor without the need to photocopy and handle physical documents. Electronic information can be bought and sold on "black networks" such as Black-Net with complete secrecy and anonymity—a safe harbor for engaging in both corporate and government espionage. The keys that unlock a corporation's files may be lost, corrupted, or held hostage for ransom, thus rendering valuable information inaccessible.

When considering the threats posed by cryptography, it is important to recognize that only the use of encryption for confidentiality, including anonymity, presents a problem. The use of cryptography for data integrity and authentication, including digital signatures, is not a threat. Indeed, by strengthening the integrity of evidence and binding it to its source, cryptographic tools for authentication are a forensic aid to criminal investigations. They also help enforce accountability. Because different cryptographic methods can be employed for confidentiality and authentication, any safeguards that might be placed on encryption to counter the threats need not affect authentication mechanisms or system protocols that rely on authentication to protect against system intrusions, forgeries, and substitution of malicious code.

The Drift toward Crypto Anarchy

Crypto anarchy can be viewed as the proliferation of cryptography that provides the benefits of confidentiality protection but does nothing about its harms. It is government-proof encryption that denies access to the government even under a court order or other legal order. It has no safeguards to protect users and their organizations from accidents and abuse. It is like an automobile with no brakes, no seat belts, no pollution controls, no license plate, and no way of getting in after you've locked your keys in the car.

The crypto-anarchist position is that cyberspace is on a nonstop drift toward crypto anarchy. Powerful encryption algorithms—including the Data Encryption Standard (DES), triple-DES, RSA, and IDEA—are readily available at no charge through Internet servers as stand-alone programs or as part of packages providing file or electronic mail encryption and digital signatures. Among these, PGP, which uses RSA and IDEA for encrypting files and electronic mail messages, has become particularly popular. Software that will turn an ordinary PC into a secure phone is posted on the Internet for free downloading. These systems have no mechanisms for accommodating authorized government decryption. Export controls have little effect, as the programs can be posted in countries that have no such controls.

In addition to the free encryption programs being distributed on the Net, encryption is becoming a basic service integrated into commercial applications packages and network products. The IP Security Working Group of the Internet Engineering Task Force has written a document that calls for all compliant IPv6 (Internet Protocol, version 6) implementations to incorporate DES cryptography.

Anonymous remailers, which allow users to send or post messages without disclosing their identity or host system, have also become popular on the Internet. May reports that there are about twenty cypherpunk-style remailers on the Internet, with more being added monthly. These remailers allow unlimited nesting of remailing, with PGP encryption at each nesting level. Anonymous digital cash, which would provide untraceability of electronic payments, is on the horizon.

The potential harms of cryptography have already begun to appear. As the result of interviews I conducted in May 1995, I found numerous cases where investigative agencies had encountered encrypted communications and computer files. These cases involved child pornography, customs violations, drugs, espionage, embezzlement, murder, obstruction of justice, tax protesters, and terrorism. At the International Cryptography Institute held in Washington in September 1995, FBI Director Louis Freeh reported that encryption had been encountered in a terrorism investigation in the Philippines involving an alleged plot to assassinate Pope John Paul II and bomb a U.S. airliner.[5]

AccessData Corp., a company in Orem, Utah, that specializes in providing software and services to help law enforcement agencies and companies recover data that has been locked out through encryption, reports receiving about a dozen and a half calls a day from companies with inaccessible data. About one half dozen of these calls result from disgruntled employees who leave employment under extreme situations and refuse to cooperate in any transitional stage by leaving necessary keys (typically in the form of passwords). Another half dozen result when employees die or leave on good terms but simply forget to leave their keys. The third half dozen result from loss of keys by current employees.

The Emergence of Key Escrow as an Alternative

The benefits of strong cryptography can be realized without following the crypto-anarchy path to social disorder. One promising alternative is *key escrow encryption*, also called *escrowed encryption*.[6] The idea is to combine strong encryption with an emergency decryption capability. This is accomplished by linking encrypted data to a data-recovery key that facilitates decryption. This key need not be (and typically is not) the one used for normal decryption, but it must provide access to that key. The data-recovery key is held by a trusted fiduciary, which could conceivably be a governmental agency, court, or trusted and bonded private organization. A key might be split among several such agencies. Organizations registered with an escrow agent can acquire their own keys for emergency decryption. An investigative or intelligence agency seeking access to communications or stored files makes application through appropriate procedures (which normally includes getting a court order) and, on compliance, is issued the key. Legitimate privacy interests are protected through access procedures, auditing, and other safeguards.

In April 1993, as a response to the rising need for and use of encryption products, the Clinton administration announced a new initiative to promote encryption in a way that would not prohibit lawful decryption when investigative agencies are authorized to intercept communications or search computer files.[7] Government agencies were directed to develop a comprehensive encryption policy that would accommodate the privacy and security needs of citizens and businesses, the ability of authorized government officials to access communications and data under proper court or other legal order, the effective and timely use of modern technology to build the National Information Infrastructure, and the need of U.S. companies to manufacture and export high-technology products. The goal was not to prevent citizens from having access to encryption or "to stigmatize cryptography as something only criminals would use."[8] As part of this encryption initiative, the government developed an escrowed encryption chip called the Clipper Chip.

Each Clipper Chip has a unique key that is programmed onto the chip and used to recover data encrypted by that chip. This key is split into two components, and the two components are held by two separate government agencies—the National Institute of Standards and Technology and the Department of Treasury Automated Systems Division. Clipper's data encryption algorithm, Skipjack, is a classified algorithm designed by the National Security Agency.[9] It has a key size of 80 bits. The general specifications for the Clipper Chip were adopted in February 1994 as the Escrowed Encryption Standard (EES),[10] which is a voluntary government standard for telephone communications, including voice, fax, and data. Implementations of the EES are required to use tamper-resistant hardware to protect the classified algorithms. The chip and associated key escrow system have been designed with extensive safeguards, including two-person control and auditing, to protect against any unauthorized use of keys.[11] Clipper's key escrow system does not provide user data-recovery services.

The National Security Agency also designed a more advanced chip called Capstone as part of the Multilevel Information System Security Initiative (MISSI). Capstone implements the EES plus algorithms for the Digital Signature Standard (DSS) and for establishing session keys. It has been embedded in the Fortezza card (a PCMCIA card), where it is used to provide the cryptographic services needed for communications and file security. The private keys used for key establishment and digital signatures, which are stored on the Fortezza card, are not stored in Clipper's key escrow system. They are, however, escrowed with the user's public-key certificate authority so that they can be recovered in case the card becomes corrupted. This allows encrypted files and previously received electronic mail messages to be read. Fortezza cards are available with or without a modem capability. The modem cards allow encryption and decryption to be performed as part of the communications protocols or as independent service calls (for example, for encrypting the content of an e-mail message or file).

The government has not been alone in its pursuit of key-escrow technology. Some type of key escrow is a feature or option of several commercial products including Fisher Watchdog®, Nortel's Entrust, PC Security Stoplock KE, RSA Secure™, and TECSEC Veil™. Escrowing is done within the user's organization and serves primarily to protect against data loss.

Several companies have proposed designs for commercial key escrow systems where the escrow agents could be trusted third parties that provide emergency decryption services for both registered users and authorized government officials. Such escrow agents might be licensed, with licenses granted to organizations demonstrating the capability to administer key-escrow encryption and safeguard keys and other sensitive information. Some of the proposed systems have been designed with the objective of being suitable for international use.

One such example is a proposal from Bankers Trust for an international commercial key escrow system for secure communications.[12] Their proposal uses a combination of hardware and software, unclassified algorithms, and public-key cryptography for key establishment and key escrow functions. Each user has a trusted encryption device, a public-private signature key pair, and a public-private encryption key pair that is used for establishing session keys and for data recovery. The private encryption keys are escrowed through a device registration process, and may be split among several escrow agents.

Trusted Information Systems (TIS) has proposed a commercial software key escrow system intended primarily for file encryption.[13] A commercial entity serves as a key escrow agent and operates a data-recovery center. To use the services of a particular center, a user must register with the center. Emergency decryption is possible through a key that is private to the center. The key is not released to users or the government; instead, the center participates in the decryption of each file that is encrypted under a distinct file encryption key. TIS would franchise its data-recovery centers to interested organizations. National Semiconductor and TIS have jointly proposed Commercial Automated Key Escrow (CAKE), which combines a CAKE-enabled PersonaCard™ token (National's PCMCIA cryptographic card) with a TIS data-recovery center.[14] The goal is an exportable, strong encryption alternative using accepted public encryption algorithms such as DES, triple DES, and RSA.

Under current U.S. export regulations, encryption products with key lengths greater than 40 bits are not generally exportable when used for confidentiality protection. One of the attractions of key escrow encryption is that by providing a mechanism for authorized government decryption, it can enable the export of products with strong encryption. For example, Clipper and Capstone devices are generally exportable, even though the encryption algorithm is strong and uses 80-bit keys. Commercial key escrow approaches that use some form of hardware token are good candidates for export as they can provide reasonable protection against modifications to bypass the key escrow functions. The Bankers Trust and National and TIS proposals take that approach. Fortress U & T, Ltd. also has proposed a token-based approach to key escrow.[15]

Hardware encryption generally offers greater security than software. Nevertheless, there is a large market for software encryption. On August 17, 1995, the Clinton administration announced a proposal to allow ready export of software encryption products with key lengths up to 64 bits when combined with an acceptable key escrow capability. This policy would allow export of DES, for example, which uses 56-bit keys, but not triple DES. Keys would be held by government-approved trusted parties within the private sector, where they would support both user data recovery and legitimate government decryption. The proposal was expected to be implemented in early 1996.

Key escrow encryption has been a topic of growing interest in the research community (most of this work is reviewed in the works cited in note 6). Silvio Micali's proposal for "fair cryptosystems"[16] has influenced several designs, including the Bankers Trust proposal. Karlsruhe

University's TESS system uses smart cards for user keys that are escrowed.[17] A proposal from Royal Holloway integrates escrow with the trusted third parties that serve as certificate authorities.[18]

Some type of escrow facility might be used to control anonymity services as well as encryption. For example, escrow could be used with digital cash and anonymous remailers to ensure traceability when there is a court order or other legal authorization for information about the originator of a transaction. Ernie Brickell, Peter Gemmell, and David Kravitz propose a system for electronic cash that would incorporate trustee-based tracing in an otherwise anonymous cash system.[19]

Alternatives to Key Escrow

Key escrow is not the only way of accommodating authorized government access. Another approach is weak encryption. The data encryption keys are short enough that a key can be determined by trying all possibilities. From the user's perspective, key escrow encryption has an advantage over weak encryption because it allows the use of strong encryption algorithms that are not vulnerable to attack. However, for applications where such a high level of security is not needed, weak encryption offers a less costly alternative. A disadvantage of weak encryption (unless it is extremely weak) from a law-enforcement perspective is that it can preclude real-time decryption in an emergency situation (such as kidnaping).

A third approach is link encryption. Communications are encrypted between network nodes but not across nodes. Thus, plaintext communications can be accessed in the network-switching nodes. One major advantage of link encryption is that it allows someone with a cellular phone to protect the over-the-air connection into the phone system without requiring that the other party have a compatible encryption device or, indeed, use any encryption at all. Global System for Mobile (GSM), a worldwide standard for mobile radio telecommunications, encrypts communications transmitted over the radio link, but they are decrypted before being transmitted through the rest of the network. The disadvantage of link encryption is that plaintext data are exposed in, potentially, many intermediate nodes. By contrast, key escrow encryption can support secure end-to-end encryption.

Crypto Anarchy Is Not Inevitable

In the United States, there are no restrictions on the import, manufacture, or use of cryptographic products (except that government agencies are required to use government standards). The question is: Are such controls needed, or will voluntary key escrow, combined with weak encryption and link encryption where appropriate, be sufficient to avoid crypto anarchy?

Several factors will facilitate the adoption of key escrow. Because key escrow products will be exportable, under appropriate conditions vendors will have a strong incentive to adopt key escrow, as it will enable them to integrate strong cryptography into a single product line for both domestic and international sales. Currently, vendors must either install weak cryptography, which does not meet the needs of many customers, or develop two sets of products, which greatly increases costs and prohibits interoperability between domestic and foreign customers. Users will have an incentive to purchase key escrow products because such products will protect them against lost or damaged keys. The government's own commitment to key escrow will ensure a large market for escrowed encryption products. As the market develops, many users will choose key escrow products to communicate with those using such products. Concern over the social consequences of crypto anarchy will also motivate some people to develop or use key escrow products. Finally, the adoption of key escrow might be facilitated by legislation that would specify the qualifications, responsibilities, and liabilities of government-approved escrow agents. This legislation could define unlawful acts relating to the compromise or abuse of escrowed keys (such as deliberately releasing a key to someone who is not authorized to receive it). Such legislation could ensure that at least approved escrow agents satisfy the requirements of users and the government. It also could allay the privacy concerns of those using approved escrow agents.

International interest in key escrow will also contribute to its success. There is growing recognition on the part of governments and businesses worldwide of the potential of key escrow to meet the needs of both users and law enforcement. In addition to providing confidentiality and emergency backup decryption, escrowed encryption is seen as a way of overcoming export restrictions, common to many countries, which have limited the international availability of strong encryption to protect national security interests. With key escrow, strong exportable cryptography can be standardized and made available internationally to support the information security needs of international business. Key escrow could be a service provided by trusted parties that manage the public-key infrastructure and issue X.509 certificates. Some products and proposals for key escrow use this approach.

At a meeting sponsored by the Organization for Economic Development (OECD) and the International Chamber of Commerce (ICC) in December 1995 in Paris, representatives from the international business community and member governments agreed to work together to develop encryption policy guidelines based on agreed on principles that accommodate their mutual interests. The INFOSEC Business Advisory Group (IBAG) issued a statement of seventeen principles that its members believe can form the basis of a detailed agreement.[20] IBAG is an association of associations (mostly European) representing the information security interests of users.

The IBAG principles acknowledge the right of businesses and individuals to protect their information and the right of law-abiding governments to intercept and lawfully seize information when there is no practical alternative. Businesses and individuals would lodge keys with trusted parties who would be liable for any loss or damage resulting from compromise or misuse of those keys. The trusted parties could be independently accredited entities or accredited entities within a company. The keys would be available to businesses and individuals on proof of ownership and to governments and law-enforcement agencies under due process of law and for a limited time frame. The process of obtaining and using keys would be auditable. Governments would be responsible for ensuring that international agreements would allow access to keys held outside national jurisdiction. The principles call for industry to develop open, voluntary, consensus, international standards and for governments, businesses, and individuals to work together to define the requirements for those standards. The standards would allow choices about algorithm, mode of operation, key length, and implementation in hardware or software. Products conforming to the standards would not be subject to restrictions on import or use and would be generally exportable.

EUROBIT (European Association of Manufacturers of Business Machines and Information Technology Industry), ITAC (Information Technology Industry Association of Canada), ITI (Information Technology Industry Council, U.S.), and JEIDA (Japan Electronic Industry Development Association) also issued a statement of principles for global cryptography policy at the OECD meeting.[21] The quadripartite group accounts for more than 90 percent of the worldwide revenue in information technology. Acknowledging the needs of both users and governments, their principles call for harmonization of national cryptography policies and industry-led international standards.

It is conceivable that domestic and international efforts will be sufficient to avoid crypto anarchy, particularly with support from the international business community. However, it is possible that they will not be enough. Many companies are developing products with strong encryption that do not accommodate government access, standards groups are adopting nonkey escrow standards, and software encryption packages such as PGP are rapidly proliferating on the Internet, which is due, in part, to crypto anarchists whose goal is to lock out the government. Since key escrow adds to the development and operation costs of encryption products, the price advantage of unescrowed encryption products could also be a factor that might undermine the success of a completely voluntary approach. If escrow is integrated into the public key infrastructure, however, cost might not be a significant factor.

Considering the explosive growth of telecommunications and the encryption market, it will be necessary to closely watch the impact of encryption on law enforcement. If government-proof encryption begins to undermine the ability of law-enforcement agencies to carry out their missions and fight organized crime and terrorism, then legislative controls over encryption technology may be desirable. One possibility would be to license encryption products but not their use. Licenses could be granted only for products that reasonably satisfy law-enforcement and national security requirements for emergency decryption and provide privacy protections for users. The exact requirements might be those that evolve from the current efforts of the Organization for Economic Cooperation and Development and international business community to develop common principles and standards. The manufacture, distribution, import, and export of unlicensed encryption products would be illegal, but no particular method of encryption would be mandated. Individuals would be allowed to develop their own encryption systems for personal or educational use without obtaining licenses, though they could not distribute them to others. France and Russia have adopted licensing programs, though of a somewhat different nature. Both countries require licenses to use encryption.

Under this licensing program, commercial encryption products, including programs distributed through public network servers, would comply with government regulations. These products would not support absolute privacy or completely anonymous transactions. Mainstream applications would assure accountability and protect societal and organizational interests. Although noncompliant products might be distributed through underground servers and bulletin boards, such products would not interoperate with licensed ones, so their use would be limited.

Such a licensing approach would not prevent the use of government-proof encryption products by criminals and terrorists. They could develop their own or acquire the products illegally. But licensing would make it considerably more difficult than it is at present. Had such controls been adopted several years ago—before programs such as DES and PGP were posted on the Internet—the encryption products on the market today would support key escrow or some other method for government access. It would not be possible to acquire strong, government-proof encryption from reputable vendors or network file servers. The encryption products available through underground servers and the black market would most likely not possess as high a quality as products developed through the legitimate market. Underground products could have security vulnerabilities or be less user friendly. They would not be integrated into standard applications or network software.

Summary

Crypto anarchy is an international threat that has been stimulated by international communications systems including telephones and the

Internet. Addressing this threat requires an international approach that provides for both secure international communications crossing national boundaries and electronic surveillance by governments of criminal and terrorist activity taking place within their jurisdictions. The adoption of an international approach is critical to avoid a situation where the use of encryption seriously endangers the ability of law-enforcement agencies, worldwide, to fight terrorism and crime. The result will not be world-wide suppression of communications and encryption tools, as May asserts, but rather the responsible use of such tools so that they do not lead to social disorder. Our information superways require responsible conduct just as our interstate highways do.

Key escrow encryption has emerged as one approach that can meet the confidentiality and data-recovery needs of organizations while allowing authorized government access to fight terrorism and crime. It can facilitate the promulgation of standards and products that support the information security requirements of the global information infrastructure. The governments of the OECD nations are working with the international business community to find specific approaches that are mutually agreeable.

Notes

Thanks to Bill Baugh and Peter Denning for helpful comments on a draft of this chapter.

1. Tim May, "Crypto Anarchy and Virtual Communities," *Internet Security* (April 1995): 4–12 (chapter 7 in this volume).

2. Friedrich Hayek, *The Fatal Conceit: The Errors of Socialism*, ed. W. W. Bartley III (Chicago: University of Chicago Press, 1988).

3. Jim Warren, "Is Phil Zimmermann Being Persecuted? Why? By Whom? Who's Next?," *Internet Security* (April 1995): 15–21.

4. Secure Computing Corporation, "Answers to Frequently Asked Questions about Network Security," Roseville, MN, October 1994; William R. Cheswick and Stephen M. Bellovin, *Firewalls and Internet Security: Repelling the Wily Hacker* (Reading, MA: Addison-Wesley, 1994).

5. Louis J. Freeh, Keynote talk at International Cryptography Institute, Washington, DC, September 1995, available at http://www.fbi.gov/crypto.htm.

6. For a description of the characteristics of key-escrow encryption systems and different proposals, see Dorothy E. Denning and Dennis K. Branstad, "A Taxon-

omy of Key Escrow Encryption," *Communications of the Association for Computing Machinery* (March 1996). More detailed descriptions of thirty systems can be found at http://www.cosc.georgetown.edu/~denning/crypto. See also Dorothy E. Denning, "Key Escrow Encryption: The Third Paradigm," *Computer Security Journal* (Summer 1995), and Dorothy E. Denning, "Critical Factors of Key Escrow Encryption Systems," *Proceedings of the Eighteenth National Information Systems Security Conference, Baltimore, October 1995.*

7. Statement by the Press Secretary, White House, April 16, 1993.

8. John A. Thomas, "Can the FBI Stop Private Cryptography?," *Internet Security* (April 1995): 13–14.

9. Because the algorithm is classified and not open to public review, outside experts were invited to examine the algorithm and report their findings to the public. See Ernest F. Brickell, Dorothy E. Denning, Stephen T. Kent, David P. Maher, and Walter Tuchman, "The SKIPJACK Review, Interim Report: The SKIPJACK Algorithm," July 28, 1993, available at http://www.cosc.georgetown.edu/~denning/crypto.

10. National Institute for Standards and Technology, "Escrowed Encryption Standard (EES)," Federal Information Processing Standards Publication (FIPS PUB) 185 (1994).

11. For a technical description of the Clipper Chip and its key escrow system, see Dorothy E. Denning and Miles Smid, "Key Escrowing Today," *IEEE Communications* 32, no. 9 (September 1994): 58–68. For a less technical description and discussion of some of the issues surrounding Clipper, see Dorothy E. Denning, "The Case for Clipper," *MIT Technology Review* (July 1995): 48–55. Both articles can be accessed at http://www.cosc.georgetown.edu/~denning/crypto.

12. Bankers Trust Electronic Commerce, "Private Key Escrow System," paper presented at the Software Publishers Association and Advanced Engineering Applications Cryptography Policy Workshop, August 17, 1995, and at the International Cryptography Institute 1995: Global Challenges, September 21–22, 1995.

13. Stephen T. Walker, Steven B. Lipner, Carl M. Ellison, and David M. Balenson, "Commercial Key Escrow," *Communications of the Association for Computing Machinery* (March 1996). Also available from Trusted Information Systems, Inc., Glenwood, MD.

14. William B. Sweet and Stephen T. Walker, "Commercial Automated Key Escrow (CAKE): An Exportable Strong Encryption Alternative," National Semiconductor, iPower Business Unit, Sunnyvale, CA, June 4, 1995.

15. Carmi Gressel, Ran Granot, and Itai Dror, "International Cryptographic Communication without Key Escrow: KISS—Keep the Invaders (of Privacy) Socially Sane," paper presented at the International Cryptography Institute 1995: Global Challenges, September 21–22, 1995.

16. Silvio Micali, "Fair Cryptosystems," MIT/LCS/TR-579.c, Laboratory for Computer Science, Massachusetts Institute of Technology, Cambridge, MA, August 1994.

17. Thomas Beth, Hans-Joachim Knoblock, Marcus Otten, Gustavus J. Simmons, and Peer Wichmann, "Clipper Repair Kit: Towards Acceptable Key Escrow Systems," *Proceedings of the Second Association for Computing Machinery Conference on Communications and Computer Security*: (1994).

18. Nigel Jefferies, Chris Mitchell, and Michael Walker, "A Proposed Architecture for Trusted Third Party Services," Royal Holloway, University of London, 1995.

19. Ernie Brickell, Peter Gemmell, and David Kravitz, "Trustee-Based Tracing Extensions to Anonymous Cash and the Making of Anonymous Change," *Proceedings of the Sixth Annual Association for Computing Machinery/SIAM Symposium on Discrete Algorithms* (1995): 457–466.

20. INFOSEC Business Advisory Group (IBAG) Statement, available at http://www.cosc.georgetown.edu/~denning/crypto.

21. EUROBIT-ITAC-ITI-JEIDA Statement, available at http://www.cosc.georgetown.edu/~denning/crypto.

10

Afterword to "The Future of Cryptography"

Dorothy E. Denning

Since I revised the above article (see chapter 9) in January 1996, the cryptographic landscape has changed significantly. The Clinton administration liberalized export controls later that year and then again in 1998 and 1999. Although key escrow played a significant role in the ninety-six liberalizations, it all but disappeared with the ninety-nine changes. Now companies can export strong encryption without providing any hooks for the government at all. There is a large market for key escrow/recovery for stored data, but it is as a means of protecting companies from internal loss of data rather than accommodating law-enforcement needs. There is practically no market for key escrow with transient communications.

Besides being woefully out-of-date, the article is overly alarmist. My more recent research on encryption and crime, summarized in chapter 12, "Hiding Crimes in Cyberspace," found that whereas encryption has posed significant problems for law enforcement, even derailing some investigations, the situation in no way resembles anarchy. In most of the cases with which I am familiar, law-enforcement succeeded in obtaining the evidence they needed for conviction. The situation does not call for domestic controls on cryptography, and I do not advocate their enactment. For a more thorough treatment of cryptography policy, see my book *Information Warfare and Security* (Reading, MA: Addison Wesley, 1999) or the National Research Council's *Cryptography's Role in Securing the Information Society* (Washington, DC: National Academy Press, 1996).

11

Re: Denning's Crypto Anarchy

Duncan Frissell

[Excerpts from Dorothy E. Denning's "The Future of Cryptography" (chapter 9 in this book), revised January 6, 1996, are followed by Duncan Frissell's comments in square brackets.]

Although May limply asserts that anarchy does not mean lawlessness and social disorder, the absence of government would lead to exactly these states of chaos.

[Tim is rarely given to limp assertions. I haven't seen him spend much time arguing about the exact social arrangements of a free society following the crypto revolution. He has merely pointed out the results of the technology.]

I do not want to live in an anarchistic society—if such could be called a society at all—and I doubt many would.

[Whatever happens, there will always be plenty of cults around (perhaps even one called the Government of the United States of America) to which anyone will be free to belong and at the altars of which one will be free to worship. In fact, the deregulation of human interaction will make it easier for more oppressive cults to exist than is possible today as long as they keep to themselves. There will be no shortage of people willing to tell their followers what to do. Nothing will stop anyone from joining such a society.]

A growing number of people are attracted to the market liberalism envisioned by Jefferson, Hayek, and many others but not to anarchy. Thus, the crypto anarchists' claims come close to asserting that the technology will take us to an outcome that most of us would not choose.

[Still up for negotiation is how liberal a market we will want. The growing power of markets and (traditional) liberal ideas is the result of the growing wealth and power of individuals around the world. Crypto anarchists merely point out that the shape of future market societies is no longer in the hands of "The Authorities" but is rather in the hands of those trading on the market; i.e., everyone on earth.]

This is the claim that I want to address here. I do not accept crypto anarchy as the inevitable outcome. A new paradigm of cryptography—key escrow—is emerging and gaining acceptance in industry.

[That is what remains to be seen.]

The drawbacks of cryptography are frequently overlooked as well. The widespread availability of unbreakable encryption coupled with anonymous services could lead to a situation where practically all communications are immune from lawful interception (wiretaps) '

[My thoughts are immune from 'lawful interception' as are everyone else's, and yet the world survives. Thought is communication within the brain. Communication is 'thought' between brains. The world which has survived private thoughts can survive private communications. The whole concept of controlling communications is a bit obsolete, in any case. In past eras, the only social threat came from large masses of men (hence the desire to intercept and control communications), whereas today any individual can do more damage than a large group in the past.]

and documents from lawful search and seizure, and where all electronic transactions are beyond the reach of any government regulation or oversight. The consequences of this to public safety and social and economic stability could be devastating.

[See the recent joint study by the Cato Institute, the Fraser Institute, and nine other think tanks worldwide showing that there is a strong positive correlation between nations with free economies and nations with wealth. There seems little doubt that total economic deregulation is a good thing. We shall certainly have the chance to test that hypothesis in coming years. I haven't seen any nation harmed so far by having too free an economy.]

With the government essentially locked out, computers and telecommunications systems would become safe havens for criminal activity. Even May himself acknowledges that crypto anarchy provides a means for tax evasion, money laundering, espionage (with digital dead drops),

[That is, keeping your own money, transferring funds, and research. Sounds like activities that should not be the concern of others?]

contract killings,

[Contract killings may be easier, although *government* killings will be harder since governments may lack the resources to do as much of that sort of thing as they have done before. (From 1917 to 1989, communist governments murdered someone every thirty seconds—a total of some sixty million people.) In addition, those who fear they may be the subject of contract killings can use pseudonyms, locational ambiguity, and untraceable communications to make themselves harder to find and thus to kill.]

and implementation of data havens for storing and marketing illegal or controversial material.

[Last time I looked, controversial material was legal to possess and transmit. Illegal information will no longer be illegal if its transmission can't be stopped since utterly unenforceable laws tend to go away (see sodomy).]

Encryption also threatens national security by interfering with foreign intelligence operations. The United States, along with many other countries, imposes export controls on encryption technology to lessen this threat.

[Of course if the United States is weakened by the growth of (really) free markets, its enemies will be as well so foreign threats will automatically diminish.]

Cryptography poses a threat to organizations and individuals too. With encryption, an employee of a company can sell proprietary electronic information to a competitor without the need to photocopy and handle physical documents.

[This is a threat from digitization, not from encryption.]

The keys that unlock a corporation's files may be lost, corrupted, or held hostage for ransom, thus rendering valuable information inaccessible.

[Or the computers cannot be backed up, can crash, can be blown up, can be flooded, can experience disk failures, etc. This is not a problem unique to encryption. Backups and scattered sites are always necessary. High-speed networks, secure communications, and encryption make it easier to back up your systems at different locations all over the world. They help you avoid data loss; they don't contribute to it. Key splitting and private key escrow can easily protect keys.]

When considering the threats posed by cryptography, it is important to recognize that only the use of encryption for confidentiality, including anonymity, presents a problem.

[Confidentiality is the reason codes were invented in the first place. Additionally, the U.S. Supreme Court has recognized that anonymity has First Amendment protection. We have already made the social decision that anonymity is OK in many circumstances. I'm sure that all of us engage in many anonymous transactions on a daily basis, and yet the world survives.]

Crypto anarchy can be viewed as the proliferation of cryptography that provides the benefits of confidentiality protection but does nothing about its harms. It is government-proof encryption that denies access to the government even under a court order or other legal order.

[In countries that don't regularly practice torture, we have the power to disobey court orders in any case. Modern technology merely makes it easier and reduces the likelihood of punishment. Court orders are rare in any case. Seems like much ado about nothing.]

It has no safeguards to protect users and their organizations from accidents and abuse.

[This is the job of those who write software, not philosophers.]

The crypto-anarchist position is that cyberspace is on a nonstop drift toward crypto anarchy.

[I usually argue that the spread of markets is driven more by cheap tele-coms and the growth of a very efficient market infrastructure. Cryptography hasn't had much of an impact yet. I think that even without crypto, markets will swamp attempts to regulate them. And since people can move, as well, they are becoming harder to control even before any cryptorevolution.]

In addition to the free encryption programs being distributed on the Net, encryption is becoming a basic service integrated into commercial applications packages and network products. The IP Security Working Group of the Internet Engineering Task Force has written a document that calls for all compliant IPv6 (Internet Protocol, version 6) implementations to incorporate DES cryptography.

[The Net belongs to its customers, and as owners they will probably decide to secure their property. Sounds enormously democratic to me.]

The potential harms of cryptography have already begun to appear. As the result of interviews I conducted in May 1995, I found numerous cases where investigative agencies had encountered encrypted communications and computer files. These cases involved child pornography,

[Possession of a bunch of zeros and ones.]

customs violations,

[Free trade.]

drugs,

[The retail pharmaceutical trade.]

espionage,

[Research.]

embezzlement,

[Finally, a crime.]

murder,

[Another crime. Can you give us the details of a murder investigation blocked by cryptography? We don't need any names.]

obstruction of justice,

[Refusal to make things easy for prosecutors—a *real* crime. This wasn't Hillary by any chance, was it?]

tax protesters,

[You mean tax evaders, don't you? As far as I know, protesting taxes is a legal activity.]

and terrorism.

[State-sponsored or private?]

At the International Cryptography Institute held in Washington in September 1995, FBI Director Louis Freeh reported that encryption had been encountered in a terrorism investigation in the Philippines involving an alleged plot to assassinate Pope John Paul II and bomb a U.S. airliner.

[But the perp was caught anyway. Is this the same Louis Freeh who thinks that the loss (by him) of a government cellphone is just as bad as the FBI issuing shoot-to-kill orders against American citizens before even trying to arrest them (since he punished both with a letter of reprimand)?]

AccessData Corp., a company in Orem, Utah, that specializes in providing software and services to help law enforcement agencies and companies recover data that has been locked out through encryption, reports receiving about a dozen and a half calls a day from companies with inaccessible data.

[Sounds like poor system design. I'm not sure that advising others how to safely store their business records has anything to do with law enforcement, however.]

The idea is to combine strong encryption with an emergency decryption capability. This is accomplished by linking encrypted data to a data-recovery key that facilitates decryption. This key need not be (and typically is not) the one used for normal decryption, but it must provide access to that key. The data-recovery key is held by a trusted fiduciary, which could conceivably be a governmental agency, court, or trusted and bonded private organization. A key might be split among several such agencies.

[Why would a government agency or a court be the best entity to provide business services? If I'm looking for someone to install a LAN in my office, I don't immediately think to call the Post Office and get them to bid on the job. Business services like data backup and recovery are much more likely to be efficiently accomplished by a private contractor.]

Organizations registered with an escrow agent can acquire their own keys for emergency decryption. An investigative or intelligence agency seeking access to communications or stored files makes application through appropriate procedures (which normally includes getting a court order) and, on compliance, is issued the key.

[But what if it turns out that my chosen escrow agent is located outside the jurisdiction of the court? Surely you don't want to cause any North American Free Trade Agreement or General Agreement on Tariffs and Trade problems here. The World Trade Organization might declare your encryption policy to be an unfair trade practice.]

Legitimate privacy interests are protected through access procedures, auditing, and other safeguards.

[But what if some of us want better protection than bureaucratic promises and procedures. Some people in the past who relied on government promises and procedures has led some of us to end up in crowded "shower" rooms trying to extract oxygen from diesel exhaust.].

In April 1993, as a response to a rising need for and use of encryption products, the Clinton administration announced a new initiative to promote encryption in a way that would not prohibit lawful decryption when investigative agencies are authorized to intercept communications or search computer files.

[And a rousing success it was.]

The IBAG principles acknowledge the right of businesses and individuals to protect their information and the right of law-abiding governments to intercept and lawfully seize information when there is no practical alternative.

[Is a communist dictatorship a "law-abiding government"?]

The principles call for industry to develop open, voluntary, consensus, international standards and for governments, businesses, and individuals to work together to define the requirements for those standards. The standards would allow choices about algorithm, mode of operation, key length, and implementation in hardware or software. Products conforming to the standards would not be subject to restrictions on import or use and would be generally exportable.

[Gee, I thought that was what we were doing.]

It is conceivable that domestic and international efforts will be sufficient to avoid crypto anarchy, particularly with support from the international business community. However, it is possible that they will not be enough. Many companies are developing products with strong encryption that do not accommodate government access, standards groups are adopting nonkey escrow standards, and software encryption packages such as PGP are rapidly proliferating on the Internet, which is due, in part, to the crypto anarchists whose goal is to lock out the government. Since key escrow adds to the development and operation costs of encryption products, the price advantage of unescrowed encryption products could also be a factor that might undermine the success of a completely voluntary approach.

[Sounds like the voluntary cooperation of human beings in international markets is just humming right along isn't it? It seems that a lot of market participants are voting with their feet for strong crypto. The System is the Solution.]

Under this licensing program, commercial encryption products, including programs distributed through public network servers, would comply with government regulations.

[Isn't a "public network server" just a server that is made world readable? Since there will be (conservatively) 100 million "public network servers" online in a few years, won't enforcement be a trifle difficult?]

Such a licensing approach would not prevent the use of government-proof encryption products by criminals and terrorists. They could develop their own or acquire the products illegally. But licensing would make it considerably more difficult than it is at present. Had such controls been adopted several years ago—before programs such as DES and PGP were posted on the Internet—the encryption products on the market today would support key escrow or some other method for government access.

[As I recall, wasn't public key encryption developed in spite of the fact that the National Security Agency had in place an unofficial ban on cryptographic research? The NSA's ban failed. Since you are not proposing to outlaw such research, what makes you think that mere distribution controls will work?]

It would not be possible to acquire strong, government-proof encryption from reputable vendors or network file servers. The encryption products available through underground servers and the black market would most likely not possess as high a quality as products developed through the legitimate market.

[The Internet itself runs primarily on software developed on the open market from noncommercial sources without slick packaging. It seems to have met with some market acceptance in spite of the lack of shrink-wrap packaging.]

Crypto anarchy is an international threat that has been stimulated by international communications systems, including telephones and the Internet. Addressing this threat requires an international approach that provides for both secure international communications crossing national boundaries and electronic surveillance by governments of criminal and terrorist activity taking place within their jurisdictions.

[It's nice to be noticed. How, exactly, is this voluntary, international, standards regime going to deal with the desire of different governments to control different communications? Look at the problems: some governments want to ban American movies, the Asian *Wall Street Journal*, books on the health of former heads of state, public records of sensational murder trials, phone calls made using callback services, financial wire services, novels by leftist coreligionists living in England, e-mail containing the English word for sexual intercourse (if readable by children), directions on where to obtain an abortion in London, etc. And all these governments will want to crack private transmissions in order to find those responsible for these "crimes." This is going to be a hell of a challenge for a voluntary, international standards regime. I think it is probably beyond the capabilities of such an institution to mediate among all of these competing desires to control the communications of others.]

"BTW if one spellchecks the word *unescrowed* (as in *unescrowed encryption*), one is likely to encounter the suggested replacement *unscrewed* (as in *unscrewed encryption*).

12

Hiding Crimes in Cyberspace[1]

Dorothy E. Denning and William E. Baugh Jr.

Introduction

The growth of telecommunications and electronic commerce has led to a growing commercial market for digital encryption technologies. Business needs encryption to protect intellectual property and to establish secure links with their partners, suppliers, and customers. Banks need it to ensure the confidentiality and authenticity of financial transactions. Law enforcement needs it to stop those under investigation from intercepting police communications and obstructing investigations. Individuals need it to protect their private communications and confidential data. Encryption is critical to building a secure and trusted global information infrastructure for communications and electronic commerce.

Encryption also gives criminals and terrorists a powerful tool for concealing their activities. It can make it impossible for law-enforcement agencies to obtain the evidence needed for a conviction or the intelligence vital to criminal investigations. It can frustrate communications intercepts, which have played a significant role in averting terrorist attacks and in gathering information about specific transnational threats, including terrorism, drug trafficking, and organized crime (White House 1995). It can delay investigations and add to their cost.

The use of encryption to hide criminal activity is not new. The April 1970 issue of the *FBI Law Enforcement Bulletin* reports on several cases

This chapter originally appeared in *Information, Communication and Society* 2, no. 3 (Autumn 1999), and in B. D. Loader and D. Thomas, eds., *Cybercrime: Law Enforcement in the Information Age* (New York: Routledge, 1999). Reprinted by permission of the authors and the publisher. © 1999, Routledge.

where law-enforcement agencies had to break codes to obtain evidence or prevent violations of the law. None of the cases, however, involved electronic information or computers. Relatively simple substitution ciphers were used to conceal speech.

Digital computers have changed the landscape considerably. Encryption and other advanced technologies increasingly are used, with direct impact on law enforcement. If all communications and stored information in criminal cases were encrypted, it would be a nightmare for investigators. It would not be feasible to decrypt everything, even if technically possible. How would law-enforcement agencies know where to spend limited resources?

We address here the use of encryption and other information technologies to hide criminal activities. Numerous case studies are presented for illustration. We first examine encryption and the options available to law enforcement for dealing with it. Next, we discuss a variety of other tools for concealing information—passwords, digital compression, steganography, remote storage, and audit disabling. Finally, we discuss tools for hiding crimes through anonymity—anonymous remailers, anonymous digital cash, computer penetration and looping, cellular phone cloning, and cellular phone cards.

Encryption in Crime and Terrorism

This section describes criminal use of encryption in four domains—voice, fax, and data communications; electronic mail; files stored on the computers of individual criminals and criminal enterprises; and information posted in public places on computer networks.

Voice, Fax, and Real-Time Data Communications

Criminals can use encryption to make their real-time communications inaccessible to law enforcement. The effect is to deny law enforcement one of the most valuable tools in fighting organized crime—the court-ordered wiretap. In March 1997, the director of the Federal Bureau of Investigation, Louis J. Freeh, testified that the FBI was unable to assist with five requests for decryption assistance in communications intercepts in 1995 and twelve in 1996 (U.S. Congress 1997a). Such wiretaps can be extremely valuable as they capture the subjects' own words, which generally holds up much better in court than information acquired from informants, for example, who are often criminals themselves and extremely unreliable. Wiretaps also provide valuable information regarding the intentions, plans, and members of criminal conspiracies and in providing leads in criminal investigations. Drug cartels and organizations rely heavily on communications networks; monitoring of these networks has been critical for identifying those at the executive level and for uncovering the organizations' illegal proceeds. Communications intercepts have also been useful in terrorism cases, sometimes helping to avoid a deadly attack. They have helped prevent the bombing of a foreign consulate in the United States and a rocket attempt against a U.S. ally, among other things (U.S. Congress 1997a).

There is little case information in the public domain on the use of communications encryption devices by criminal enterprises. The Cali cartel is reputed to be using sophisticated encryption to conceal their telephone communications. Communications devices seized from the cartel in 1995 included radios that distort voices, video phones that provide visual authentication of the caller's identity, and instruments for scrambling transmissions from computer modems (Grabosky and Smith 1998).

We understand that some terrorist groups are using high-frequency encrypted voice/data links with state sponsors of terrorism. Hamas reportedly is using encrypted Internet communications to transmit maps, pictures, and other details pertaining to terrorist attacks. The Israeli General Security Service believes that most of the data is being sent to the Hamas worldwide center in Great Britain (IINS 1997).

The lack of universal interoperability and cost of telephone encryption devices—several hundred dollars for a device that provides strong security—has likely slowed their adoption by criminal enterprises. The problems to law enforcement could get worse as prices drop and Internet telephony becomes more common. Criminals can conduct encrypted voice conversations over the Internet at little or no cost. This impact on law enforcement, however, may be balanced by the emergence of digital cellular communications. These phones encrypt the radio links between the mobile devices and base stations, which is where the communications are most vulnerable to eavesdroppers. Elsewhere, the communications travel in the clear (or are separately encrypted while traversing micro-wave or satellite links), making court-ordered interception possible in the switches. The advantage to users is that they can protect their local over-the-air communications even if the parties they are conversing with are using phones with no encryption or with incompatible methods of encryption. The benefit to law enforcement is that plaintext can be inter-cepted in the base stations or switches. Although there are devices for achieving end-to-end encryption with cellular phones, they are more costly and require compatible devices at both ends.

Hackers use encryption to protect their communications on Internet Relay Chat (IRC) channels from interception. They have also installed their own encryption software on computers they have penetrated. The software is then used to set up a secure channel between the hacker's PC and the compromised machine. This has complicated, but not precluded, investigations.

Electronic Mail

Law-enforcement agencies have encountered encrypted e-mail and files in investigations of pedophiles and child pornography, including the FBI's Innocent Images national child pornography investigation. In many cases, the subjects were using Pretty Good Privacy (PGP) to encrypt files and e-mail. PGP uses conventional cryptography for data encryption and public-key cryptography for key distribution. The investigators thought this group favored PGP because they are generally educated, technically knowledgeable, and heavy Internet users. PGP is universally available on the Internet, and they can download it for free. Investigators say, however, that most child pornography traded on the Internet is not encrypted.

One hacker used encrypted e-mail to facilitate the sale of credit card numbers he had stolen from an Internet service provider and two other companies doing business on the Web. According to Richard Power, edi-torial director of the Computer Security Institute, Carlos Felipe Salgado Jr. had acquired nearly a hundred thousand card numbers by penetrat-ing the computers from an account he had compromised at the Univer-sity of California at San Francisco. Using commonly available hacking tools, he exploited known security flaws to go around firewalls and bypass encryption and other security measures. Boasting about his exploits on Internet Relay Chat, Salgado, who used the code name SMAK, made the mistake of offering to sell his booty to someone on the Internet. He conducted online negotiations using encrypted e-mail and received initial payments via anonymous Western Union wire transfer. Unknown to him, he had walked right into an FBI sting. After making two small buys and checking the legitimacy of the card numbers, FBI agents arranged a meeting at San Francisco airport. Salgado was to turn over the credit card numbers in exchange for $260,000. He arrived with an encrypted CD-ROM containing about a hundred thousand credit card numbers and a paperback copy of Mario Puzo's *The Last Don*. The key to decrypting the data was given by the first letter of each sentence in the first paragraph on page 128. Salgado was arrested and waived his rights. In June 1997, he was indicted on three counts of computer crime fraud and two counts of trafficking in stolen credit cards. In August, he pled guilty to four of the five counts. Had he not been caught, the losses to the credit card companies could have run from $10 million to over $100 million (Power 1997).

We were told of another case in which a terrorist group that was attacking businesses and state officials used encryption to conceal their messages. At the time the authorities intercepted the communications, they were unable to decrypt the messages, although they did perform some traffic analysis to determine who was talking with whom. Later they found the key on the hard disk of a seized computer, but only after breaking through additional layers of encryption, compression, and password protection. The messages were said to have been a great help to the investigating task force. We also received an anonymous report of a group of terrorists encrypting their e-mail with PGP.

Stored Data

In many criminal cases, documents and other papers found at a subject's premises provide evidence crucial for successful prosecution. Increasingly, this information is stored electronically on computers. Computers themselves have posed major challenges to law enforcement, and encryption has only compounded these challenges.

The FBI found encrypted files on the laptop computer of Ramsey Yousef, a member of the international terrorist group responsible for bombing the World Trade Center in 1994 and a Manila Air airliner in late 1995. These files, which were successfully decrypted, contained information pertaining to further plans to blow up eleven U.S.-owned commercial airliners in the Far East (U.S. Congress 1997a). Although much of the information was also available in unencrypted documents, the case illustrates the potential threat of encryption to public safety if authorities cannot get information about a planned attack and some of the conspirators are still at large.

Successful decryption of electronic records can be important to an investigation. Such was the case when Japanese authorities seized the computers of the Aum Shinrikyo cult—the group responsible for gassing the Tokyo subway in March 1995, killing twelve people and injuring six thousand more (Kaplan and Marshall 1996). The cult had stored its records on computers, encrypted with RSA. Authorities were able to decrypt the files after finding the key on a floppy disk. The encrypted files contained evidence that was said to be crucial to the investigation, including plans and intentions to deploy weapons of mass destruction in Japan and the United States.

In the Aum cult case, the authorities were lucky to find the key on a disk. In other cases, the subjects turned over their keys. For example, the Dallas Police Department encountered encrypted data in the investigation of a national drug ring that was operating in several states and dealing in Ecstasy. A member of the ring, residing within their jurisdiction, had encrypted his address book. He turned over the password, enabling the police to decrypt the file. Meanwhile, however, the subject was out on bond and alerted his associates, so the decrypted information was not as useful as it might have been. The detective handling the case said that in the ten years he had been working drug cases, this was the only time he had encountered encryption and that he rarely even encountered computers. He noted that the Ecstasy dealers were into computers more than other types of drug dealers, most likely because they were younger and better educated. They were using the Internet for sales, but they were not encrypting electronic mail. The detective also noted that the big drug dealers were not encrypting phone calls. Instead, they were swapping phones (using cloned phones; see later discussion) to stay ahead of law enforcement (Manning 1997).[2]

In many cases, investigators have had to break the encryption system to get at the data. For example, when the FBI seized the computers of

Central Intelligence Agency spy Aldrich Ames, they found encrypted computer files but no keys. Fortunately, Ames had used standard commercial off-the-shelf software, and the investigator handling the computer evidence was able to break the codes using software supplied by AccessData Corporation of Orem, Utah. The key was Ames's Russian code name, KOLOKOL (bell). According to investigators, failure to recover the encrypted data would have weakened the case. Ames was eventually convicted of espionage against the United States (CSI 1997).[3]

Code breaking is not always so easy. In his book about convicted hacker Kevin Poulsen, Jonathan Littman reported that Poulsen had encrypted files documenting everything from the wiretaps he had discovered to the dossiers he had compiled about his enemies. The files were said to have been encrypted several times using the "Defense Encryption Standard." According to Littman, a Department of Energy supercomputer was used to find the key, a task that took several months at an estimated cost of hundreds of thousands of dollars. The effort apparently paid off, however, yielding nearly ten thousand pages of evidence (Littman 1997).

A substantial effort was also required to break the encryption software used by the 1996 New York subway bomber, Edward J. Leary. In that case, the result yielded child pornography and personal information that was not particularly useful to the case. Investigators, however, retrieved other evidence from the computer that was used at the trial. Leary was found guilty and sentenced to ninety-four years in jail.

Timeliness is critical in some investigations. Several years ago, a Bolivian terrorist organization assassinated four U.S. Marines, and AccessData was brought in to decrypt files seized from a safe house. With only twenty-four hours to perform this task, they decrypted the custom-encrypted files in twelve hours, and the case ended with one of the largest drug busts in Bolivian history. The terrorists were caught and put in jail (CSI 1997). In such cases, an effort that requires months or years to complete might be useless.

In other cases, the ability to successfully decrypt files proved unessential, as when a Durham priest was sentenced to six years in jail for sexually assaulting minors and distributing child pornography (Akdeniz, n.d.). The priest was part of an international pedophile ring that communicated and exchanged images over the Internet. When U.K. authorities seized his computers, they found files of encrypted messages. The encryption was successfully broken; however, the decrypted data did not affect the case.

Even when decrypted material has little or no investigative value, considerable resources are wasted reaching that determination. If all information were encrypted, it would be extremely difficult for law enforcement to decide where to spend precious resources. It would not be practical or even possible to decrypt everything. Yet if nothing were decrypted, many criminals would go free.

Some investigations have been derailed by encryption. For example, at one university, the investigation of a professor thought to be trafficking in child pornography was aborted because the campus police could not decrypt his files. In another case, an employee of a company copied proprietary software to a floppy disk, took the disk home, and then stored the file on his computer encrypted under PGP. Evidently, his intention was to use the software to offer competing services, which were valued at tens of millions of dollars annually (the software itself cost over a million dollars to develop). At the time we heard about the case, the authorities had not determined the passphrase needed to decrypt the files. Information contained in logs had led them to suspect the file was the pilfered software.

At Senate hearings in September 1997, Jeffery Herig, special agent with the Florida Department of Law Enforcement, testified that the department was unable to access protected files within a personal finance program in an embezzlement case at Florida State University. He said the files could possibly hold useful information concerning the location of the embezzled funds (U.S. Congress 1997b).

Herig also reported that they had encountered unbreakable encryption in a U.S. Customs case involving an illegal, worldwide advance-fee scheme. At least three hundred victims were allegedly bilked out of over $60 million. Herig said they had encountered three different encryption systems. Although they were able to defeat the first two, they were unsuccessful with the third. The vendor told them that there were no backdoors. "Although I have been able to access some of the encrypted data in this case," Herig said, "we know there is a substantial amount of incriminating evidence which has not been recovered" (U.S. Congress 1997b).

In early 1997, we were told that Dutch organized crime groups had received encryption support from a group of skilled hackers who themselves used PGP and PGPfone to encrypt their communications. The hackers had supplied the mobsters with palmtop computers on which they installed Secure Device, a Dutch software product for encrypting data with IDEA. The palmtops served as an unmarked police/intelligence vehicles database. In 1995, the Amsterdam police captured a PC in the possession of one organized crime member. The PC contained an encrypted partition, which they were unable to recover at the time. Nevertheless, there was sufficient other evidence for conviction. The disk, which was encrypted with a U.S. product, was eventually decrypted in 1997 and found to be of little interest.

There have been a few reported cases of company insiders using encryption as a tool of extortion. The employees or former employees threatened to withhold the keys to encrypted data unless payment was made. In these cases, encryption is not used to conceal evidence of crimes but rather to intimidate the organization. We are not aware of any extortion attempts of this nature that succeeded.

The use of encryption by the victims of crime can also pose a problem for law enforcement. At hearings in June 1997, Senator Charles Grassley told of an eleven-year-old boy in the Denver area who committed suicide after being sexually molested. The boy left behind a personal organizer, which investigators believed might contain information about the man whom his mother believed molested him. The organizer was encrypted, however, and the police were unable to crack the password. The investigation had been on hold since February 1996.

In April 1998, the FBI's Computer Analysis Response Team (CART) forensics laboratory started collecting data on computer forensics cases handled at headquarters or in one of the FBI's field offices. As of December 9, they had received 299 examination reporting forms, of which twelve (4 percent) indicated use of encryption.[4] This is slightly lower than CART's estimate of 5 to 6 percent for 1996 (Denning and Baugh 1997). There are at least three possible explanations. One is that the 1996 estimate, which was made before the FBI began collecting hard data, was somewhat high. A second is that as computers have become more common and user friendly, they are increasingly being used by criminals who lack the knowledge or skills to encrypt their files. Hence, the percentage of computer forensics cases involving encryption is staying about the same or decreasing even as the total number of forensics cases (and encryption cases) is growing. A third is that the early reports are skewed; as more come in, the percentage could approach 5 to 6 percent.

Public Postings

Criminals can use encryption to communicate in secrecy through open forums such as computer bulletin boards and Internet Web sites. Although many people might see the garbled messages, only those with the key would be able to determine the plaintext.

This technique was used by an extortionist who threatened to kill Microsoft president and chief executive officer Bill Gates in spring 1997.[5] The extortionist transmitted messages to Gates via letter and asked Gates to acknowledge acceptance by posting a specified message on the America Online Netgirl bulletin board. Gates then received a letter with instructions to open an account for a Mr. Robert M. Rath in a Luxemburg bank and to transfer $5,246,827.62 to that account. The money was to be transferred by April 26 "to avoid dying, among other things." Gates was reminded that April 26 was his daughter's birthday. The letter came with a disk that contained an image of the entertainer Elvira and the key to a simple substitution cipher. Gates was told to use the code to encrypt instructions for accessing the Rath account via telephone or facsimile. He was then to attach the ciphertext to the bottom of the image and post the image to numerous image libraries within the Photography Forum of America Online (AOL). The graphic image with ciphertext was uploaded to AOL at the direction of the FBI on April 25.

Although Gates complied with the requests, he did not lose his money. The extortion threat was traced to Adam Quinn Pletcher in Long Grove, Illinois. On May 9, Pletcher admitted writing and mailing the threatening letters (there were four altogether) to Gates.

Law Enforcement Options

The majority of investigations we heard about were not stopped by encryption. Authorities obtained the key by consent, found it on disk, or cracked the system in some way—for example, by guessing a password or exploiting a weakness in the overall system. Alternatively, they used other evidence such as printed copies of encrypted documents, other paper documents, unencrypted conversations and files, witnesses, and information acquired through other, more intrusive, surveillance technologies such as bugs. We emphasize, however, that these were cases involving computer searches and seizures, not wiretaps. This section discusses the options available to law enforcement for dealing with encryption.

Getting the Key from the Subject

In many cases, subjects have cooperated with the police and disclosed their keys or passwords, sometimes as part of a plea bargain. One hacker who had encrypted his files with the Colorful File System confessed to his crimes and revealed his CFS passphrase:

ifyoucanreadthisyoumustbeerikdale—**oragoodcypherpunk

He (Erik) wanted to speed the process along. The decrypted files contained evidence that was important to the case.[6]

A question that frequently arises is whether a court can compel the disclosure of plaintext or keys or whether the defendants are protected by the Fifth Amendment. Philip Reitinger, an attorney with the Department of Justice Computer Crime Unit, studied this question and concluded that a grand jury subpoena can direct the production of plaintext or of documents that reveal keys, although a limited form of immunity may be required (Reitinger 1996). He left open the question of whether law enforcement could compel production of a key that has been memorized but not recorded. He also observed that faced with the choice of providing a key that unlocks incriminating evidence or risking contempt of court, many will choose the latter and claim loss of memory or destruction of the key.

In *People v. Price* in Yolo County, California Superior Court prosecutors successfully compelled production of the passphrase protecting the defendant's PGP key. In this case, however, the key was not sought for the purpose of acquiring evidence for conviction but rather to determine whether the defendant's computer should be released from police custody. He had already been convicted of annoying children and wanted his computer back. The police argued it should not be released as there was reason to believe it contained contraband, specifically PGP-encrypted files containing child pornography. This determination was based on the existence of a pair of files named "Boys.gif" and "Boys.pgp" (when PGP encrypts a plaintext file, it automatically gives the ciphertext file the same name but with the extension ".pgp").[7]

The defendant was unsuccessful in arguing a Fifth Amendment privilege. The prosecution argued that the contents of the file had already been uttered and, therefore, were not protected under the Fifth Amendment. As long as prosecutors did not try to tie the defendant to the file by virtue of his knowing the passphrase, no incrimination was implied by disclosing the passphrase.

To handle the passphrase, a court clerk was sworn in as a special master. An investigator activated the PGP program to the point where it prompted for the passphrase. He left the room while the defendant disclosed the passphrase to the special master, who typed it into the computer. The investigator was then brought back into the room to hit the Enter key and complete the decryption process. As expected, child pornography fell out. The judge then ordered the computer, its peripherals, and all diskettes destroyed. The defendant argued that the computer contained research material, but the judge admonished him for commingling it with the contraband.

Getting Access through a Third Party

Some encryption products have a key recovery system that enables access to plaintext through a means other than the normal decryption process. The key needed to decrypt the data is recovered using information stored with the ciphertext plus information held by a trusted agent, which could be an officer of the organization owning the data or a third party. The primary objective is to protect organizations and individuals using strong encryption from loss or destruction of encryption keys, which could render valuable data inaccessible.

Key recovery systems can accommodate lawful investigations by proving authorities with a means of acquiring the keys needed. If the keys are held by a third party, this can be done without the knowledge of the criminal group under investigation. Of course, if criminal enterprises operate their own recovery services, law enforcement may be no better off. Indeed, they could be worse off because the encryption will be much stronger, possibly uncrackable, and the criminals might not cooperate with the authorities. Moreover, with wiretaps, which must be performed surreptitiously to have value, investigators cannot go to the subjects and ask for keys to tap their lines. Key recovery systems could also encourage the use of encryption in organized crime to protect electronic files, as criminal enterprises need not worry about loss of keys.

Because of the potential benefits of key recovery to law enforcement, the Clinton administration has encouraged the development of key recovery products by offering an export advantages to companies making such products. Beginning in December 1996, products with key recovery systems could be readily exported with unlimited key lengths. The administration has retained restrictions on nonrecoverable products that use keys longer than 56 bits, but even here export controls have been liberalized to allow ready export under certain conditions.

Breaking the Codes

It is often possible to obtain the key needed to decrypt data by exploiting a weakness in the encryption algorithm, implementation, key management system, or some other system component. Indeed, there are software tools on the Internet for cracking the encryption in many commercial applications. One site on the World Wide Web[8] lists freeware crackers and products from AccessData Corp. and CRAK Software for Microsoft Word, Excel, and Money; WordPerfect, Data Perfect, and Professional Write; Lotus 1-2-3 and Quattro Pro; Paradox; PKZIP; Symantex Q&A; and Quicken.

Eric Thompson, president of AccessData, reported that his company had a recovery rate of 80 to 85 percent with the encryption in large-scale commercial commodity software applications. He also noted that 90 percent of the systems are broken somewhere other than at the crypto engine level—for example, in the way the text is preprocessed (CSI 1997). A passphrase or key might be found in the swap space on disk.

In those cases where there is no shortcut attack, the key might be determined by brute-force search—that is, by trying all possible keys until one is found that yields known plaintext or, if that is not available, meaningful data. Keys are represented as strings of 0s and 1s (bits), so this means trying every possible bit combination. This is relatively easy if the keys are no more than 40 bits, and somewhat longer keys can be broken given enough horsepower. In July 1998, John Gilmore, a computer privacy and civil liberties activist, and Paul Kocher, president of Cryptography Research in California, won $10,000 for designing a supercomputer that broke a 56-bit DES challenge cipher in record time—in their case, fifty-six hours or less than three days. The EFF DES Cracker was built by a team of about a dozen computer researchers with funds from the Electronic Frontier Foundation. It took less than a year to build and cost less than $250,000. It tested keys at a rate of almost a hundred billion per second (EFF 1998; Markoff 1998).

Unfortunately, criminals can protect against such searches by using methods that take longer keys—say, 128 bits with the RC4, RC5, or IDEA encryption algorithm or 168 bits with Triple DES. Because each additional bit doubles the number of candidates to try, a brute-force search quickly becomes intractable. To crack a 64-bit key, it would take ten EFF DES Crackers operating for an entire year. At 128 bits, it is totally infeasible to break a key by brute force, even if all the computers in the world are put to the task. To break one in a year would require, say, one trillion computers (more than a hundred computers for every person on the globe), each running ten billion times faster than the EFF DES Cracker. Put another way, it would require the equivalent of ten billion trillion DES Crackers! Many products, including PGP, use 128-bit keys or longer.

With many encryption systems (for example, PGP), a user's private key (which unlocks message keys) is computed from or protected by a passphrase chosen by the user. In that case, it may be easier to brute-force the password than the key because it will be limited to ASCII characters and be less random than an arbitrary stream of bits. Eric Thompson reports that the odds are about even of successfully guessing a password. They use a variety of techniques, including Markov chains, phonetic generation algorithms, and concatenation of small words (CSI 1997).

Often, investigators will find multiple encryption systems on a subject's computer. For example, PGP might be used for e-mail, while an application's built-in encryption might be used to protect documents within the application. In those cases, the subject might use the same password with all systems. If investigators can break one because the overall system is weak, they might be able to break the other, more difficult system by trying the same password.

To help law enforcement develop the capability to stay abreast of new technologies, including encryption, the Federal Bureau of Investigation proposes establishing a technical support center. The center would maintain a close working relationship with the encryption vendors. The Clinton administration announced support for the center in its September 1998 update on encryption policy (White House 1998).

One issue raised by the development and use of tools for breaking codes is how law enforcement can protect its sources and methods. If investigators must reveal in court the exact methods used to decipher a message, future use of such methods could be jeopardized.

Finding an Access Point
Another strategy for acquiring plaintext is to find an access point that provides direct access to the plaintext before encryption or after decryption. In the area of communications, a router or switch might offer such access to communications that traverse the switch. If the communications are encrypted on links coming into and going out of the switch but in the clear as they pass through the switch, then a wiretap placed in the switch will give access to the plaintext communications. We noted earlier how digital cellular communications could be intercepted in this manner, while at the same time offering users considerably greater security and privacy than offered by analog phones that do not use encryption.

Network encryption systems that offer access points of this nature are given an export advantage over those that do not (White House 1998). The approach was initially called a "private doorbell" approach to distinguish it from one that uses key recovery agents (Corcoran 1998; Cisco Systems 1998). Now it is considered a form of recoverable encryption.

For stored data, Codex Data Systems of Bardonia, New York, advertises a product called Data Interception by Remote Transmission (DIRT), which is designed to allow remote monitoring of a subject's personal computer by law-enforcement and other intelligence-gathering agencies. Once DIRT is installed on the subject's machine, the software will surreptitiously log keystrokes and transmit captured data to a predetermined Internet address that is monitored and decoded by DIRT Command Center Software. DIRT add-ons include remote file access, real-time capture of keystrokes, remote screen capture, and remote audio and video capture. The software could be used to capture a password and read encrypted e-mail traffic and files.

When All Else Fails

The inability to break through encryption does not always spell doom. Investigators may find printed copies of encrypted documents. They may find the original plaintext version of an encrypted file, for example, if the subject forgot to delete the original file or if it was not thoroughly erased from the disk. They may obtain incriminating information from unencrypted conversations, witnesses, informants, and hidden microphones. They may conduct an undercover or sting operation to catch the subject. These other methods do not guarantee success, however.

If there is sufficient evidence of some crime but not the one believed to be concealed by encryption, a conviction may be possible on lesser charges. This happened in Maryland when police encountered an encrypted file in a drug case. Allegations were raised that the subject had been involved in document counterfeiting, and file names were consistent with formal documents. Efforts to decrypt the files failed, however, so the conviction was on the drug charges only.[9]

In another case, a fifteen-year-old boy came to the child abuse bureau of the Sacramento County Sheriff's Department with his mother, who desired to file a complaint against an adult who had met her son in person, befriended the boy and his friends and bought them pizza. The man had sold her son $500 to $1,000 worth of hardware and software for $1 and given him lewd pictures on floppy disks. The man subsequently mailed her son pornographic material on floppy disk and sent her son pornographic files over the Internet using America Online. After three months of investigation, a search warrant was issued against a man in Campbell, California, and the adoption process of a nine-year-old boy was stopped. Eventually, the subject was arrested, but by this time he had purchased another computer system and traveled to England to visit another boy. Within ten days of acquiring the system, he had started experimenting with different encryption systems, eventually settling on PGP. He had encrypted a directory on the system. There was information indicating that the subject was engaged in serious corporate espionage, and it was thought that the encrypted files might have contained evidence of that activity. The Sheriffs Department was never able to decrypt the files, however, and after the subject tried unsuccessfully to put a contract out on the victim from jail, he pled no contest to multiple counts of distribution of harmful material to a juvenile and the attempt to influence, dissuade, or harm a victim/witness.[10]

If encryption precludes access to all evidence of wrongdoing, then a case is dropped (assuming other methods of investigation have failed as well). Several cases that had been aborted or put on hold because of encryption were noted earlier.

Other Technologies for Hiding Evidence

The modern criminal has access to a variety of tools other than encryption for concealing information.

Passwords

Criminals, like law-abiding persons, often password-protect their machines to keep others out. In one gambling operation with connections to New York's Gambino, Genovese, and Colombo crime families, bookies had password-protected a computer used to cover bets at the rate of $65 million a year (Ramo 1996). After discovering that the password was one of the henchmen's mother's name, the cops found ten thousand digital betting slips worth $10 million.

Another gambling enterprise operated multiple sites linked by a computer system, with drop-offs and pick-ups spanning three California counties. The ring leader managed his records with a commercial accounting program, using a password to control access to his files.

Although the software manufacturer refused to assist law enforcement, police investigators were able to gain access by zeroing out the passwords in the data files. They found the daily take on bets, payoffs, persons involved, amounts due and paid or owed, and so forth. The printed files showed the results of four years of bookmaking and resulted in a plea of guilty to the original charges and a sizeable payment of back taxes, both state and federal.[11]

Passwords are encountered much more often than encryption in computer forensics cases. Of the 299 computer examination reports received by the FBI's CART between April and December 1998, sixty (20 percent) indicated use of passwords. This was five times as many as had indicated use of encryption.[12]

Digital Compression

Digital compression is normally used to reduce the size of a file or communication without losing information content, or at least significant content. The greatest reductions are normally achieved with audio, image, and video data; however, substantial savings are possible even with text data. Compression can benefit the criminal trying to hide information in two ways. First, it makes the task of identifying and accessing information more difficult for the police conducting a wiretap or seizing files. Second, when used prior to encryption, it can make cracking an otherwise weak cipher difficult. This is because the compressed data is more random in appearance than the original data, making it less susceptible to techniques that exploit the redundancy in languages and multimedia formats.

Steganography

Steganography refers to methods of hiding of secret data in other data such that its existence is even concealed. One class of methods encodes the secret data in the low-order bit positions of image, sound, or video files. There are several tools for doing this, many of which can be downloaded for free off the Internet. With S-tools, for example, the user hides a file of secret data in an image by dragging the file over the image. The software will optionally encrypt the data before hiding it for an extra layer of security. S-tools will also hide data in sound files or in the unallocated sectors of a disk.

There have been a few reported cases of criminals using steganography to facilitate their crimes. One credit card thief, for example, used it to hide stolen card numbers on a hacked Web page. He replaced bullets on the page with images that looked the same but contained the credit card numbers, which he then offered to associates. This case illustrates the potential of using Web images as "digital dead drops" for information brokering. Only a handful of people need know the drop exists.

Steganography can be used to hide the existence of files on a computer's hard disk. Ross Anderson, Roger Needham, and Adi Shamir propose a steganographic file system that would make a file invisible to anyone who does not know the file name and a password. An attacker who does not know this information gains no knowledge about whether the file exists, even given complete access to all the hardware and software. One simple approach creates cover files so that the user's hidden files are the exclusive or (XOR) of a subset of the cover files. The subset is chosen by the user's password (Anderson, Needham, and Shamir 1998).

Remote Storage

Criminals can hide data by storing it on remote hosts—for example, a file server at their Internet Service Provider (ISP). Jim McMahon, former head of the High Technology Crimes Detail of the San Jose Police Department, reported that he had personally seen suspects hiding criminal data on nonlocal disks, often at ISP locations but sometimes on the systems of innocent third parties with poor security, leaving them open to intrusions and subsequent abuse. Eugene Schultz, former manager of the Department of Energy's Computer Incident Advisory Capability, said that a group of hackers from the Netherlands had taken so much information from Defense Department computers that they could not store it all on their own disks. So they broke into systems at Bowling Green University and the University of Chicago and downloaded the information to these sites, figuring they could transfer it somewhere else later.[13] Software pirates have been known to stash their pilfered files in hidden directories on systems they have hacked.

Data can be hidden on removable disks and kept in a physical location away from the computers. Don Delaney, a detective with the New York State Police, told us in early 1997 that in one Russian organized crime case involving more than $100 million in state sales-tax evasion, money laundering, gasoline bootlegging, and enterprise corruption, police had to obtain amendments to their search warrants to seize disks and records from handbags and locked briefcases in the offices at two locations. After an exhaustive six-month review of all computer evidence, they determined that the largest amount of the most damaging evidence was on the diskettes. The crooks did their work in Excel and then saved it on floppies. The lesson they learned from this was to execute the search warrant with everyone present and look for disks in areas where personal property is kept. As storage technologies continue to get smaller, criminals will have even more options for hiding data.

Audit Disabling

Most systems keep a log of activity on the system. Perpetrators of computer crimes have, in many cases, disabled the auditing or deleted the audit records pertaining to their activity. The hacking tool RootKit, for example, contains Trojan horse system utilities that conceal the presence of the hacker and disable auditing. ZAP is another tool for erasing audit records. Both of these can be downloaded for free on the Internet.

Concealing Crimes through Anonymity

Crimes can be concealed by hiding behind a cloak of anonymity. A variety of technologies are available.

Anonymous Remailers

An anonymous remailer is a service that allows someone to send an electronic mail message without the receiver knowing the sender's identity. The remailer may keep enough information about the sender to enable the receiver to reply to the message by way of the remailer. To illustrate, suppose Alice wishes to send an anonymous e-mail message to Bob. Instead of e-mailing to Bob directly, Alice sends the message to a remailer (an e-mail server), which strips off the headers and forwards the contents to Bob. When Bob gets the message, he sees that it came via the remailer, but he cannot tell who the sender was. Some remailers give users pseudonyms so that recipients can reply to messages by way of the remailer. The remailer forwards the replies to the owners of the pseudonyms. These pseudo-anonymous remailers do not provide total anonymity because the remailer knows who the parties are. Other remailers offer full anonymity, but they cannot support replies. All they do is act as a mail forwarder.

A remailer can accumulate batches of messages before forwarding them to their destinations. That way, if someone is intercepting encrypted Internet messages for the purpose of traffic analysis, the eavesdropper would not be able to deduce who is talking to whom.

There are numerous anonymous and pseudo-anonymous remailers on the Internet. Some provide encryption services (typically using PGP) in addition to mail forwarding so that messages transmitted to and from the remailer can be encrypted. Users who don't trust the remailers can forward their messages through multiple remailers.

Anonymous remailers allow persons to engage in criminal activity while concealing their identities. President Clinton, for example, has received e-mail death threats that were routed through anonymous remailers. In one case involving remailers, an extortionist threatened to fly a model airplane into the jet engine of an airplane during takeoff at a German airport, the objective being to cause the plane to crash. The threats were sent as e-mail through an anonymous remailer in the United States. The messages were traced to introductory accounts on America Online, but the person had provided bogus names and credit card numbers. He was caught, however, before carrying out his threat.[14]

Anonymous Digital Cash

Digital cash enables users to buy and sell information goods and services. It is particularly useful with small transactions, serving the role of hard currency. Some methods allow users to make transactions with complete anonymity; others allow traceability under exigent circumstances—for example, a court order.

Total anonymity affords criminals the ability to launder money and engage in other illegal activity in ways that circumvent law enforcement. Combined with encryption or steganography and anonymous remailers, digital cash could be used to traffic in stolen intellectual property on the Web or to extort money from victims.

In May 1993, Timothy May (1996b) wrote an essay about a hypothetical organization, BlackNet, which would buy and sell information using a combination of public-key cryptography, anonymous remailers, and anonymous digital cash:

> BlackNet can make anonymous deposits to the bank account of your choice, where local banking laws permit, can mail cash directly ..., or can credit you in CryptoCredits, the internal currency of BlackNet.... If you are interested, do *not* attempt to contact us directly (you'll be wasting your time), and do *not* post anything that contains your name, your e-mail address, etc. Rather, compose your message, encrypt it with the public key of BlackNet (included below), and use an anonymous remailer chain of one or more links to post this encrypted, anonymized message on one of the locations listed.

Although May said he wrote the essay to point out the difficulty of "bottling up" new technologies (May 1996a), rumors spread shortly after May's essay appeared on the Internet of actual BlackNets being used for the purpose of selling stolen trade secrets.

In an essay called "Assassination Politics," James Dalton Bell suggested using cyber betting pools to kill off Internal Revenue Service (IRS) agents and other "hated government employees and officeholders" (Bell 1996). The idea was simple: using the Internet, encryption, and untraceable digital cash, anyone could contribute anonymously to a pool of digital cash. The person, presumably the assassin, correctly guessing the victim's time of death wins. After spending nearly two years peddling his ideas on Internet discussion groups and mailing lists, Bell was arrested and pled guilty to two felony charges: obstructing and impeding the IRS and falsely using a social security number with the intent to deceive. In his plea agreement, he admitted to conducting a "stink bomb" attack on an IRS office in Vancouver (McCullah 1997).[15] He also disclosed the passphrase required to decrypt e-mail messages that had been sent to Bell by his associates encrypted under PGP.

Although Bell did not implement any betting pools, an anonymous message was posted to the Cypherpunks Internet mailing list announcing an Assassination Politics Bot (program) called Dead Lucky that did. The message also listed four potential targets. A related message pointed to an interactive Web page titled Dead Lucky, which contained the statement "If you can correctly predict the date and time of death of others, then you can win large prizes payable in untaxable, untraceable eca$h." The page also stated "Contest will officially begin after Posting of Rules and Announcement of Official Starting Date (Until then it is for Entertainment Purposes Only)." Another anonymous message posted to

Cypherpunks had the subject "Encrypted InterNet DEATH THREAT!!! / ATTN: Ninth District Judges / PASSWORD: sog." The PGP encrypted message, when decrypted with "sog," contained death threats and a claim to authorship of the Assassination Bot. Investigators linked the messages and Bot to an individual by the name of Carl Edward Johnson. In August 1998, a warrant was issued charging Johnson with threatening "to kill certain law enforcement officers and judges of the United States, with intent to impede, intimidate, or interfere with said officers and judges on account of their official duties."[16]

Computer Penetrations and Looping
By breaking into someone's computer account and issuing commands from that account, a criminal can hide behind the account holder's identity. In one such case, two hackers allegedly penetrated the computers of Strong Capital Management and sent out 250,000 ads with fraudulent headers that bore the company's name. The ads were for online strip-tease services ('cyberstripping'), computer equipment, and sports betting. SCM filed a $125 million lawsuit against the hackers, demanding penalties of $5,000 per message.

Hackers can make it difficult for investigators to discover their true identity by using a technique called *looping*. Instead of penetrating a particular system directly, they can enter one system, use that system as a springboard to penetrate another, use the second system to penetrate a third, and so forth, eventually reaching their target system. The effect is to conceal the intruder's location and complicate an investigation. In order to trace the connection, investigators need the help of systems administrators along the path. If the path crosses several national borders, getting that cooperation may be impossible.

Cellular Phones and Cloning
Drug lords, gangsters, and other criminals regularly use "cloned" cell phones to evade the police. Typically, they buy the phones in bulk and discard them after use. A top Cali cartel manager might use as many as thirty-five different cell phones a day (Ramo 1996). In one case involving the Colombia cartel, DEA officials discovered an unusual number of calls to Colombia on their phone bills. It turned out that cartel operatives had cloned the DEA's own number! Some cloned phones, called *lifetime*

phones, hold up to 99 stolen numbers. New numbers can be programmed into the phone from a keypad, allowing the user to switch to a different cloned number for each call. With cloning, whether cellular communications are encrypted may have little impact on law enforcement, as they do not even know which numbers to tap.

Digital cellular phones use stronger methods of authentication that protect against cloning. As this technology replaces analog cell phones, cloning may be less of a problem for law enforcement.

Cellular Phone Cards

A similar problem occurs with cellular phone cards. These prepaid cards, which are inserted into a mobile phone, specify a telephone number and amount of air time. In Sweden, phone cards can be purchased anonymously, which has made wiretapping impossible. The narcotics police have asked that purchasers be required to register in a database that would be accessible to the police (Minow 1997). A similar card is used in France; however, buyers must show an identification card at the time of purchase. In Italy, a prepaid card must be linked to an identity, which must be linked to an owner.

Conclusions

Criminals and terrorists are using encryption and other advanced technologies to hide their activities. Indications are that use of these technologies will continue and expand, with a growing impact on law enforcement. Although the majority of investigations we heard about were not stopped by encryption, we heard about a few cases that were effectively derailed or put on hold by encryption. Even when the encryption was broken, however, it delayed investigations, sometimes by months or years, and added to their cost, in a few cases costing agencies hundreds of thousands of dollars to crack open encrypted files.

Efforts to decrypt data for law-enforcement agencies or corporations in need of recovering from lost keys have been largely successful because of weaknesses in the systems as a whole. That success rate is likely to drop, however, as vendors integrate stronger encryption into their products and get smarter about security. It is not possible to break well-designed cryptosystems that use key lengths of 128 bits or more. It is not just a matter of paying enough money or getting enough people on the Internet to help out. The resources simply do not exist—anywhere.

Most of the investigators we talked to said that they had not yet detected substantial use of encryption by large organized crime groups. This can be attributed to several factors, including the difficulty and overhead of using encryption (particularly the personnel time involved) and a general sense that their environments are already reasonably isolated and protected from law enforcement.

Maria Christina Ascents, who runs the Italian state police's crime and technology center, said that the Italian Mafia is increasingly looking to use encryption to help protect it from the government. She cited encryption as their greatest limit on investigations and noted that instead of hiring cryptographers to create their codes, mobsters download copies of Pretty Good Privacy (PGP) off the Internet (Ramo 1996).

As the population becomes better educated about technology and encryption, more and more criminals will have the knowledge and skills needed to evade law enforcement, particularly given the ease with which unbreakable, user-friendly software encryption can be distributed and obtained on the Internet. We recommend ongoing collection of data on the use of encryption and other advanced technologies in crime. We need to know how encryption is impacting cases—whether it is broken or circumvented, whether cases are successfully investigated and prosecuted despite encryption and costs to investigators.

Encryption is a critical international issue with severe impact and benefits to business and order. National policy must recognize not only the threat to law enforcement and intelligence operations, but also the need to protect the intellectual property and economic competitiveness of industry. Encryption policy must also respect consumer needs for encryption and basic human rights, including privacy and freedom of expression. Addressing all of these interests is enormously challenging.

Notes

1. The chapter is an update of a study we conducted in 1997 at the invitation of the U.S. Working Group on Organized Crime, National Strategy Information Center, Washington, DC.

2. Additional information was provided by Detective R. J. Montemayor in the Dallas Police Department.

3. The key used by Ames was disclosed to us by Robert Reynard on February 18, 1998.

4. Data provided by CART on December 9, 1998.

5. U.S. District Court, Northern District of Illinois, Eastern Division, Search Warrant, Case Number 97-157M, May 8, 1997; United States v. Adam Quinn Pletcher, U.S. District Court, Western District of Washington at Seattle, Magistrate's Docket No. Case No. 97-179M, May 9, 1997.

6. Byron W. Thompson, presentation at HTCIA-FBI Training Seminar, Perspectives on Computer Crime, November 12–13, 1998.

7. Information on this case was provided by Fred B. Cotton of SEARCH Group, Inc. Cotton was the investigator who activated the PGP program on the defendant's computer.

8. http://www.hiwaay.net/boklr/bsw_crak.html as of February 1997.

9. This case was reported to us by Howard Schmidt.

10. This case was reported by Brian Kennedy of the Sacramento County Sheriff's Department.

11. This case was first reported to us on February 22, 1997, by Jim McMahon, former head of the High Technology Crimes Detail of the San Jose Police Department. We received additional information from Robert Reynard on June 10, 1998.

12. Data provided by CART on December 9, 1998.

13. Communication from Eugene Schultz, May 15, 1998.

14. Presentation by Christoph Fischer at Georgetown University, July 22, 1998.

15. http://jya.com/jimbell3.htm.

16. United States v. Carl Edward Johnson, Warrant for Arrest, Case No. 98-430M, U.S. District Court, Western District of Washington, August 19, 1998.

References

Akdeniz, Y. n.d. "Regulation of Child Pornography on the Internet." http://www.leads.ac.uk/law/pgs/yaman/child.htm.

Anderson, R., R. Needham, and A. Shamir. 1998. "The Steganographic File System." Paper presented at the Workshop on Information Hiding, Portland, OR, April 14–17.

Bell, James Dalton. 1996. "Assassination Politics." In Winn Schwartau, ed., *Information Warfare* (2nd ed., pp. 420–425). New York: Thunder's Mouth Press.

Cisco Systems. 1998. "Thirteen High-Tech Leaders Support Alternative Solution to Network Encryption Stalemate." Press release, July 13.

Corcoran, E. 1998. "Breakthrough Possible in Battle over Encryption Technology." *Washington Post*, July 12, p. A8.

CSI. 1997. "Can Your Crypto Be Turned against You? An interview with Eric Thompson of AccessData." *Computer Security Alert*, no. 167, February.

Denning, D. E., and W. E. Baugh, Jr. 1997. "Encryption and Evolving Technologies as Tools of Organized Crime and Terrorism." National Strategy Information Center, Washington, DC, July.

Electronic Frontier Foundation (EFF). 1998. " 'EFF DES Cracker' Machine Brings Honesty to Crypto Debate." Press release, July 17.

Federal Bureau of Investigation (FBI). 1970. "Crime and Cryptology." *FBI Law Enforcement Bulletin*, April 13–14.

Fischer, C. 1998. Presentation at Georgetown University, July 22.

Grabosky, P. N., and R. G. Smith. 1998. *Crime in the Digital Age: Controlling Telecommunications and Cyberspace Illegalities*. New Brunswick, N.J.: Transaction.

IINS News Service. 1997. "Hamas Using Internet for Attack Instructions." Israel, September 28.

Kaplan, D. E., and A. Marshall. 1996. *The Cult at the End of the World*.: The Terrifying Story of the Aum Doomsday Cult, from the Subways of Tokyo to the Nuclear Arserals of Russia (New York: Crown).

Littman, J. 1997. *The Watchman: The Twisted Life and Crimes of Serial Hacker Kevin Poulson*. Boston: Little, Brown.

Manning, W. M. 1997. "Should You Be on the Net?" *FBI Law Enforcement Bulletin*, January 18–22.

Markoff, J. 1998. "U.S. Data-Scrambling Code Cracked with Homemade Equipment." *New York Times*, July 17.

May, T. C. 1996a "BlackNet Worries." In Peter Ludlow ed., *High Noon on the Electronic Frontier* (pp. 245–249). Cambrige: MIT Press.

May, T. C. 1996b. "Introduction to BlackNet." In P. Ludlow, ed., *High Noon on the Electronic Frontier* (pp. 241–243). Cambridge: MIT Press.

McCullah, D. 1997. "IRS Raids a Cypherpunk." *Netly News*; accessed April 4.

Minow, M. 1997. "Swedish Narcotics Police Demand Telephone Card Database." *Risks-Forum Digest*, 19, no. 7; accessed April 14.

Power, R. 1997. "CSI Special Report: Salgado Case Reveals Darkside of Electronic Commerce." *Computer Security Alert*, no. 174, September.

Ramo, J. C. 1996. "Crime Online." *Time Digital*, September 23, pp. 28–32.

Reitinger, P. R. 1996. "Compelled Production of Plaintext and Keys." *University of Chicago Legal Forum* (1996): 171–206.

U.S. Congress. 1997a. Statement of Louis J. Freeh, Director FBI, "Impact of Encryption on Law Enforcement and Public Safety," testimony before the Senate Committee on Commerce, Science, and Transportation, March 19.

U.S. Congress. 1997b. Jeffrey A. Herig, Special Agent, Florida Department of Law Enforcement, "The Encryption Debate: Criminals, Terrorists, and the Security Needs of Business and Industry," testimony before the Senate Judiciary Subcommittee on Technology, Terrorism, and Government Information, September 3.

White House. 1995. Remarks by the President to Staff of the CIA and Intelligence Community, Central Intelligence Agency, McLean, VA, July 14.

White House. 1998. "Administration Updates Encryption Policy." Statement by the Press Secretary and fact sheet, September.

III

Shifting Borders: How VR Is Claiming Jurisdiction from RL

13

Law and Borders: The Rise of Law in Cyberspace

David R. Johnson and David G. Post

Introduction

Global computer-based communications cut across territorial borders, creating a new realm of human activity and undermining the feasibility—and legitimacy—of applying laws based on geographic boundaries. While these electronic communications play havoc with geographic boundaries, a new boundary—made up of the screens and passwords that separate the virtual world from the "real world" of atoms—emerges. This new boundary defines a distinct cyberspace that needs and can create new law and legal institutions of its own. Territorially-based lawmaking and law-enforcing authorities find this new environment deeply threatening. But established territorial authorities may yet learn to defer to the self-regulatory efforts of cyberspace participants who care most deeply about this new digital trade in ideas, information, and services. Separated from doctrine tied to territorial jurisdictions, new rules will emerge, in a variety of online spaces, to govern a wide range of new phenomena that have no clear parallel in the nonvirtual world. These new rules will play the role of law by defining legal personhood and property, resolving disputes, and crystallizing a collective conversation about core values.

This chapter has appeared in the *Stanford Law Review* 48 and in electronic form in *First Monday* (http://www.firstmonday.dk/issues/issue1/index.html). Reprinted by permission of the authors. © 1996, David R. Johnson and David G. Post.

Breaking Down Territorial Borders

Territorial Borders in the "Real World"

We take for granted a world in which geographical borders—lines separating physical spaces—are of primary importance in determining legal rights and responsibilities: "All law is prima facie territorial."[1] Territorial borders, generally speaking, delineate areas within which different sets of legal rules apply. There has until now been a general correspondence between borders drawn in physical space (between nation states or other political entities) and borders in "law space." For example, if we were to superimpose a "law map" (delineating areas where different rules apply to particular behaviors) onto a political map of the world, the two maps would overlap to a significant degree, with clusters of homogeneous applicable law and legal institutions fitting within existing physical borders, distinct from neighboring homogeneous clusters.

The Trademark Example   Consider a specific example to which we will refer throughout this chapter: trademark law—schemes for the protection of the associations between words or images and particular commercial enterprises. Trademark law is distinctly based on geographical separations.[2] Trademark rights typically arise within a given country, usually on the basis of use of a mark on physical goods or in connection with the provision of services in specific locations within that country. Different countries have different trademark laws, with important differences on matters as central as whether the same name can be used in different lines of business. In the United States, the same name can even be used for the same line of business if there is sufficient geographic separation of use to avoid confusion.[3] In fact, many local stores, restaurants, and businesses have identical names that do not interfere with each other because their customers do not overlap. The physical cues provided by different lines of business allow most marks to be used in multiple lines of commerce without dilution of the other users' rights.[4] There is no global registration scheme;[5] protection of a particularly famous mark on a global basis requires registration in each country. A trademark owner must therefore also be constantly alert to territory-based claims of abandonment and to dilution arising from uses of confusingly similar marks and must master the different procedural and jurisdictional laws of various countries that apply in each such instance.

When Geographic Boundaries for Law Make Sense   Physical borders are not, of course, simply arbitrary creations. Although they may be based on historical accident, geographic borders for law make sense in the real world. Their relationship to the development and enforcement of legal rules is logically based on a number of related considerations:

• *Power*   Control over physical space and the people and things located in that space is a defining attribute of sovereignty and statehood.[6] Lawmaking requires some mechanism for law enforcement, which in turn depends (to a large extent) on the ability to exercise physical control over and to impose coercive sanctions on law violators. For example, the U.S. government does not impose its trademark law on a Brazilian business operating in Brazil, at least in part because imposing sanctions on the Brazilian business would require assertion of physical control over those responsible for the operation of that business. Such an assertion of control would conflict with the Brazilian government's recognized monopoly on the use of force over its citizens.[7]

• *Effects*   The correspondence between physical boundaries and boundaries in "law space" also reflects a deeply rooted relationship between physical proximity and the effects of any particular behavior. That is, Brazilian trademark law governs the use of marks in Brazil because that use has a more direct impact on persons and assets located within that geographic territory than anywhere else. For example, the existence of a large sign over "Jones's Restaurant" in Rio de Janeiro is unlikely to have an impact on the operation of "Jones's Restaurant" in Oslo, Norway, for we may assume that there is no substantial overlap between the customers or competitors of these two entities. Protection of the former's trademark does not—and probably should not—affect the protection afforded the latter's.

• *Legitimacy*   We generally accept the notion that the persons within a geographically defined border are the ultimate source of lawmaking authority for activities within that border.[8] The "consent of the governed" implies that those subject to a set of laws must have a role in their formulation. By virtue of the preceding considerations, the category of persons subject to a sovereign's laws and most deeply affected by those laws will consist primarily of individuals who are located in particular physical spaces. Similarly, allocation of responsibility among levels of government proceeds on the assumption that, for many legal problems, physical proximity between the responsible authority and those most directly affected by the law will improve the quality of decision making and that it is easier to determine the will of those individuals in physical proximity to one another.

• *Notice*   Physical boundaries are also appropriate for the delineation of "law space" in the physical world because they can give notice that the rules change when the boundaries are crossed. Proper boundaries have signposts that provide warning that we will be required, after crossing, to abide by different rules, and physical boundaries—lines on the geographical map—are generally well equipped to serve this signpost function.[9]

The Absence of Territorial Borders in Cyberspace

Cyberspace radically undermines the relationship between legally significant (online) phenomena and physical location. The rise of the global computer network is destroying the link between geographical location and (1) the power of local governments to assert control over online behavior, (2) the effects of online behavior on individuals or things, (3) the legitimacy of the efforts of a local sovereign to enforce rules applicable to global phenomena, and (4) the ability of physical location to give notice of which sets of rules apply. The Net thus radically subverts a system of rule making based on borders between physical spaces, at least with respect to the claim that cyberspace should naturally be governed by territorially defined rules.

Cyberspace has no territorial boundaries because the cost and speed of message transmission on the Net is almost entirely independent of physical location. Messages can be transmitted from any physical location to any other location without degradation, decay, or substantial delay and without any physical cues or barriers that might otherwise keep certain geographically remote places and people separate from one another.[10] The Net enables transactions between people who do not know and, in many cases, cannot know the physical location of the other party. Location remains vitally important, but only within a virtual space consisting of the "addresses" of the machines between which messages and information are routed. The system is indifferent to the physical location of those machines, and there is no necessary connection between an Internet address and a physical jurisdiction.

Although a domain name, when initially assigned to a given machine, may be associated with a particular Internet protocol address corresponding to the territory within which the machine is physically located (e.g., a .uk domain name extension), the machine may move in physical space without any movement in the logical domain name space of the Net. Or, alternatively, the owner of the domain name might request that the name become associated with an entirely different machine, in a different physical location.[11] Thus, a server with a *.uk* domain name may not necessarily be located in the United Kingdom, a server with a *.com* domain name may be anywhere, and users, generally speaking, are not even aware of the location of the server that stores the content that they read. Physical borders no longer can function as signposts informing individuals of the obligations assumed by entering into a new, legally significant place because individuals are unaware of the existence of those borders as they move through virtual space.

The power to control activity in cyberspace has only the most tenuous connections to physical location. Many governments first respond to electronic communications crossing their territorial borders by trying to stop or regulate that flow of information as it crosses their borders.[12] Rather than deferring to efforts by participants in online transactions to regulate their own affairs, many governments establish trade barriers, seek to tax any border-crossing cargo, and respond especially sympathetically to claims that information coming into the jurisdiction might prove harmful to local residents. Efforts to stem the flow increase as online information becomes more important to local citizens. In particular, resistance to transborder data flow (TDF) reflects the concerns of sovereign nations that the development and use of TDF's will undermine their "informational sovereignty,"[13] will negatively impact on the privacy of local citizens,[14] and will upset private-property interests in information.[15] Even local governments in the United States have expressed concern about their loss of control over information and transactions flowing across their borders.[16]

But efforts to control the flow of electronic information across physical borders—to map local regulation and physical boundaries onto cyberspace—are likely to prove futile, at least in countries that hope to participate in global commerce.[17] Individual electrons can easily, and without any realistic prospect of detection, "enter" any sovereign's territory. The volume of electronic communications crossing territorial boundaries is just too great in relation to the resources available to government authorities to permit meaningful control.

U.S. Customs officials have generally given up. They assert jurisdiction only over the physical goods that cross the geographic borders they guard and claim no right to force declarations of the value of materials transmitted by modem.[18] Banking and securities regulators seem likely to lose their battle to impose local regulations on a global financial marketplace.[19] And state attorneys general face serious challenges in seeking to intercept the electrons that transmit the kinds of consumer fraud that, if conducted physically within the local jurisdiction, would be more easily shut down.

Faced with their inability to control the flow of electrons across physical borders, some authorities strive to inject their boundaries into the new electronic medium through filtering mechanisms and the establishment of electronic barriers.[20] Others have been quick to assert the right to regulate all online trade insofar as it might adversely impact local citizens. The attorney general of Minnesota, for example, has asserted the right to regulate gambling that occurs on a foreign Web page that was accessed and brought into the state by a local resident.[21] The New Jersey securities regulatory agency has similarly asserted the right to shut down any offending Web page accessible from within the state.[22]

But such protective schemes will likely fail as well. First, the determined seeker of prohibited communications can simply reconfigure his connection so as to appear to reside in a different location, outside the particular locality, state, or country. Because the Net is engineered to work on the basis of logical, not geographical, locations, any attempt to defeat the independence of messages from physical locations would be as futile as an effort to tie an atom and a bit together. And, moreover, assertions of lawmaking authority over Net activities on the ground that those activities constitute entry into the physical jurisdiction can just as easily be made by any territory-based authority.

If Minnesota law applies to gambling operations conducted on the World Wide Web because such operations foreseeably affect Minnesota residents, so, too, must the law of any physical jurisdiction from which those operations can be accessed. By asserting a right to regulate whatever its citizens may access on the Net, these local authorities are laying the predicate for an argument that Singapore or Iraq or any other sovereign can regulate the activities of U.S. companies operating in cyberspace from a location physically within the United States. All such Web-based activity, in this view, must be subject simultaneously to the laws of all territorial sovereigns.

Nor are the effects of online activities tied to geographically proximate locations. Information available on the World Wide Web is available simultaneously to anyone with a connection to the global network. The notion that the effects of an activity taking place on that Web site radiate from a physical location over a geographic map in concentric circles of decreasing intensity, however sensible that may be in the nonvirtual world, is incoherent when applied to Cyberspace. A Web site physically located in Brazil, to continue with that example, has no more of an effect on individuals in Brazil than does a Web site physically located in Belgium or Belize that is accessible in Brazil. Usenet discussion groups, to take another example, consist of continuously changing collections of messages that are routed from one network to another, with no centralized location at all; they exist, in effect, everywhere, nowhere in particular, and only on the Net.[23]

Nor can the legitimacy of any rules governing online activities be naturally traced to a geographically situated polity. There is no geographically localized set of constituents with a stronger claim to regulate it than any other local group; the strongest claim to control comes from the participants themselves, and they could be anywhere.

The rise of an electronic medium that disregards geographical boundaries also throws the law into disarray by creating entirely new phenomena that need to become the subject of clear legal rules but that cannot be governed, satisfactorily, by any current territorial sovereign. For example, electronic communications create vast new quantities of transactional records and pose serious questions regarding the nature and adequacy of privacy protections. Yet the communications that create these records may pass through or even simultaneously exist in many different territorial jurisdictions.[24] What substantive law should we apply to protect this new, vulnerable body of transactional data?[25] May a French policeman lawfully access the records of communications traveling across the Net from the United States to Japan? Similarly, whether it is permissible for a commercial entity to publish a record of all of any given individual's postings to Usenet newsgroups, or whether it is permissible to implement an interactive Web page application that inspects a user's "bookmarks" to determine which other pages that user has visited, are questions not readily addressed by existing legal regimes—both because the phenomena are novel and because any given local territorial sovereign cannot readily control the relevant, globally dispersed, actors and actions.[26]

Because events on the Net occur everywhere but nowhere in particular, are engaged in by online personas who are both "real" (possessing reputations, able to perform services, and deploy intellectual assets) and "intangible" (not necessarily or traceably tied to any particular person in the physical sense) and concern "things" (messages, databases, standing relationships) that are not necessarily separated from one another by any physical boundaries, no physical jurisdiction has a more compelling claim than any other to subject these events exclusively to its laws.

The Trademark Example   The question who should regulate or control Net domain names presents an illustration of the difficulties faced by territory-based lawmaking. The engineers who created the Net devised a domain name system that associates numerical machine addresses with easier-to-remember names. Thus, an Internet Protocol machine address like *36.21.0.69* can be derived, by means of a lookup table, from *leland.stanford.edu.*

Certain letter extensions (*.com*, *.edu*, *.org*, and *.net*) have developed as global domains with no association to any particular geographic area.[27] Although the Net creators designed this system as a convenience, it rapidly developed commercial value because it allows customers to learn and remember the location of particular Web pages or e-mail addresses. Currently, domain names are registered with specific parties that echo the information to domain name servers around the world. Registration generally occurs on a first-come, first-served basis,[28] generating a new type of property akin to trademark rights but without inherent ties to the trademark law of any individual country. Defining rights in this new, valuable property presents many questions, including those relating to transferability, conditions for ownership (such as payment of registration fees), duration of ownership rights, and forfeiture in the event of abandonment, however defined. Who should make these rules?

Consider the placement of a "traditional" trademark on the face of a World Wide Web page. This page can be accessed instantly from any location connected to the Net. It is not clear that any given country's trademark authorities possess, or should possess, jurisdiction over such placements. Otherwise, any use of a trademark on the Net would be subject simultaneously to the jurisdiction of every country. Should a Web page advertising a local business in Illinois be deemed to infringe a trademark in Brazil just because the page can be accessed freely from Brazil? Large U.S. companies may be upset by the appearance on the Web of names and symbols that overlap with their valid U.S.-registered trademarks.

But these same names and symbols could also be validly registered by another party in Mexico whose "infringing" marks are now, suddenly, accessible from within the United States. Upholding a claim of infringement or dilution launched by the holder of a U.S.-registered trademark, solely on the basis of a conflicting mark on the Net, exposes that same trademark holder to claims from other countries when the use of their U.S.-registered mark on the Web would allegedly infringe a similar mark in those foreign jurisdictions.

Migration of Other Regulated Conduct to the Net   Almost everything involving the transfer of information can be done online—education, health care, banking, the provision of intangible services, all forms of publishing, and the practice of law. The laws regulating many of these activities have developed as distinctly local and territorial. Local authorities certify teachers, charter banks with authorized "branches," and license doctors and lawyers. The law has in essence presumed that the activities conducted by these regulated persons cannot be performed without being tied to a physical body or building subject to regulation by the territorial sovereign authority and that the effects of those activities are most distinctly felt in geographically circumscribed areas. These distinctly local regulations cannot be preserved once these activities are conducted by globally dispersed parties through the Net. When many trades can be practiced in a manner that is unrelated to the physical location of the participants, these local regulatory structures will either delay the development of the new medium or, more likely, be superseded by new structures that better fit the online phenomena in question.[29]

Any insistence on "reducing" all online transactions to a legal analysis based in geographic terms presents, in effect, a new "mind-body" problem on a global scale. We know that the activities that have traditionally been the subject of regulation must still be engaged in by real people who are, after all, at distinct physical locations. But the interactions of these people now somehow transcend those physical locations. The Net enables forms of interaction in which the shipment of tangible items across geographic boundaries is irrelevant and in which the location of the participants does not matter. Efforts to determine where the events in question occur are decidedly misguided, if not altogether futile.

A New Boundary for Cyberspace

Although geographic boundaries may be irrelevant in defining a legal regime for cyberspace, a more legally significant border for the "law space" of the Net consists of the screens and passwords that separate the tangible from the virtual world. Traditional legal doctrine treats the Net as a mere transmission medium that facilitates the exchange of messages sent from one legally significant geographical location to another, each of which has its own applicable laws. Yet trying to tie the laws of any particular territorial sovereign to transactions on the Net or even trying to analyze the legal consequences of Net-based commerce as if each transaction occurred geographically somewhere in particular is most unsatisfying.

Cyberspace as a Place

Many of the jurisdictional and substantive quandaries raised by border-crossing electronic communications could be resolved by one simple principle: conceiving of cyberspace as a distinct "place" for purposes of legal analysis by recognizing a legally significant border between cyberspace and the "real world." Using this new approach, we would no longer ask the unanswerable question of "where" in the geographical world a Net-based transaction occurred. Instead, the more salient questions become: What rules are best suited to the often unique characteristics of this new place and the expectations of those who are engaged in various activities there? What mechanisms exist or need to be developed to determine the content of those rules and the mechanisms by which they can enforced?

Answers to these questions will permit the development of rules better suited to the new phenomena in question, more likely to be made by those who understand and participate in those phenomena, and more likely to be enforced by means that the new global communications media make available and effective.

The New Boundary is Real   Treating cyberspace as a separate "space" to which distinct laws apply should come naturally because entry into this world of stored online communications occurs through a screen and (usually) a "password" boundary.[30] There is a "placeness" to cyberspace because the messages accessed there are persistent and accessible to many people.[31] You know when you are "there." No one accidentally strays across the border into cyberspace.[32] To be sure, cyberspace is not a homogeneous place; groups and activities found at various online locations possess their own unique characteristics and distinctions, and each area will likely develop its own set of distinct rules.[33] But the line that separates online transactions from our dealings in the real world is just as distinct as the physical boundaries between our territorial governments—perhaps more so.[34]

Crossing into cyberspace is a meaningful act that would make application of a distinct "law of cyberspace" fair to those who pass over the electronic boundary. As noted, a primary function and characteristic of a border or boundary is its ability to be perceived by the one who crosses it.[35] As regulatory structures evolve to govern cyberspace-based transactions, it will be much easier to be certain which of those rules apply to your activities online than to determine which territorial-based authority might apply its laws to your conduct. For example, you would know to abide by the "terms of service" established by CompuServe or America Online when you are in their online territory rather than guess whether

Germany, or Tennessee, or the SEC will succeed in asserting its right to regulate your activities and those of the "placeless" online personas with whom you communicate.

The Trademark Example   The ultimate question of who should set the rules for uses of names on the Net presents an apt microcosm for examining the relationship between the Net and territorial-based legal systems. There is nothing more fundamental, legally, than a name or identity: the right to legally recognized personhood is a predicate for the amassing of capital, including the reputational and financial capital, that arises from sustained interactions. The domain name system and other online uses of names and symbols tied to reputations and virtual locations exist operationally only on the Net. These names can, of course, be printed on paper or embodied in physical form and shipped across geographic borders. But such physical uses should be distinguished from electronic use of such names in cyberspace because publishing a name or symbol on the Net is not the same as intentional distribution to any particular jurisdiction. Instead, use of a name or symbol on the Net is like distribution to all jurisdictions simultaneously. Recall that the non-country-specific domain names like *.com*, and *.edu* lead to the establishment of online addresses on a global basis. And through such widespread use, the global domain names gained proprietary value. In this context, assertion by any local jurisdiction of the right to set the rules applicable to the domain-name space is an illegitimate extraterritorial power grab.

Conceiving of the Net as a separate place for purposes of legal analysis will have great simplifying effects. For example, a global registration system for all domain names and reputationally significant names and symbols used on the Net would become possible. Such a Net-based regime could take account of the special claims of owners of strong global marks (as used on physical goods) and "grandfather" these owners' rights to the use of their strong marks in the newly opened online territory. But a Net-based global registration system could also fully account for the true nature of the Net by treating the use of marks on Web pages as a global phenomenon, by assessing the likelihood of confusion and dilution in the online context in which such confusion would actually occur, and by harmonizing any rules with applicable engineering criteria, such as optimizing the overall size of the domain name space.

A distinct set of rules applicable to trademarks in cyberspace would greatly simplify matters by providing a basis to resist the inconsistent and conflicting assertions of geographically local prerogatives. If one country objects to the use of a mark on the Web that conflicts with a locally registered mark, the rebuttal would be that the mark has not been used inside the country at all but only on the Web. If a company wants to know where to register its use of a symbol on the Net or to check for conflicting prior uses of its mark, the answer will be obvious and cost effective—the designated registration authority for the relevant portion of the Net itself. If we need to develop rules governing abandonment, dilution, and conditions on uses of particular types of domain names and addresses, those rules—applicable specifically to cyberspace—will be able to reflect the special characteristics of this new electronic medium.[36]

Other Cyberspace Regimes

Once we take cyberspace seriously as a distinct place for purposes of legal analysis, many opportunities to clarify and simplify the rules applicable to online transactions become available.

Defamation Law   Treating messages on the Net as transmissions from one place to another has created a quandary for those concerned about liability for defamation: messages may be transmitted between countries with very different laws, and liability may be imposed on the basis of "publication" in multiple jurisdictions with varying standards.[37] In contrast, the approach that treats the global network as a separate place would consider any allegedly defamatory message to have been published only "on the Net" (or in some distinct subsidiary area thereof)—at least until such time as distribution on paper occurs.[38]

This recharacterization makes more sense. A person who uploads a potentially defamatory statement would be able more readily to determine the rules applicable to his own actions. Moreover, because the Net has distinct characteristics, including an enhanced ability of the allegedly defamed person to reply, the rules of defamation developed for the Net could take into account these technological capabilities—perhaps by requiring that the opportunity for reply be taken advantage of in lieu of monetary compensation for certain defamatory Net-based messages.[39] The distinct characteristics of the Net could also be taken into account when applying and adapting the "public figure" doctrine in a context that is both global and highly compartmentalized and that blurs the distinction between private and public spaces.

Regulation of Net-Based Professional Activities   The simplifying effect of "taking cyberspace seriously" likewise arises in the context of regimes for regulating professional activities. As noted, traditional regulation insists that professionals be licensed by every territorial jurisdiction where they provide services.[40]

This requirement is infeasible when professional services are dispensed over the Net and potentially provided in numerous jurisdictions. Establishing certification regimes that apply only to such activities on the Net would greatly simplify matters. Such regulations would take into account the special features of Net-based professional activities like telemedicine or global law practice by including the need to avoid any special risks caused by giving online medical advice in the absence of direct physical contact with a patient or by answering a question regarding geographically local law from a remote location.[41] Using this new approach, we could override the efforts of local school boards to license online educational institutions, treating attendance by students at online institutions as a form of "leaving home for school" rather than characterizing the offering of education online as prosecutable distribution of disfavored materials into a potentially unwelcoming community that asserts local licensing authority.

Fraud and Antitrust   Even an example that might otherwise be thought to favor the assertion of jurisdiction by a local sovereign—protection of local citizens from fraud and antitrust violations—shows the beneficial effects of a cyberspace legal regime. How should we analyze "markets" for antitrust and consumer protection purposes when the companies at issue do business only through the World Wide Web?

Cyberspace could be treated as a distinct marketplace for purposes of assessing concentration and market power. Concentration in geographic markets would be relevant only in the rare cases in which such market power could be inappropriately leveraged to obtain power in online markets—for example, by conditioning access to the Net by local citizens on their buying services from the same company (such as a phone company) online. Claims regarding a right to access to particular online services, as distinct from claims to access particular physical pipelines, would remain tenuous as long as it is possible to create a new online service instantly in any corner of an expanding online space.[42]

Consumer-protection doctrines could also develop differently online—to take into account the fact that anyone reading an online ad is only a mouse click away from guidance from consumer protection agencies and discussions with other consumers. Can Minnesota prohibit the establishment of a Ponzi scheme on a Web page physically based in the Cayman Islands but accessed by Minnesota citizens through the Net? Under the proposed new approach to regulation of online activities, the answer is clearly no. Minnesota has no special right to prohibit such activities. The state lacks enforcement power, cannot show specially targeted effects, and does not speak for the community with the most legitimate claim to self-governance. But that does not mean that fraud might not be made "illegal" in at least large areas of cyberspace. Those who establish and use online systems have a interest in preserving the safety of their electronic territory and preventing crime. They are more likely to be able to enforce their own rules. And, as more fully discussed below, insofar as a consensually based "law of the Net" needs to obtain respect and deference from local sovereigns, new Net-based lawmaking institutions have an incentive to avoid fostering activities that threaten the vital interests of territorial governments.

Copyright Law   We suggest, not without some trepidation, that "taking cyberspace seriously" could clarify the current intense debate about how to apply copyright law principles in the digital age. In the absence of global agreement on applicable copyright principles, the jurisdictional problems inherent in any attempt to apply territorially-based copyright regimes to electronic works simultaneously available everywhere on the globe are profound. As Jane Ginsburg has noted:

A key feature of the GII [Global Information Infrastructure] is its ability to render works of authorship pervasively and simultaneously accessible throughout the world.

The principle of territoriality becomes problematic if it means that posting a work on the GII calls into play the laws of every country in which the work may be received when ... these laws may differ substantively.

Should the rights in a work be determined by a multiplicity of inconsistent legal regimes when the work is simultaneously communicated to scores of countries? Simply taking into account one country's laws, the complexity of placing works in a digital network is already daunting; should the task be further burdened by an obligation to assess the impact of the laws of every country where the work might be received? Put more bluntly, for works on the GII, there will be no physical territoriality.... Without physical territoriality, can legal territoriality persist?[43]

But treating cyberspace as a distinct place for purposes of legal analysis does more than resolve the conflicting claims of different jurisdictions: it also allows the development of new doctrines that take into account the special characteristics of the online "place." The basic justification for copyright protection is that bestowing an exclusive property right to control the reproduction and distribution of works on authors will increase the supply of such works by offering authors a financial incentive to engage in the effort required for their creation.[44] But even in the "real world," much creative expression is entirely independent of this incentive structure because the author's primary reward has more to do with acceptance in a community and the accumulation of reputational capital through wide dissemination than it does with the licensing and sale of individual copies of works.[45] And that may be more generally true of authorship in Cyberspace; because authors can now, for the first time in history, deliver copies of their creations instantaneously and at virtually no cost anywhere in the world, one might expect authors to devise new modes of operation that take advantage of, rather than work counter to, this fundamental characteristics of the new environment.[46]

One such strategy has already begun to emerge—giving away information at no charge or what might be called the "Netscape strategy"[47]— as a means of building up reputational capital that can subsequently be converted into income (for example, by means of the sale of services). As Esther Dyson has written:

Controlling copies (once created by the author or by a third party) becomes a complex challenge. You can either control something very tightly, limiting distribution to a small, trusted group, or you can rest assured that eventually your product will find its way to a large nonpaying audience—if anyone cares to have it in the first place....

.Much chargeable value will be in certification of authenticity and reliability, not in the content. Brand name, identity, and other marks of value will be important; so will security of supply. Customers will pay for a stream of information and content from a trusted source. For example, the umbrella of the *New York Times* sanctifies the words of its reporters. The content churned out by *Times* reporters is valuable because the reporters undergo quality-control, and because others believe them....

The trick is to control not the copies of your work but instead a relationship with the customers—subscriptions or membership. And that's often what the customers want, because they see it as an assurance of a continuing supply of reliable, timely content.[48]

A profound shift of this kind in regard to authorial incentives fundamentally alters the applicable balance between the costs and benefits of copyright protection in cyberspace, calling for a reappraisal of long-standing principles.[49] So, too, do other unique characteristics of Cyberspace severely challenge traditional copyright concepts.[50] The very ubiquity of file "copying"—the fact that one cannot access any information whatsoever in a computer-mediated environment without making a "copy" of that information[51]—implies that any simple-minded attempt to map traditional notions of "copying" onto cyberspace transactions will have perverse results.[52] Application of the "first sale" doctrine (allowing the purchaser of a copyrighted work to freely resell the copy she purchased) is problematic when the transfer of a lawfully owned copy technically involves the making of a new copy before the old one is eliminated,[53] as is defining "fair use" when a work's size is indeterminate, ranging from (1) an individual paragraph sold separately on demand in response to searches to (2) the entire database from which the paragraph originates, something never sold as a whole unit.[54]

Treating cyberspace as a distinct location allows for the development of new forms of intellectual property law, applicable only on the Net, that would properly focus attention on these unique characteristics of this new, distinct place while preserving doctrines that apply to works embodied in physical collections (like books) or displayed in legally significant physical places (like theaters). Current debates about applying copyright law to the Net often do, implicitly, treat it as a distinct space, at least insofar as commercial copyright owners somewhat inaccurately refer to it as a "lawless" place.[55] The civility of the debate might improve if everyone assumed the Net should have an appropriately different law, including a special law for unauthorized transfers of works from one realm to the other; we could, in other words, regulate the smuggling of works created in the physical world, by treating the unauthorized uploading of a copy of such works to the Net as infringement. This new approach would help promoters of electronic commerce focus on developing incentive-producing rules to encourage authorized transfers into cyberspace of works not available now, while also reassuring owners of existing copyrights to valuable works that changes in the copyright law for the Net would not require changing laws applicable to distributing physical works. It would also permit the development of new doctrines of implied license and fair use that, as to works first created on the Net or imported with the author's permission, appropriately allow the transmission and copying necessary to facilitate their use within the electronic realm.[56]

Will Responsible Self-Regulatory Structures Emerge on the Net? The Trademark Example

Even if we agree that new rules should apply to online phenomena, questions remain about who sets the rules and how they are enforced. We believe the Net can develop its own effective legal institutions.

In order for the domain-name space to be administered by a legal authority that is not territorially based, new lawmaking institutions will have to develop. Many questions that arise in setting up this system will need answers—decisions about whether to create a new top-level domain, whether online addresses belong to users or service providers,[57] and whether one name impermissibly interferes with another, thus confusing the public and diluting the value of the preexisting name.[58] The new system must also include procedures to give notice in conflicting claims, to resolve these claims, and to assess appropriate remedies (including, possibly, compensation) in cases of wrongful use. If the Cyberspace equivalent of eminent domain develops, questions may arise over how to compensate individuals when certain domain names are destroyed or redeployed for the public good of the Net community.[59]

Someone must also decide threshold membership issues for cyberspace citizens, including how much users must disclose (and to whom) about their real-world identities to use e-mail addresses and domain names for commercial purposes. Implied throughout this discussion is the recognition that these rules will only be meaningful and enforceable if cyberspace citizens view whomever makes these decisions as a legitimate governing body.

Experience suggests that the community of online users and service providers is up to the task of developing a self-governance system.[60] The current domain-name system evolved from decisions made by engineers and the practices of Internet service providers.[61] Now that trademark owners are threatening the company that administers the registration system, the same engineers who established the original domain-name standards are again deliberating whether to alter the domain-name system to take these new policy issues into account.[62] Who has the ultimate right to control policy in this area remains unclear.[63]

Every system operator who dispenses a password imposes at least some requirements as conditions of continuing access, including paying bills on time or remaining a member of a group entitled to access (such as students at a university).[64] System operators (sysops) have an extremely powerful enforcement tool at their disposal to enforce such rules—banishment.[65] Moreover, communities of users have marshaled plenty of enforcement weapons to induce wrongdoers to comply with local conventions, such as rules against flaming,[66] shunning,[67] mailbombs, and more.[68] And both sysops and users have begun explicitly to recognize that formulating and enforcing such rules should be a matter for principled discussion, not an act of will by whoever has control of the power switch.[69]

While many of these new rules and customs apply only to specific, local areas of the global network, some standards apply through technical protocols on a nearly universal basis. And widespread agreement already exists about core principles of "netiquette" in mailing lists and discussion groups[70]—although, admittedly, new users have a slow learning curve, and the Net offers little formal "public education" regarding applicable norms.[71] Dispute-resolution mechanisms suited to this new environment also seem certain to prosper.[72] Cyberspace is anything but anarchic; its distinct rule sets are becoming more robust every day.

Perhaps the most apt analogy to the rise of a separate law of cyberspace is the origin of the law merchant—a distinct set of rules that developed with the new, boundary-crossing trade of the Middle Ages.[73] Merchants could not resolve their disputes by taking them to the local noble, whose established feudal law concerned mainly land claims. Nor could the local lord easily establish meaningful rules for a sphere of activity he barely understood, executed in locations beyond his control. The result of this jurisdictional confusion, arising from a then-novel form of boundary-crossing communications, was the development of a new legal system—lex mercatoria.[74] The people who cared most about and best understood their new creation formed and championed this new law, which did not destroy or replace existing law regarding more territorially-based transactions (such as transferring land ownership). Arguably, exactly the same type of phenomenon is developing in cyberspace right now.[75]

Governments cannot stop electronic communications coming across their borders, even if they want to do so. Nor can they credibly claim a right to regulate the Net based on supposed local harms caused by activities that originate outside their borders and that travel electronically to many different nations. One nation's legal institutions should not, therefore, monopolize rule making for the entire Net. Even so, established authorities likely will continue to claim that they must analyze and regulate the new online phenomena in terms of some physical locations. After all, the people engaged in online communications still inhabit the material world. And, so the argument goes, local legal authorities must have authority to remedy the problems created in the physical world by those acting on the Net. The rise of responsible lawmaking institutions within cyberspace, however, will weigh heavily against arguments that would claim that the Net is "lawless" and thus tie regulation of online trade to physical jurisdictions. As noted, sysops acting alone or collectively have the power of banishment to control wrongful actions online.[76] Thus, for online activities that minimally impact the vital interests of sovereigns, the self-regulating structures of cyberspace seem better suited than local authorities to deal with the Net's legal issues.[77]

Local Authorities, Foreign Rules: Reconciling Conflicts

What should happen when conflicts arise between the local territorial law (applicable to persons or entities by virtue of their location in a particular area of physical space) and the law applicable to particular activities on the Net? The doctrine of "comity," as well as principles applied when delegating authority to self-regulatory organizations provide us with guidance for reconciling such disputes.

The doctrine of comity, in the U.S. Supreme Court's classic formulation, is "the recognition which one nation allows within its territory to the legislative, executive, or judicial acts of another nation, having due regard both to international duty and convenience, and to the rights of its own citizens or of other persons who are under the protections of its law."[78]

It is incorporated into the principles set forth in the Restatement (Third) of Foreign Relations Law of the United States, in particular Section 403, which provides that "a state may not exercise jurisdiction to prescribe law with respect to a person or activity having connections with another state when the exercise of such jurisdiction is unreasonable"[79] and that when a conflict between the laws of two states arises, "each state has an obligation to evaluate its own as well as the other state's interest in exercising jurisdiction [and] should defer to the other state if that state's interest is clearly greater."[80]

It arose as an attempt to mitigate some of the harsher features of a world in which lawmaking is an attribute of control over physical space but in which persons, things, and actions may move across physical boundaries, and it functions as a constraint on the strict application of territorial principles that attempts to reconcile "the principle of absolute territorial sovereignty [with] the fact that intercourse between nations often demand[s] the recognition of one sovereign's lawmaking acts in the forum of another."[81] In general, comity reflects the view that those who care more deeply about and better understand the disputed activity should determine the outcome. Accordingly, it may be ideally suited to handle, by extension, the new conflicts between the aterritorial nature of cyberspace activities and the legitimate needs of territorial sovereigns and of those whose interests they protect on the other side of the cyberspace border. This doctrine does not disable territorial sovereigns from protecting the interests of those individuals located within their spheres of control, but it calls on them to exercise a significant degree of restraint when doing so.

Local officials handling conflicts can also learn from the many examples of delegating authority to self-regulatory organizations. Churches are allowed to make religious law.[82] Clubs and social organizations can, within broad limits, define rules that govern activities within their spheres of interest.[83] Securities exchanges can establish commercial rules, so long as they protect the vital interests of the surrounding communities. In these cases, government has seen the wisdom of allocating rule-making functions to those who best understand a complex phenomenon and who have an interest in ensuring the growth and health of their shared enterprise.

Cyberspace represents a new permutation of the underlying issue: how much should local authorities defer to a new, self-regulating activity arising independently of local control and reaching beyond the limited physical boundaries of the sovereign? This mixing of both tangible and intangible boundaries leads to a convergence of the intellectual categories of comity in international relations and the local delegation by a sovereign to self-regulatory groups. In applying both the doctrine of "comity" and the idea of "delegation"[84] to cyberspace, a local sovereign is called on to defer to the self-regulatory judgments of a population partly, but not wholly, composed of its own subjects.[85]

Despite the seeming contradiction of a sovereign deferring to the authority of those who are not its own subjects, such a policy makes sense, especially in light of the underlying purposes of both doctrines. Comity and delegation represent the wise conservation of governmental resources and allocate decisions to those who most fully understand the special needs and characteristics of a particular "sphere" of being. Although cyberspace represents a new sphere that cuts across national boundaries, the fundamental principle remains.

If the sysops and users who collectively inhabit and control a particular area of the Net want to establish special rules to govern conduct there, and if that rule set does not fundamentally impinge on the vital interests of others who never visit this new space, then the law of sovereigns in the physical world should defer to this new form of self-government.

Consider, once again, the trademark example. A U.S. government representative has stated that, since the government paid for the initial development and administration of the domain-name system, it "owns" the right to control policy decisions regarding the creation and use of such names.[86] Obviously, government funds, in addition to individual efforts on a global scale, created this valuable and finite new asset. But the government's claim based on its investment is not particularly convincing. In fact, the United States may be asserting its right to control the policies governing the domain-name space primarily because it fears that any other authority over the Net might force it to pay again for the ".gov" and ".mil" domain names used by governmental entities.[87] To assuage these concerns, a Net-based authority should concede to the governments on this point. For example, it should accommodate the military's strong interest in remaining free to regulate and use its ".mil" addresses.[88] A new Net-based standards-making authority should also accommodate the government's interests in retaining its own untaxed domain names and prohibiting counterfeiting. Given responsible restraint by the Net-based authority and the development of an effective self-regulatory scheme, the government might well then decide that it should not spend its finite resources trying to wrest effective control of nongovernmental domain names away from those who care most about facilitating the growth of online trade.

Because controlling the flow of electrons across physical boundaries is so difficult, a local jurisdiction that seeks to prevent its citizens from accessing specific materials must either outlaw all access to the Net—thereby cutting itself off from the new global trade—or seek to impose its will on the Net as a whole. This would be the modern equivalent of a local lord in medieval times either trying to prevent the silk trade from passing through his boundaries (to the dismay of local customers and merchants) or purporting to assert jurisdiction over the known world. It may be most difficult to envision local territorial sovereigns deferring to the law of the Net when the perceived threat to local interests arises from the very free flow of information that is the Net's most fundamental characteristic—when, for example, local sovereigns assert an interest in seeing that their citizens are not adversely affected by information that the local jurisdiction deems harmful but that is freely (and lawfully) available elsewhere. Examples include the German government's attempts to prevent its citizens access to prohibited materials[89] or the prosecution of a California bulletin board operator for making material offensive to local "community standards" available for downloading in Tennessee.[90]

Local sovereigns may insist that their interest (in protecting their citizens from harm) is paramount and easily outweighs any purported interest in making this kind of material freely available. But the opposing interest is not simply the interest in seeing that individuals have access to ostensibly obscene material, it is the "meta-interest" of Net citizens in preserving the global free flow of information.

If there is one central principle on which all local authorities within the Net should agree, it must be that territorially local claims to restrict online transactions (in ways unrelated to vital and localized interests of a territorial government) should be resisted. This is the Net equivalent of the First Amendment, a principle already recognized in the form of the international human rights doctrine protecting the right to communicate.[91]

Participants in the new online trade must oppose external regulation designed to obstruct this flow. This naturally central principle of online law bears importantly on the "comity" analysis because it makes clear that the need to preserve a free flow of information across the Net is just as vital to the interests of the Net as the need to protect local citizens against the impacts of unwelcome information may appear from the perspective of a local territorial sovereign.[92] For the Net to realize its full promise, online rule-making authorities must not respect the claims of territorial sovereigns to restrict online communications when unrelated to vital and localized governmental interests.

Internal Diversity

One of a border's key characteristics is that it slows the interchange of people, things, and information across its divide. Arguably, distinct sets of legal rules can develop and persist only where effective boundaries exist. The development of a true "law of cyberspace," therefore, depends on a dividing line between this new online territory and the nonvirtual world. Our argument so far has been that the new sphere online is cut off, at least to some extent, from rule-making institutions in the material world and requires the creation of a distinct law applicable just to the online sphere.

But we hasten to add that cyberspace is not, behind that border, a homogeneous or uniform territory behind that border, where information flows without further impediment. Although it is meaningless to speak of a French or Armenian portion of cyberspace because the physical borders dividing French or Armenian territory from their neighbors cannot generally be mapped onto the flow of information in cyberspace, the Net has other kinds of internal borders delineating many distinct internal locations that slow or block the flow of information.

Distinct names and (virtual) addresses, special passwords, entry fees, and visual cues—software boundaries—can distinguish subsidiary areas from one another. The Usenet newsgroup alt.religion.scientology is distinct from alt.misc.legal, and each of which is distinct from a chatroom on Compuserve or America Online, which, in turn, is distinct from the Cyberspace Law Institute listserver or Counsel Connect. Users can access these different forums only through distinct addresses or phone numbers, often navigating through login screens, the use of passwords, or the payment of fees. Indeed, the ease with which internal borders, consisting entirely of software protocols, can be constructed is one of cyberspace's most remarkable and salient characteristics; setting up a new Usenet newsgroup or a listserver discussion group requires little more than a few lines of code.[93]

The separation of subsidiary "territories" or spheres of activity within cyberspace and the barriers to exchanging information across these internal borders allow for the development of distinct rule sets and for the divergence of those rule sets over time.[94] The processes underlying biological evolution provide a useful analogy.[95] Speciation—the emergence over time of multiple, distinct constellations of genetic information from a single, original group—cannot occur when the original population freely exchanges information (in the form of genetic material) among its members.

In other words, a single, freely interbreeding population of organisms cannot divide into genetically distinct populations. While the genetic material in the population changes over time, it does so more or less uniformly (for example, the population of the species *Homo erectus* becomes a population of *Homo sapiens*) and cannot give rise to more than one contemporaneous, distinct genetic set. Speciation requires, at a minimum, some barrier to the interchange of genetic material between subsets of the original homogeneous population. Ordinarily, a physical barrier suffices to prevent one subgroup from exchanging genetic data with another. Once this "border" is in place, divergence within the "gene pool"—the aggregate of the underlying genetic information—in each of the two subpopulations can occur.[96] Over time, this divergence may be substantial enough that even when the physical barrier disappears, the two subgroups can no longer exchange genetic material—that is, they have become separate species.

Rules, like genetic material, are self-replicating information.[97] The internal borders within cyberspace will thus allow for differentiation among distinct constellations of such information—in this case, rule sets rather than species. Content or conduct acceptable in one area of the Net may be banned in another. Institutions that resolve disputes in one area of cyberspace may not gain support or legitimacy in others. Local sysops can, by contract, impose differing default rules regarding who has the right, under certain conditions, to replicate and redistribute materials that originate with others. While cyberspace's reliance on bits instead of atoms may make physical boundaries more permeable, the boundaries delineating digital online "spheres of being" may become less permeable. Securing online systems from unauthorized intruders may prove an easier task than sealing physical borders from unwanted immigration.[98] Groups can establish online corporate entities or membership clubs that tightly control participation in, or even public knowledge of, their own affairs.

Such groups can reach agreement on or modify these rules more rapidly via online communications. Accordingly, the rule sets applicable to the online world may quickly evolve away from those applicable to more traditional spheres and develop greater variation among the sets.

How this process of differentiation and evolution will proceed is one of the more complex and fascinating questions about law in cyberspace —and a subject beyond the scope of this chapter. We should point out, however, an important normative dimension to the proliferation of these internal boundaries between distinct communities and distinct rule sets and the process by which law will evolve in cyberspace. Cyberspace may be an important forum for the development of new connections between imdividuals and mechanisms of self-governance by which individuals attain an increasingly elusive sense of community. Commenting on the erosion of national sovereignty in the modern world and the failure of the existing system of nation states to cultivate a civic voice, a moral connection between the individual and the community (or communities) in which she is embedded, Sandel has written:

The hope for self-government today lies not in relocating sovereignty but in dispersing it. The most promising alternative to the sovereign state is not a cosmopolitan community based on the solidarity of humankind but a multiplicity of communities and political bodies—some more extensive than nations and some less—among which sovereignty is diffused. Only a politics that disperses sovereignty both upward [to transnational institutions] and downward can combine the power required to rival global market forces with the differentiation required of a public life that hopes to inspire the allegiance of its citizens.... If the nation cannot summon more than a minimal commonality, it is unlikely that the global community can do better, at least on its own. A more promising basis for a democratic politics that reaches beyond nations is a revitalized civic life nourished in the more particular communities we inhabit. In the age of NAFTA the politics of neighborhood matters more, not less.[99]

Furthermore, the ease with which individuals can move between different rule sets in cyberspace has important implications for any contractarian political philosophy deriving a justification of the state's exercise of coercive power over its citizens from their consent to the exercise of that power. In the nonvirtual world, this consent has a strong fictional element: "State reliance on consent inferred from someone merely remaining in the state is particularly unrealistic. An individual's unwillingness to incur the extraordinary costs of leaving his or her birthplace should not be treated as a consensual undertaking to obey state authority."[100]

To be sure, citizens of France, dissatisfied with French law and preferring, say, Armenian rules, can try to persuade their compatriots and local decision makers of the superiority of the Armenian rule set.[101] However, their "exit" option, in Albert Hirschman's terms, is limited by the need to physically relocate to Armenia to take advantage of that rule set.[102]

In contrast, in cyberspace, any given user has a more accessible exit option, in terms of moving from one virtual environment's rule set to another's, thus providing a more legitimate "selection mechanism" by which differing rule sets will evolve over time.[103]

The ability of inhabitants of cyberspace to cross borders at will between legally significant territories, many times in a single day, is unsettling. This power seems to undercut the validity of developing distinct laws for online culture and commerce: how can these rules be "law" if participants can literally turn them on and off with a switch? Frequent online travel might subject relatively mobile human beings to a far larger number of rule sets than they would encounter traveling through the physical world over the same period. Established authorities, contemplating the rise of a new law applicable to online activities, might object that we cannot easily live in a world with too many different sources and types of law, particularly those made by private (nongovernmental) parties, without breeding confusion and allowing antisocial actors to escape effective regulation.

But the speed with which we can cross legally meaningful borders or adopt and then shed legally significant roles should not reduce our willingness to recognize multiple rule sets. Rapid travel between spheres of being does not detract from the distinctiveness of the boundaries, as long as participants realize the rules are changing. Nor does it detract from the appropriateness of rules applying within any given place, any more than changing commercial or organizational roles in the physical world detracts from a person's ability to obey and distinguish rules as a member of many different institutional affiliations and to know which rules are appropriate for which roles.[104] Nor does it lower the enforceability of any given rule set within its appropriate boundaries, as long as groups can control unauthorized boundary crossing of groups or messages.

Alternating between different legal identities many times during a day may confuse those for whom cyberspace remains an alien territory, but for those for whom cyberspace is a more natural habitat in which they spend increasing amounts of time, it may become second nature. Legal systems must learn to accommodate a more mobile kind of legal person.[105]

Conclusion

Global electronic communications have created new spaces in which distinct rule sets will evolve. We can reconcile the new law created in this space with current territorially-based legal systems by treating it as a distinct doctrine, applicable to a clearly demarcated sphere, created primarily by legitimate, self-regulatory processes, and entitled to appropriate deference—but also subject to limitations when it oversteps its appropriate sphere.

The law of any given place must take into account the special characteristics of the space it regulates and the types of persons, places, and things found there. Just as a country's jurisprudence reflects its unique historical experience and culture, the law of cyberspace will reflect its special character, which differs markedly from anything found in the physical world. For example, the law of the Net must deal with persons who "exist" in cyberspace only in the form of an e-mail address and whose purported identity may or may not accurately correspond to physical characteristics in the real world. In fact, an e-mail address might not even belong to a single person. Accordingly, if cyberspace law is to recognize the nature of its "subjects," it cannot rest on the same doctrines that give geography-based sovereigns jurisdiction over "whole," locatable, physical persons. The law of the Net must be prepared to deal with persons who manifest themselves only by means of a particular ID, user account, or domain name.

Moreover, if rights and duties attach to an account itself, rather than to an underlying real-world person, traditional concepts such as "equality," "discrimination," or even "rights and duties" may not work as we normally understand them. New angles on these ideas may develop. For example, when AOL users joined the Net in large numbers, other cyberspace users often ridiculed them based on the *.aol* tag on their e-mail addresses—a form of "domainism" that might be discouraged by new forms of Netiquette. If a doctrine of cyberspace law accords rights to users, we will need to decide whether those rights adhere only to particular types of online appearances, as distinct from attaching to particular individuals in the real world.

Similarly, the types of "properties" that can become the subject of legal discussion in cyberspace will differ from real-world real estate or tangible objects. For example, in the real world the physical covers of a book delineate the boundaries of a "work" for purposes of copyright law.[106] Those limits may disappear entirely when the same materials are part of a large electronic database. Thus, we may have to change the fair-use doctrine in copyright law that previously depended on calculating what portion of the physical work was copied.[107] Similarly, a Web page's "location" in cyberspace may take on a value unrelated to the physical place where the disk holding that Web page resides, and efforts to regulate Web pages by attempting to control physical objects may only cause the relevant bits to move from one place to another. On the other hand, the boundaries set by URLs (Uniform Resource Locators, the location of a document on the World Wide Web) may need special protection against confiscation or confusingly similar addresses. And, because these online "places" may contain offensive material, we may need rules requiring (or allowing) groups to post certain signs or markings at these places' outer borders.

The boundaries that separate persons and things behave differently in the virtual world but are nonetheless legally significant. Messages posted under one e-mail name will not affect the reputation of another e-mail address, even if the same physical person authors both messages. Materials separated by a password will be accessible to different sets of users, even if those materials physically exist on the very same hard drive. A user's claim to a right to a particular online identity or to redress when that identity's reputation suffers harm may be valid even if that identity does not correspond exactly to that of any single person in the real world.[108]

Clear boundaries make law possible, encouraging rapid differentiation between rule sets and defining the subjects of legal discussion. New abilities to travel or exchange information rapidly across old borders may change the legal frame of reference and require fundamental changes in legal institutions. Fundamental activities of lawmaking—accommodating conflicting claims, defining property rights, establishing rules to guide conduct, enforcing those rules, and resolving disputes—remain very much alive within the newly defined, intangible territory of cyberspace. At the same time, the newly emerging law challenges the core idea of a current lawmaking authority—the territorial nation state, with substantial but legally restrained powers.

If the rules of cyberspace thus emerge from consensually based rule sets, and the subjects of such laws remain free to move among many differing online spaces, then considering the actions of cyberspace's system administrators as the exercise of a power akin to "sovereignty" may be inappropriate. Under a legal framework where the top level imposes physical order on those below it and depends for its continued effectiveness on the inability of its citizens to fight back or leave the territory, the legal and political doctrines we have evolved over the centuries are essential to constrain such power. In that situation, where exit is impossible, costly, or painful, then a right to a voice for the people is essential. But when the "persons" in question are not whole people, when their "property" is intangible and portable, and when all concerned may readily escape a jurisdiction they do not find empowering, the relationship between the "citizen" and the "state" changes radically. Law, defined as a thoughtful group conversation about core values, will persist. But it will not, could not, and should not be the same law as that applicable to physical, geographically-defined territories.

Notes

The authors wish to thank Becky Burr, Larry Downes, Henry J. Perritt, Jr., and Ron Plesser, as well as the other Fellows of the Cyberspace Law Institute (Jerry Berman, John Brown, Bill Burrington, Esther Dyson, David Farber, Ken Freeling, A. Michael Froomkin, Robert Gellman, I. Trotter Hardy, Ethan Katsh, Lawrence Lessig, Bill Marmon, Lance Rose, Marc Rotenberg, Pamela Samuelson, and Eugene Volokh), CLI Codirectors Carey Heckman, John Podesta, and Peggy Radin, and Jim Campbell, for their assistance in the formulation of these ideas. The usual disclaimer, of course, applies: the authors alone are responsible for errors, omissions, misstatements, and misunderstandings set forth in the following.

1. *American Banana Co. v. United Fruit Co.*, 213 U.S. 347, 357 (1909) (holding that as a general rule of construction, any statute is presumed to be intended to operate within the territorial limits of the sovereign).

2. See 1A Jerome Gilson, Trademark Protection and Practice sec. 9.01 (1991); Dan L. Burk, Trademarks Along the Infobahn: A First Look at the Emerging Law of Cybermarks, 1 U. Rich. J.L. & Tech. 1 (1995), available at http://www.urich.edu/~jolt/v1i1/burk.html; Jeffrey M. Samuels & Linda B. Samuels, The Changing Landscape of International Trademark Law, 27 G.W.J. Int'l L. & Econ. 433 (1993–94).

3. *Dawn Donut Co. v. Hart's Food Stores*, 267 F.2d 358 (2d Cir. 1959) (holding that the owner of a registered trademark may not enjoin another's use of that mark in a geographically separate market if the holder of the registered mark does not intend to expand into that market).

4. See, e.g., *California Fruit Growers Exchange v. Sunkist Baking Co.*, 166 F.2d 971 (7th Cir. 1947) (permitting Sunkist fruits and Sunkist bakery products); *Restaurant Lutece v. Houbigant, Inc.*, 593 F. Supp. 588 (D.N.J. 1984) (denying a preliminary injunction by the restaurant Lutece against Lutece cosmetics).

5. Clark W. Lackert, International Efforts Against Trademark Counterfeiting, Colum. Bus. L. Rev. 161 (1988); Samuels & Samuels, supra note 2, at 433.

6. Restatement (Third) of Foreign Relations Law of the United States sec. 201 (1987) ("Under international law, a state is an entity that has a defined territory and a permanent population, under the control of its own government"); id. sec. 402 (a state has "jurisdiction to prescribe law with respect to (1)(a) conduct that, wholly or in substantial part, takes place within its territory; (b) the status of persons, or interests in things, present within its territory; (c) conduct outside its territory that has or is intended to have substantial effect within its territory"); see also Lea Brilmayer, Consent, Contract, and Territory, 74 *Minn. L. Rev.* 1, 11–12 (1989) (noting the significance of state authority derived from sovereignty over physical territory in the context of social contract theory).

7. The ability of the sovereign to claim personal jurisdiction over a particular party, for instance, turns on the party's relationship to the physical jurisdiction over which the sovereign has control, such as the presence of the party or assets belonging to the party within the jurisdiction or the activities of the party that are directed to persons or things within the jurisdiction. Similarly, the law chosen to apply to a contract, tort, or criminal action has historically been influenced primarily by the physical location of the parties or the deed in question. See generally Henry H. Perritt Jr., Jurisdiction in Cyberspace (October 28, 1995) (unpublished manuscript on file with the Stanford Law Review); Henry H. Perritt Jr. Law and the Information Superhighway, ch. 12 (1996).

8. Declaration on Principles of International Law Concerning Friendly Relations and Cooperation Among States in Accordance with the Charter of the United Nations, G.A. Res. 2625, 35th Sess. (1970); Declaration of the Inadmissibility of Intervention into the Domestic Affairs of States, G.A. Res. 2131, 30th Sess. (1965). See also Brilmayer, supra note 6, at 6 (discussing contractarian theories of state sovereignty and legitimacy).

9. The exception proves this rule: we feel outrage when a journalist who crosses a territorial boundary without any signs is imprisoned for any supposed offense against the local state. Some signposts are culturally understood conventions that accompany entry into specialized places, such as courtrooms, office buildings, and churches. But not all signposts and boundaries dividing different rule sets are based in geography or physical location. Sets of different rules may apply when the affected parties play particular roles, such as members of self-regulatory organizations, agents of corporate entities, and so forth. Henry H. Perritt Jr., Self-governing Electronic Communities, 36–49, 59–60 (1995) (on file with the Stanford Law Review). But even these roles are most often clearly marked by cues of dress or formal signatures that give warning of the applicable rules. See text at notes 72 and 79.

10. As Woody Allen once quipped: "Space is nature's way of keeping everything from happening to you." Although there is distance in online space, it behaves differently from distance in real space. See generally M. Ethan Katsh, The Electronic Media and the Transformation of Law, 92–94 (1989); M. Ethan Katsh, Law in a Digital World 57–59, 218 (1995).

11. See Burk, supra note 2, at 12–14, for a general description of the Domain Naming System; see also Randy Bush, Brian Carpenter & Jon Postel, Delegation of International Top-Level Domains, Internet-Draft ymbk-itld-admin-00, available at http://www.internic.net; RFC 882, Domain Names—Concepts and Facilities, available at ftp://ds.internic.net/rfc/rfc882.txt; RFC 883, Domain Names —Implementation and Specifications, available at ftp://ds.internic.net/rfc/rfc883.txt.

12. See Jon Auerbach, Fences in Cyberspace: Governments Move to Limit Free Flow of the Internet, Boston Globe, Feb. 1, 1996, at 1 (surveying "digital Balkanization" of the Internet through government censorship and filtration); Seth Faison, Chinese Cruise Internet, Wary of Watchdogs, N.Y. Times, Feb. 5, 1995, at A1; see also infra, note 20 (describing the German government's attempts to interrupt German citizens' access to certain Usenet discussion groups); see generally Anne Wells Branscomb, "Jurisdictional Quandaries for Global Networks," Linda M. Harasim (ed.), in Global Networks: Computers and International Communication (1993) (exploring efforts to exercise jurisdictional control over electronic information services).

13. Anthony Paul Miller, Teleinformatics, Transborder Data Flows and the Emerging Struggle for Information: An Introduction to the Arrival of the New Information Age, 20 Colum. J.L. & Soc. Probs. 89, 107–08, 127–32 (1986) (exploring the willingness of some national governments to forego the benefits of unregulated TDFs to protect their political, social, and cultural interests).

14. Id. at 105–07, 111–18 (suggesting that the data-storage capabilities and anonymity of information technologies have prompted the Organization for Economic Cooperation and Development (OECD) and governments throughout Western Europe to restrict the content of TDFs to protect individual and corporate privacy).

15. Id. at 109–11 (noting the drive, particularly among computer software developers, to curb the threat that TDFs pose to intellectual property rights); see also Book Publishers Worry About Threat of Internet, N.Y. Times, Mar. 18, 1996, at A1 (describing appearance of Le Grand Secret, a book about former French President François Mitterand, on the Internet despite its ban in France, and the general concern of book publishers about unauthorized Internet distributions).

16. For example, A. Jared Silverman, former chief of the New Jersey Bureau of Securities, expressed concern about the ability of the State to protect its residents against fraudulent schemes if it does not assert the right to regulate every online securities offering accessible, via the Net, from within the State. See also Gregory Spears, Cops and Robbers on the Net, Kiplinger's Pers. Fin. Mag., Feb. 1995, at 56 (surveying responses to online investment scams). Moreover, various state attorneys general have expressed concern about gambling and consumer fraud reaching their state's residents over the Net. See note 21, infra.

17. The difficulty of policing an electronic border may have something to do with its relative length. See comment of Peter Martin, NewJuris Electronic Conference 13, (Sept. 22, 1993) (discussing cyberspace's "near infinite bound-

ary" with territorial jurisdictions). Physical roads and ports linking sovereign territories are few in number, and geographical boundaries can be fenced and policed. In contrast, the number of starting points for an electronic "trip" out of a given country is staggering, consisting of every telephone capable of connecting outside the territory. Even if electronic communications are concentrated into high-volume connections, a customs house opened on an electronic border would cause a massive traffic jam, threatening the very electronic commerce such facilities were constructed to encourage.

18. Cf. Information Infrastructure Task Force, Intellectual Property and the National Information Infrastructure: The Report of the Working Group on Intellectual Property Rights, 221 (1995) ("White Paper") (discussing cross-border transmission of copies of copyrighted works): "Although we recognize that the U.S. Customs Service cannot, for all practical purposes, enforce a prohibition on importation by transmission, given the global dimensions of the information infrastructure of the future, it is important that copyright owners have the other remedies for infringements of this type available to them." Id. Ironically, the Voice of America cannot prevent the information it places on the Net from doubling back into the United States, even though this domestic dissemination violates the 1948 Smith-Mundt Act. John Schwartz, Over the Net and Around the Law, Wash. Post, Jan. 14, 1995, at C1.

19. See Walter B. Wriston, The Twilight of Sovereignty (1992) (examining the challenges to sovereignty posed by the information revolution): "Technology has made us a "global" community in the literal sense of the word. Whether we are ready or not, mankind now has a completely integrated international financial and information marketplace capable of moving money and ideas to any place on this planet in minutes. Capital will go where it is wanted and stay where it is well treated. It will flee from manipulation or onerous regulation of its value or use, and no government power can restrain it for long." Id. at 61–62.

For example, the Securities and Exchange Commission has taken the position that securities offerings "that occur outside the United States" are not subject to the registration requirements of Section 5 of the Securities Act of 1933, even if United States residents are the purchasers in the overseas market. See SEC Rule 90; see also Rule 903 (for offers and sales to be deemed to "occur outside the United States," there must be, inter alia, "no directed selling efforts ... made in the United States"); Rule 902(b)(1) (defining "directed selling efforts" as "any activity undertaken for the purpose of, or that could reasonably be expected to have the effect of, conditioning the market in the United States" for the securities in question). If, as many predict, trading on physical exchanges increasingly gives way to computerized trading over the Net (see, e.g., Therese H. Maynard, What Is an e-Exchange? Proprietary Electronic Securities Trading Systems and the Statutory Definition of an Exchange, 49 Wash. & Lee L. Rev., 833, 362 (1992); Lewis D. Solomon & Louise Corso, The Impact of Technology on the Trading of Securities, 24 J. Marshall L. Rev. 299, 318–19 (1991)), this rule will inevitably become increasingly difficult to apply on a coherent basis. Where, in such a market, does the offer occur? Can information about the offering placed on the

World Wide Web "reasonably be expected to have the effect of conditioning the market in the United States" for the securities in question? See generally Solomon & Corso, Supra, at 330. The authors wish to thank Professor Merritt Fox, whose talk, titled "The Political Economy of Statutory Reach: U.S. Disclosure Rules for a Globalizing Market for Securities" (Georgetown University Law Center, March 6, 1996) drew our attention to these questions in this context.

20. For example, German authorities, seeking to prevent violations of that country's laws against distribution of pornographic material, ordered CompuServe to disable access by German residents to certain global Usenet newsgroups that would otherwise be accessible through that commercial service. See Karen Kaplan, Germany Forces Online Service to Censor Internet, L.A. Times, Dec. 29, 1995, at A1; Why Free-Wheeling Internet Puts Teutonic Wall over Porn, Christian Sci. Monitor, Jan. 4, 1996, at 1; Cyberporn Debate Goes International: Germany Pulls the Shade on CompuServe, Internet, Wash. Post, Jan. 1, 1996, at F13 (describing efforts by a local Bavarian police force had the effect of requiring CompuServe to temporarily cut off the availability of news groups to its entire audience, at least until a way could be developed to prevent delivery of specified groups to the German audience). Anyone inside Germany with an Internet connection could easily find a way to access the prohibited news groups during the ban. Auerbach, supra note 12, at 15. Although initially compliant, CompuServe subsequently rescinded the ban on most of the files by sending parents a new program to choose for themselves what items to restrict. CompuServe Ends Access Suspension: It Reopens All But Five Adult-Oriented Newsgroups. Parents Can Now Block Offensive Material, *L.A. Times*, Feb. 14, 1996, at D1.

Similarly, Tennessee may insist (indirectly, through enforcement of a federal law that defers to local community standards) that an electronic bulletin board in California install filters that prevent offensive screens from being displayed to users in Tennessee if it is to avoid liability under local obscenity standards in Tennessee. See *United States v. Thomas*—F.3d—, 1996 W.L. 30477 (6th Cir. 1996) (affirming the convictions of a California couple for violations of federal obscenity laws stemming from electronic bulletin board postings made by the couple in California but accessible from and offensive to the community standards of Tennessee). See generally Electronic Frontier Foundation, A Virtual Amicus Brief in the Amateur Action Case (Aug. 11, 1995), available at http://www.eff.org/pub/Legal/Cases/AABBS_Thomases_Memphis/Old/aa_eff_vbrief.html. The bulletin board in this case had very clear warnings and password protection. This intangible boundary limited entrance to only those who voluntarily desired to see the materials and accepted the system operator's rules. It is our contention that posting offensive materials in areas where unwilling readers may come across them inadvertently raises different problems that are better dealt with by those who understand the technology involved rather than by extrapolating from the conflicting laws of multiple geographic jurisdictions. See text accompanying notes 64–69 supra.

21. The Minnesota attorney general's office distributed a Warning to All Internet Users and Providers (available at http://www.state.mn.us/cbranch/ag/memo/txt),

stating that "[p]ersons outside of Minnesota who transmit information via the Internet knowing that information will be disseminated in Minnesota are subject to jurisdiction in Minnesota courts for violations of state criminal and civil laws." Id. (emphasis omitted). The conclusion rested on the Minnesota general criminal jurisdiction statute, which provides that "a person may be convicted and sentenced under the law of this State if the person ... (3) Being without the state, intentionally causes a result within the state prohibited by the criminal laws of this State." Minn. Stat. Ann. sec. 609.025 (1987). Minnesota also began civil proceedings against Wagernet, a Nevada gambling business that posted an Internet advertisement for online gambling services. See Complaint, Minnesota v. Granite Gate Resorts (1995) (No. 9507227), available at http://www.state.mn.us/ebranch/ag/ggcom.txt. The Florida attorney general, by contrast, contends that it is illegal to use the Web to gamble from within Florida but concedes that the attorney general's office should not waste time trying to enforce the unenforceable. 95-70 Op. Fla. Att'y Gen. (1995), available at http://legal.firn.edu/units/opinions/95-70.html. For a general discussion of these pronouncements, see Mark Eckenwiler, States Get Entangled in the Web, Legal Times, Jan. 22. 1996, at S35.

22. See State Regulators Crack Down on "Information Highway" Scams, Daily Rep. for Exec. (BNA), July 1, 1994, available in Westlaw, BNA-DER database, 1994 DER 125 at d16.

23. See David G. Post, The State of Nature and the First Internet War, Reason Apr. 1996, at 30–31 (describing the operation of the alt.religion.scientology Usenet group, noting that "Usenet groups like alt.religion.scientology come into existence when someone ... sends a proposal to establish the group to the specific newsgroup (named 'alt.config') set up for receiving such proposals. The operators of each of the thousands of computer networks hooked up to the Internet are then free to carry, or to ignore, the proposed group. If a network chooses to carry the newsgroup, its computers will be instructed to make the alt.religion.scientology 'feed,' i.e., the stream of messages posted to alt.religion.scientology arriving from other participating networks, accessible to its users, who can read—and, if they wish, add to—this stream before it is passed along to the next network in the worldwide chain. It's a completely decentralized organism—in technical terms, a 'e-distributed database'—whose content is constantly changing as it moves silently around the globe from network to network and machine to machine, never settling down in any one legal jurisdiction, or on any one computer"). See generally What Is Usenet? and Answers to Frequently Asked Questions About Usenet, available at http://www.smartpages.com/bngfaqs/news/announce/newusers/top.html.

24. European countries are trying to protect data regarding their citizens by banning the export of information for processing in countries that do not afford sufficient protections. See Peter Blume, "An EEC Policy for Data Protection," 11 Computer L.J. 399 (1992); Joseph I. Rosenbaum, The European Commission's Draft Directive on Data Protection, 33 Jurimetrics 1 (1992); Symposium, Data Protection and the European Union's Directive, 80 Iowa L. Rev. 431 (1995). But

the data regarding their citizens' activities may not be subject to their control: it may originate as a result of actions recorded on servers outside their boundaries.

25. See Joel R. Reidenberg, The Privacy Obstacle Course: Hurdling Barriers to Transnational Financial Services, 60 Fordham L. Rev. S137 (1992); David Post, Hansel and Gretel in Cyberspace, Am. Law., Oct. 1995, at 110.

26. Privacy, at least, is a relatively familiar concept, susceptible of definition on the Net by reference to analogies with mail systems, telephone calls, and print publication of invasive materials. But many new issues posed by phenomena unique to the Net are not familiar. Because electronic communications are not necessarily tied to real-world identities, new questions arise about the rights to continued existence or to protection of the reputation of a pseudonym. The potential to launch a computer virus or to "spam the Net" by sending multiple offpoint messages to newsgroups, for example, creates a need to define rules governing online behavior. When large numbers of people collaborate across the Net to create services or works of value, we will face the question whether they have formed a corporate entity or partnership—with rights and duties of its own that are distinct from those of the individual participants—in a context in which there may have been no registration with any particular geographic authority and the rights of any such authority to regulate that new legal person remain unsettled.

27. See note 11 supra.

28. Conflicts between domain names and registered trademarks have caused Network Solutions, Inc. (NSI), the agent for registration of domain names in the United States, to require that registrants "represent and warrant" that they have the right to a requested domain name and promise to "defend, indemnify, and hold harmless" NSI for any claims stemming from use or registration of the requested name. See Network Solution, Inc., NSI Domain Name Dispute Policy Statement (Revision 01, effective Nov. 23, 1995), available at ftp://rs.internic.net/policy/internic/internic-domain-4.txt. For a useful overview of the domain-name registration system and of the tensions between trademark rights and domain names, see Gary W. Hamilton, Trademarks on the Internet: Confusion, Collusion or Dilution?, 4 Tex. Intell. Prop. L.J. 1 (1995). See also Proceedings of the NSF/DNCEI & Harvard Information Infrastructure Project, Internet Names, Numbers, and Beyond: Issues in the Coordination, Privatization, and Internationalization of the Internet, Nov. 20, 1995, available at http://ksgwww.harvard.edu/iip/nsfmin1.html (discussing protection of the "trademark community" on the Net).

29. David R. Johnson, The Internet vs. the Local Character of the Law: The Electronic Web Ties Iowa and New York into One Big System, Legal Times, Dec. 5, 1994, at S32 (predicting the transformation of "local" regulation on the Net).

30. Cf. David R. Johnson, Traveling in Cyberspace, Legal Times, Apr. 3, 1995, at 26.

31. Indeed, the persistence and accessibility of electronic messages create such a sense of "placeness" that meetings in cyberspace may become a viable alternative to meetings in physical space. See I. Trotter Hardy, "Electronic Conferences:

The Report of an Experiment," 6 Harv. J. Law & Tech. 213, 232–34 (1993) (discussing the advantages of e-mail conferences). In contrast, there is no "telespace" because the conversations we conduct by telephone disappear when the parties hang up. Voicemail creates an aural version of electronic mail, but it is not part of an interconnected system that you can travel through, by hypertext links or otherwise, to a range of public and semipublic locations.

32. Some information products combine a local CD-ROM with online access to provide updated information. But even these products typically provide some onscreen indication when the user is going online. Failure to provide notice might well be deemed fraudulent, particularly if additional charges for use of the online system were imposed. In any event, a product that brings information to the screen from an online location, without disclosing the online connection to the user, should not be characterized as having allowed the user to visit a legally significant user visit to online space. Visiting a space implies some knowledge that you are there.

33. See infra pp. 275 ff. (discussing internal differentiation among rule sets in different online areas).

34. See infra note 98.

35. Having a noticeable border may be a prerequisite to the establishment of any legal regime that can claim to be separate from preexisting regimes. If someone acting in any given space has no warning that the rules have changed, the legitimacy of any attempt to enforce a distinctive system of law is fatally weakened. No geography-based sovereign could plausibly claim to have jurisdiction over a territory with secret boundaries. And no self-regulatory organization could assert its prerogatives while making it hard for members and nonmembers to tell each other apart or disguising when they were (or were not) playing their membership-related roles.

36. For example, we will have to take into account the desire of participants in online communications for pseudonymity. This will affect the extent to which information about the applicant's identity must be disclosed to obtain a valid address registration. See David G. Post, Pooling Intellectual Capital: Thoughts on Anonymity, Pseudonymity, and Limited Liability in Cyberspace, U. Chi. Legal F. (forthcoming), available at http://www_law.lib.uchicago.edu/forum/, also available at http://www.cli.org/DPost/paper8.htm (discussing the value of pseudonymous communications); A. Michael Froomkin, Flood Control on the Information Ocean: Living with Anonymity, Digital Cash, and Distributed Databases (Dec. 4, 1995) (unpublished manuscript on file with the Stanford Law Review), available at http://www.law.miami.edu/~froomkin (exploring the use and possible regulation of computer-aided anonymity); A. Michael Froomkin, Anonymity and Its Enmities, 1995 J. of Online Law art. 4, available at http://www.law.cornell.edu/jol/jol.table.html (discussing the mechanics of anonymity and how it affects the creation of pseudonymous personalities and communication on the Net). And any registration and conflict-resolution scheme will have to take into account the particular ways in which Internet addresses and names

are viewed in the marketplace. If shorter names are valued more highly (jones.com being more valuable than jones@isp.members.directory.com), this new form of "domain envy" will have to be considered in developing applicable policy.

37. See, e.g., Henry H. Perritt Jr., Tort Liability, the First Amendment, and Equal Access to Electronic Networks, 5 Harv. J.L. & Tech. 65, 106–08 (1992) (assessing the applicability of the tort of libel to network users and operators); Michael Smyth & Nick Braithwaite, First U.K. Bulletin Board Defamation Suit Brought, Nat'l L.J., Sept. 19, 1994, at C10 (noting that English courts may be a more attractive forum for plaintiffs charging defamation in cyberspace).

38. Subsequent distribution of printed versions might be characterized as publication without undermining the benefits of applying this new doctrine. It is much easier to determine who has taken such action and where (in physical space) it occurred, and the party who engages in physical distribution of defamatory works has much clearer warning regarding the nature of the act and the applicability of the laws of a particular territorial state.

39. Edward A. Cavazos, Computer Bulletin Board Systems and the Right of Reply: Redefining Defamation Liability for a New Technology, 12 Rev. Lit. 231, 243–47 (1992). This right-of-reply doctrine might apply differently to different areas of the Net, depending on whether these areas do in fact offer a meaningful opportunity to respond to defamatory messages.

40. In the context of "telemedicine," early efforts to avoid this result seem to take the form of allowing doctors to interact with other doctors in consultations, requiring compliance with local regulations only when the doctor deals directly with a patient. See Howard J. Young & Robert J. Waters, Arent Fox Kitner Plotkin & Kahn, Licensure Barriers to the Interstate Use of Telemedicine (1995) available at http://www.arentfox.com/newslett/tele1b.htm. The regulation of lawyers is muddled: regulations are sometimes based on where the lawyer's office is (as in the case of Texas's regulation of advertising), sometimes based on the content of legal advice, and sometimes based on the nature and location of the client. See Katsh, supra note 10, at 178–81.

41. Indeed, practicing the law of the Net itself presumably requires qualifications unrelated to those imposed by local bars.

42. In this, as in other matters, it is critical to distinguish the different layers of the "protocol stack." It may be possible to establish power with regard to physical connections. It is much harder to do so with respect to the logical connections that exist at the applications layer.

43. Jane C. Ginsburg, Global Use/Territorial Rights: Private International Law questions of the Global Information Infrastructure, J. Copyright Soc'y 318, 319–20 (1995).

44. See generally David Friedman, Standards as Intellectual Property, 19 U. Dayton L. Rev. 1109 (1994); William Landes & Richard Posner, An Economic Analysis of Copyright Law, 18 J. Legal Stud. 325 (1989).

45. For example, the creative output of lawyers and law professors—law review articles, briefs and other pleadings, and the like—may well be determined largely by factors completely unrelated to the availability or unavailability of copyright protection for those works because that category of authors, generally speaking, obtains reputational benefits from wide dissemination that far outweigh the benefits that could be obtained from licensing individual copies. See Stephen Breyer, The Uneasy Case for Copyright: A Study of Copyright in Books, Photocopies, and Computer Programs, 84 Harv. L. Rev. 281, 293–309 (1970), for an analysis of the incentive structure in the scholarly publishing market; see also Howard P. Tuckman & Jack Leahey, What Is an Article Worth?, 83 J. Pol. Econ. 951 (1975).

46. There is a large and diverse literature on the new kinds of authorship that are likely to emerge in cyberspace as a function of the interactive nature of the medium, the ease with which digital information can be manipulated, and new searching and linking capabilities. Among the more insightful pieces in this vein are Pamela Samuelson, Digital Media and the Changing Face of Intellectual Property Law, 16 Rutgers Comp. & Tech. L.J. 323 (1990); Ethan Katsh, Law in a Digital Age, chaps. 4, 8, and 9 (1994); Eugene Volokh, Cheap Speech, 94 Yale. L.J. 1805 (1994); and Sherry Turkle, The Second Self: Computers and the Human Spirit (1984).

47. Netscape Corp. gave away, at no charge, over four million copies of their Web browser; it is estimated that they now control over 70 percent of the Web browser market, which they have managed to leverage into dominance in the Web server software market, sufficient to enable them to launch one of the most successful Initial Public Offering in the history of the United States. See Netscape IPO Booted Up: Debut of Hot Stock Stuns Wall Street Veterans, Boston Globe, Aug. 10, 1995, at 37; With Internet Cachet, Not Profit, A New Stock Is Wall St.'s Darling, N.Y. Times, Aug. 10, 1995, at 1. Other companies are following Netscape's lead; for example, RealAudio, Inc. is distributing software designed to allow Web browsers to play sound files in real time over the Internet, presumably in the hopes of similarly establishing a dominant market position in the server market. See http://www.realaudio.com.

48. Esther Dyson, Intellectual Value, Wired (Aug. 1995).

49. David G. Post, Who Owns the Copy Right? Opportunities and Opportunism on the Global Network 2–3 (Oct. 29, 1995) (unpublished manuscript on file with the Stanford Law Review).

50. See Jane C. Ginsburg, Putting Cars on the Information Superhighway: Authors, Exploiters, and Copyright in Cyberspace, 95 Colum. L. Rev. 1466, 1488 (1995) (concluding that authors enjoy rights whose effective enforcement in cyberspace is today rather uncertain); David G. Post, New Wine, Old Bottles: The Evanescent Copy, Am. Law., May 1995, at 103.

51. See David G. Post, White Paper Blues: Copyright and the National Information Infrastructure, Legal Times, Apr. 8, 1996, at ("For example, 'browsing' on the World Wide Web necessarily involves the creation of numerous 'copies' of

information; first, a message is transmitted from Computer A to (remote) Computer B, requesting that Computer B send a copy of a particular file (e.g., the 'home page' stored on Computer B) back to Computer A. When the request is received by Computer B, a copy of the requested file is made and transmitted back to Computer A (where it is copied again—'loaded' into memory—and displayed). And the manner in which messages travel across the Internet to reach their intended recipient(s)—via intermediary computers known as 'routers,' at each of which the message is 'read' by means of 'copying' the message into the computer's memory—[involve] ... innumerable separate acts of ... 'reproduction.' File copying is not merely inexpensive in cyberspace, it is ubiquitous; and it is not merely ubiquitous, it is indispensable.... Were you to equip your computer with a 'copy lock'—an imaginary device that will prevent the reproduction of any and all information now stored in the computer in any form—it will, essentially, stop functioning").

52. See Jessica Litman, The Exclusive Right to Read, 13 Cardozo Arts & Ent. L.J. 29, 40–42 (1994) (noting that under a view that "one reproduces a work every time one reads it into a computer's random access memory ... any act of reading or viewing [a digital] work would require the use of a computer and would, under this interpretation, involve an actionable reproduction"); Pamela Samuelson, The Copyright Grab, Wired, Jan. 1996, at 137 (same); Pamela Samuelson, Legally Speaking: Intellectual Property Rights and the Global Information Economy, 39 Commun. Assoc. Comp. Machinery 23, 24 (1996) (browsing of digital works potentially infringing if "temporary copying that must occur in a computer's memory to enable users to read documents" is considered "reproduction" within meaning of Copyright Act); Post, supra note 50, at 103–04 ("If the very act of getting a document to your screen is considered the 'making of a copy' within the meaning of the Copyright Act, then a high proportion of the millions of messages traveling over the Internet each day potentially infringes on the right of some file creator ... to control the making of copies. And, if the very act reading such documents on line involves copying, then some form of a license ... would, in this view, be required for virtually every one of those message transmissions").

53. Neel Chatterjee, Imperishable Intellectual Creations: Use Limits of the First Sale Doctrine, 5 Fordham Intell. Prop. Media & Ent. L.J. 383, 384, 415–18 (1995) (discussing an Information Infrastructure Task Force proposal to exclude transmissions from the first-sale doctrine).

54. See, e.g., Telerate Systems v. Cars, 689 F. Supp. 221, 229 (S.D.N.Y. 1988) (finding that copying a "few pages" of a 20,000-page database was substantial enough to weigh against fair use).

55. Benjamin Wittes, A (Nearly) Lawless Frontier: The Rapid Pace of Change in 1994 Left the Law Chasing Technology on the Information Superhighway, Am. Law., Jan. 3, 1995, at 1.

56. For example, we could adopt rules that make the "caching" of Web pages presumptively permissible, absent an explicit agreement, rather than adopting

the standard copyright doctrine to the contrary (caching involves copying Web pages to a hard drive so that future trips to the site take less time to complete). Because making "cached" copies in computer memory is essential to speed up the operation of the Web, and because respecting express limits or retractions on any implied license allowing caching would clog up the free flow of information, we should adopt a rule favoring browsing. See Cyberspace Law Institute, Caching and Copyright Protections (Sept. 1, 1995), available at http://www.ll.georgetown.edu/cli.html; Post, supra note 49 (proposing a new rule for caching Web pages); Samuelson, supra note 52, at 26–27 (discussing copyright issues raised by file caching).

57. See text accompanying note 11 supra for an explanations of the domain-name system.

58. This danger of confusion exists whether the name conflicts with "real-world" trademark uses or only other online uses. To be sure, whoever decides these questions must consider the views of geography-based authorities when online names interfere with the existing trademarks of physical goods. But they must also decide ownership questions about online identities with addresses, names, and logos having no application offline. The views of territory-based authorities would appear to have less bearing in this context.

59. Domain-name space may raise the question of whether the Net should develop an online equivalent of eminent domain. Newly discovered public needs, such as to use a particular domain or to eliminate it to establish a new system, could interfere with "investment-backed expectations." To keep geography-based trademark authorities at bay, Net authorities may need to grandfather in strong global trademarks and prevent those who acquired certain domain names on a first-come, first-served basis from engaging in holdups—a responsible foreign policy to ward off overregulation by local sovereigns. The impact on individuals of these efforts to pursue the greater good may be require mandatory compensation. Who will pay and how remains unclear.

60. See David G. Post, Anarchy, State, and the Internet: An Essay on Law-Making in Cyberspace, 1995 J. Online L. art. 3, 10, available at http://www.law.cornell.edu/jol/jol.table.html. [Chapter 14 in this volume.]

61. A. M. Rutkowski, Internet Names, Numbers and Beyond: Issues in the Coordination, Privatization, and Internationalization of the Internet (Nov. 20, 1995) (on file with the Stanford Law Review) (identifying issues associated with the administration of Internet names and numbers).

62. David W. Maher, Trademarks on the Internet: Who's in Charge? (Feb. 14, 1996), available at http://www.aldea.com/cix/maher.html (arguing that trademark owners have a stake in the Net that must be taken into account).

63. See text accompanying note 86 infra regarding recent claims by the U.S. government.

64. Typical rules also require refraining from actions that threaten the value of the online space or increase the risk that the system operator will face legal trou-

ble in the real world. Many coherent online communities also have rules preserving the special character of their online spaces, rules governing posted messages, rules discouraging "flaming" (sending an insulting message) or "spamming" (sending the same message to multiple newsgroups), and even rules mandating certain professional qualifications for participants.

65. See Robert L. Dunne, Deterring Unauthorized Access to Computers: Controlling Behavior in Cyberspace Through a Contract Law Paradigm, 35 Jurimetrics J. 1, 12 (1994) (suggesting that system-operator agreements to banish offenders would deter unauthorized computer access more effectively than current criminal sanctions).

66. See John Seabrook, My First Flame, New Yorker, June 6, 1994, at 70 (describing the online phenomenon of flaming, where a user loses "self-control and write[s] a message that uses derogatory, obscene, or inappropriate language").

67. A computer user shuns another by refusing to receive messages from that person (or, more generally, by employing a software program known as a "kill file" to automatically deflect any e-mail messages from a specified address).

68. Computer users "mailbomb" a victim by sending a large number of junk electronic mail messages with the goal of overloading the receiving computer or at least inconveniencing the receiver.

69. Jennifer Mnookin, Virtual(ly) Law: A Case Study of the Emergence of Law on LambdaMOO (May 15, 1995) (unpublished manuscript on file with the Stanford Law Review) (describing the emergence of a legal system in the LambdaMOO virtual community). [Chapter 16 in this volume.]

70. Joanne Goode and Maggie Johnson, Putting Out the Flames: The Etiquette and Law of E-Mail, Online, Nov. 1991, at 61 (suggesting guidelines for using electronic mail and networking; S. Hambridge, Request for Comments: 1855, Netiquette Guidelines (Oct. 1995), available at ftp://ds.internic.net/rfc/rfc1855.txt.

71. James Barron, It's Time to Mind Your E-Manners, N.Y. Times, Jan. 11, 1995, at C1.

72. See Henry H. Perritt Jr., Dispute Resolution in Electronic Network Communities, 38 Vill. L. Rev. 349, 398–99 (1993) (proposing an alternative dispute resolution mechanism that could be implemented by a computer network service provider); Henry H. Perritt Jr., President Clinton's National Information Infrastructure Initiative: Community Regained?, 69 Chi.-Kent L. Rev. 991, 995–1022 (1994) (advocating the use of new information technology to facilitate dispute resolution); I. Trotter Hardy, The Proper Legal Regime for "Cyberspace," 55 U. Pitt. L. Rev. 993, 1051–53. One such dispute-resolution service, the Virtual Magistrate, has already arisen on the Net. See http:\\vmag.law.vill.edu:8080.

73. See Hardy, supra note 72, at 1020 (Law Merchant was "simply an enforceable set of customary practices that inured to the benefit of merchants, and that was reasonably uniform across all the jurisdictions involved in the [medieval]

trade fairs"); Leon E. Trakman, The Law Merchant: The Evolution of Commercial Law 11–12 (1983) (the law merchant was "a system of law that did ... not
rest exclusively on the institutions and local customs of any particular country,
but consisted of certain principles of equity and usages of trade which general
convenience and a common sense of justice have established to regulate the dealings of merchants and mariners in all the commercial countries of the civilized
world").

Benson describes the development of the Law Merchant as follows: "With the
fall of the Roman Empire, commercial activities in Europe were almost nonexistent relative to what had occurred before and what would come after. Things
began to change in the eleventh and twelfth centuries [with the] emergence of a
class of professional merchants. There were significant barriers to overcome
before substantial interregional and inter-national trade could develop, however.
Merchants spoke different languages and had different cultural backgrounds.
Beyond that, geographic distances frequently prevented direct communication,
let alone the building of strong interpersonal bonds that would facilitate trust.
Numerous middlemen were often required to bring about an exchange.... All of
this, in the face of localized, often contradictory laws and business practices, produced hostility towards foreign commercial customs and led to mercantile confrontations. There was a clear need for Law as a 'elanguage of interaction.'"
Bruce L. Benson, The Spontaneous Evolution of Commercial Law, 55 S. Econ. J.
644, 646–67 (1989). See also Perritt, supra note 9, at 46–49.

74. See Benson, supra note 73, at 647 ("[D]uring this period, because of the
need for uniform laws of commerce to facilitate international trade, "... the basic
concepts and institutions of modern Western mercantile law—lex mercatoria
—were formed, and, even more important, it was then that mercantile law in the
West first came to be viewed as an integrated, developing system, a body of law."
Virtually every aspect of commercial transactions in all of Europe (and in cases
even outside Europe) were "governed" by this body of law after the eleventh century.... This body of law was voluntarily produced, voluntarily adjudicated and
voluntarily enforced. In fact, it had to be. There was no other potential source of
such law, including state coercion").

75. See Perritt, supra note 9, at 49; Hardy, supra note 72, at 1019 ("The parallels [between the development of the Law Merchant and] cyberspace are strong.
Many people interact frequently over networks, but not always with the same
people each time so that advance contractual relations are not always practical.
Commercial transactions will more and more take place in cyberspace, and more
and more those transactions will cross national boundaries and implicate different bodies of law. Speedy resolution of disputes will be as desirable as it was in
the Middle Ages! The means of an informal court system are in place in the form
of online discussion groups and electronic mail. A 'Law Cyberspace' coexisting
with existing laws would be an eminently practical and efficient way of handling
commerce in the networked world"); Post, supra note 60, at par. 43 and n. 15.

76. This enforcement tool is not perfect—any more than the tool of banishing
merchants from the medieval trade fairs was perfect for the development of the

Law Merchant. See Paul R. Milgrom, Douglass C. North & Barry R. Weingast, The Role of Institutions in the Revival of Trade: The Law Merchant, Private Judges, and the Champagne Fairs, 2 Econ. & Pol. 1 (1990) (describing the use of banishment and other enforcement mechanisms prior to the rise of the state). Individuals intent on wrongdoing may be able to sneak back on the Net or into a particular online area with a new identity. But the enforcement tools used by legal authorities in the real world also have limits. We do not refrain from recognizing the sovereignty of our territorial governments just because they cannot fully control their physical borders or all of the actions of their citizens.

77. The social philosopher Michael Sandel has made a similar point in writing of the need for new transnational lawmaking institutions if the "loss of mastery and the erosion of community that lie at the heart of democracy's discontent" is to be alleviated: "In a world where capital and goods, information and images, pollution and people, flow across national boundaries with unprecedented ease, politics must assume transnational, even global, forms, if only to keep up. Otherwise, economic power will go unchecked by democratically sanctioned political power.... We cannot hope to govern the global economy without transnational political institutions." Michael Sandel, America's Search for a New Public Philosophy, Atlantic Monthly, March 1996, at 72–73 (emphasis added). See also infra, text at note 99, for additional parallels between our arguments and Sandel's.

78. Hilton v. Guyot, 115 U.S. 113, 163–64 (1995). See also Lauritzen v. Larsen, 345 U.S. 571, 582 (1953) ("International or maritime law ... aims at stability and order through usages which considerations of comity, reciprocity and long-range interest have developed to define the domain which each nation will claim as its own"); Mitsubishi Motors v. Soler Chrysler-Plymouth, 473 U.S. 614 (1985); see also The Bremen v. Zapata Off-Shore Co., 407 U.S. 1 (1972). Good general treatments of the comity doctrine can be found in Swanson, Comity, International Dispute Resolution Agreements, and the Supreme Court, 21 Law & Pol'y in Int'l Bus. 333 (1990); Joel R. Paul, Comity in International Law, 32 Harv. Int'l L.J. 1 (1991); Hessel Yntema, The Comity Doctrine, 65 Mich. L. Rev. 9 (1966); James S. Campbell, New Law for New International Trade 5 (Dec. 3, 1993) (on file with the Stanford Law Review); Mark W. Janis, An Introduction to International Law 250 ff. (1988); Lea Brilmayer, Conflict of Laws: Foundations and Future Directions 145–90 (1991).

79. Restatement (Third) of Foreign Relations Law of the United States sec. 403(1) (1987).

80. Id. at sec. 403(3).

81. Harold G. Maier, Remarks, 84 Proc. Am. Soc. Int'l L. 339, 339 (1990); id. at 340 (principle of comity informs the "interest-balancing" choice-of-law principles in the Restatement); Paul, supra note 78, at 12 (comity arose out of "[t]he need for a more sophisticated system of conflicts ... in connection with the emergence of the nation state and the rise of commerce that brought different nationalities into more frequent contact and conflict with one another"); id. at 45–48

(noting that although the relationship between the "classical doctrine of comity" and the Restatement's principle of "reasonableness" is uncertain, the former "retains a significant function in the Restatement"); id. at 54 (the comity principle "mitigates the inherent tension between principles of territorial exclusivity and sovereign equality"); cf. Campbell, supra note 78, at 6 (the Supreme Court's comity jurisprudence "inquires, in cases involving international trade, what values facilitate that trade. Trading nations have a common interest in supporting these values, and therefore national agencies—courts, legislators, administrators—should seek to respect, and thereby strengthen, these values as they engage in the processes of law formation").

82. Cf. Adam Gopnik, The Virtual Bishop, New Yorker, March 18, 1996, at 63 ("Of course, the primitive Church was a kind of Internet itself, which was one of the reasons it was so difficult for the Roman Empire to combat it. The early Christians understood that what was most important was not to claim physical power in a physical place but to establish a network of believers—to be on line,' " quoting French Bishop Jacques Gaillot).

83. Perritt, supra note 9, at 42. Cf. Michael Walzer, Spheres of Justice: A Defense of Pluralism and Equality 281–83 (1983) (discussing differences between different spheres of power and authority).

84. The idea of "delegation" is something of a fiction. But legal fictions have a way of becoming persuasive and therefore real. See, e.g., Lon L. Fuller, Legal Fictions 55 (1967). Self-regulatory bodies evolve independently of the state and derive their authority from the sovereign only insofar as the sovereign, after the fact, claims and exercises a monopoly over the use of force.

85. See generally Henry H. Perritt Jr., Computer Crimes and Torts in the Global Information Infrastructure: Intermediaries and Jurisdiction (Oct. 12, 1995) (on file with the Stanford Law Review).

86. See Maher, supra note 62 (noting the "arrogance" of the Federal Networking Council's position on this issue).

87. Cf. id. (noting that while other groups faced fees for new domain names, "[s]pecial arrangements are made for users of '.gov' and '.edu' ").

88. See id. (noting "[t]he .mil domain is excluded" from the jurisdiction of the private corporation that administers the registration of domain names).

89. See supra note 20.

90. See id.

91. See Jonathan Graubert, What's News: A Progressive Framework for Evaluating the International Debate Over the News, 77 Cal. L. Rev 629, 633 (1989) ("The guiding principle in international communications since World War II has been the U.S.-inspired goal of a 'free flow of information.' According to this principle, '[f]reedom of information implies the right to gather, transmit and publish news anywhere and everywhere without fetters'") (citing G.A. Res. 59(I), 1(2), U.N. GAOR Resolutions at 95, U.N. Doc. A/64/Add. 1 (1947). The free-flow-of-information principle has been defined as a necessary part of freedom of opinion

and expression. See Article 19 of the Universal Declaration of Human Rights, G.A. Res. 217(III)A, 3(1) U.N. GAOR Resolutions at 71, 74–75, U.N. Doc. A/810 (1948) (stating that freedom of expression includes "freedom to hold opinions without interference and to seek, receive and impart information and ideas through any media and regardless of frontiers").

92. Moreover, the right of individuals to participate in various online realms depends critically on their obtaining information about those realms. Insofar as any territorial government merely claims moral superiority of its laws and values, it is not well situated to oppose a free flow of information that might lead its citizens to disagree, for this would be the equivalent of defending ignorance as a necessary ingredient of preservation of the values espoused by the local state. This view is unlikely to persuade external rulemakers who do not share those values.

93. Listservers, for example, can be set up on any network (or Internet) server by means of simple instructions given to one of several widely available software programs (listproc or majordomo). A Usenet discussion group in the alt. hierarchy can be established by sending a simple request to the alt.config newsgroup. See sources cited supra note 23. Cyberspace not only permits the effective delineation of internal boundaries between different online spaces but also allows for effective delineation of distinct online roles within different spheres of activity and as to which different rules apply. In the nonvirtual world, we slip in and out of such roles frequently; the rules applicable to the behavior of a single individual, in a single territorial jurisdiction, may change as he moves between different legally significant persona (acting as an employee, a member of a church, a parent, or the officer of a corporation, for example). Cyberspace may make the boundaries between these different roles easier to maintain, insofar as explicit "tags"—distinct "signature files," or screen names—can relatively easily be attached to messages originating from the author's different roles.

94. Post, supra note 60, art. 3, at par. 7 (asserting that the individual network "organizations" will probably determine the substantive rule making for cyberspace); David R. Johnson & Kevin A. Marks, Mapping Electronic Data Communications onto Existing Legal Metaphors: Should We Let Our Conscience (and Our Contracts) Be Our Guide?, 38 Vill. L. Rev. 487, 489–89 (1993) (explaining that communication service providers, owners of disks carrying centralized databases, and people presiding over electronic discussion groups have the power to select applicable rules).

95. For illuminating discussions of the many parallels between biological evolution and social evolution in Cyberspace, see Kevin Kelly, Out of Control: The Law of Neo-Biological Civilization (1994); John Lienhard, Reflections on Information, Biology, and Community, 32 Hous. L. Rev. 303 (1995); Michael Schrage, Revolutionary Evolutionist, Wired (July 1995).

96. This geographic barrier merely permits divergence to occur; it does not guarantee it. Specification will occur, for example, only if the two divided subpopulations are subject to different selection pressures or at least one of them is small

enough to accrue significant random changes in its gene pool ("genetic drift"). For good, nontechnical descriptions of evolutionary theory, see Daniel C. Dennett, Darwin's Dangerous Idea: Evolution and the Meanings of Life (1995); John Maynard-Smith, Did Darwin Get It Right? Essays on Games, Sex, and Evolution (1989); John Maynard-Smith, On Evolution (1972); George C. Williams, Adaptation and Natural Selection: A Critique of Some Current Evolutionary Thought (1966).

97. To survive, rules must be passed on somehow, whether in the form of "case reports" or other interindividual or intergenerational methods. See Richard Dawkins, The Selfish Gene (1989). General parallels between biological evolution and the evolution of legal rules are discussed in Friedrich Hayek, 1 Law, Legislation, and Liberty at 44–49 (1973); Friedrich Hayek, The Constitution of Liberty 56–61 (1960); see generally Tom W. Bell, Polycentric Law, 7 Humane Stud. Rev. (available at http://osf1.gmu.edu/~ihs/w91issues.html).

98. Cyberspace, as M. Ethan Katsh has written, is a "software world" where "code is the Law." M. Ethan Katsh, Software Worlds and the First Amendment: Virtual Doorkeepers in Cyberspace, Univ. of Chi. Legal F. (forthcoming), quoting William Mitchell, City of Bits (1995): "To a considerable extent, networks really are what software allows them to be. The Internet is not a network but a set of communications protocols.... [T]he Internet is software. Similarly, the World Wide Web is not anything tangible. It is client-server software that permits machines linked on a network to share and work with information on any of the connected machines." Id. at 7. See also Post, supra note 60, at par. 16 ("networks are not merely governed by substantive rules of conduct, they have no existence apart from such rules"). And software specifications can be unforgiving (as anyone who has tried to send an e-mail message to an incorrectly spelled network recipient can attest): "Entry of messages into, and routing of messages across, digitally based electronic networks ... are controlled by more effective protocols [than generally govern nonelectronic communications networks in the 'real world']: each network's technical specifications (typically embodied in software or switching mechanisms) constitute rules that precisely distinguish between compliant and non-compliant messages. This boundary [is not an] artificial construct because the rules are effectively self-enforcing. To put the matter simply, you can't 'almost' be on the Georgetown University LAN or America Online—you are either transmitting LAN- or AOL-compliant messages or you are not." Id. at par. 20 (emphasis added). Thus, individual network communities can be configured, by means of unique specifications of this kind, to bar all (or some specified portion of) internetwork traffic with relative ease.

99. Sandel, supra note 77, at 73–74 (emphasis added).

100. Brilmayer, supra note 6, at 5.

101. In Albert Hirschman's terms, they have a "voice" in the development of French law, at least to the extent that French lawmaking institutions represent and are affected by citizen participation. Albert O. Hirschman, Exit, Voice and Loyalty 106–19 (1970); cf. Richard A. Epstein, Exit Rights Under Federalism,

Law & Contemp. Probs. at 147, 151–65 (Winter 1992) (discussing the ability of exit rights to constrain governmental power and the limitations of such rights).

102. According to Post, supra note 23, at 33: "There has always been a strong fictional element to using this notion of a social contract as a rationale for a sovereign's legitimacy. When exactly did you or I consent to be bound by the U.S. Constitution? At best, that consent can only be inferred indirectly, from our continued presence within the U.S. borders—the love-it-or-leave-it, vote-with-your-feet theory of political legitimacy. But by that token, is Saddam Hussein's rule legitimate, as least as to those Iraqis who have 'consented' in this fashion? Have the Zairois consented to Mobutu's rule? In the world of atoms, we simply cannot ignore the fact that real movement of real people is not always so easy, and that most people can hardly be charged with having chosen the jurisdiction in which they live or the laws that they are made to obey. But in cyberspace, there is an infinite amount of space, and movement between online communities is entirely frictionless. Here, there really is the opportunity to obtain consent to a social contract; virtual communities can be established with their own particular rule-sets, power to maintain a degree of order and to banish wrongdoers can be lodged, or not, in particular individuals or groups, and those who find the rules oppressive or unfair may simply leave and join another community (or start their own)."

103. The ease with which individuals may move between communities (or inhabit multiple communities simultaneously) also implies that cyberspace may provide conditions necessary and sufficient for something more closely resembling the optimal collective production of a particular set of goods—namely, laws—than can be achieved in the real world. Cyberspace may closely approximate the idealized model for the allocation of local goods and services set forth by Charles Tiebout, see Charles Tiebout, A Pure Theory of Local Expenditures, 64 J. Pol. Econ. 416 (1956), in which optimal allocation of locally produced public goods is provided by small jurisdictions competing for mobile residents. The Tiebout model of intergovernmental competition has four components: (1) a perfectly elastic supply of jurisdictions, (2) costless mobility of individuals among jurisdictions, (3) full information about the attributes of all jurisdictions, and (4) no interjurisdictional externalities. See Robert P. Inman & Daniel L. Rubinfeld, The Political Economy of Federalism, Working Paper No. 94-15, Boalt Hall Program in Law and Economics (1994), at 11–16, reprinted in D. Mueller (ed.), Developments in Public Choice (1995). (As Inman and Rubinfeld demonstrate, a fifth assumption of the Tiebout model—the provision of public goods with a "congestible technology" such that the per capita cost of providing each level of a public good first decreases and then increases as more individuals move into the jurisdiction—is not necessary for the model. Id. at 13.) In a Tieboutian world, "each locality provides a package of local public goods consistent with the preferences of its residents (consumer-voters). Residents whose preferences remain unsatisfied by a particular locality's package of goods and services would (costlessly) move.... Escape from undesirable packages of goods and services is feasible as a result of two explicit characteristics of the Tiebout model: absence

of externalities and mobility of residents." Clayton P. Gillette, In Partial Praise of Dillon's Rule, or, Can Public Choice Theory Justify Local Government Law?, 67 Chi.-Kent L. Rev. 959, 969 (1991). We suggest that cyberspace may be a closer approximation to ideal Tieboutian competition between rule sets than exists in the nonvirtual world, a consequence of (1) the low cost of establishing an online "jurisdiction," see text at note 72, (2) the ease of exit from online communities, (3) the relative ease of acquiring information about the practices of online communities, and (4) the greater impermeability of the internal, software-mediated boundaries between online communities in cyberspace, see supra note 98, which may mitigate (at least to some extent) the problem of intercommunity externalities.

104. The Net may need new metarules for transporting information across these borders. For example, the members of the LambdaMOO multiuser domain debated at length whether to permit the use of information obtained from the virtual discussion group out in the "real world." See Mnookin, supra note 69, at 20–21. Various online systems have rules about copying or reposting materials from one online area to another. For example, the terms of service for Counsel Connect contains the following rules for acceptable copying:

[M]embers who submit material shall be deemed to (I) grant to ... subscribers to the system a paid up, perpetual, world-wide irrevocable license to use, copy, and redistribute such materials and any portions thereof and any derivative works therefrom.... Each member agrees, as a condition of such license, (I) not to remove identifying source information from verbatim copies of member-supplied materials ... and (ii) not to reproduce portions thereof in any way that identifies the source but fails to describe accurately the nature and source of any modification, alteration thereto or selection therefrom.... B. Notwithstanding the licenses granted by members and information suppliers, subscribers ... shall not engage in systematic, substantial and regular replication of materials supplied to the system by a commercial publisher ... where the effect of such actions is to provide another person who is not an authorized subscriber to such materials with a substantial substitute for such a subscription.

Terms and Conditions for Use of Counsel Connect (on file with the Stanford Law Review). America Online's Terms of Service Agreement contain a somewhat similar clause:

4. Rights and Responsibilities
(a) Content ... [Members]Acknowledge that (I) AOL contains information, software, photos, video, graphics, music, sounds and other material and services (collectively, "Content").... AOL permits access to Content that is protected by copyrights, trademarks, and other proprietary (including intellectual property) rights.... [Members'] use of Content shall be governed by applicable copyright and other intellectual property laws.... By submitting Content to and "Public Area" ... [members] automatically grant ... AOL Inc. the royalty free, perpetual, irrevocable, non-exclusive right and license to use, reproduce, modify, adapt, publish, translate, create derivative works from, distribute, perform and display such Content (in whole or part) worldwide.

AOL Inc.'s Terms of Service Agreement (on file with the Stanford Law Review).

105. See Sandel, supra note 77, at 74 ("Self-government today ... requires a politics that plays itself out in a multiplicity of settings, from neighborhoods to nations to the world as a whole. Such a politics requires citizens who can abide the ambiguity associated with divided sovereignty, who can think and act as multiply situated selves"); see also Sherry Turkle, Life on the Screen: Identity in the Age of the Internet (1995); Sherry Turkle, The Second Self: Computers and the Human Spirit 95 (1984). To be sure, sophisticated analysis even of traditional legal doctrines suggests that we appear before the law only in certain partial, conditional roles. Joseph Vining, Legal Identity: The Coming of Age of Public Law 139–69 (1978). But this partial and conditional nature of "persons" who hold rights and duties is more pronounced in cyberspace.

106. See Chatterjee, supra note 53, at 425 n. 142 (noting that "[o]riginal copyright paradigms were created to protect only physical books").

107. Electronic information can be dispensed in any sized serving, ranging from a few words to an entire database. If we use the database as a whole as our measure, then any user's selection will be an insignificant portion. In contrast, if we tried to use the traditional boundaries of the book's cover, the user cannot observe this standard; in some cases it is an entirely theoretical boundary, with respect to material only dispensed from the database. This case demonstrates again that the absence of physical borders setting off distinct "works" in cyberspace undermines the utility of doctrines like copyright law that are based on the existence of such boundaries in the real world.

108. Whether the law should consider that interest to be a property right or a right on behalf of the persona in question remains undecided.

14

Anarchy, State, and the Internet: An Essay on Lawmaking in Cyberspace

David G. Post

Introduction

Increasing attention is currently paid to important and interesting questions about the rules that will, or should, govern behavior within the global networked environment: What shape should copyright protection take in a world of instantaneous, costless, and undetectable copying? Should the First Amendment be interpreted to encompass a right to post anonymous messages or commercial messages across Usenet groups or a right to send encrypted messages that are, for all intents and purposes, immune to eavesdropping by law enforcement? What standard of liability should be imposed on system operators in regard to the availability of "obscene" material on their systems?

This focus on the substantive content of legal rules reflects, at least in part, what Oliver Williamson has called "legal centralism."[1] A "centralist" inquiry focuses on alternative sets of substantive laws—with an eye toward determining which set is optimal in terms of some predefined criterion, such as aggregate welfare. This is an entirely appropriate model for an inquiry where some lawmaking body—typically a sovereign government—is in a position to choose the optimal set of laws.

My focus in this chapter, however, is elsewhere. To the extent that the global network proves relatively resistant to centralized control—and I believe that it will so prove, for some of the reasons addressed below—the question "Which copyright law is 'best'?" must at least be sup-

This chapter originally appeared in the *Journal of Online Law* (http://www.warthog.cc.wm.edu/law/publications/jol/post.html). Reprinted by permission of the author. © 1995, David G. Post.

plemented by the question "What are the forces that govern the legal system's trajectory through 'rule-space,' and which configuration(s) of copyright law is likely to emerge from the operation of those forces over time?"[2] Before we try to answer the substantive questions—before we try to decide what the "best" copyright law for the global network might look like—we should pause to consider some necessarily antecedent questions: What mechanisms exist whereby such a law could be implemented? Who can make and enforce the rules in cyberspace, whatever the substantive content of those rules might be?

What follows is a rough sketch of the reasons that these are particularly interesting and rich questions in the context of electronic networks and a framework that may help to structure the inquiry into law and lawmaking on the global network. Cyberspace has itself already demonstrated the immense power of collective intellectual efforts, and I offer this essay in the hopes of spurring others to think about these important questions in new and fruitful ways.[3]

Lawmaking and Social Control in Network Communities

Robert C. Ellickson's framework for behavioral controls is a useful starting point for a discussion of the various forces governing individual behavior in electronic networks.[4] Ellickson identifies five "controllers" that can provide substantive rules governing an individual's behavior: the actor himself or herself, other individuals being acted on, nonhierarchically organized social forces, hierarchically organized nongovernmental organizations, and, finally, government (that is, a hierarchical organization "widely regarded as having the legitimate authority to inflict detriments on persons within its geographically defined jurisdiction who have not necessarily voluntarily submitted themselves to its authority").[5] Ellickson's descriptive labels for each controller's substantive rules, and the rewards and punishments through which each enforces those rules, are set forth in table 14.1.

For an illustration of the application of this framework, consider the various rules that combine to determine the frequency with which a particular behavior—say, the transmission of messages containing any of the Federal Communications Commission's "seven dirty words"—might

Table 14.1
Ellickson's five Controllers that provide substantive rules governing behavior

Controller	Substantive Rules	Sanctions
The actor	Personal ethics	Self-sanction
Second-party controllers (i.e., the person acted on)	Contractual provisions	Various self-help mechanisms
Nonhierarchically organized social forces	Social norms	Social sanctions
Hierarchically organized nongovernmental organizations	Organization rules	Organization sanctions
Governments	Law	State enforcement, coercive sanctions

occur on my university's local area network.[6] Each network participant may have a personal ethical position in regard to the propriety or impropriety of such messages.

One can imagine (not terribly realistically, perhaps, in this context) bilateral agreements between network users regarding the use of particular words in e-mail messages or in files stored on the network or even self-help (in the form of authorized or unauthorized file deletion) by individual network users. Each of these is, in turn, at least partially determined by each user's response to various social forces such as cultural or professional norms. Formal or informal organization rules, promulgated by the network administrators (that is, by Georgetown University itself), may apply to this conduct, as may federal or state laws regarding the transmission of "obscene" messages.

The question I am here addressing (whose rules will govern behavior in cyberspace?) can thus be rephrased: How does the competition among these controllers proceed? What are the "controller-selecting rules"[7] that determine which controller's rules take precedence in the event of conflict? To take a concrete example, how would the Communications Decency Act recently introduced in the U.S. Senate[8] affect the frequency with which "indecent" or "obscene" communications appear in any particular network community if the proscriptions in that Act conflicted with other behavioral "controllers" within that community? And most specifically, what are the special characteristics of electronic networks that might influence the way in which these controller-selecting rules operate?

The Nature of Networks

Networks (electronic or otherwise) are particular kinds of "organizations" that are not merely capable of promulgating substantive rules of conduct; their very essence defined by such rules—in this case, the *network protocols*. Accordingly, the person or entity in a position to dictate the content of these network protocols is, in the first instance at least, a primary rule maker in regard to behavior on the network.

What we call *cyberspace* can be characterized as a multitude of individual but interconnected electronic communications networks—for example, individual BBS systems, Prodigy, the Georgetown University LAN, the Cyberia discussion list, or the network of machines that can communicate across the World Wide Web. Communication networks of any kind (a number of individuals meeting together in a room, the network comprising the people who read this essay, or the network of computers communicating on America Online) are defined at a minimum by a set of rules—the network protocols—specifying (1) the medium through which messages can travel, (2) the characteristics of the messages that are permitted to enter the network, and (3) the manner in which messages are routed through this medium to network members.

A group of children playing the game of "telephone," for example, constitutes a network, as do the participants in a university seminar presentation. In both, the network protocols require audible sounds transmitted through the atmosphere (though at low volume in the case of "telephone"). Each network has its own message origination and routing rules; in "telephone," messages originate with the child on one side of the room and are routed from one child to the child immediately adjacent. At the seminar, the rules may require that all messages originate from the speaker ("No questions until I'm finished") from whom they are routed simultaneously to all participants ("Can you hear me in the back row?").

Similarly, the local area network at Georgetown University on which I am composing this essay requires that messages be transmitted through special cabling installed in our building and further that those messages obey certain formatting and coding conventions, embodied in the LAN operating system software, that will allow them to be appropriately managed by the central LAN server.

In one sense, then, networks are not merely governed by substantive rules of conduct; they have no existence apart from such rules. Viewed in this light, the network protocols have a kind of first-order competitive advantage over other controllers in regard to the behavior that occurs there by virtue of their ability to control entry onto the network by excluding behavior that is inconsistent with the message entry rules. Accordingly, the person or entity in a position to dictate the content of these network protocols is, in the first instance at least, a primary rule maker in regard to behavior on the network.

This is, admittedly, something of a definitional trick in regard to most ordinary networks and is unlikely to illuminate behavioral questions of real interest because the boundary between being "on" and "off" the network has little objective meaning with respect to whatever questions we are likely to have about the frequency with which particular behaviors manifest themselves. For example, suppose that during our game of telephone one of the children stands up and says, in an inappropriately loud voice: "This is a stupid game. Here's what the message is: 'Johnny and Susie were holding hands in class yesterday.'"

If we are interested in how these children behave on the "telephone game" network, we can ignore this comment. Because it violates the network protocols, we can simply deem it to have occurred "off the network." But that is unlikely to help us understand the children's behavior in any meaningful sense. The other children have heard the message and have observed this conduct, even though it took place "off the network." To the extent that this particular network is largely an artificial construct existing almost exclusively in the mind of the observer, the fact that in some technical sense the protocols exclude this particular behavior will have few, if any, meaningful consequences.

Entry of messages into, and routing of messages across, digital electronic networks, however, are controlled by more effective protocols than in our game-of-"telephone" example: each network's technical specifications (typically embodied in software or switching mechanisms) constitute rules that precisely distinguish between compliant and noncompliant messages. This boundary is less easily dismissed as an artificial construct because the rules are effectively self-enforcing. To put the matter simply, you can't "almost" be on the Georgetown University LAN or America Online: you are either transmitting LAN- or AOL-compliant messages or you are not.

As a consequence, the ability of this control mechanism to impose its rules on network conduct is considerably less trivial for electronic networks than for their nonelectronic counterparts because permissible behavior can be more precisely demarcated from that which is impermissible. Any discussion of rule making in cyberspace therefore should begin by looking at the role of the entities and institutions defining the network protocols because this level of organizational controller has what might be termed "competitive advantages" over other controllers in electronic network communities.

Are these network technical specifications, then, part of the "law of cyberspace"? I believe that they are—or at least that it would be profitable to analyze them as such. On the one hand, they would appear to govern a fairly narrow range of what we might want to call "behavior." Whether one is using an HTML-compliant Internet browser, even or odd parity to communicate over a network, fixed- or variable-length message packets, or the SMTP mail-routing protocol, would not appear to have much to do with the behavioral questions of copyright infringement, transmission of obscene messages, fraud, and the like that we're really interested in when we speak of the "law of cyberspace." Because network technical specifications generally operate on those message characteristics unrelated to message content, they might appear to be of little relevance to our understanding of the constraints on behaviors that can be defined only with reference to precisely that content.

But we shouldn't dismiss them quite so quickly as entirely irrelevant to our inquiry because these technical specifications may reach further down into message content and meaning than one might think at first glance. It is easy to overlook the fact that the message traffic over digital networks consists entirely of strings of binary digits. In this environment, the line between the meaning contained in message transmissions, and the purely technical contours of those messages, is blurred indeed.

One can hardly imagine, to be sure, a rule regarding, say, fraudulent transactions that would be capable of digital embodiment in these engineering specifications. One can imagine, however, a digital embodiment of rules regarding other activities (for example, the transmission of anonymous messages or encrypted files) that can be more easily expressed in digital form and thereby enforced at the level of the technical network specifications. The scope for digitizing behavioral rules represents a particularly fruitful avenue of inquiry in any attempt to determine the role that these specifications may play in setting the rules of conduct on these networks.[9]

And note also that these digitally embodied network specifications are not the only means by which the network organization controller can impose its rules regarding permissible or prohibited network behaviors. Any centralized network architecture involving a single location through which all messages must pass—whether it is a client-server LAN or a moderated Internet newsgroup—allows for the examination of all transmissions for compliance with specific behavioral rules. That is, whether or not Georgetown University's LAN can implement in its operating system software a rule excluding "obscene" messages, the LAN administrator can, though perhaps at significant cost, screen all messages for compliance with a rule prohibiting such transmissions.[10] Similarly, a discussion group moderator can announce and enforce a rule providing that any messages not meeting certain criteria of relevance to the group's focus, taste, or propriety will be deleted.

My thesis, then, is that this controller—the individual network "organizations" themselves—possesses at least certain inherent advantages in the competition for rule-making precedence in cyberspace and that this controller is therefore potentially the locus for much of the substantive rule making that will take place there. *Potentially* is the operative word. Saying that cyberspace may consist of a large number of individual networks, each with its own rules (about, for example, the propriety of obscene text and the definition of *obscenity*) does not tell us whether the law of cyberspace will in the aggregate consist of a diverse set of such rules or will converge on a single, or a small number, of such rules. To analyze that question we need to examine one additional feature of the competition among controllers.

The competition among controllers is asymmetric, at least insofar as the state holds a monopoly on the imposition of coercive sanctions on controllers lower down in the controller hierarchy. The state's ability to impose its substantive law by means of such sanctions, however, is substantially constrained by the existence of the global Internet itself, which provides a credible exit strategy for networks and other lower-order controllers.

There is something of an asymmetry in the ranking of controllers, at least insofar as the state has a monopoly on the use of coercive sanctions when faced with violations of whatever rules it promulgates. Thus, we can speak of the ability of this controller to impose its laws on the individuals, contracting parties, or organizations lower down in the controller hierarchy, but not vice versa. Neither individual actors, contracting parties, nor organizations can similarly impose their preferred substantive rules on the state where the state's laws are in conflict with theirs. The effectiveness of the state's sanctions, generally speaking, is an inverse function of the ease with which the lower-order controllers can "exit" from the regime defined by those laws—by evading detection of rule—violating behavior, evading the state-imposed sanctions for such violations, or somehow withdrawing from the rule-making jurisdiction of the state as controller.[11]

This notion of "exit" may be generalized to apply across the entire controller hierarchy—that is, it may be useful to think of each controller possessing the ability to impose its rules on lower-order controllers, each of whom needs to rely on some form of exit to counter that imposition. Thus, the organization by whom I am employed, Georgetown University, can impose its rules regarding proper faculty conduct on my behavior, subject to my ability to evade detection should I behave in contravention of those rules, my ability to evade the sanctions that Georgetown imposes in the event such behavior is detected, and, finally, my ability to obtain substantially equivalent employment elsewhere and thereby leave Georgetown's jurisdiction entirely.

Returning, then, to our question of diversity and uniformity of network rule sets, imposition of governmental laws on those individual network rule sets is one way that a measure of rule uniformity may emerge in cyberspace. The state will experience obvious difficulties in attempting to monitor the behavior of individual network users, who are numerous and dispersed across many such networks. Because each such network functions as a gatekeeper for its users in cyberspace, however, we might expect that governments will try to rely instead on their ability to impose coercive sanctions on network administrators (and thereby on the network rules) to implement their own particular preferred set of rules on behavior in this environment.[12]

The extent to which this will occur, and the substantive areas in which this strategy is most likely to be tried and in which it is most likely to be effective, are important and complex questions, the full explication of which is far beyond the scope of this chapter. I have, again, a single observation that may shed some light here: the existence of the global internetwork functions as a significant constraint on any sovereign's ability to implement this strategy.

The Internet, like any network, is not a physical object with a tangible existence but is itself a set of network protocols that has been adopted by a large number of individual networks allowing the transfer of information among them. There may well be no principle more important for understanding rule making in cyberspace than that of distinguishing between the Internet as a whole and the individual networks that are its component members. It is indeed the interplay between the vast number of largely centralized individual networks and the decentralized internetwork through which they can communicate that will prove to be of fundamental importance in determining the efficacy with which state law can be imposed on individual network communities.[13]

The state's ability to impose sanctions on law violators is fundamentally constrained by the need for physical proximity and physical control. This is by no means an absolute constraint. Mechanisms do exist, of course, whereby individual sovereigns can impose their rules on persons or entities not physically present in the area over which the sovereign has control.

Such mechanisms, however, entail additional enforcement costs—both the direct costs of projecting sovereign power extraterritorially and the costs of coordinating and harmonizing the legal regimes of competing sovereigns. Thus, United States law is not ordinarily applicable to, nor can the United States ordinarily apply sanctions on, a network operator in, say, Singapore. Attempts by the United States to go around these limitations require either some means of obtaining control over the network operator or its assets, or some measure of cooperation with state authorities in Singapore or other jurisdictions where the operator maintains physical assets on which judgments can be executed.

The Internet, of course, is multijurisdictional in the obvious sense that messages can travel from a network in Washington to one in Singapore, Kazakhstan, or anywhere on the globe where computers have access to the Internet's medium of communication. But the Internet is not merely multijurisdictional; it is almost ajurisdictional: physical location and physical boundaries are irrelevant in this networked environment in a way that has, I believe, no parallel elsewhere.

Moving through the World Wide Web, for example, by following hypertext links from one Internet site to another, the user is almost completely indifferent (and, indeed, may have no way of knowing) whether the file she is viewing resides on a computer down the street or across the globe. Similarly, whether control of the Cyberia listserver is exercised by a computer in Williamsburg, Virginia, or Williams Corner, New South Wales, has almost no effect on the functional capabilities of that particular network or the ease with which any individual with Internet access can participate in the activities taking place on that network.

This independence from geographical constraints results both from the electronic nature of the message transmission (which largely decouples the physical distance between communicating machines from message travel times) and, more significantly, from the decentralized design of the Internet. Because the Internet, unlike most of its constituent networks, was designed without a centralized control mechanism or any single location through which all internetwork traffic must travel, all network nodes are effectively equipotent, each equally capable of performing the key internetwork message routing functions.

As a consequence, the Internet itself is an "exit strategy" for individual network rule makers in two senses. First, the Internet allows one to exit by evading detection. Decentralization implies that the costs of monitoring behavior are substantially higher and rule-violative behavior substantially more difficult to detect than would be the case under a centralized internetwork design.

The second sense pertains to exit by withdrawal from jurisdictional control—the relocation of rule-violative behavior so that it is outside the jurisdiction of any physically-based sovereign. Should a particular network rule set be incompatible with the law of sovereign X, the network rule set itself can, with relative ease, be transferred elsewhere on the internetwork, outside of the sovereign's jurisdictional boundaries. Georgetown University, that is, may indeed choose to implement a particular rule prohibiting the transmission of certain kinds of pornographic images across the Georgetown LAN, and it may well do so because the District of Columbia, or the United States, government has forced it to do so (that is, has decided to impose sanctions on networks within its jurisdictional control that do not implement such rules). And Georgetown may indeed be able to enforce this prohibition in regard to its own network, subject to whatever difficulties it may encounter in trying to detect violations of this rule.

The effect of Georgetown's rules on the behavior itself, however (on the availability of pornographic images and the frequency with which such images are transmitted across the aggregated internetwork) may be considerably attenuated or even nonexistent. To the extent that those conducting this behavior on the Georgetown LAN can, by virtue of their access to the Internet, equally easily access some other network whose rules are not subject to the control of the District of Columbia or United States, this rule set and the images themselves can migrate to the less restrictive jurisdiction.

Conclusion

The model sketched out above implies that although each individual network can be constrained from "above" in regard to the rule sets that it can or cannot adopt, the aggregate range of such rule sets in cyberspace will be far less susceptible to such control. A kind of competition between individual networks to design and implement rule sets that are compatible with the preferences of individual internetwork users will thus materialize in a new and largely unregulated, because largely unregulatable, market for rules. The outcome of the individual decisions within this market—the aggregated choices of individual users seeking particular network rule sets most to their liking—will therefore, to a significant extent, determine the contours of the "law of cyberspace."

What kind of rules will emerge from this process? We have almost no experience with unregulated markets for social control rules and hence have little basis for predicting the criteria that people are likely to use in choosing among these alternative rule sets and to predict the outcome of this competition.[14] Two points seem clear, however. First, the prospect of relatively unfettered individual choice among competing sets of rules is surely an attractive prospect, to the extent that what emerges represents the rules that people have voluntarily chosen to adopt rather than rules that have been imposed by others on them.

Second, rules governing behavior in individual networks may generate negative externalities in regard to participants in other networks in much the same way that an individual geographical community's laws (regarding, say, water pollution) can impose costs on neighboring communities.[15] All communities may benefit from an agreement establishing a rule prohibiting polluting activities, but absent a means to enforce that agreement it may be in each individual community's interests to "cheat." This, of course, is the familiar Prisoner's Dilemma, and to the extent that my description of rule making in cyberspace is accurate, there may be no more important task facing those interested in the future course of cyberspace than to develop ways in which this coordination problem can be solved with a minimum of interference with the freedom of individuals to choose the rules under which they wish to operate.

Notes

I want to thank the many participants on the discussion groups on Lexis Counsel Connect, as well as on the Cyberia listserver, for their innumerable interesting and instructive comments, which have helped me formulate some of the ideas expressed in this essay. A version of this chapter was delivered at the Georgetown University Faculty Research Seminar, and I thank participants in that forum—Avery Katz, Marc Rotenberg, Steve Salop, and Warren Schwartz in particular—as well as Eugene Volokh for helpful comments on earlier drafts. The ideas expressed, and all remaining errors are, of course, my responsibility alone.

1. Oliver W. Williamson, Credible Commitments: Using Hostages to Support Exchange, 73 Am. Econ. Rev. 519, 520, 537 (1983). The legal centralist tradition is cogently criticized in Robert C. Ellickson, Order Without Law: How Neighbors Settle Disputes 137–47 (1991); Robert D. Cooter, Decentralized Law for a Complex Economy, 23 Sw. U.L. Rev. 443 (1994); Robert D. Cooter, Structural Adjudication and the New Law Merchant: A Model of Decentralized Law, 14 Intl J.L. & Amp. Econ. 215 (1994).

2. Evolutionary biology illustrates these differences in approach. To understand why cockroaches are the way they are, biologists do not begin with questions of the form "What is the optimally designed cockroach?" or "Would a cockroach with eight legs or one capable of photosynthesis be a 'better' cockroach?" Those questions might well be appropriate if we were in the business of designing some organism to do cockroachlike things. But biological evolution proceeds without a central design authority that chooses among alternative versions of the cockroach, and questions regarding "optimal cockroach design" make no sense until an antecedent question—"What is the process by which changes in cockroach design are implemented?"—is satisfactorily answered. To explain why cockroaches are the way they are or to predict what they will look like in the future, evolutionary biologists must begin with a theory of how evolution proceeds and then ask, "Can we explain the features of the cockroach by reference to the working of those evolutionary forces?" (and "If not, do our theory of the way evolution proceeds and our understanding of the problems faced by the cockroach need to be revised?"). Identification of the optimum is still of interest, to be sure, but only in the context of asking whether these forces are likely to produce a system at or close to this optimum. For a discussion of these issues, see David G. Post, Is the Optimization Approach the Optimal Approach to Primate Foraging?, in P. Rodman & J. Cant (eds.), Adaptations for Foraging in Nonhuman Primates (1984).

3. I do not mean to suggest that I am the first person to look at this metaquestion of lawmaking in cyberspace. See, e.g., I. Trotter Hardy, The Proper Legal Regime for Cyberspace, 55 U. Pitt. L. Rev. 993 (1994); David R. Johnson & Kevin A. Marks, Mapping Electronic Data Communications onto Existing Legal Metaphors: Should We Let Our Conscience (and Our Contracts) Be Our Guide?, 38 Vill. L. Rev. 487 (1993).

4. Ellickson, supra note 1, at 123–36.

5. Ellickson, supra note 1, at 127, citing Frank I. Michelman, States' Rights and States' Roles: Permutations of "Sovereignty" in National League of Cities v. Usery, 86 Yale L.J. 1165, 1167 (1977).

6. I use the example of the Georgetown University local area network throughout this chapter purely, it should be stressed, for illustrative purposes.

7. In Ellickson's words, "In a society replete with governments, private organizations, social forces, contractual arrangements, and individuals potentially capable of self-control, there must be rules that decide, for each domain of

human activity, the division of social-control labor among the various controllers. Controller-selecting rules perform this function." Ellickson, supra note 1, at 135.

8. The Communications Decency Act of 1995, S. 314, was introduced on February 1, 1995, by Senator Exon and would subject to criminal and civil liability anyone who "transmits or otherwise makes available" by means of a "telephone or telecommunications device" any "obscene, lewd, lascivious, filthy, or indecent" comment. This has occasioned much controversy; relevant materials can be located at the Electronic Frontier Foundation World Wide Web site.

9. To take another example, the design of the next generation of the hypertext transfer protocol (HTTP)—the set of specifications permitting transmission of World Wide Web documents—is currently being considered by the Internet Engineering Task Force. One of the design goals under consideration for implementation within this new version of HTTP would optimize the *caching* of World Wide Web pages. Caching involves downloading and copying Web pages off of their host machines and onto intermediate servers (a LAN server, for example, or some other individual network host), which enables those users with direct connections to that intermediate host to access those pages without the need to wait for files to be transferred over the Internet. Caching, of course, raises difficult questions under U.S. copyright law. If storing a Web page in a cache constitutes the making of a "copy"—as it well might under the view of such cases as MAI Systems Corp. v. Peak Computer, 991 F.2d 511 (9th Cir. 1993), and Advanced Computer Services v. MA Systems Corp., 845 F. Supp. 356 (E.D. Va. 1994), holding that transitory fixation in RAM constitutes copying for purposes of the Copyright Act—then each instance of caching constitutes prima facie copyright infringement. My point here is not to debate whether copyright law should be interpreted in this manner but rather to note that anyone interested in that question must take a long look at the new HTTP standards, for any view of the copyright rules that will govern on the Internet that does not take these technical rules regarding permissible copying into account will necessarily be sorely deficient.

10. One is reminded of the report that Prodigy examines all electronic mail transmissions for the purpose of identifying those that contain any of the FCC's "seven dirty words," an activity made possible by the centralized architecture of the Prodigy network.

11. The general notion of "exit" derives from Albert O. Hirschman, Exit, Voice, and Loyalty: Responses to Decline in Firms, Organizations, and States (1990).

12. I believe that the controversy spawned by recent attempts to define the liability standards that will be applicable to network administrators and system operators in regard to individual instances of defamation, libel, copyright infringement, and the transmission of obscene material reflects this phenomenon. The few recent court cases that have addressed this issue—e.g., Cubby v. Compuserve, 776 F. Supp. 135 (S.D.N.Y 1991) (holding that a computer service providing subscribers access to an electronic library of news publications inde-

pendently managed for the service was not liable for defamatory statements made in those publications), and Playboy Enterprises v. Frena, 839 F. Supp. 1552 (M.D. Fla. 1993) (holding that the operator of a computer bulletin board was liable for copyright infringement of magazine photographs uploaded by bulletin board users)—have engendered mountains of commentary. See, e.g., Henry H. Perritt Jr., Tort Liability, the First Amendment, and Equal Access to Electronic Networks, 5 Harv. J.L. & Amp. Tech. 65 (1992); Eric Schlacter, Cyberspace, the Free Market and the Free Marketplace of Ideas: Recognizing Legal Differences in Computer Bulletin Board Functions, 16 Hastings Comm./Ent. L.J. 87 (1993); Henry H. Perritt Jr., Metaphors for Understanding Rights and Responsibilities in Network Communities: Print Shops, Barons, Sheriffs, and Bureaucracies; David J. Loundy, E-Law: Legal Issues Affecting Computer Information Systems and System Operator Liability, 3 Alb. L.J. Sci. & Amp. Tech. 79 (1993).

13. The literature on the Internet, and specifically Internet architecture, is vast. I have found the following particularly helpful. Henry H. Perritt Jr., What Is the Internet; John S. Quarterman, The Matrix: Computer Networks and Conferencing Systems Worldwide (1990); Krol & Hoffman, What Is the Internet, Internet Engineering Task Force RFC 1462; Andy Johnson-Laird, The Internet: The Good, the Bad, and the Ugly, Paper presented at the Computer Law Association Annual Meeting, September 29, 1994 (available from the author at andy@jli.portland.or.us); Andy Reinhardt, Building the Data Highway, 19 Byte 46 (1994).

14. The development of the medieval law merchant may represent a close historical analogue to the market for rules in cyberspace, inasmuch as it represents an example of unregulated and unconstrained rule making in the absence of state control. See Hardy, supra note 3, at 1019–21; Paul R. Milgrom, Douglas C. North & Barry R. Weingast, The Role of Institutions in the Revival of Trade: The Law Merchant, Private Judges, and the Champagne Fairs, 2 Econ. & Amp. Pol. 1 (1990); Bruce L. Benson, Customary Law as Social Contract, 3 Const. Pol. Econ. 1 (1992).

15. Imagine, for example, a network in which a "no copyrights will be recognized" rule is declared. Such a rule may be beneficial to all network participants but may impose costs on nonparticipants (that is, individuals who hold intellectual property that has value under other rule sets but whose value is diminished because of the free copying available to the network participants).

15

Prop 13 Meets the Internet: How State and Local Government Finances Are Becoming Road Kill on the Information Superhighway

Nathan Newman

The 1990s have been a time of increasing debate over turning more federal functions of government over to states, cities and counties. While much of the battle between Democrats and Republican forces led by Newt Gingrich focused on the amount of money to spend on such functions, largely undebated was whether state and local governments had a revenue base that could deal with the demands being handed to them.

What is clear is that, while many local governments gained some temporary stability in the boom of the mid-90s after years of cities like New York and Los Angeles teetering on the edge of bankruptcy, the new technology of the Internet and the global economic changes accompanying it promise to deal a final body blow to the financial security of local governments. Local governments could once count on local economic development to produce local jobs where local employees could spend money in local stores, thereby generating local tax revenue for further development. This virtuous cycle has been fatally undermined by the new technology of cyberspace. Even as many states and local areas hope for increased revenue due to high-technology-based growth, it becomes harder and harder for local government to capture much of that growth in local tax revenue. There is an irony (or more specifically a strategy) that Newt Gingrich, the leader of the conservative movement to hand government responsibilities to local government, was also the foremost congressional promoter of Tofflerian views of a "third-wave" economy

This chapter is a revised version of chapter 6 of his University of California, Berkeley, dissertation. Reprinted by permission of the author. © Nathan Newman, 2001.

—the very high-tech global economy that was rendering local governments unable to deal with taxation of increasingly global commerce.

This chapter will outline not only the fiscal squeeze on local sales taxes due to networking technology, but how that squeeze follows the pattern set by Proposition 13 and other property-tax-limitation measures that themselves responded to the earlier wave of increasing global speculation in local housing markets. The pressures of responding to the global economy have fractured the ability of local government to effectively push forward long-term economic development, and as rich communities have increasingly abandoned participation and financial contributions to shared regional economic development, economic inequality has increased between communities within regions. This "opt-out" by rich communities over shared investment through local government parallels the opt-out by the wealthy from the local banking, power, and phone systems that had once promoted some degree of equity within regions.

A House of Cards

The key to the fiscal crisis facing local governments is the expansion of interstate retail sales of goods ranging from computers to Christmas sweaters, sales that go untaxed due to a 1967 U.S. Supreme Court ruling barring such state taxes on interstate commerce. That fact is good news for the consumer (and often a key sales advantage of mail-order and Internet sales outfits) but is a potential catastrophe for the state and local governments dependent on sales-tax revenue.

By 1994, states were already losing at least $3.3 billion in revenue each year because of retail sales that have migrated to mail-order businesses, as estimated by the U.S. Advisory Commission on Intergovernmental Relations (an agency that brings together representatives of state governments to improve the effect of federal policy on the states.)[1] And that estimate is based on pre-Internet technology. With the growth of the Internet and on-line sales, consumer access to a nationwide and worldwide marketplace is expanding exponentially. At a push of a button, consumers increasingly have access to the lowest-priced goods nationwide and, with the bonus of avoiding sales taxes, interstate sales promise to explode over the Internet, leaving state and local government in tatters.

Ironically, California, at the heart of the new Internet technology, is likely to feel the most severe effects of this change. Because of Proposition 13's limits on property-tax revenue, state and local governments in California are extremely dependent on sales taxes to fund their budgets, so any increase in untaxed interstate sales at the expense of local retail will be magnified there. Wally Dean, mayor of Cupertino (the birthplace of Apple Computer) in 1995, summed up the shock his government colleagues would soon be feeling as Internet sales took off in the next few years, undermining their traditional tax and economic development goals:

The thing that scares us is that cities are run on local sales tax; if stuff is sold on the Internet, there's no sales tax. It's a house of cards for government finances. This could be the Achilles heel for state and local government. And it's an invisible problem. The average retailer has no clue what a computer is .... it's not in their vocabulary. It's changing that where you once had a manufacturer selling to a wholesaler to a retailer. If this gets hot, you'll have a manufacturer going on the Internet and selling directly to the mass market—bypassing the sales tax. We once built city government on local manufacturers and sales: you didn't think globally. This will mess with a lot of people's heads.[2]

How Real Is the Danger of the Internet to Local Taxes?

There has also been an explosion of business-to-business sales over the Internet (most of it taxed normally, for reasons detailed later in this chapter). Computer companies like Cisco lead the way with over $1 billion in on-line sales in 1996 and companies like General Electric moved $1 billion alone in contracting on-line. Retail sales on-line have lagged behind these amounts, with an estimated $200 million in direct Internet sales in 1994 exploding exponentially each year to reach $2.6 billion in total retail sales by 1997.[3] Business web sites exploded in the period with 34 percent of Fortune 500 companies having a Web site in 1995 growing to 80 percent by the end of 1996. Computer-related products have led the way on retail Internet sales, with Dell computers, a pioneer in mail-order leading on the Web with $3 million per day of PC sales by 1998.[4] Non-computer companies pioneering use of the Web included restaurants like the Virginia Diner which does 75 percent of its business by mail and used a Web page to expand its reach globally[5] along with compact disk companies and stores pioneering direct sales of automobiles over the Net. One of the most remarkable retail success stories on the Net became, of all things, a bookstore. Started in 1995, Amazon.com, an Internet-only store based in Seattle, would be making $16 million in sales by the first quarter of 1997 with sales doubling each quarter. (Its summer 1997 IPO would raise $54 million.) While books might be a retro success, Amazon.com's ability to list 2.5 million in-print books (which it in turn orders from book publishers and warehouses on demand from retail customers) far outstrips the available books at local bookstores. This highlights the advantages of online stores that can virtually bring together all the products a consumer might desire. Combined with search engines, online reviews, and discounts, Amazon.com became a symbol of the promise of online commerce and the threat to local retail merchants.[6]

Even where sales are not made directly over the Net, an expanded online presence has made it easier for many companies to expand and build trust in traditional mail-order operations, even if the final sale ultimately happens over the telephone. Mark Masotto of CommerceNet observed, "Clearly, you'll see more and more stories emerging of how putting information on the Internet is reducing the number of phone calls and number of brochures distributed. There are intangibles of being able to provide information twenty-four hours a day and not having to have people on the phone all the time to service an international market. The medium provides much more possibility to do interactive support: you can read and search information, immediately pull up the information you are interested in rather than looking through a whole catalog of information. It makes the person reading the information more effective in finding information."[7]

While full security for Internet transactions has come slower than many companies had hoped, Internet sales have still jumped at such a high rate that fully secure payment schemes promise advances in Internet commerce far beyond the most technologically optimistic earlier predictions.

As Internet commerce grows into the tens and hundreds of billions of dollars range in the coming decade, this will just add to the revenue losses by local governments on interstate retail sales. Presently, well over $200 billion in interstate sales, most of it free of sales tax, is generated

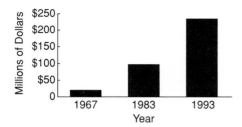

Figure 15.1
Total mail order sales, 1967 to 1993

by mail-order merchandisers, video marketers, credit card processors, and similar companies that operate without local offices.[8] Driven by an earlier generation of telecommunications and computer technology advances, the mail-order industry has grown phenomenally in the last few decades. Total mail-order sales grew from only $2.4 billion in 1967 to over $237 billion in sales by 1993, extraordinary growth even when accounting for inflation[9] (see figure 15.1).

At the same time, sales taxes have emerged as a big revenue source for state governments and often an even larger source of revenue for local governments. Beginning in the early 1980s, the federal government began to cut funding to the states, forcing state and local governments to pay for more and more services out of local budgets. Sales taxes often became the revenue of choice. De facto, state governments substituted local sales taxes for federal income taxes cut in the early Reagan years. Fully forty-four states (and the District of Columbia) now impose taxes on retail sales, revenue that accounts for 25 percent of states' annual income. With income taxes increasingly hard to increase and with tax limitation laws like Proposition 13 making it harder to raise property taxes, sales taxes have become the most attractive way to raise local revenues.[10] By 1997 states were raising $132.2 billion from sales taxes, one-third of their total revenue, whereas in 1950 sales taxes had been just 20 percent of revenue.[11]

These two trends—more out-of-state sales and a greater dependence by local governments on sales taxes—are now on a collision course. Even if smaller out-of-state mail firms are ignored, the U.S. Advisory Commission on Intergovernmental Relations has estimated that $3.3 billion in sales taxes are lost each year by states. Nine states lost over $100 million in 1994 revenue, with California's loss of $483 million topping the list (see table 15.1). These amounts represent 2.4 percent of total sales-tax collections.[12] As mail-order sales grow under the impact of the Internet and other technologies, the impact is likely to become even more severe. In a report released by the National Governors Association in association in 1997, the increasingly loss of sales tax revenue because of the new technology was cited, along with federal cuts in Medicaid, as one of the top budgetary threats to state government finances.[13]

For many local governments that suffered budget cutbacks throughout the 1980s and early 1990s, the effect could be even more devastating. While many cities in Silicon Valley became more flush with funds from the economic boom due to the Internet, this new stability hardly made up for the cuts suffered during the bad times. After slashing budgets by $293 million a year in the early 1990s, Santa Clara County finally balanced its budget in 1997 with an $8 million surplus[14]—hardly making a dint toward restoring funds previously cut despite the economic boom. And the irony is that Santa Clara County, encompassing much of Silicon Valley, is one of the California counties most vulnerable to lost sales-tax revenue.

At the county level, Santa Clara County actually outpaces the larger Los Angeles, San Diego, and Orange Counties in the percentage of tax revenue coming from sales taxes and in the total revenue from sales taxes, despite the larger population sizes of those other counties. Cities are even more vulnerable than counties, with many smaller cities receiving almost all tax revenue from the sales tax. It is not surprising that the mayor of Cupertino was ahead of the curve in worrying about this threat to his city's finances: Cupertino depends on sales taxes for 81 percent of all taxes collected in the city, making it one of the most sales-tax-dependent cities in California. Even including nontax revenue sources such as state aid, fines, and service charges for utilities, Cupertino still depends on the sales tax for 45 percent of city revenues. However, in absolute terms it is clear that the large urban cities like Los Angeles, San Francisco, San Diego, and San Jose have billions in revenue at threat from the new technology. (See tables 15.2 and 15.3 for the most vulner-

Table 15.1
Total tax lost by states to mail order, 1994

State	Untaxed Sales (millions of dollars)	State	Untaxed Sales (millions of dollars)
Alabama	$48.6	Montana	0.0
Alaska	0.0	Nebraska	17.4
Arizona	44.4	Nevada	17.4
Arkansas	19.6	New Hampshire	0.0
California	482.8	New Jersey	112.2
Colorado	47.9	New Mexico	16.8
Connecticut	50.4	New York	359.4
Delaware	0.0	North Carolina	71.1
District of Columbia	9.9	North Dakota	5.8
Florida	168.9	Ohio	116.3
Georgia	72.9	Oklahoma	41.8
Hawaii	9.8	Oregon	0.0
Idaho	9.7	Pennsylvania	145.0
Illinois	233.1	Rhode Island	14.2
Indiana	54.5	South Carolina	31.3
Iowa	28.3	South Dakota	7.3
Kansas	33.5	Tennessee	68.8
Kentucky	41.7	Texas	235.2
Louisiana	61.9	Utah	16.8
Maine	13.3	Vermont	6.0
Maryland	60.1	Virginia	59.9
Massachusetts	69.0	Washington	76.2
Michigan	108.4	West Virginia	18.6
Minnesota	53.1	Wisconsin	46.6
Mississippi	28.0	Wyoming	4.4
Missouri	63.5	Total, all states	$3,301.5

Source: U.S. Advisory Commission on Intergovernmental Relations, *Taxation of Interstate Mail Order Sales: 1994 Revenue Estimates* (Washington, DC: Government Printing Office, 1994).

Table 15.2

California counties most vulnerable to sales Tax Losses, 1993

A.   Top ten vulnerable counties by total sales taxes

	Total Sales Taxes (millions of dollars)	Taxes from Sales Tax (percentage)
Sacramento	95.5	29
Santa Clara	78.8	17
Los Angeles	75.3	3
Kern	22.9	12
Riverside	21.1	8
San Bernadino	19.2	7
San Diego	17.3	4
Orange	16.4	3
Alameda	12.1	4
Monterey	11.7	16

B.   Top ten vulnerable counties by sales taxes as a percentage of all county taxes

	Taxes from Sales Tax (percentage)	Total Sales Taxes (millions of dollars)
Mariposa	56	4.1
Sacramento	29	95.5
Del Norte	25	0.8
Plumas	24	1.7
Mendocino	23	5.6
Trinity	23	0.7
Nevada	21	4.4
Tuolumne	21	3.4
Alpine	20	0.3
Santa Clara	17	78.8

Source: Municipal Analysis Services, *Governments of California: 1993 Annual Financial and Employee Analysis* (Austin, TX: MAS, 1993).

Table 15.3
California cities most vulnerable to sales tax losses, 1993

A.   Top ten most vulnerable cities by sales taxes as a percentage of all city taxes

	Taxes from Sales Tax (percentage)	Total Sales Taxes (millions of dollars)
Colma	98	4.2
Bellflower	92	5.3
Cupertino	81	9.4
Mammoth Lakes	78	3.1
Capitola	73	3.8
El Cajon	72	14.5
Carmel by the Sea	72	4.4
Ukiah	71	2.3
Lakewood	70	8.0
Hesperia	70	3.2

B.   Top ten most vulnerable cities by total sales taxes

	Total Sales Tax (millions of dollars)	Taxes from Sales Tax (percentage)
Los Angeles	778.3	42
San Francisco	235.7	25
San Diego	193.4	52
San Jose	148.6	46
Sacramento	92.8	59
Long Beach	78.6	49
Oakland	63.8	30
Anaheim	61.0	56
Fresno	51.9	48
Torrance	50.2	64

Source: Municipal Analysis Services, *Governments of California: 1993 Annual Financial and Employee Analysis* (Austin, TX: MAS, 1993).

able cities and counties as measured by absolute sales-tax amounts collected and as a percentage of local taxes derived from sales taxes.)[15]

Why States Can't Collect Mail-Order Taxes: The *Quill* Decision

The obvious response to the loss of mail-order and Internet-based sales taxes would be to allow states to tax such sales directly. However, the U.S. Supreme Court in its 1967 *National Bellas Hess v. Department of Revenue* decision prohibited states from taxing out-of-state companies selling to state residents, basing its decision on the Commerce Clause of the U.S. Constitution. The heart of that clause of the Constitution is to take regulation of commerce, including taxation, away from the control of local government in cases where the scale of that commerce has grown beyond the confines of one state. In the case of mail order, the view of the Court was that businesses operating in one state could not be taxed by another state merely because residents of that other state were buying the company's products through the federal mail system. With the explosion of mail order commerce and the ubiquity of catalogs, direct marketing and other changes in technology to reach customers, there had been some hope in states that the Supreme Court might alter what was considered "in-state" commerce, but in its May 1992 *Quill Corp. v. North Dakota* decision, the Supreme Court reaffirmed that mail-order firms were exempt from state sales taxes. By creating an extremely tough standard in defining in-state sales, technically called *nexus* in the law, the Supreme Court made it clear that Internet-based sales would be treated as out-of-state, tax-free transactions.

In a sense, Quill Corp., which at the center of the 1992 decision, exemplifies the danger states face from out-of-state sales and new networking technology. Quill is based in Delaware with offices and warehouses in Illinois, California and Georgia. Quill sells office supplies, stationery, and equipment, offering over 9,500 different products ranging from paper clips to computers, with annual sales in excess of $340 million in 1992, making Quill one of the largest mail-order companies in the country, just behind L. L. Bean and Lands' End.[16]

Quill solicits business through its numerous catalogs and flyers, advertisement in nationally distributed "card packs," in national periodicals, and through telephone solicitations. Of the more that 200,000 orders that Quill was receiving by the time of the court decision in 1992, approximately half were by telephone. The remaining half, however, were received by mail, fax, telex, and, increasingly, direct computer contact. Utilizing computer technologies to expand its business, Quill leased computer software that permitted customers to directly contact Quill's computers for direct orders.[17] Quill rapidly supplemented this with online ordering through a Web site as the Internet took off.

When the state of North Dakota attempted to impose state sales taxes on Quill, the state argued to the courts that the nature of direct marketing had created a "ubiquitous presence" in the state through the mail, telephone, and electronic solicitations in the state far beyond what the Supreme Court had envisioned when it banned interstate sales taxes in its 1967 decision. If states were to survive as fiscal units, the state basically argued, the courts had to recognize that the new technology made companies a part of the local economy just as much as if they had sales people in the downtown mall. But in the *Quill* decision, the Supreme Court held to its "bright-line" rule that physical presence by company personnel in a state was required to trigger sales taxes. The logic was that without such personnel present, the company was receiving no benefits from state services so it need not pay taxes. Thus Quill would pay taxes in Delaware, Illinois, California, and Georgia, where it had employees, but in no other states.[18]

So, rather than the new technologies of direct marketing making companies more subject to sales taxes as they collapse geographic distances for their customers, the use of toll-free numbers, computer databases, and the Internet itself would allow direct marketing companies to further dispense with the need for placing sales personnel, inventory, or showrooms within most states. Such technologies would actually help such companies avoid creating the physical presence that would trigger the "nexus" that would force them to collect sales taxes. As Internet Web pages located on servers in far-distant states increasingly replace catalogs mailed to people's homes, it is clear that the physical connection between retailers and states trying to tax them will increasingly recede even farther.

Why Saving the Sales Tax Requires More Intrusive Government Regulation

The irony of the movement toward local control and decentralizing government is that the increased dependence on local taxes and revenue in an increasingly global retail market is pushing governments towards policies of more burdensome regulation on business and more intrusive government on the individual in order to collect those out-of-state sales taxes. As local regions becoming increasingly artificial boundaries for government jurisdiction, even more jerry-rigged regulations are attempted to salvage regional financial health.

In the *Quill* decision, the Supreme Court did leave open the option that, while the states could not unilaterally impose sales taxes on interstate commerce, the Congress itself could establish such a tax and remit the proceeds to the respective states. Senator Dale Bumpers (Democrat from Arkansas) was author of the tax Fairness for Main Street Business Act of 1994, which would have established such a tax, but the bill failed in the face of opposition from the Direct Marketing Association and allied business and consumer groups, including the American Council of the Blind, Disabled American Veterans, and the National Alliance of Senior Citizens.[19] An earlier similar bill introduced in the House of Representatives back in 1989 never made it out of committee in the face of half a million angry letters to members of Congress generated by the same direct-mail technology used by the industry in generating its business nationwide.[20] In late 1997, local governments and representatives of the Direct Marketing Association were close to an agreement where firms would voluntarily collect sales taxes for states in exchange for limits on state audits and the right to expand their presence within target states without invoking nexus for tax purposes. However, when the imminent deal was reported about in the *New York Times*, the affluent customers of direct retailers like L. L. Bean generated such a volume of complaining phone calls to the retailers that they backed out of the deal.[21] With new legislation moving forward in Congress by 1997, sponsored by Californian Republican Chris Cox, to firmly prohibit states from collecting revenue on Internet-based retail sales, it was clear that any hopes for states collecting on interstate sales was dimming. The worry of Congress was in promoting global commerce on the Internet, not preserving the fiscal survival of local budgets (an issue we will return to at the end of this article in discussing the Cox bill in the context of states and economic development).

Aside from the pleas of shut-ins and the disabled, the heart of the argument against compelling the collection of local sales taxes by direct marketers is the administrative burden of national marketing being subject to the ever-changing tax laws of thousands of separate government jurisdictions. With forty-six states, the District of Columbia, and more than six thousand counties, cities, and school districts each collecting their own sales taxes, the complexity of tracking tax rates in each area and dealing with local government authorities would overwhelm many businesses.[22] Some argue that the computers that allow direct mail to boom could be used to ease the burden of calculating the tax costs, but the burden of dealing with so many separate government authorities remains.

Arnold Miller, treasurer of Quill, argued in the company's legal brief against the "untold hardship" of paying deposits, quarterly returns, and dealing with audits in many jurisdictions. Miller had once worked at Sears Roebuck and Co., which through its stores had nexus in all states, and noted that Sears underwent at least five audits at any time. Sears could endure the burden because they could afford 25 professionals dealing solely with tax issues, a luxury smaller direct marketing firms could not afford.[23] And while local tax issues were probably not the only reason, Sears discontinued its mail-order catalog business in 1993 in favor of licensing its database of customers and addresses to specialty catalogs like Hanover Direct of Weehawken, New Jersey, a company that escapes nexus in other states and thereby avoids sales-tax burdens.[24] When Spiegel, the largest catalog direct marketer in the United States, acquired retailers Honeybee and Eddie Bauer, it suddenly was hit with nexus in thirty-four states. "You really do need a lot of computer power," noted Spiegel investor relations officer Debby Koopman. "For example, some states like Massachusetts and Connecticut exclude clothing mail-order sales up to a certain amount, say $75. Other states have one rate for shoes that are classed as clothing and another for shoes that are classed as athletic equipment."[25] The exact costs of forcing companies to collect sales taxes in all jurisdictions is unclear, but estimates place the costs at a 10 to 20 percent increase in operating costs to comply,[26] while other analyses estimate it costs out-of-state companies 50 percent more to collect the same sales taxes as in-state local retailers. All of this is aside from any extra costs of filing statements with all the different government jurisdictions.[27]

The other alternative to having retail companies collect taxes is to have states directly tax consumers on a "use tax" in place of a sales tax. States can already legally do this, and they can step up their efforts to collect use taxes directly from end consumers. Companies with resale permits in any state are already required in their routine sales-tax audits to prove they pay tax on everything purchased for their own use. And for individuals, some states are already using computerized records from U.S. Customs to bill residents for purchases made abroad that are subject to use taxes. The Software Industry Coalition, one of the main Silicon Valley voices in the sales-tax debate, advocated that all states add a line to their state income-tax forms specifically for sales tax on goods purchased out-of-state, thereby transferring the burden of sales-tax collection (and possible audits by the government) from business to the consumer.[28]

To collect such taxes from individuals, some have suggested that states could begin collecting information on sales directly from private sources such as individual credit card and checking account records. No state has dared to do this, but legislators may move in that direction if their sales-tax revenues continue to fall. Some states, like California, prohibit such actions with strong privacy guarantees in their state constitutions. But in other places, we have the specter of a consumption-based equivalent of the Internal Revenue Service appearing to audit individual purchases.[29] This intrusion of government into peoples' private lives would be an ironic result of the decentralization promoted by conservatives in the name of "getting government off peoples' backs."

Sales Taxes and the Effects on the Poor

The other major problem with the increasing use of the sales tax as a revenue source is its disproportionate burden on the poor and working families. Beyond lobbying on behalf of their own economic self-interest,

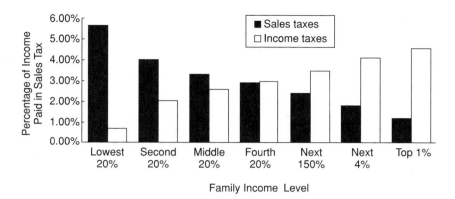

Figure 15.2
State and local taxes in 1991 as share of income for a family of four

direct marketers trumpet the burdens on the elderly, the disabled, and poorer rural residents of taxing mail-order sales. While there is a certain cynicism in this "concern" by the Direct Marketing Association as they have trotted out allies from the disabled and elderly communities before the US Congress, there is also a strong truth to their argument that taxing consumer sales impacts the poor more than anyone else.

Study after study has shown the regressive nature of sales taxes as a revenue source. The most comprehensive study was by Citizens for Tax Justice in their 1991 report *A Far Cry from Fair*. In that survey of all taxes collected by local governments, the report argued that "excessive reliance on sales and excise taxes is certainly the hallmark of regressive taxation." Across the country, the report found that in 1991 the poorest 20 percent of families were paying 5.7 percent of their income in state sales taxes, while the richest 1 percent paid only 1.2 percent of their income in sales taxes: the poor paid nearly five times the tax rate paid by the rich (see Figure 15.2). This contrasts sharply with the much more progressive state income tax. Across the country, the average state personal income tax for a family of four is only 0.7 percent for the poorest 20 percent of residents and 4.6 percent of the income of the richest 1 percent.[30]

Because of the regressive nature of sales taxes, states that depend on them, such as Washington and Texas, have the highest tax rates in the country for the poor. Including in property taxes (which burden the poor as part of their rent), total state and local taxes in Washington state were 17.4 percent of the income of the poorest 20 percent. Contrast that with neighboring Oregon, which has a state income tax and where the poorest 20 percent paid only 9.8 percent of their income in state and local taxes. The results are clear that depending on sales taxes leads to the heaviest taxation burdens on those least able to pay.

Many analysts worry that Internet sales are making this tax inequality worse, since upper-income taxpayers with computers have increasing access to a world of tax-free goods ordered over the Internet, while those with fewest resources are stuck buying locally and paying sales taxes on their purchases. The Center on Budget and Policy Priorities has argued that untaxed Internet sales "create a vicious cycle leading to an ever more regressive sales tax. The erosion of the sales tax base resulting from online purchasing by businesses and affluent consumers would force states and localities to raise sales tax rates, encouraging more online buying, forcing further rounds of rate increases, until the lowest-income population groups unable to buy online would be left paying an ever-greater share of sales taxes."[31]

Technology, Suburbanization, and Prop 13

While the economic losses and regressive tax burden due to dependence on sales taxes is a prime concern for regional economic planners, the deeper problem is the fracturing of the tax base as cities find themselves having to more desperately compete for retail outlet revenue rather than cooperate in expanding general growth. As cities polarize over this competition, it further increases inequality within regions and, given the regressive nature of sales taxes, increases overall inequality.

Before turning to how this regional competition for sales tax is undermining economic development, it is important to understand the context of this problem in a longer history of regional polarization around tax policy and development. With California's growth over the last decades, the polarization there was most intense. This polarization culminated in Prop 13's passage in 1978 based on an earlier round of technology-induced economic changes that skewed and then exploded regional fiscal stability and planning.

In the postwar period, property taxes, not sales taxes, were the key tax source for local governments. The economic expansion of the 1950s and 1960s not only created economic growth by increasing the number of home owners but created the funding base for continued local expansion of services through this new class of property taxpayers. Homeowners, construction workers, community builders, and regional development as a whole supported each other in a virtuous cycle of expansion.[32] However, the economic and technological changes of the late 1960s and 1970s undermined that virtuous cycle and fractured the political unity that had supported broadly distributed growth.

The same computer and communication technology that was allowing the new middle classes to take their money out of local banks and invest in the global markets was also creating the global investment markets that prowled the country for local property investments as a hedge against the inflation of the 1970s. Investors in the US and around the globe were playing increasingly speculative games in the housing market, especially in the booming growth cities of California. Housing prices began to escalate wildly, setting the stage for the coming tax revolt of Prop 13 and its sisters across the country. Where housing inflation in the 1950s and 60s had been two-thirds of general inflation, in the 1970s that relationship reversed. In some areas of California, housing prices that had been increasing 2 to 3 percent every year in the mid-1960s increased 2 to 3 percent *every month* by 1976.[33]

It was not just financial speculation that drove these housing prices upward but a new dynamic of slow-growth politics and "suburban separatism" that began to dry up available development areas, increasing the premium on housing prices of those areas that were developed. Especially in the upper-middle-class communities of the new high-tech millionaires, slow-growth ordinances began springing up and were copied on down the economic scale. By 1975, most cities and counties in California had some form of growth-control policies, thereby vastly increasingly the value of uncontrolled land. Speculation exploded, and in extreme cases, such as Orange County, almost half of all single-family homes built were bought by speculators.[34]

Mike Davis in his book *City of Quartz* contrasts the "Keynesian suburbanization" of the 1960s and early 1970s, where local finance supported local growth, with the "new Octopus" of giant developers pulling in financial backing from global markets. With the price of land rising dramatically, many of the old railroad companies and industrial concerns found their landholdings to be their most valuable resource. Developing land often became their new economic focus. These new developers came into increasing political confrontation with the new upper-income suburbanites who were developing their own strategies to maintain their incomes while severing their ties to general growth politics of the region. The goal of these new suburbanites was to slow development in their own communities to preserve their quality of life and escape the economic burden of providing services to new residents, particularly poor residents of the region. This clash between developer and suburbanite elites would culminate in the battle over Prop 13. In its aftermath, both elites would sever almost all remaining alliances with working-class and urban forces that had once fueled general growth politics.[35]

Beginning in the 1950s, wealth and racial divisions had fueled the creation of an escalating number of municipal incorporations divided from urban core areas. Previously, homeowner covenants and organizations had enforced racial segregation while keeping most citizens within the same fiscal and political jurisdiction. When the Supreme Court declared such covenants illegal in the 1940s, the old homeowner associations began to mobilize to find new strategies for racial separation, which would soon be joined with the goal of fiscal separation from the poor as well. In the past, separate incorporation of a municipality had been a possibility only for the wealthiest enclaves like Beverly Hills, but the passage in California of the 1956 Bradley-Burns Act radically changed the fiscal calculus of incorporation. Bradley-Burns allowed any local government to collect a 1 percent sales tax exclusively for its own use, a key tool for suburban separatism where fringe areas with a shopping center could now finance city government without needing much of a property tax. This was combined with new arrangements by local governments to have counties contract (usually at cut rates) to perform basic services, leaving the new towns with control of zoning without the fiscal hassles of managing most services. As Davis argues, "Sacramento [the capital of California] licensed suburban governments to pay for their contracted county services with regressive sales revenues rather than progressive property taxes—a direct subsidy to suburban separatism at the expense of the weakened tax bases of primate cities."[36] The first step on local dependence on sales taxes had begun.

Upper-income homeowners began exiting cities to avoid paying the standard taxes to support urban infrastructure. Davis notes the distinct "gradient" of home values between each incorporation with lower-middle-class, middle-class, upper-middle-class, and wealthy communities neatly divided by the new jurisdictional lines of incorporation and zoning. With poor people and their need for services zoned out of these new towns, this fiscal zoning would help suck jobs out of the inner city to these minimal-service, low-tax areas. Racial and income divides would expand between these jurisdictions. As well, federal and state spending on highways and other traditional urban spending would facilitate this fiscal succession by providing the critical infrastructure that once required regional growth alliances and planning. And by creating divisions between municipalities, capital investors interested in development could now more easily demand economic concessions from weaker fiscal units desperate for new revenue sources following the departure of the upper-income municipal residents.[37]

What is striking is that just as massive regulation was necessary for that same upper-income elite to secede from common banking and utilities systems in regions, it took strong government regulation to assist them in preserving their segregated residential enclaves. From providing them their own sales taxes apart from shared revenue streams to assisting them in delivering basic services separate from regional systems, the state and federal governments nurtured these enclaves. And these upper-income homeowners, normally advocates of free markets in other aspects of the economy, would promote what conservative commentator George Will labeled "Sunbelt Bolshevism"[38] in their extensive system of land regulation, growth controls, and other zoning to undermine housing markets that might otherwise have brought "undesirables" into their municipal districts.

At the same time it was a combination of government action (and refusal to take action) in support of the developer interests that put the suburban separatists on a collision course with growth economics, leading to the further splintering of economic development due to Proposition 13. Even as money-market funds and other new financial tools were leveraging personal savings out of local finance markets into speculative global markets, thereby naturally fueling intensified investments in real estate, the government actually began expanding subsidies for real estate, adding fuel to an already growing speculative fire. Through an alphabet soup of institutions—FNMA, GNMA, FHLMC, REITs—in combination with a range of tax advantages, the government was encouraging new flows of capital to bid up the price of housing throughout the 1970s.[39] The Federal Home Loan Bank Board was well aware that housing was being increasingly priced out of the reach of average homeowners, but it refused to do anything other than issue toothless warning to the savings and loan institutions it governed not to lend to speculators who did not plan to reside in property they were buying. Tighter regulation or a windfall profits tax on speculation could have gone a long way toward cooling the speculation that was turning housing from a prop of regional growth economics into a plaything for global investing.[40]

The result of the clash between speculation and suburban slow-growth controls was that in the four years before passage of Proposition 13 in 1978, property taxes on California homeowners doubled. By 1978, the typical homeowner was paying four times as much for property taxes as for mortgage payments.[41] Compounding the indignity for property taxpayers, the state government was running a budget surplus of $3 billion, which Governor Jerry Brown was neither spending on social programs nor returning as a tax cut but was instead sitting on as proof of his fiscal responsibility.

The Prop 13 results were not foreordained; the earliest roots of the tax revolt were among lower-middle-class property owners feeling the economic squeeze; they were open to alliances that could have been more economically populist. But in both California and Massachusetts (where a similar Prop 2 1/2 was passed soon after Prop 13), initial attempts by progressive tax-reform activists to ally with those squeezed by these new global forces of speculation were abandoned in favor of alliances with developers and big business in what became the last hurrah in California of the old broad-based growth coalition. In the fight against Proposition 13, social spending liberals and unions were joined by the broad economic elite of the state, from Bank of America to the California Tax-payers Association, the main lobby for large corporations. The California Republican Party even refused to endorse Proposition 13. The alliance by progressives with the increasingly global banks and developers, however, meant that no alternative solution to the tax pressures on lower-income homeowners was pushed forcefully.

This, in turn, left the way open for upper-middle-class homeowners in rich communities like Sherman Oaks to give a more conservative bent to the tax revolt. Clarence Lo, in his classic study of the class dynamics of the Proposition 13 battle, describes how

upper-middle class homeowners drove down from the scenic hills of the Palos Verdes peninsula ... back to the unwashed Toyota Tercels gridlocking Ventura Boulevard [where] they mingled with the K-Mart shoppers of Van Nuys.... Joining the less affluent in mass meetings, the homeowners of Rolling Hills Estates and Sherman Oaks eventually took the lead in organizing and shaping the entire tax limitation movement.[42]

The new tax revolt was linked to anti-school-busing movements and other political campaigns that race-baited welfare programs. With the help of right-wing politicians like Howard Jarvis, this alliance of suburban separatists would surge to an overwhelming margin of victory, 65–35 percent. Despite the racial overtones of the tax-revolt movements, the reality of a broad-based problem with property taxes was shown in a victory where even 42 percent of African Americans voted for the measure.

However, Proposition 13 would have devastating effects on local governments' financial stability, especially those in poor inner-city areas, and would lead to the final fracture of any growth alliances between city and suburb, and, as important, between the global economic investors and their traditional urban-union partners in regional growth alliances. Large corporations had opposed Prop 13, partly fearing it would be followed by a round of increases in corporate and bank taxes to make up for the shortfall. When that populist reaction failed to appear, they began to enjoy their economic windfall from the tax revolt, and much of the corporate elite shifted political allegiances to the emerging Reaganite tax revolt nationally. Of the $5.5 billion in taxes cut by Proposition 13, $3.5 billion went to businesses and landlords, a model of corporate enrichment that would be replicated nationally. While particular battles over development would be fought between the suburban separatists and the corporate developers, they soon made peace over a shared enthusiasm over the mutual benefits they received from the tax revolt. (At the same time, the results of cumulative tax changes, including increases in social security taxes, meant that between 1977 and 1990, the poorest 90 percent of taxpayers ended up paying more, not less, in taxes than before the "tax revolt.")[43]

Sales Taxes and the Distortions of Economic Development

Lenny Goldberg, the head of the progressive California Tax Reform Association in the 1990s, has written that "The most noted irony of Proposition 13 is the extent to which it decimated the fiscal powers of local government and transferred power decisively to Sacramento—an irony because the major source of tax problem in 1978 was Sacramento, not local government."[44] After worries about local control, the post–Prop 13 result was, to take one example, a change from state government supplying less than 25 percent of school funding before the tax initiative to the state supplying over two-thirds of school funding by the 1990s. Local government lost almost all fiscal power to leverage new growth and the divisions between the fractured municipal jurisdictions made regional economic planning a near impossibility.

The shift from property taxes to sales taxes as the main source of local tax revenue created further distortions and perversities in how economic development impacted upon communities. The inflexibility of Proposition 13's funding formulas (all property is assessed at its 1975 value or whenever it last changed hands, adjusted for inflation by no more than 2 percent each year) meant that governments could not capture most of the results of growth as reflected in increasing property values. Since new-housing developments often would not pay for themselves, especially over the long term as the inflation-adjusted value of taxes paid would fall, local governments began increasing up-front fees on construction—$3 billion a year in California in fees with an average of $10,000 per unit. Essentially, while the old homeowners who pushed Prop 13 would reap a massive capital gains windfall, new homebuyers (including any inner-city residents seeking to move to the suburbs) would have to prepay a large share of development costs. Since growth could not generate the tax revenue needed to sustain many of the social services and amenities that once accompanied such growth, from schools to parks to museums, Proposition 13 further justified slow-growth policies. And since commercial property is covered by Prop 13, the measure breeds inefficient uses of property by businesses that survive only because they are paying so much less in property taxes than new businesses that have to pay dramatically higher taxes.[45]

With Californians paying less in property taxes (in real dollars) than they did back in 1977, and 75 percent less in property taxes than if Prop 13 had never been passed, local governments have had to increasingly depend on sales taxes to pay for social services of all kinds. This has led to a desperate competition between cities for the location of retail outlets, a competition that itself not only prevents strong regional cooperation but itself undermines revenue as cities financially subsidize such outlets. Even as Silicon Valley boomed, cities like San Jose still found themselves subsidizing retail expansion as the simplest way to capture the fruits of that growth. *The San Jose Mercury News* highlighted the example of San Jose offering the electronics superstore Fry's Electronics a no-interest loan amounting to a $1 million subsidy. The paper bemoaned the fact that "reliance on sales tax leads some cities to favor building superstores over industries that offer good-paying jobs. It discourages cities from adding housing, since more residents mean more city costs but not necessarily more revenue."[46]

Greg LeRoy, now research director at the Service Employees International Union, described in his book *No More Candy Store* how local and state government subsidies create a desperate competition for the location of retail establishments with little evidence that such subsidies create any new jobs overall; they merely move them from one location to another. The tax revolt that started in 1978 has just accelerated that trend of subsidies. LeRoy notes that in 1977, only nine states gave tax credits for research and development; by 1993, thirty-four states did. In 1977, only eight states allowed cities and counties to lend for construction, and now forty-five do; only twenty states gave low-interest, tax-exempt revenue-bond loans, now forty-four do; only twenty-one states gave corporate income-tax exemptions, now thirty-six do.[47] In the

March 1995 Federal Reserve of Minneapolis economic newsletter *The Region*, Melvin Burstein and Arthur Rolnick (general counsel and director of research respectively for the bank) argued that in regards to the competition between states over economic subsidies:

> Though it is rational for individual states to compete for specific businesses, the overall economy is worse off for their efforts. Economists have found that if states are prohibited from competing for specific businesses there will be more public and private goods for all citizens to consume .... In general, it can be shown that the optimal tax (the tax that distorts the least) is one that is uniformly applied to all businesses. Allowing states to have a discriminatory tax policy, one that is based on location preferences or degree of mobility, therefore, will result in the overall economy yielding fewer private and public goods.[48]

While six states have begun prohibiting cities from using tax subsidies purely to lure retail across municipal borders and some try to block subsidies to "footloose" companies, only one city, Gary, Indiana, has an ordinance that specifically denies tax abatements to projects that will relocate jobs from other cities. Unfortunately, the federal government has contributed to such wasteful relocation subsidies, since its biggest job programs (such as Industrial Revenue Bonds, the Department of Housing and Urban Development's Community Development Block Grants, and most Commerce Department programs) have no rules against using such funds to encourage relocation. Only two small job subsidy programs have such rules, but states and cities can elude the rules by shuffling money from other federal sources to fund questionable projects.[49]

The competition for retail has created a ludicrous distortion of economic development patterns, as cities have had to desperately bid for successive waves of retail evolution. First, shopping in urban centers gave way to downtown retail in the suburbs. Then, downtowns began to weaken in the face of movement to concentrated suburban malls. Now, general-purpose department stores in malls are giving way to discount "big-box" retailers like Home Depot and Toys 'R' Us. There was once some expectation that a residential population would generate proportionate retail revenues. Now, competing cities work to attract discount giants that suck in business from a whole region, often devastating the more dispersed retail stores that local governments depend on for financing their budgets. An extreme example is the small city of Emeryville,

California, which has attracted a large number of discount retailers. Emeryville now has over five times the retail sales per resident as surrounding cities like Oakland, whose own retail businesses have suffered from the competition.

Direct marketing through phone, cable, or the Internet takes this economic cannibalism to a new level. Cities and states are fighting to attract "call centers" to service direct-marketing companies, since such jobs are seen as nontoxic and "high tech." To cite one example, Oklahoma has done well in replacing lost oil-patch jobs with telecom-based jobs, but the price has been massive subsidies to encourage companies to locate in the state. Oklahoma offers tax incentives, including a law exempting business from sales tax on 800 numbers, WATS, and private-line systems. There is one-stop environmental permitting, tax exemptions on distribution facilities, and major support for training and retraining workers. Data-processing firms get a five-year property-tax exemption.[50] In pursuit of jobs, other states and local areas have created similar subsidies. In the end, they merely subsidize the flight of local retail business to tax-exempt mail order.

Even though all local governments as a whole lose out in this competition, the hope for the individual areas is that jobs from such call centers will be long lasting and that the gain in long-term jobs will offset the cost in local subsidies. But even that hope may wither in the face of new technologies. Bruce Lowenthal, Tandem Corporation's program manager for electronic commerce over the Internet, predicts that the Internet will eliminate the need for much of the work done by such call centers. The Internet will be an "interface" for finding out what customers need and letting them directly indicate what they want. Presently, "Such 'interfaces' are done by data-entry clerks," argues Lowenthal. "So many call centers may be replaced. You'll still need some people to deal with hysterical customers, but that's about it."[51] The whole industry of entry-level data clerks at call centers may melt away, leaving only a much smaller set of more specialized troubleshooters. With companies like Federal Express and Quill allowing business customers to place orders electronically, the elimination of data-entry positions is already in motion.

State governments are already fighting to attract electronic and Internet-based commerce, starting another round of self-inflicted revenue loss in pursuit. In 1994, the state of California quietly passed a law, AB 72, sponsored by Assemblyman Johan Klehs, that allows out-of-state businesses to advertise on online services based in California without thereby being subject to state sales taxes. This law was passed at the request of Apple Computer, which feared that its now defunct online commercial service, E-World, would lose out to commercial services based in other states that could promise tax-free sales in California. So even as Silicon Valley cities are losing local tax revenue, Silicon Valley businesses like Apple Computer were leading the way in the hemorrhage of online sales tax revenue.

Mack Hicks, vice-president of electronic services delivery at Bank of America and chair of CommerceNet in 1995, summarized the economic development logic of the new online services:

If the Bay Area wanted to be the information area, we should call ourselves an Information-Tax-Free Zone, and we'd clean up. Everyone's trying to figure out how to tax it because it crosses borders. It's too young to tax. If they tax it, they'll kill it. How are you going to tax goods when they're ordered over the Internet? You could tax the money, but what if it's bartered? If I'm in Tennessee, I log onto a server in Ireland, I buy software with a credit card based in California, the software is delivered. Which taxes should be paid—import taxes, sales tax, etc.? What a mess.[52]

It was out of this priority of promoting growth of the industry over the fiscal needs of regions that Internet companies began promoting the "Internet Tax Freedom Bill," sponsored by Congressman Chris Cox (R-CA) and Senator Ron Wyden (Democrat from Oregon) to exempt all online transactions from local taxes. As Cox aide Peter Uhlmann argued, the priority of Congress is to "help ensure that state, local and foreign tax policies don't interfere with the potential for economic growth over the Internet."[53] As with bank, utility, and telecommunications "deregulation," local power over economic development has to be reduced to serve the ambitions of industries looking to global markets.

In the fight over the Internet Tax Freedom Bill, local governments represented by the National League of Cities and National Governors' Association fiercely criticized the federal government for preempting their tax powers and businesses that would see only an acceleration of their tax disadvantages versus mail-order businesses. Brian O'Neill, head of the

National League of Cities, condemned Congress harshly: "This is unfair to Main Street business people. This is as un-American as it gets."[54]

While local governments worried that the bill would institutionalize tax losses from Internet sales, they were outraged that the ambiguity of the language banning taxes on Internet transactions would likely repeal existing taxes on a range of local telecommunications. Most versions of the bill would repeal taxes in twelve states collected on local Internet service providers. But the real worry was that the bill, by banning "indirect" taxes on the Internet, might be used by courts to repeal local taxes on telephone service, especially as more and more phone calls were projected to use Internet protocols in coming years. This would cost local governments billions of dollars and give further advantage to Internet-based telecommunications at the expense of local phone companies serving non-Internet users.[55] In the end, the more limited three-year moratorium on new Net taxes that finally passed in 1998 has postponed the legislative debate.

Conclusion

The loss of local control over sales and telecommunications taxes adds to the general fracturing of local economic development due to the interaction of technological and the increasingly global economy. All of this should coerce a reevaluation of the push to decentralization of government responsibilities to local government. Such responsibility makes little sense in a world where multinational corporations often outpower whole states in total assets and can pit local governments against each other in the competition for jobs and local revenue. While much information-age rhetoric harkens to images of small firms and decentralization, the reality is that soon-to-be trillion-dollar corporations are straddling the globe. Even modest-sized enterprises operate more and more on a global basis. Faced with such a disparity in power and the fracturing of the ability of such governments to cooperate easily, local governments can hardly be expected to devise fair and efficient systems of taxation that can deliver the social goods and economic development needed. The result is that the poor and working class face increased tax burdens under such decentralized revenue approaches. The rise of national and global commerce calls for national and even global revenue approaches. While the microchip may be getting smaller, the plane of economic activity encouraged by this technology is national and global. Our tax systems must scale our tax systems to reflect this reality.

Notes

1. U.S. Advisory Commission on Intergovernmental Relations, *Taxation of Interstate Mail Order Sales: 1994 Revenue Estimates* (Washington, DC: Government Printing Office, 1994), p. SR-18.

2. Interview with Wally Dean, April 5, 1995.

3. Tim W. Ferguson, "Web Grab? If It Moves, Tax It: State and Local Governments Smell Revenue in the Internet," *Forbes*, March 9, 1998.

4. Christopher Anderson, "In Search of the Perfect Market," *The Economist*, May 10, 1997.

5. Tom Watson, "Click Here for a Slab of Peanut Pie," *Restaurant Business*, March 20, 1995, pp. 15–18.

6. N.a., "A River Runs through It," *The Economist*, May 10, 1997 (http://www.jrnet.com/open/ec3.html).

7. Interview with Mark Masotto, n.d.

8. James Srodes, "Murdering Mail Order," *Financial World*, March 31, 1992, pp. 64–67.

9. Daniel O'Connell, "U.S. Supreme Court Reviews State and Local Taxation Issues," *CPA Journal* 62, no. 3 (March 1992): 16–21.

10. Srodes, "Murdering Mail Order."

11. David Cay Johnston, "Online Sales Collide With Off-line Tax Questions," *New York Times*, November 10, 1997.

12. U.S. Advisory Commission, *Taxation of Interstate Mail Order Sales*, p. SR-18.

13. Richard Stevenson, "Governors Stress Tax Cuts and Austerity," *New York Times*, May 8, 1997.

14. Maria Alicia Gaura, "Santa Clara County Coffers Should Jingle with $8 Million Surplus: Lower Welfare Costs, Higher Property Values—$8 Million Surplus," *San Francisco Chronicle*, February 17, 1998.

15. Figures are from Municipal Analysis Services, *Governments of California: 1993 Annual Financial and Employee Analysis* (Austin: Municipal Analysis Services, 1993). Note that San Francisco is unique in that it does not differentiate between city and county borders, unlike with Los Angeles and San Diego, where the county and city borders are separate.

16. U.S. Advisory Commission, *Taxation of Interstate Mail Order Sales*.

17. O'Connell, "U.S. Supreme Court Reviews."

18. Richard W. Genetelli, David B. Zigman, and Cesar E. Bencosmer, "Recent U.S. Supreme Court Decisions on State and Local Tax Issues," *CPA Journal* 62, no. 11 (November 1992): 38–44.

19. Grego Gattuso, "Tax Fairness Act Unfair: DMA," *Direct Marketing* 57, no. 2 (June 1994): 6.

20. Brett Glass, "The Real Cost of Mail-Order PCs," *InfoWorld*, December 2, 1991, pp. 45–46.

21. David Cay Johnston, "Sales Tax Proposal Angers Mail-Order Customers," *New York Times*, November 7, 1997.

22. Gattuso, "Tax Fairness Act Unfair."

23. Glass, "The Real Cost of Mail-Order PCs."

24. Cyndee Miller, "Catalogs Alive, Thriving," *Marketing News*, February 28, 1994, pp. 1, 6.

25. Srodes, "Murdering Mail Order."

26. John R. Gwaltney, "Fallacies of Sales-Tax Loophole for Mail-Order Firms," *Small Business Reports* 15, no. 4 (April): 26–29.

27. Srodes, "Murdering Mail Order."

28. Kaye K. Caldwell, "Solving State and Local Use Tax Collection Problems: A Necessary First Step before Dealing with Use Tax Problems of Electronic Commerce," discussion draft by Software Industry Coalition, 1996.

29. Glass, "The Real Cost of Mail-Order PCs."

30. Citizens for Tax Justice, *A Far Cry From Fair: CTJ's Guide to State Tax Reform* (Washington, DC: Citizens for Tax Justice and Institute for Taxation and Economic Policy, 1991).

31. Michael Mazerov and Iris J. Lay, "A Federal 'Moratorium' on Internet Commerce Taxes Would Erode State and Local Revenues and Shift Burdens to Lower-Income Households," report by the Center on Budget and Policy Priorities, May 11, 1998.

32. Anders Schneiderman, "The Hidden Handout," Ph.D. dissertation, University of California, Berkeley, 1995.

33. Ned Eichler, *The Merchant Builders* (Cambridge, MA: MIT Press, 1982), pp. 219, 259.

34. Robert Kuttner, *Revolt of the Haves: Tax Rebellions and Hard Times* (New York: Simon and Schuster, 1980), p. 51.

35. Mike Davis, *City of Quartz: Excavating the Future in Los Angeles* (New York: Vintage Books, 1990), pp. 130–31.

36. Davis, *City of Quartz*, p. 166.

37. John R. Logan and Harvey L. Molotch, *Urban Fortunes: The Political Economy of Place* (Berkeley: University of California Press, 1988), p. 187.

38. George Will, "'Slow Growth' Is the Liberalism of the Privileged," *New York Times*, August 30, 1987.

39. Martin Mayer, *The Builders: Houses, People, Neighborhoods, Governments, Money* (New York: Norton, 1978).

40. Schneiderman, *The Hidden Handout*, chap. 6.

41. Lenny Goldberg, *Taxation with Representation: A Citizen's Guide to Reforming Proposition 13* (Sacramento: California Tax Reform Association and New California Alliance, November 1991).

42. Clarence Y. H. Lo, *Small Property versus Big Government: Social Origins of the Property Tax Revolt* (Berkeley: University of California Press, 1990), p. 154.

43. Kuttner, *Revolt of the Haves*, pp. 42–43.

44. Goldberg, *Taxation with Representation*, pp. 42–43.

45. Goldberg, *Taxation with Representation*, pp. 50, 78.

46. "Tax Facts: The System Sets Cities Up to Be Squeezed By Superstores" [editorial], *San Jose Mercury News*, July 24, 1995.

47. Greg LeRoy, "No More Candy Store: States Move to End Corporate Welfare as We Know It," *Dollars & Sense*, no. 199 (May–June 1995): 10.

48. Melvin L. Burstein and Arthur J. Rolnick, "Congress Should End the Economic War among the States," *Federal Reserve Bank of Minneapolis: The Region* 9, no. 1 (March 1995): 3–20.

49. LeRoy, "No More Candy Store."

50. Curt Harler, "Why Governments Want Your Network Center," *Communications News* 29, no. 12 (December 1992): 30.

51. Interview with Bruce Lowenthal, Tandem, July 21, 1995.

52. Interview with Mack Hicks, June 22, 1995.

53. "Bill to Prohibit Internet Taxation Moving Forward," *Reuters New Media*, March 12, 1997.

54. "Lawmakers Criticize Internet Bill," *Associated Press*, March 10, 1998.

55. Ferguson, "Web Grab?"

IV

The Emergence of Law and Governance Structures in Cyberspace

16

Virtual(ly) Law: The Emergence of Law in LambdaMOO

Jennifer L. Mnookin

Law is a resource in signification that enables us to submit, rejoice, struggle, pervert, mock, disgrace, humiliate, or dignify.
—Robert Cover[1]

Thus, the problem ... concerns both how we should imagine society and how we may recast it in the mold of the imagination.
—Roberto Unger[2]

An Introduction to LambdaMOO

This chapter takes a journey through the looking glass to examine the legal system that has emerged in an online community, a virtual society that both reflects and refracts reality as we know it. This parallel universe cannot be found on any conventional map; indeed, it has no material existence at all, except as the contents of a database stored on a computer. Yet this world is visited, explored, and transformed hundreds of times daily by people sitting at keyboards all across the country, even across the globe.

This uncanny Wonderland is called LambdaMOO: it is a virtual reality, a community located online and accessible only by computer. LambdaMOO is one of the longest lived and most popular of the more than 350 text-based virtual realities available via the Internet.[3] MOOs and their cousins, MUDs,[4] are real-time, interactive conferencing programs, spaces in which many people can carry on conversations at the

This chapter originally appeared online in the *Journal of Computer-Mediated Communication* 2, no. 1 (June 1996). Reprinted by permission of the author. © 1996, Jennifer L. Mnookin.

same time. Unlike some other conferencing spaces—such as a party line on a telephone or a chatroom on the Internet—MOOs and MUDs are based in physical, spatial metaphors; they are virtual worlds in which to wander. A visitor to LambdaMOO, for example, arrives inside the coat closet of a house; the visitor may walk around the house's rooms, explore a garden maze, take a stroll over to the museum, or visit a bar and order a drink.[5] In each space, the visitor's computer screen shows a textual description of the room (but no graphics) and lists the room's other inhabitants. The visitor can talk to everyone else in the room, interact with objects in the room, whisper a message to one particular person in the room, or page someone logged onto the MOO but located somewhere else.

LambdaMOO began in October 1990, created by Pavel Curtis, a researcher at Xerox PARC (Palo Alto Research Center).[6] Since that time it has become one of the most popular of the MOOs and MUDS; it has about six thousand registered characters and a lengthy waiting list of people who wish for a character of their own.[7] Some participants drop by infrequently;[8] others spend dozens of hours a week in LambdaMOO. Frequently, hundreds of people are logged on at once: LambdaMOO is thus a full-fledged virtual community.[9] To visit LambdaMOO one need only telnet to its site at lambda.moo.mud.org, port 8888. Anyone can visit LambdaMOO as a guest;[10] to take up residence there in a more permanent fashion, one must request a character, provide a functioning electronic mail address, and take a place on the waiting list.[11]

Descriptions and activities in LambdaMOO are both realistic and fantastic. On a typical afternoon a visitor might find half a dozen characters clustered in the kitchen of a sprawling house. These characters could well range from the ordinary—such as a college kid with a ripped teeshirt —to the impossible—perhaps a rainbow-colored dragon or a "spivak," a being without gender. New arrivals are greeted with a friendly wave or a nod; old friends bid farewell by hugging each other warmly. Inhabitants of LambdaMOO sit around and socialize, ride helicopters and moonbeams, even teleport themselves instantaneously from one place to another or take an elevator from California to China. Experienced players also build their own rooms and spaces within the MOO or, using object-oriented programming methods, create objects that they and other players can manipulate or expand or "verbs" that allow characters to interact in novel ways. Participants in the MOO are literally building their own universe room by room. At the same time, they are building their own social structure, as well as their own legal system. Indeed, LambdaMOO has had for several years a system for enacting legislation as well as mechanisms for dispute resolution. This chapter focuses on this nascent legal system that has begun to emerge within Lambda-MOO's confines.

Before we turn to look at LambdaMOO's legal system, however, it is worth asking why this strange land of make-believe deserves sustained analysis. Some might dismiss the community as merely the product of a few thousand virtuosos of the virtual engaged in a gigantic game of "Let's Pretend." No doubt more than a few readers suspect that this kooky online universe is no more worthy of serious consideration than a rotisserie baseball league, a student government, or any other activity that might be undertaken substantially by college students with too much time on their hands. Why, then, is a look at the emergence of law in LambdaMOO worthwhile?

First, the study of LambdaMOO is an exercise in legal anthropology, a chance to examine a legal order separate from our own that has received no scholarly attention. There has been a great deal of inflated rhetoric about the lawlessness of cyberspace and both celebration and criticism of the supposed lack of formal rules or law. It is thus worthwhile to look closely at a virtual community in the process of inventing its own law. In addition, the emergence of law in LambdaMOO can give us insight into the close relation between social and legal constitution. That is, we can see the ways in which LambdaMOO denizens have brought law into existence as they have fashioned their community, and indeed, the ways in which participants' understandings of the nature of LambdaMOO and the nature of Lambda Law have become inextricably intertwined.

As discussed later, moreover, law has become a central mechanism through which LambdaMOO participants understand LambdaMOO itself. For some, the existence of law provides the proof that Lambda-MOO is a veritable community, whereas for others, LambdaMOO's legal system indicates that something has gone awry in this virtual play space. At the same time, participants struggle over basic questions about what shape their society's legal structures should have. These flashes of self-consciousness about the status of law and its institutional embodiments make LambdaMOO an especially interesting site for this exercise in legal anthropology. In the "real world," rare are the moments in which society's members engage in critical reflection about the nature of the legal and social institutions that constrain and structure inhabitants' lives. We might see this kind of flux after a revolution or following a tremendous institutional shake-up. But it is not part of our ordinary experience of law. We in the United States rarely ask, "Should we have a Supreme Court?" or "What should precedents mean?" Looking at LambdaMOO lets us witness precisely these kinds of debates over law in a society in which legal institutions are being instantiated for the first time. LambdaMOO thus provides an opportunity to see concretely how participants are creating both social and legal order within a virtual sphere.[12]

But there is a second reason that a look at LambdaMOO and its legal system may be worthwhile. The structure of LambdaMOO mirrors the theoretical vision of legal scholar Roberto Unger to a significant degree. Unger, a principal proponent of critical legal studies and a leading legal and social theorist, elaborates in his three-volume work *Politics* a vision of society that resonates powerfully with LambdaMOO. *Politics* is intended as an elaboration of what Unger sees as a basic tenet of modern social thought—the notion "that society is made and imagined, that it is a human artifact, rather than the expression of an underlying social order."[13] Unger claims that although numerous theories—most notably both liberalism and Marxism—have proclaimed this antinaturalistic premise, they have not sustained it. His work endeavors to offer a radical vision of human emancipation that transcends both traditional liberal and Marxist approaches by centering on "an effort to take the antinaturalistic idea of society to the extreme."[14] Although this is not the place for an extended analysis of Unger's social theory, what is interesting for our purposes is that LambdaMOO is a reification of an antinaturalistic theory of society: it is antinaturalism literally made into a thing.

This claim, of course, needs to be investigated further. To make sense of this claim we must first take a closer look at the structure of Lambda-

MOO. LambdaMOO is a society made up entirely of text, a world generated by computer code. From descriptions of characters to political processes, all of LambdaMOO is constituted through words, based in language. Rooms, people, objects, technology, and politics: all consist of nothing but words and signs. In LambdaMOO, it is not just communication that takes place in and through language but the material substrate of LambdaMOO itself, its physical spaces and manipulable objects, its social institutions and political processes. In LambdaMOO, *there is no extralinguistic reality*. In real life, action may be intelligible only through a linguistic filter; in LambdaMOO, reality is quite literally nothing but language.

One of the most interesting consequences of LambdaMOO's basis in language is that it is structurally unconstrained by the laws of nature. To give just one example, in LambdaMOO in no way is biology destiny; that is, a LambdaMOO character need not correspond to a person's real-life identity. People can make and remake themselves, choosing their gender[15] and the details of their online presentation.[16] They need not even present themselves as human. Of equal significance, LambdaMOO need not be bound by the institutional structures of "real life" (or, as it is often known within the MOO, RL). LambdaMOO takes to the hilt the notion of reality as a social construction. Antinaturalism is, in this sense, a shared premise of the community. Within LambdaMOO, it is far more obvious than in real life that social structures are made rather than given—that they are constructed out of the actions and assumptions of the participants. In this virtual society, to change the code is to change the world; reality is bounded only by the imagination. In other words, LambdaMOO offers the potential to be an imaginative space, an environment within which social structures and legal mechanisms may be creatively constructed and reconstructed. The legal system of LambdaMOO can be, quite literally, whatever the players make of it.

Thus, in LambdaMOO the constructedness of society is itself transparent: it is patently obvious that social institutions, hierarchies, and legal mechanisms are malleable human products, not inflexible natural structures or the inevitable result of an evolutionary script. Unger wrote that supporters of an antinaturalistic and antinecessitarian social theory "see the formative contexts of social life ... or the procedural frameworks of problem solving and interest accommodation ... as nothing but frozen politics: conflicts interrupted or contained. They want to deprive these frameworks or contexts of their aura of higher necessity or authority. Above all, they want to affirm that things can be otherwise."[17] It is inherent to the very structure of LambdaMOO that "things can be otherwise." In a world of words, it is impossible to believe that particular social structures are natural or necessary.

In fact, LambdaMOO may take the notion of antinaturalism even further than Unger does, for it is not only the realm of the social that is obviously constructed but the realm of the "natural" as well. Or to put it differently, in a society bounded only by imagination, there is no tenable distinction between the natural and the social: both are equally subject to human invention and reinvention. As a result, there are no inherent, inflexible organizational constraints in LambdaMOO—except those brought into existence by the participants themselves. To whatever extent social structures (or conceptions of nature) in LambdaMOO become rigid or congealed or taken for granted as necessary and inevitable, it is not because of some higher necessity or authority but rather because they have been built *into* constraints by the participants.

That LambdaMOO is the literal embodiment of Ungerian social theory does not, however, necessarily mean that politics in LambdaMOO will mirror Unger's ideals. For Unger, the antinaturalistic quality of society is, at root, a premise. On this premise he builds his conception of the kind of society we should construct. To put it simply, Unger argues that we should strive to change the character of our formative frameworks and social structures to make them less entrenched and more subject to revision and remaking. Although he does not believe that we can create a society entirely *without* structures, Unger advocates the construction of structures that are more plastic and malleable, easier to disrupt.[18] In short, he argues that we should endeavor to make our social structures less structure-like, to make them into what he terms "structure-denying structures."[19]

Just because LambdaMOO embodies Unger's antinaturalistic premise does not necessarily mean that it will (or should) develop the kind of relation between society and social structure that Unger envisions. As discussed later, LambdaMOO's citizens are divided on exactly the question of how entrenched and permanent, or how difficult to disrupt and revise, their legal and social structures should be. Indeed, the Lambda-MOO experience, as a kind of laboratory experiment that lets us see Ungerian social theory in action, offers an empirical challenge to Unger's optimism about the innovative institutional structures that may emerge from taking antinaturalism seriously.

The clear affinity between Ungerian social theory and LambdaMOO suggests that looking at the kinds of social structures that have emerged in a society that takes antinaturalism to its extreme is a worthwhile project. Moreover, it implies that looking at the forms of institutional experimentation in this virtual space might offer an interesting perspective on institutional experimentation in real life as well. It is just possible that LambdaMOO and spaces like it can serve as both virtual laboratories and virtual looking glasses. Law within LambdaMOO might turn out to reveal something about law outside of LambdaMOO as well.

The next section looks closely at the emergence of law within Lambda-MOO through the early part of 1996. This section examines the rise of the legislative system, the nature of the mechanisms for resolving disputes, and the kinds of disputes that have arisen within the MOO. It also looks at a central debate over the nature of law within LambdaMOO: many players wish to make Lambda Law better defined, more structured, and increasingly formalized, whereas a number of other participants want it to become less formal and legalistic or even hope to abolish it altogether. The third section examines the appropriate relation between law within LambdaMOO and law outside of it.[20] How should law in the "real world" relate to law within virtual environments? This section briefly sketches a number of possible ways of modeling the relationship between Lambda Law and real-world law and argues that the best model is the one that gives LambdaMOO the greatest possible amount of legal autonomy—and thus the greatest potential for becoming an imaginative space for legal experimentation. Finally, an epilogue discusses some more recent changes in the structure of LambdaMOO and offers some final musings on law and politics in this virtual community.

Law and Politics in LambdaMOO

In its early days, LambdaMOO was an oligarchy without any formal system for resolving controversies or establishing rules. The oligarchs—

MOO founder Pavel Curtis, as well as several other players who had participated in LambdaMOO since its infancy—were known as *wizards*. They were responsible for both technical integrity and social control on the MOO. The wizards were benevolent dictators. They set the rules of conduct within the MOO. They decided when to increase a player's quota (the quantity of disk space reserved for objects and spaces of her creation). They attempted to resolve disputes among players. Occasionally the *wizardocracy* meted out punishment, the most extreme form of which was to *recycle* (destroy) a player for incorrigibly antisocial behavior.

The Creation of a Legislative System

In early 1993, Pavel Curtis, the archwizard, wrote a memo to inform the MOO populace that its social structure was about to be transformed. As LambdaMOO expanded, the wizards

were fighting an increasingly losing battle to control and accommodate and soothe a larger and larger, more and more complex community. We were trying to take responsibility for, now, the behavior and mores of over 800 people a week, connecting from almost 30 countries of the world. We were frustrated, many of the players were frustrated; the center could not hold.

You can probably see where this is leading.

I realize now that the LambdaMOO community has attained a level of complexity and diversity that I've actually been waiting and hoping for since four hackers and I first set out to build this place: this society has left the nest.

I believe that there is no longer a place here for wizard mothers, guarding the nest and trying to discipline the chicks for their own good. It is time for the wizards to give up on the "mother" role and to begin relating to this society as a group of adults with independent motivations and goals.

So, as the last social decision we make for you, and whether or not you independent adults wish it, the wizards are pulling out of the discipline/manners/ arbitration business; we're handing the burden and freedom of that role to the society at large....

My personal model is that the wizards should move into the role of systems programmers: our job is to keep the MOO running well and getting better in a purely technical sense. That implies, though, that we're responsible for keeping people from getting "unauthorized" access; in particular, we still have to try to keep others from getting wizard bits since the functional integrity of the entire MOO is clearly at risk otherwise....

It's a brave new world outside the nest, and I am very much looking forward to exploring it with the rest of you. To those of you who have noted that I have the ability to shut down the MOO at any moment, that my finger is, after all, the one on the boot button: you have nothing to fear on that score for the foreseeable future; only an utter fool would put an end to such an exciting social experiment at so crucial a time in its evolution.[21]

In what Curtis hoped would be "the last socio-technical decision imposed on LambdaMOO by wizardly fiat," the oligarchs instituted a petition system, a process through which the players in LambdaMOO could enact legislation for themselves.

Any LambdaMOO resident who meets certain minimal criteria[22] can initiate a petition for making a sociotechnical change in LambdaMOO. The scope of changes that can be made by petition is broad: any modification that requires technical action to reach a social goal. For example, a petition might request the creation of a truly escape-proof jail, a modification in the character-creation process, or a transformation of the petitions mechanism itself.[23] When a player creates a petition, a mailing list is simultaneously created, to be used by all LambdaMOOers for debating the merits of the proposal.[24] Players who support the goals of the petition, or who at least believe that the petition presents an issue worthy of consideration by the Lambda populace as a whole, may choose to attach their signatures to the petition. When a petition gets at least ten signatures, its creator can submit it to the wizards for "vetting." A wizard's decision to vet is supposed to be based on five criteria—that the petition be (1) appropriate subject matter for petitions, (2) sufficiently precise that the wizard can understand how to implement it, (3) technically feasible, (4) not likely to jeopardize the functional integrity of the MOO, and (5) not likely to conflict with real-world laws or regulations. Wizards are supposed to base their decisions exclusively on these five criteria, and they are explicitly prohibited from refusing to vet on the basis of their personal opinions regarding the soundness of the proposals. Once vetted, a petition needs a certain number of signatures (5 percent of the average total vote count on all ballots) to be transformed into an open ballot, and if the signatures are not received within a given amount of time, the petition expires. Ballots are open for voting for two weeks and must pass by a two to one margin to be implemented.

The inauguration of the petitions process transformed LambdaMOO from an aristocracy into a partly democratic technocracy. Wizards continued to be appointed, not elected; only the Archwizard could promote a player to wizard status. Although Lambda laws were supposed to apply equally to all, there were no mechanisms for holding wizards or their actions accountable to the population at large.[25] Officially, wizards had become mere implementers of the popular will. But implementation is far from self-executing. The power to implement—to transform the language of a petition into computer code—is necessarily the power to interpret and shape whatever is being implemented.[26] Moreover, the wizards still had technical powers and access to information denied to the rest of LambdaMOO.[27] Even if they pledged to use these abilities only for the public good and only when explicitly told to by mechanisms like the petitions process, their special abilities gave them power over the MOO. Indeed, wizards have often been referred to—only half-jokingly—as gods.

The wizards' functions, with regard to the petitions process, might be analogized to a cross between an administrative agency and a higher court. Like an administrative agency, the wizards are responsible for the actual implementation of legislation. (However, unlike the rule-making process undertaken by an administrative agency *after* a piece of legislation has passed, the wizards write their implementation notes *before* the petition is voted on so voters can see in advance, at least to a certain extent, what actions will result if any given petition is passed.) When wizards decide whether to vet a petition, they are acting in a capacity similar to that of judges engaged in judicial review, except that vetting takes place before the voting rather than after the legislation has been passed. (If judges had the power to issue advisory opinions about constitutionality when legislation was still under consideration, this would be akin to the vetting process.) The vetting process frequently has multiple iterations: a wizard may refuse to vet, explaining the refusal in a letter to the petition's public mailing list; the petition's author can then revise the petition in light of the wizard's comments and resubmit it. This back-and-forth process will continue until a wizard vets or the author gives up and decides to pursue the petition no longer.

LambdaMOO's petitions process illustrates both the politics of technology and the technology of politics. Transforming the virtual world in any significant and enforceable way requires changes in the computer code.[28] Moreover, politics in LambdaMOO cannot be seen as a mere superstructure nor understood as entirely distinct from technology. Rather, politics in LambdaMOO is implemented *through* technology. Political conceptions can be embedded within the technological constructions of the virtual environment.[29] That is, ideas about politics can even be hardwired into the society via technology. For example, to prevent people from signing petitions without so much as glancing at them, a player may not sign without first scrolling through a petition beginning to end.[30] Currently, voters are allowed to change their votes as often as they like throughout the voting period, but the breakdown of yes and no votes is not available to voters until after the voting period has closed. Voting in LambdaMOO is not required.[31]

All these aspects of the voting system reflect a certain conception of the relation between the individual and the political sphere, a conception of informed individuals who voluntarily participate within a system in which strategic voting is discouraged. We can easily imagine, however, the technologies of LambdaMOO being used to implement alternative conceptions of voting. For example, it would not be difficult to implement a system in which players were obligated to vote or one in which strategic alliances were encouraged because the names of voters on each side and the vote tallies were both revealed and revisable while the voting period was underway.[32] The range of what is possible is broad indeed when every petition is a textual "object" and every political process is, in essence, created by a programming routine. The point is that in LambdaMOO it is far more apparent than in real life the extent to which choices about the design of the political process are just that: choices. As one LambdaMOO character put it,

LambdaMOO isn't a "closed" or "homeostatic" system—we're not stuck with anything.... All legislation that exists at LambdaMOO has been created in a vacuum where no one could predict how it would actually function with living, breathing human beings "living the law." People make mistakes. Foolish people are those that don't recognize that mistakes can be corrected. In virtual reality they can be undone![33]

In LambdaMOO, it is transparently obvious that political processes are humanly made artifacts, and it is thus equally obvious that they are subject to revision. We see once again the dramatic homology between politics in LambdaMOO and Roberto Unger's theoretical vision. In LambdaMOO, plasticity comes naturally.

Lambda Law in Action
As of February 1, 1996, the voters of LambdaMOO had approved forty-four ballots. The ballots concerned a number of LambdaMOO's important social issues—procedures for increasing or transferring quota,[34] mechanisms for attempting to limit LambdaMOO's population explosion,[35] the creation of a verb allowing experienced players to "boot" guests off the system for an hour if visitors behave in inappropriate or annoying ways,[36] the creation of a way for players to ban players they dislike from using their objects or visiting their rooms;[37] and the inclusion of a paragraph in the "help manners" text stating that sexual harassment is "not tolerated by the LambdaMOO community" and may result "in permanent expulsion."[38] Other passed ballots include a referendum declaring that the petition and balloting system is legitimate,[39] a petition declaring that a homophobic petition would be burned in effigy,[40] and a declaration that no petition may "bribe" signatories by providing special or differential treatment to those who supported the measure by signing the petition.[41]

Dispute Resolution in LambdaMOO
The petitions process was also used to establish a system of dispute resolution. LambdaMOO's arbitration system is staffed by volunteers; participants who have been a member of the community for at least four months may offer their services. Every member of LambdaMOO is bound by the arbitration system, including wizards.[42] Any player can initiate a dispute against any other individual player. The person calling for the dispute must have experienced an actual injury, interpreted broadly; making this determination is within the arbitrator's discretion. The two disputants must agree on an arbitrator from among those who have volunteered for the case; if they cannot agree, an arbitrator will be assigned at random. Other interested players can join an ongoing dispute, but a party cannot initiate a dispute against more than one player or initiate two disputes simultaneously. A mailing list is established for each dispute; anyone who wishes to comment on the facts or the process or any other aspect may contribute to the mailing list.[43] Arbitrators hear both sides, collect information, and post their decisions to the mailing list. They are "encouraged, but not required to solicit advice on the handling of the case from others."[44] Although the parties cannot appeal the deci-

sion, it is reviewed by the other arbitrators. If more arbitrators vote against the decision than uphold it, it is overturned,[45] and, depending on the circumstances, the same arbitrator tries again or a new one is appointed. Trials in absentia are discouraged but permissible.[46]

Arbitrators have a broad array of remedies. They may "call for almost any action *within the MOO.*"[47] They may modify either player's quota, recycle any of their objects, or reduce their powers. They may ban either party from the MOO for a period of time or order a character to engage in community service.[48] They may even order the most extreme of punishments—"toading," LambdaMOO's name for the virtual death penalty.[49] Indeed, there are only two significant limits on the power of arbitrators: (1) they may take action only with respect to the two parties; they may neither propose a punishment that would infringe on the rights of other players nor call for a new law as the result of the arbitration; and (2) their proposed actions must take place within LambdaMOO itself; the punishment cannot require any real-life activity. In practical terms, however, this first limitation on arbitrators' power is a serious issue for two reasons. First, it means that except by providing potentially persuasive examples of community norms, disputes have no precedential value. Other than community enforcement through the "overturn" mechanism, there is no system for ensuring that similarly situated disputants are treated in the same manner. Moreover, and even more significantly, when a dispute illustrates a structural problem within the MOO, the arbitrator is limited to resolving the specific instance of the problem. Arbitration thus cannot be used to resolve the more basic structural issue that underlay and perhaps generated the particular dispute. Arbitrators cannot prohibit the population in general from taking any action, nor can an arbitrator use a dispute to change social policy or make institutional reforms.

So what do people fight about in LambdaMOO? Two of the most significant areas of contention and debate have been the nature of property rights within the MOO and the tension between free speech and harassment.

Property Rights   To what extent do Lambda residents own the objects they create within the MOO? To what extent should the creator of a room or object be able to control who uses it and how? Can especially useful objects be appropriated in the interest of the common good? Several ballots and disputes have revolved around these issues of property rights. For example, in *Margeaux v. Yib*, Yib refused to allow a helicopter pad created by Margeaux a place in her list of outdoor rooms. Yib claimed that this list was her own creation and that she should therefore be allowed to use her own criteria for judging inclusions. She intended her criteria to be reasonable and would include any outdoor room so long as it was "themely"—that is, so long as it reasonably related to the theme of outdoor air transportation and had an appropriate outdoor look and feel. In Yib's view, Margeaux's helipad—made of swiss cheese and connected to the second floor of her house—was not sufficiently outdoorslike to warrant inclusion.

Margeaux argued that Yib's list was not a privately owned object but a public utility. (In essence, Yib's list provided the basis for the in-MOO aviation system; if one's spaces were not on the list, it would be quite difficult for anyone with a form of air transportation to fly over them or land there.) In Margeuax's words, "it's NOT Yib's system anymore. It's a public transportation system now."[50] The problem was, as one player put it, "What is a public object? And if an object becomes 'public' ([and it is] still undefined as to what that means or when this occurs), who has control of the object? Does its author/creator? Does that author suddenly have to follow guidelines ([that are] also undefined)?"[51]

The dispute itself did not solve any of the thorny definitional issues (indeed, under the rules of Lambda arbitration it could not address such broader issues). However, Margeaux and Yib compromised; Yib agreed to publish her standards for including landing pads and modified the code so that people could land on their own helipads regardless of whether they were listed in Yib's catalog.

Another property-related dispute concerned a player who created object after object and then immediately destroyed them to get access to objects with particular numbers.[52] (He wanted what he saw as a "magic" number: 93939.) Every object in LambdaMOO, from a player to a mailing list, is associated with a number; basically, these numbers are distributed sequentially. In this player's efforts to get the particular number he wanted, he wasted hundreds of object numbers. The argument against his behavior was essentially that these numbers are a shared resource, a

Lambda commons, and he was violating the norms necessary for their shared use and enjoyment by the community. The player was punished by having some of his programming powers temporarily removed.[53]

Issues related to property rights have generated petitions as well as disputes. One character wrote a petition that would have granted him ownership of numerous objects that belonged to other people. He explained his reasoning: "I'm not an anarchist. I'm a libertarian. I believe in property rights. In fact, I fight for them. However, while I realize that this is an actual society where people interact and have real relationships, it's *still* just a 'virtual' world. Why not toy with anarchy a bit? It's fun. It's also interesting that I'm using a democratic system for my anarchistic means."[54]

A number of players appreciated this character's effort to thumb his virtual nose at the system, whereas others roundly criticized the petition as "an idiotic waste of resources."[55] Even its supporters acknowledged that the ballot was "a joke" and had no chance of passing,[56] and indeed it did not pass. But part of the discomfort of its opponents stemmed from the way it would have transferred property via petition. Another proposed petition would have allowed MOO characters to write wills to dispose of their property if they should be recycled for any reason or commit "MOOicide."[57] (At the time the petition was proposed, one of the wizards served as the "grim reaper" and made decisions about what happened to the property of characters who were reaped.) The central argument articulated in favor of will creation emphasized that it was a proper component of property rights: characters should have some control over the uses to which their property was put even if they permanently left the MOO.[58] This petition would have allowed characters to designate items for destruction or preservation in case of their MOO death and to bequeath their property to specific individuals or prohibit certain individuals from acquiring it.[59] References to real-world intellectual property issues abounded in the discussion of this petition—the nature of copyright protection, whether volatile computer memory counted as "fixed in a tangible medium" under the copyright color, whether it violated the spirit of intellectual property protection to expel someone from the MOO and nonetheless make use of the programming undertaken by the banished character.

Disputes about property in LambdaMOO are less common and less heated than disputes about speech. Nonetheless, serious issues have been raised about the nature of property ownership within the MOO. If someone writes code and makes it available to the public, is the author then accountable to the public in any way? To what extent should the creators of rooms and objects be allowed to control who uses them and how? Should stealing someone's code be considered a punishable offense? The residents of LambdaMOO continue to wrestle with these questions about the nature of property within their virtual world.

Speech Rights and Harassment   Disputes involving the issues of free speech and harassment are both more frequent and more acrimonious than disputes arising over property rights. In *Abaxas v. lucifuge2*, for example, a player initiated a dispute against a character who was frequently insulting other players and using "violent" verbs against them. In particular, lucifuge2 was repeatedly using these verbs to move other players without their permission to unpleasant places within Lambda-MOO such as "the cinder pile" and "Hell." In this case, nearly everyone agreed that lucifuge2's behavior was obnoxious; the question was one of appropriate punishment. The issue was further complicated when it became clear that the human being behind the character lucifuge2 had already been disciplined several times under other character names for nearly identical behavior. Despite his past offenses, a number of people felt strongly that the use of the most severe forms of punishment such as toading or the revelation of real-life information about the character, was not an appropriate penalty for such behavior. They pointed out that players could easily protect themselves from lucifuge2's shenanigans through simple defensive measures; therefore, no matter how obnoxious lucifuge2's behavior may have been, severe punishment was not warranted.

What are these defensive measures that a victim could have used? In LambdaMOO, any player can "gag" any other player (or object); issuing the "@gag" command prevents the gagged player's words from appearing on the issuer's screen. This command affects only the issuer; it has no effect on what the gagged player can say to anyone else. Another command allows a player to "refuse" the speech or commands of a character. For example, a player can refuse to receive paged messages from someone[60] or refuse to be moved from one place to another by someone else. Anyone who gagged or refused moves from lucifuge2 would, in effect, become immune to his harassment.[61]

Some of the debate in this case, and in other similar instances, centered on the appropriate response to "verb abuse," as it is called on Lambda-MOO. Many believed that the responsibility clearly lay with whomever used the offending verbs. The arbitrator in *Abraxas* described an interview he had with a character who had been verb-abused by lucifuge2: "[This character] feels that this sort of constant, mindless use of violently emoting verbs that move players involuntarily has created an environment of harassment that directly imposes on her ability freely to enjoy public areas of the MOO.... [She] also wanted to state that no player should be forced to @gag offensive players ... since that would have the effect of leaving them vulnerable to spoofing from that player which would result in one being demeaned in front of one's friends and guests."[62]

Others, however, emphasized that behavior like lucifuge2's, although irritating, should nonetheless be viewed as protected speech. As one player put it, "Don't like the way lucifuge talks? Got a filthy mouth? Tough shit, so do a lot of us. Gag him if you don't like it. I don't advocate toading the Jesus-preachers that show up from time to time, as personally offensive as I may find them. This place is supposed to protect free speech."[63]

In another dispute in which similar issues arose, a commentator tersely summarized the two positions: "Those who do not believe in dealing with MOO criminals directly would argue that these crimes could be solved by such commands as '@refuse all from ⟨perpetrator⟩.' Others [liken] commands like '@refuse all from ⟨perp⟩' to taking a painkiller and wearing a blindfold while getting raped."[64]

A third position was that "abusive" verbs should be prohibited altogether or their programmers should be responsible for their use. In one player's words, "This kind of behavior (i.e., using verbs to move characters) should be prevented by disabling the verbs in question. If the verbs are available for public consumption, who is to decide how much use is 'too much'? What legitimate use does the 'sewer' or 'fireball' verb have?"[65] As another wrote,

In an instance such as this, I do believe the responsibility lies with [the character who built the verbs in question]. His [verb] serves no purpose that I can tell other than to harass players. This isn't an instance where we have a kid who has written his own harassment verbs. [He] gave tacit permission (and we, the community, in turn, give [him] permission when we don't hold him accountable for creating objects that only function to annoy others, and leave ourselves in the role of having to educate his 'customers') to this player by allowing him access to his [creations]. And because this community is so transient, [with] players of varying ages continually joining, I foresee this as being a constant problem for the dispute [resolution] process.[66]

In the end, lucifuge2 was given a player status invented specifically for this dispute: his powers were sharply curtailed for a two-month period. The creator of this new status described it as follows: "This is the Time Out Player Class, named for the way my 4-year-old's day care deals with unruly children. They are sent to 'time out' to contemplate their behavior."[67] While taking his "time out," lucifuge2 was allowed to participate in LambdaMOO, but his activities were restricted: he was denied access to all verbs other than those necessary for basic communication, and he lacked the power to "gag" or "refuse" other players. He did, however, retain the right to initiate a dispute if he were the victim of harassment.

This dispute and the many other speech-related disputes that have come about on LambdaMOO illustrate the difficulty of separating the categories of speech and action within the MOO. One player can type words onto his keyboard, and these words—this speech—results in another player's forcible removal to another place in the MOO—an action. Moreover, players in LambdaMOO may "spoof" each other.[68] As a general term, spoofing refers to unattributed speech within the MOO. But spoofing may also be used by one character to impersonate another. If a character makes offensive remarks in the LambdaMOO living room, he is, it would seem, speaking. But what if the character, by spoofing, makes it appear that *somebody else* is making those offensive remarks, somebody who is not actually typing the words onto the keyboard at all? Is this speech, or is it action? Should this distinction be important within LambdaMOO?

There continues to be substantial disagreement within LambdaMOO about the appropriate balance between freedom of speech and protection from unwanted speech. Ballots at each extreme have been proposed. One proposal, for example, recognized freedom of speech as a "basic right" and prohibited any disputes that were based on "solely the content of speech," such as, presumably, disputes based on charges of sexual harassment or hate speech.[69] Disagreement ensued over whether by the terms of the petition spoofing would—or should—be included within the category of protected speech; indeed, no consensus was reached regarding the status of spoofing should the ballot come to pass. As it turned out, the ballot was voted down, with 337 nays and 269 yeas.

An antirape measure illustrates the opposite extreme. This proposal was spurred in part by an incident, infamous in LambdaMOO, in which a character named Mr. Bungle spoofed several players in a public space, forcing them to engage in violent sex acts and making it appear that they were acting voluntarily.[70] This petition recommended that toading, or permanent expulsion, become the recommended punishment for confirmed virtual rapists. The ballot tried to distinguish between speech and action within the MOO. This attempt led to a complex set of definitions:

A virtual "rape," also known as "MOOrape," is defined within LambdaMOO as a sexually related act of a violent or acutely debasing or profoundly humiliating nature against a character who has not explicitly consented to the interaction. Any act that explicitly references the nonconsensual, involuntary exposure, manipulation, or touching of sexual organs of or by a character is considered an act of this nature.

An "act" is considered, for the purposes of this petition, to be a use of "emote" (locally or remotely), a spoof, or a use of another verb performing the equivalent presentation, whether by a character or by an object controlled by a character.

The use of "say," "page," and "whisper" ... and other functionality creating an equivalent sense of quotation generally are not considered "acts" under this petition; they are considered "speech." Notes, mail messages, descriptions, and other public media of communication within LambdaMOO that provide a sense of quotation or written expression rather than conveying action are also forms of "speech." This petition should not be interpreted to abridge freedom of speech within LambdaMOO community standards. Communications in the form of speech might still be considered offensive and harassing but generally are not considered virtual rape unless they explicitly and provokingly reference a character performing the actions associated with rape.[71]

The author of this petition attempted, through these definitions, to make a distinction between those words that give a "sense of quotation" and those that give a sense of action or activity. The debate over this ballot included extended discussion of whether this distinction between speech and action was coherent and whether, even if coherent, it was the proper basis for determining the severity of punishment. In the end, the ballot had a high turnout and received support from a majority of voters but not from the two-thirds supermajority necessary for passage. The final tally was 541 in favor and 379 against, with 167 abstentions.

Arbitrators' Techniques

Authority through Dialogue   Like many real-life trial judges, the arbitrators of LambdaMOO seem willing to go to great lengths to avoid being overturned. Recall that commentary—on the accusation, on the process, on the arbitrator's competence, on the appropriate penalty—is not only allowed but structurally encouraged through the existence of the dispute-related mailing list to which any member of the community may contribute.[72] One strategy that arbitrators use to minimize their chances of being overturned is to seek out a wide range of opinion before making a decision. Arbitrators frequently submit to the mailing list their proposed resolution, in unofficial form, asking for suggestions and comments. This provides the arbitrator with a chance to see if the community backs the proposed approach to the dispute and an opportunity to argue with and perhaps persuade those unhappy with the chosen sanction. The dialogic nature of most LambdaMOO arbitrations is one of their most notable features. There is typically a great deal of give and take and animated discussion among the parties, the arbitrator, and other members of the community. Rarely do arbitrators maintain judicial distance during disputes; they participate, argue, explain their rationales, and even change their minds. Indeed, the ensuing discussion often prompts the arbitrator to modify the proposed penalty. (For example, in two of the cases involving lucifuge, the arbitrator changed the punishment in light of the discussion on the dispute's mailing list. In *Abraxas v. lucifuge2* the sanction changed from revealing the character's site information to enrolling him for two months in "time-out." In another case involving the same typist, *Basshead v. Lucifuge*, the punishment changed from temporary banishment to permanent expulsion.)[73]

Formal Language But the dialogic nature of the dispute-resolution process can strain the system. Dispute mailing lists can turn into shouting matches. Moreover, arbitrators sometimes feel frustrated by the influence the community wields over the sanction, especially when the arbitrator alone has been privy to all of the evidence on both sides. As one arbitrator explained, turning in his resignation, "Frankly, I don't want to go into a situation where I have to consider the opinions of masses over my better judgment having been the *only* one to hear *both* sides of the story."[74]

These concerns have led some arbitrators to pursue a second strategy, in addition to or in place of participatory dialogue—formalization: that is, some arbitrators attempt to gain legitimacy for their decisions by using lawyerly language and issuing official-sounding findings of fact. For example, the arbitrator in *Basshead* issued a very precise, legalistic set of rulings regarding who would be allowed to join the dispute, explaining: "I realize these rulings may appear somewhat formalistic, but serious measures against lucifuge have been requested, and I intend this process to be beyond criticism to the extent I can possibly manage it."[75] Formal speech and an attention to process can give the adjudicatory process authority; it can imply that the procedure was fair and beyond reproach. It is an attempt to be official by sounding official—not an outlandish strategy in a society consisting solely of text.[76]

Directions for Lambda Law: Formalization and Resistance

This tendency toward formalization may occur institutionally as well as individually. It is not limited to specific arbitrators or even to arbitrators as a group. Rather, the entire LambdaMOO legal system is at a crossroads. Many believe that the current regime has proved itself to be unworkable. Disputes are frequent and acrimonious. Frustration levels are high, and charges of favoritism are commonplace. Moreover, because arbitration remedies cannot extend beyond the parties to a dispute, many of the issues underlying disputes cannot adequately be addressed by the arbitration system. To be sure, the explanations for the current difficulties diverge: some blame the problems on corrupt and self-serving arbitrators, others believe the problems lie in the institutional structure, and still others view the very idea of Lambda law with suspicion.

Two very different approaches have emerged for confronting the limitations of the current system. One approach favors increased formalization of Lambda law, whereas the other wants Lambda law eliminated. Those seeking formalization hope to establish more powerful legal and adjudicatory mechanisms along with better defined rights and responsibilities for players. The other camp, by contrast, advocates a turn away from law. Throughout 1995 and into the first months of 1996, a stalemate persisted between the two camps: neither faction succeeded in mobilizing enough voters to change the system radically, but both approaches had enough support to keep their issues on the virtual table.

The Formalizers

Perhaps the most significant effort by the formalizers was their effort in the spring of 1995 to implement a Judicial Review Board (JRB), also known as the LambdaMOO Supreme Court.[77] This Board would have been an elected body responsible for interpreting any question of Lambda law and, under certain proscribed circumstances, would have acted as a court of appeals to review decisions made by wizards or LambdaMOO executive bodies. The JRB would have had jurisdiction over four kinds of cases: (1) inquiries about the proper interpretation of a clause of a petition or an existing law, (2) challenges to a wizard's decision to vet based on the procedural guidelines wizards are obligated to follow, (3) challenges to the way a wizard implemented a petition, and (4) procedural challenges to the actions of LambdaMOO governmental and quasi-governmental bodies. To have brought a case before the court, players would have needed to show a direct and specific interest in the case or to have collected fifteen signatures on a petition. The petition also declared that all ballots passed within LambdaMOO were to have the status of constitutional law and that other forms of lawmaking, should they come to exist, were *not* to be considered to be constitutional law unless they explicitly stated otherwise.

The JRB petition had three main goals. First, it aimed to provide some structural accountability for the action of wizards. Second, it hoped to provide procedural accountability for the actions taken by arbitrators or by the quota-granting Architectural Review Board. Third, as we have seen, the current system of law in LambdaMOO often renders interpretive disputes insoluble. Furious debates have arisen over such matters as whether the petition rewriting "help manners" was intended as a guideline for courteous MOOing or as enforceable law. Having an arbitration system whose resolutions have no precedential value combined with the lack of an authoritative body for resolving interpretive differences means that such disputes never attain closure. Each time a new dispute is initiated regarding, for example, sexual harassment, the arguments erupt again with as much force as ever.[78] The JRB would have provided a mechanism for achieving closure—a social structure with the authority to speak definitively.[79] Although more voters supported the measure than opposed it, the ballot on JRB failed to achieve the support of two-thirds of the voters, as required for passage.

The most ambitious formalizing effort, however, was never taken up as a ballot. This restructuring proposal, although under consideration for more than a year, never received vetting by the wizards because a number of implementation details were deemed insufficiently clear.[80] This petition would have created a "bill of rights" to protect the right to privacy, the right to control access to one's property, the right to a harassment-free environment, the right to free expression, the right to raise grievances within the judicial system, the right to propose social policy changes, and the right to due process (interpreted primarily as the right to not have any LambdaMOO database downtime count against any process with a time limit, such as the petitions process).[81] This proposal would also have constitutionalized citizens' responsibilities, ranging from the responsibility to report (and not to abuse) any breaches in security to the responsibility to respect other citizens' constitutional rights and intellectual property rights (for example, not to copy someone's code without permission). In addition, this petition would have created a legislative body—not an elected body but a forum open to anyone who wished to participate—for addressing social concerns (as opposed to technical matters). Changes to the constitution would have required a public referendum; the legislative body could not effect such changes itself.[82] The petition also specified certain minimum requirements for an adjudicative system.[83] Yet another restructuring proposal would have established a different bill of rights that ranged from the right to free expression to the right to conceive of LambdaMOO as a bounded universe. This latter bill-of-rights petition became a ballot and won support from a majority of voters but not from the two-thirds required for passage.[84]

A significant aspect of the various restructuring proposals is that they are all efforts not simply to delineate Lambda Law with more precision but to put it on a more secure foundation—that is, to make it *more* entrenched and *less* subject to revision. In particular, those proposals that explicitly aim to "constitutionalize" some aspects of Lambda Law are, in essence, efforts to make certain social structures or particular rights harder to transform or eliminate. That is, they are proposals that *increase* the force and strength of institutional constraint. In this sense, these formalizing efforts reflect precisely the impulse that Roberto Unger would wish to quell. Whereas Unger aspires to "diminish the gap between routine conflicts within a framework of social life and revolutionary struggles about that framework,"[85] these formalizing proposals aspire to a more elaborate distinction between structure and routine, a greater gap between basic institutional framework and lower-level institutional tinkering. Granted, Unger acknowledges that there can be no escape from social structure,[86] and he, too, envisions some kind of constitution, albeit one that has as its main characteristic the preservation of the right to disrupt social structures.[87]

LambdaMOO shows, however, that even in an environment in which antinaturalism is a completely shared premise of the community, there are pressures that favor structures that look *more* like structures rather than *less*. Just because LambdaMOO's residents recognize their society's antinaturalism does not mean they favor social structures that are disentrenched or more easily subject to revision. In fact, as we have seen, many of LambdaMOO's most committed players are frustrated by the plasticity of their virtual environment and desperately want to develop institutions that are more formalized and more entrenched—institutions that are structure creating rather than structure denying.

This experience in LambdaMOO suggests a flaw in any theory that presumes a *necessary* relation between the recognition of antinaturalism and the creation of social structures that are more open to disruption and transformation. It would be somewhat inconsistent for Unger himself to presume such a necessary relation: after all, one of the central themes of his work is the argument *against* necessity as an explanation for either social structures or historical change. And yet Unger believes that an understanding of society as antinaturalistic is tightly linked to the creation of more plastic, malleable, revisable social structures. He argues that his explanatory theory of society as antinaturalistic and his programmatic ideas about reshaping society "are closely connected: each supports the other, and each expresses an aspect of the vision that both share."[88] LambdaMOO, however, suggests an alternative. The formalization movement in LambdaMOO indicates that it is possible to be fully aware of antinaturalism and nonetheless want social structures that are *more* entrenched and *harder* to change. In other words, just as class consciousness does not necessarily lead to revolution, consciousness of society's constructed nature does not necessarily lead to social structures that are easier to revise and reconstruct.

The Resisters

While some members of the community expend their efforts attempting to formalize and extend Lambda Law, another faction hopes reduce or abolish its effect. In an effort to shrink Lambda Law down to size, a number of petitions and ballots have been introduced with an antiformalist, antilegalist bent. These ballots mock the formalist turn in Lambda Law and aim to add some humor to the adjudicative process. The subtext of all these ballots is: "Remember, LambdaMOO is supposed to be fun. It's a game. Can't we all lighten up a bit?" For example, one ballot proposal, Choosing Justice, would have allowed individual Lambda denizens to opt out of the system of arbitration and to choose to solve their disputes through "wiffle" instead. Each participating player would receive a "wiffle-ball"-style bat (in other words, a virtual plastic toy) to whap other participating players whom they found offensive, annoying, or otherwise deserving of whapping.[89] Any character who received a certain number of whaps would be automatically banished from LambdaMOO for a period of twenty-four hours.

Wiffle's supporters argued that it provided people with an alternative to a stifling and arbitrary adjudicative mechanism by means of a relatively small penalty "available without all the legislative brouhaha" and that it might actually increase the level of courtesy within the MOO.[90] Wiffle was also quite explicitly intended as a statement about the Lambda-legal system. As one supporter wrote, "I protest the introduction of violence into LambdaMOO society through the use of lawyers, arbitration, and legal red tape. This is a MOO, not a court of law. Support wiffle!"[91] Wiffle's detractors claimed that players would abuse their wiffle bats and gang up on people for no reason, that it was "uncivilized" and offered lynch-mob-style-justice, and that encouraging violence and self-help on LambdaMOO would lead to chaos and the unraveling of Lambda society.[92] When all was said and done, the LambdaMOO population as a whole voted down the wiffle ballot. The tally was 345 in favor and 376 against, with 268 abstensions.

Another petition proposed allowing a game of Scrabble to be an alternative dispute-resolution mechanism.[93] Some participants viewed this mechanism as especially appropriate for the MOO: "LambdaMOO is a society based almost entirely on words; [this measure provides] a form of settling disputes that takes this fact into account."[94] The Scrabble petition, however, was denied vetting because players could have concocted disputes and agreed that the winner would receive a quota increase, thus using the Scrabble game to make an end run around the proper quota-distribution channels.

One lighthearted measure proposed attaching a new description to any player who submitted a political petition that received vetting: "[Playername] is wearing a boring three piece suit and an ugly tie. [Player is] carrying a leather attaché case. On one side of the attaché case is a large sign which reads 'MOO-politician. Beware!' "[95] Any player to whom these words were attached could not remove them for a period of three weeks. Although some people found the ballot amusing and thought a little embarrassment for Lambda politicians was entirely appropriate, others claimed that it was discriminatory and mean. The ballot failed to win passage; the tally was 304 in favor, 404 against, with 253 abstaining. The most extreme antiformalist measure proposed the wholesale elimination of the arbitration system.[96] Its author advocated a return to a virtual state of nature—a system of self-help and the elimination of all enforceable, MOO-sanctioned law.[97] The debate regarding this proposal generated into name calling, and the measure failed.

These disagreements between formalizers and resisters about Lambda Law are, at their root, philosophic debates about the nature of Lambda-MOO. For both the resisters and the formalizers, anxieties about the meaning of LambdaMOO are played out in the sphere of law. For those who view the MOO as a diversion, a virtual playground, Lambda Law seems unnecessary and frustrating, an absurd bureaucratic impediment to enjoying the MOO. These participants think that the formalizers take themselves and LambdaMOO far more seriously than they ought to. Many, indeed most, of the resisters believe that LambdaMOO is, in the end, a game, a virtual reality that ought not to be mistaken for a real one.

However, it is worth pointing out that some of the law resisters opposed greater structural entrenchment in quite an Ungerian spirit. For example, one opponent of the Supreme Court proposal wrote:

We are faced, right now, with a MOO that doesn't change very much, and a proposition [in this petition] that suggests we solidify and clarify a single set of broken rules and procedures as the "legal heart" of LambdaMOO. This is directly opposite to what I feel we actually need to make this place more interesting and vibrant, what we *need* is an enhanced ability to experiment and change, in order to conduct many different social and political experiments (and to be able to exempt ourselves from most effects of others' experiments) simultaneously.[98]

By this reasoning, greater codification of law should be opposed precisely *because* it thwarts the possibilities for social and political experimentation.

For the formalizers, however, law has a double function, both pragmatic and symbolic. On the one hand, they view a legal system as a practical necessity because the society requires workable mechanisms for adjudicating disputes, enacting legislation, and establishing community standards of conduct. However, law simultaneously serves a symbolic function: if LambdaMOO has a well-defined legal system, then it *is* a society. That is, the existence of Lambda Law itself becomes proof that LambdaMOO is more than a game, that what happens there is not just recreation but the creation of a virtual community. Games have rules, but who ever heard of a game with a Supreme Court and a complex legislative system? In this sense, formalized law becomes a mechanism by which LambdaMOOers can prove that they are engaged in something grander than a role-playing game, that they are participants in a full-fledged virtual world. Law provides dispute-resolution mechanisms and legislative procedures, but it also provides something more: legitimacy.

What will be the outcome of this philosophic battle between the formalizers and the resisters? It seems that a greater proportion of MOO denizens—or at least a greater proportion of the voting population—support the formalizers than the resisters. Several of the formalizers' ballots, including the blueprint for the Judicial Review Board, received majority support from the nonabstaining voters, although none has received the necessary supermajority. By contrast, not a single one of the various antiformalist measures has been favored by a simple majority. The formalizers' support thus appears to be broader and deeper than that of the resisters. Moreover, the lack of face-to-face communication and the diversity of the LambdaMOO community suggest that informal norm-enforcement mechanisms will be hard to sustain; indeed, they have already proved hard to sustain.[99] It therefore seems likely that if LambdaMOO lasts, so will Lambda Law.

Real Law and Lambda Law: Defining the Boundaries

If Lambda Law seems likely to be a permanent feature of LambdaMOO, determining the appropriate relationship between the legal system within the virtual world and the legal systems that exist outside of it becomes an issue. What should the relationship between LambdaMOO and the legal system in the real world look like? One (admittedly unrealistic) extreme would be for the U.S. courts to recognize LambdaMOO as a separate jurisdiction. The opposite extreme would view Lambda Law as irrelevant to "real" legal determinations involving activities within the MOO. In what circumstances should events that take place within virtual space be actionable in real space?

Metaphors of MOOdom

LambdaMOO as a Social Club   If LambdaMOO were understood as the equivalent of a social club, the existence of Lambda Law would be largely irrelevant within the larger legal framework. In other words, the existence of dispute-resolution mechanisms within the MOO would have no effect on LambdaMOOers' ability to seek redress outside of the MOO for matters that took place within the MOO. Lambda Law would be like the bylaws of a social club or a university's internal regulations. Just as a social club's rules might prohibit members from engaging in certain otherwise legal behaviors within the club, Lambda Law might prohibit activities that are permissible outside of its sphere. But by this analogy, Lambda rules would not limit LambdaMOO players out-of-MOO legal options. If a university has rules prohibiting libel, and a student is libeled in the college newspaper, the student can file a lawsuit instead of, or in addition to, making use of the university's grievance procedures. The existence of internal procedures has no effect on whether the student is allowed recourse to law, nor do those procedures affect the legal standard that operates.[100] By this analogy, the laws of Lambda-MOO would have little relevance to proceedings that took place outside of the MOO, even if the events underlying the cause of action occurred within the MOO. Treating LambdaMOO like a social club suggests no compelling reason to give its organizational forms and structures any special legal recognition.

LambdaMOO as a Village   If Lambda Law were understood to be a village, exhaustion of Lambda remedies before allowing access to state remedies might be appropriate. That is, if we see LambdaMOO as a place of its own but one nested within larger geographic entities—just as a town is within a state within a country—we might want the legal system to require disputes to be addressed first at the local level before allowing them to be appealed to a higher authority. This conception would suggest a requirement of exhaustion of LambdaMOO remedies before allowing anyone to make an out-of-Lambda legal claim resulting from in-Lambda activities. Under this approach, courts would dismiss any case in which the plaintiff did not first make use of whatever remedies were available within LambdaMOO. In other words, a Lambda-MOO player could not bring suit against someone for libel that took place within LambdaMOO without first using LambdaMOO's arbitration process against the libeler. We might deem the Lambda arbitration system the functional equivalent of the court of original jurisdiction for disputes arising within LambdaMOO or, more accurately, analogize

274 Jennifer L. Mnookin

it to an administrative remedy.[101] Just as, for example, a government employee may sue for wrongful discharge only after administrative remedies have been exhausted, a LambdaMOO denizen could take out-of-MOO action only after making use of LambdaMOO's available procedures.

The problem with this approach, however, is that unlike a county court or an administrative agency, Lambda's legal institutions have no formal legal authority. They are not an arm of the state and are not recognized by it—nor are they likely to become so in the forseeable future. Therefore, courts are unlikely to take this approach with LambdaMOO—unless LambdaMOO itself requires it of its participants contractually. For example, LambdaMOO could pass a petition that would add to the text each player sees when logging in: "By connecting to this MOO, you agree to exhaust all legal remedies available within the MOO before making any activities, actions, or speech that takes place within the MOO the basis for a lawsuit anywhere outside of Lambda-MOO." Although courts would be unlikely to impose an exhaustion requirement on their own, they would probably enforce such a requirement if it were made a contractual condition of MOO participation.[102] Alternatively, LambdaMOO could follow the model established by many corporate contracts and require binding arbitration for all disputes generated within the MOO and not resolved through MOO dispute-resolution mechanisms.

LambdaMOO as a Separate Country A third approach—admittedly fanciful but nonetheless worth considering analytically—would have courts recognize LambdaMOO as a separate jurisdiction. The analogy here would be to view LambdaMOO as a separate physical space, a place of its own. Legally speaking, LambdaMOO would be equivalent to not a village within a state but another country. Viewing LambdaMOO as its own jurisdiction has some conceptual advantages. After all, where exactly are activities on LambdaMOO taking place? The database server is in California, but the characters are logging in from computers all over the country—indeed, all over the world. If LambdaMOO is a village, in what state or country is the village itself located?

To put it another way, if a player from Seattle libels a St. Louis player to players from Sussex and Syracuse, where did the libel take place— California, Washington, Missouri, England, New York? Where exactly was the tort committed? Perhaps the most satisfying answer is that the tort was committed in LambdaMOO. That is, we could view Lambda-MOO as a real place—indeed, the place where the libel occurred. If LambdaMOO were understood to be a separate jurisdictional entity, courts would generally refuse to hear disputes arising from activities taking place entirely within LambdaMOO. Just as U.S. courts lack jurisdiction over disputes among Germans taking place in Germany, they would lack jurisdiction over disputes among LambdaMOOers taking place in LambdaMOO.

In practice, of course, the possibility of courts in multiple sites, each with legitimate jurisdiction, means that the situation would be substantially more complex. If a MOOer from California injured another MOOer from California, even if California courts recognized Lambda-MOO as a separate jurisdiction, the California courts would certainly have jurisdiction. If we spin out this scenario, it soon verges on the absurd: we can imagine courts making inquiries into the adequacy of LambdaMOO remedies and determining whether to apply the doctrine of *forum non conveniens* or engaging in elaborate analysis regarding choice of law. These scenarios are, of course, farfetched. The point is that even recognizing LambdaMOO's jurisdictional independence would not ensure that disputes that arose in LambdaMOO would be resolved through LambdaMOO legal mechanisms. Now, if LambdaMOO had *exclusive* jurisdiction over all that took place in LambdaMOO, these jurisdictional issues would not arise. However, even if LambdaMOO is *like* another country, the players typing onto their computer screens are themselves located in specific, real-world, geographically located places. On what theory would a real-world court maintain that it lacked jurisdiction over the actions of a real person that took place within its boundaries? If a player located in California committed libel within LambdaMOO, a California court would seem clearly to have both personal jurisdiction and subject-matter jurisdiction over the defendant. Still, the metaphorical resonance of the recognition of LambdaMOO as a separate jurisdiction is strong; it corresponds to the instinct of many that cyberspace is elsewhere.

LambdaMOO as a Role-Playing Game A fourth approach would analogize LambdaMOO to a role-playing game—richer and more complex than Dungeons and Dragons, to be sure, but of the same ilk.[103] This analogy suggests the need to make a distinction between role and player, between the persona that someone adopts within the MOO and the person who actually types words onto a computer keyboard. If Lambda-MOO were a role-playing game, perhaps characters should be conceived as fictional creations rather than juridical entities. And fictional characters (unlike legally recognized artificial persons, such as corporations) have no legal standing. In other words, if characters are not juridical entities, they can neither sue nor be sued. Damage to fictional characters is not legally cognizable, nor can the person who controls a character sue on the *character's* behalf. (Imagine, for example, George Lucas filing a suit alleging that Luke Skywalker had been libeled. Putting aside the question of whether it is even possible to libel a fictional character, if George Lucas could show that he, George Lucas, was damaged by the libel, he might have a cause of action. But Luke Skywalker himself would not.) Therefore, to bring a civil suit based on action that took place in LambdaMOO, a plaintiff would have to show that the *person*—the typist behind the character, the human being—experienced damages. And reputational damage suffered within the MOO by the character alone would not, one imagines, count as damage experienced by the typist controlling the character.

However, the real people behind characters would be accountable for any damage their characters caused noncharacters. (The analogy here would be to an actor who assaults someone during the shooting of the film. If the assault was part of the script, and he was carrying out his role, he has not committed a legally cognizable act of violence. If the assault, however, had nothing to do with the script, the actor could not escape accountability by claiming that it was his character who committed the assault, not the actor himself.) In other words, if we return to our libel example, if one MOO character libeled another MOO character, the libeled character would not have standing to sue in a civil court. The victim of libel would therefore have no alternative but to use whatever dispute-resolution mechanisms were available to characters *within* LambdaMOO. However, if a MOO character libeled a real human being within the MOO—such as, perhaps, a person who had never even visited the MOO—and the real human being suffered damages outside of the MOO as a result of the libel, the victim would have a cause of action against the typist who controlled the libeling character.

This approach, however, rests on a clear distinction between persona and person. In reality, of course, the boundaries between character and typist are indistinct and imperfect. The real effect of positing a distinction between character and typist would be to require out-of-MOO damages before allowing a MOOer access to out-of-MOO legal system. If the MOO were analogized to a role-playing game, when a dispute arose in which the harm were confined to the MOO, only MOO remedies would be available. The claim of harm would have to spread beyond the boundaries of the game before it would be recognized at law.

We have, then, four approaches to the relation between Lambda law and the system of law outside of it. Each approach is based on a metaphor, a conception of the nature of LambdaMOO. Is LambdaMOO a social club, or is it a village? Is it more like a country or more like a role-playing game? The difficulty, of course, is that all four metaphors resonate: LambdaMOO is a hybrid. It is a fantasy space in a double sense—both a utopian space of possibility *and* an adolescent playground. It is a social club *and* a village *and* a country *and* a role-playing game. How, then, should we choose a reigning metaphor and with it a framework for the relation between Lambda law and the state-sanctioned legal system?

Laboratories for Experimentation

As has been discussed, LambdaMOO is a space in which reality is bounded only by the imagination. As social psychologist Sherry Turkle emphasized in her 1995 book, *Life on the Screen*, virtual environments such as LambdaMOO allow their participants to engage in creative self-fashioning. In MOOs, people can develop characters that emphasize usually suppressed aspects of themselves.[104] In the MOOs, they may be something or someone that they are unable to be in the physical world. People may even use the MOO to work through anxieties with origins in the real world; on occasion, MOOs may even have genuine therapeutic potential.[105] Turkle describe how virtual spaces encourage participants to play with aspects of themselves, to experiment with identity and self-presentation. But it is not only individual identities that are shaped and reshaped within a MOO but institutional identities as well. Just as players may construct themselves in novel and creative ways, they may also imaginatively construct political institutions and social forms. Turkle calls spaces such as LambdaMOO "laboratories for the construction of identity."[106] They may equally be laboratories for the construction of society. In an often-quoted dissenting opinion, Justice Louis Brandeis wrote: "It is one of the happy incidents of the federal system that a single courageous State may, if its citizens choose, serve as a laboratory; and try novel social and economic experiments without risk to the rest of the country."[107] Seventy years later, it may be virtual spaces that can best serve as laboratories for experimentation—places in which participants can test creative social, political, and legal arrangements.

As we have seen, many of the disputes within LambdaMOO have centered around issues relating to property and speech. It is worth noting that both of these topics are highly contested outside of LambdaMOO as well as within it. To what extent is information properly considered property? What should ownership look like in a society in which the most valuable resources are symbolic rather than material, words rather than things? To what extent should information be protected as private? All these questions are as central in the "real world" as in LambdaMOO. The same is true with the speech-related issues: How should the legal system protect people from unwanted speech and simultaneously allow free and open communication? Can speech alone cause injuries that should be legally recognized? Are there circumstances in which the content of speech should be regulated? Obviously, these are relevant questions in domains far outside of cyberspace. Approaches to these issues fashioned within virtual communities might, therefore, have applicability—or at least provide inspiration—outside these spaces as well.

Moreover, it is not as if the Lambda legal system has been constructed in a vacuum. It borrows from the legal systems outside of it—especially the U.S. legal system—both explicitly and implicitly. Often participants invoke notions of the law based on their (sometimes inaccurate) understanding of law in the real world. For example, nowhere in Lambda Law is there any explicit codification of either a free-speech right or a privacy right, and yet most participants presume that these rights exist within the MOO. (Ironically, it is often law resisters who most vehemently argue that free speech is sacrosanct.[108]) At a procedural and institutional level, too, we can see the tremendous extent to which U.S. legal culture influences LambdaMOOers' approaches to Lambda Law. Both in the mechanisms used by arbitrators to shore up their authority and in the structure of the Judicial Review Board, we see a turn to a process-based system for determining the legitimacy of decisions. We see an individualistic conception of property rights applied to virtual objects created by computer code. And the language used by LambdaMOO participants— such as the labeling of their proposals "the LambdaMOO Supreme Court" and the "LambdaMOO Bill of Rights"—reflects the legal culture in which they exist offline.

That people invent for themselves structures that resemble those that they know best is not surprising. The strong reliance on existing models of law, both procedural and substantive, suggests the limits of any paradigm that views virtual reality as completely set apart from real life. The structure of LambdaMOO makes it possible to change the world by changing the code, limited only by the imagination. And yet in practice, although the characters and the places may look like nothing one's seen before (the real world is sorely lacking in characters shaped like fractal dragons and offers no possibility of taking an elevator from California to China), the institutions look rather familiar. We must be careful, however, not to overstate the resemblance. Lambda Law is at once tightly linked to the culture of the real world and a kaleidoscopic transformation of it. Its relation to real law is far from simply mimetic. It is a form of legal bricolage, blending elements of "real" law—and elements of laypeople's conception of "real" law—together with institutional variations and innovative conceptions.

Potentially, then, virtual spaces such as LambdaMOO could be laboratories for experimenting with various institutional creation and creative legal standards. With this possibility in mind, I return to the question of the reigning metaphor, the best way to conceive of the relation between reality and virtuality, Lambda Law and real law. Which approach—LambdaMOO as a social club, as a village, as a country, or as a role-playing game—offers the most promise of allowing virtual communities to be laboratories for social and institutional invention? Which approach would allow for the most plasticity, the greatest flexibility for institutional refashioning?

The best metaphor turns out to be conceiving of LambdaMOO as a role-playing game. Analogizing LambdaMOO to a role-playing game ends up granting LambdaMOO participants the most freedom to experiment and, indeed, the greatest amount of legal autonomy. By emphasizing LambdaMOO's gamelike aspects, we emphasize LambdaMOO's power to make rules for itself, unconstrained by the rules that operate outside its borders. Recognizing LambdaMOO as a game, as a play space, frees participants in LambdaMOO to play—to invent and reinvent both themselves and their institutional setting. Labeling Lambda-MOO a "mere" game is the easiest way to free what happens within LambdaMOO from external legal oversight. If LambdaMOO were a social club, external legal institutions would have no reason to defer to the MOO's rules when they differed from those of society at large. If LambdaMOO were a village, when the village laws conflicted with the law of the state, state law would trump when invoked. If LambdaMOO were a country, the principle of comity would suggest that real-world courts should respect Lambda Law as legitimate; however, unless Lambda Law had exclusive jurisdiction over anything that took place in LambdaMOO, complex jurisdictional questions would arise. If Lambda-MOO were a game, though players would generally find it difficult to invoke external law when it differed from the rules of the game. A football player cannot successfully sue for a civil assault when he is tackled during a game, even though the same action in another circumstance would be actionable. When he agrees to play football, he agrees to its rules, even when they conflict with those of the general society. Similarly, LambdaMOOers would find it difficult to bring suit for actions sanctioned by the rules of the MOO, even if the same action would be prohibited outside of the MOO. Obviously, there are social limits to what society will allow in the guise of a game: "it was part of a consensual game" would hardly provide an adequate defense for murder. Nonetheless, analogizing the virtual community to a role-playing game ends up providing LambdaMOO with the greatest freedom from external legal control.

Moreover, the role-playing game metaphor suggests a useful guideline for determining when the external legal system should allow actions within Lambda to be the basis for a lawsuit. The analogy helps us recognize when "it was part of a consensual game" should *not* protect a player from liability. As has been discussed, viewing LambdaMOO as a role-playing game suggests a distinction between the role and the players, between the persona and the person. This distinction, to be sure, is not always a stable one. As Sherry Turkle points out, "MUDs blur the boundaries between self and game, self and role, self and simulation."[109] Indeed, within the MOO, there are frequently conflicts that suggest the instability of a pair of related distinctions—the distinction between the persona and the person and the distinction between Lambda life and real life.

A useful framework for determining when a player ought to be able to invoke the real-world legal system is to allow access to external law in those circumstances when these distinctions—between role and player, between MOOlife and real life—have, in fact, broken down. That is, when actions that take place within the MOO have consequences outside of the MOO, when the actions of a character damage not a persona but a person, then the person should be able to seek redress through the external legal system. Another way of articulating this principle is to emphasize that characters lack standing in court. For legal remedies to be available based on in-MOO activities, the player, not the character, must have actual damages. And these alleged damages must be in the real world, not in the MOO, before external legal remedies should be available.

These boundaries between person and persona and LambdaMOO and the world outside will inevitably break down on occasion. Within LambdaMOO there have indeed been numerous examples of this collapse. Officially, the relation between Lambda Law and the outside world is rather straightforward. The arbitration help file states, "The only RL actions which have material bearing on any case brought before Arbitration shall be: the mental processes of that typist and the fact that the typist elected to type what they did."[110] As another player put it, "I think this should be a right of all users: 'The right to treat any and all communications occurring outside the MOO as irrelevant to the MOO.'... The MOO is the MOO. It is not the outside."[111] But in practice, this can be a hard distinction to maintain. As one arbitrator wrote, struggling with this issue in a case in which the real-life activities and on-Lambda activities of the disputants were deeply entangled:

I stressed, and stress now, that I cannot act on incidents outside the db [database]. However, I can consider threats made in LM [LambdaMOO] of RL [real-life] action. [I believe in] the necessity of limiting ourselves as much as possible to the concerns *on* the MUD. [But] it is my feeling that we cannot simply ignore the existence of a problem merely because someone has decided to engage in out-of-MOO escalation. To do so, I'm afraid, would only encourage such escalation.[112]

The problem towards which the arbitrator gestures is that it is difficult to uphold a strict distinction between real-life actions and LambdaMOO actions when the participants in a dispute are fighting on both battlegrounds. If the participants have a dispute with each other *both* in real life and in LambdaMOO, for the players themselves it will be impossible to believe that the goings-on in one arena are irrelevant in the other. In other words, if the players in a dispute are equating the persona and the person—if they have, so to speak, "pierced the character veil"—it is extremely difficult for the adjudicatory system to *both* reattach the veil and resolve the dispute successfully. In one highly charged dispute, the accusations against a player included the claim that he was threatening to use information he had learned from characters on LambdaMOO to harass them in real life. Over the course of the dispute, the accused committed MOOicide; he voluntarily exiled himself from LambdaMOO. An observer commented to the victims on the irony of the outcome: "While you are *victorious* in a make-believe environment, you're still affected by him in real life!"[113]

On the one hand, there is widespread recognition within the MOO that it is impractical and inappropriate for LambdaMOO to claim jurisdiction over any aspect of real life. On the other hand, MOO players all know that sometimes the two are far from distinct. For both amity and enmity the border separating real life from virtual can be porous indeed.

The belief in the need for the LambdaMOO legal system to maintain a strict separation between reality and virtuality coexists alongside the knowledge that this separation is often chimerical. This tension leads to exchanges like the following. One player insisted:

I don't think there would be much argument about this particular issue. That if you're having a real-life problem with another player in real life, you cannot get redress in a virtual reality Arbitration program. The place to seek redress for real-life offenses is in real life. In MOO life, if you're having "virtual nature" problems with another player, you may bring the problem to Arbitration and attempt to get some peace WHERE the offense occurs, where Arbitration has "jurisdiction." But there is no crossover.

Another replied, exasperated, "How many examples of tangible crossover do you require before recognizing that they exist?"[114] The insistence on a strict separation between real life and LambdaLife is, then, a legal fiction: although it does not conform to people's lived experience, it is viewed as necessary for LambdaMOO's legal system to function at all.

Unlike the LambdaMOO legal system, the external legal system need recognize no such separation. Indeed, it is on precisely those occasions in which the separation ceases to exist—resulting in real damages to a real person—in which the legal system ought to recognize goings-on within LambdaMOO as raising legally cognizable claims. To give just a few examples: If a LambdaMOO character stole the computer code of another LambdaMOO character within the MOO and then outside of the MOO sold copies of the stolen code, even though the theft occurred within the MOO, the player from whom the MOO was stolen might have a legitimate infringement of copyright claim. Or if a LambdaMOO character libeled someone not on the MOO, the libeled person should have out-of-MOO redress available even though the speech occurred within the MOO. And clearly goings on within the MOO could be used as evidence in cases grounded in actions committed outside of the MOO. By contrast, unless the actions caused out-of-MOO damage to a real person, libel within the MOO, property theft within the MOO, or sexual harassment within the MOO or even virtual rape would not be legally cognizable outside of the MOO. Note that in order for such a system to work, psychological damage experienced by persons because of the experiences of their persona cannot be viewed as the kind of damage that would allow someone access to outside-MOO legal redress.

The point here is *not* that persona cannot suffer real harm. Rather, the question is which organizational level is best suited to adjudicating different kinds of disputes. When the harm-causing activities occur within LambdaMOO and the harm is suffered by a LambdaMOO character, the adjudicatory mechanisms of LambdaMOO provide the best institutional setting in which to settle the issue. By contrast, when the damage seeps beyond the borders of LambdaMOO, the legal institutions beyond LambdaMOO's borders are better placed to resolve the matter.

We see, therefore, that understanding LambdaMOO as a role-playing game has two useful consequences. First, it opens up the greatest possible space for institutional experimentation within LambdaMOO and thus enlarges LambdaMOO's sphere of legal autonomy. In addition, by implying a distinction between role and player, persona and person, the role-playing game analogy suggests a useful guideline for determining when disputes arising out of activities within LambdaMOO should be cognizable in out-of-MOO courts. The role-playing game analogy, then, both maximizes the possibility for LambdaMOO to operate as a laboratory for experimentation and suggests a framework for determining the boundaries of this zone of experimentation.

The irony here is that in the disagreements between the resisters and the formalizers over the existence of Lambda Law, it was the resisters who frequently emphasized that LambdaMOO was a game. For the resisters, calling Lambda Law a game implied that Lambda Law was overwrought and unnecessary. Recognizing it as a game would, many resisters thought, prevent players from taking it too seriously. Emphasizing the analogy between LambdaMOO and role-playing games need not, however, diminish LambdaMOO's seriousness. LambdaMOO can simultaneously be a virtual community and a game. In other words, LambdaMOO can be serious play.

However, we must take heed of the resisters and their presumption that Lambda Law is superfluous if LambdaMOO is merely a game. If nothing else, the resisters' viewpoint should remind us that analogizing LambdaMOO to a role-playing game for the purpose of determining its relation to the external legal world is no panacea. It provides no guarantee that LambdaMOO and places like it will, in practice, become laboratories for social experimentation. This analogy minimizes the intrusion of real-world law into LambdaMOO and thereby maximizes the space for institutional invention. The extent to which such institutional invention will actually occur within MOO spaces is another issue entirely. Of course, as we have seen, a legal and institutional structure has already emerged within LambdaMOO. Whether it will flourish remains an open question. Even if we maximize LambdaMOO's freedom to innovate, there may be substantial obstacles in place that make creative reinvention difficult to achieve. Virtual communities may find it difficult to create effective ways to enforce the laws they have created; participants may not choose to invest time and energy in institutional creation in a virtual world; irresolvable philosophical differences (such as that between the formalizers and the resisters) may lead to stagnation instead of innovation; it may be that the infinite expansibility of virtual spaces leads to fragmentation rather than creation; finally, the collective imagination and generative capacity of participants may simply not be up to the task.

LambdaMOO, then, may be a test of our collective imaginative capacity, the ultimate thought experiment. LambdaMOO is a world in which nearly anything is possible. It is a world in which destroying an institution (or a character) requires no more than tossing out some programming code, a society in which institutional creation and innovation are made real through writing. It is a society in which antinaturalism is a universally shared premise. And it is a place in which words have the potential to come to life. LambdaMOO, then, has the potential to be a utopian space of possibility. It could provide a space in which participants can remake themselves and their institutions; it could provide a standpoint from which to critique and rethink the institutional structures of the space outside the MOO.

LambdaMOO has the potential to be all these things, but it may not succeed in becoming any of them. Indeed, the actual experience of law in LambdaMOO suggests an empirical critique of Roberto Unger in two related ways. It shows us, first, the persistence of the urge for entrenched social structures, even in an intrinsically antinaturalistic society. And it illustrates further how the tensions over an intensely Ungerian question

—just how entrenched social structures ought to be—can themselves lead to stagnation rather than innovation. The very structure of Lambda-MOO provides it with the potential to be a space in which creative institutional experimentation and innovation can be enacted; simultaneously, however, the lived experience of law in LambdaMOO cautions us to be wary about the possibility of translating utopian theories into practice.

The utopian possibility—the notion of a virgin place in which we can wash away the mistakes of the past and begin anew—is a recurrent and familiar myth. From the hopes of creating a new human in the New World to the conception of the frontier as a place of freedom from the stifling constraints of society, there have been those who have believed in the possibility of transforming humanity by moving to a new space, an untouched place. Cyberspace has clearly become the latest site within this lineage of utopian dream spaces, and in this new world as surely as in the ones that have preceded it, utopian dreamers are destined to be disappointed. Nonetheless, virtual communities like LambdaMOO— odd hybrids between games and worlds, simulations and society—may yet prove to be spaces for institutional reimagining, for questioning and reshaping conceptions of self, politics, and law.

Epilogue

In 1996, the year following this essay's publication in the online *Journal of Computer-Mediated Communications*, LambdaMOO and its legal and political structures went through innumerable small transformations. For example, although the will-creation ballot discussed earlier did not pass, a subsequent ballot providing a mechanism for characters to make wills succeeded in becoming law.[115] This brief epilogue neither details nor comments on the varieties of tinkering that have taken place in the virtual community. However, attention must be called to a significant modification that altered LambdaMOO's political landscape dramatically. On May 16, 1996, the wizards announced that they were reclaiming certain aspects of social control. Recall that in 1993, the wizards proclaimed in a memo that LambdaMOO was to become a democracy—that the wizards were henceforth to act as mere technicians, implementers of the popular will, and promised to refrain from making any social decisions *sua sponte*. The 1996 memo, "LambdaMOO Takes Another Direction" (memorialized as "LTAD"), acknowledged that neither the democratic experiment nor the effort to circumscribe wizardly action had been fully successful.

The wizards had come to realize that the distinction between technical implementation and social decision making was not tenable: "Over the course of the past three and a half years, it has become obvious that this was an impossible ideal: The line between 'technical' and 'social' is not a clear one, and never can be.... So we now acknowledge and accept that we have unavoidably made some social decisions over the past three years, and inform you that we hold ourselves free to do so henceforth."[116]

The memo further explained that the wizards would hold themselves out as mere technicians no longer: "In particular, we henceforth explicitly reserve the right to make decisions that will unquestionably have social impact. We also now acknowledge that any technical decision may have social implications; we will no longer attempt to justify every action we take. Players will still have a voice, however. Your input is essential. We will keep our existing institutions for now ... but we encourage you to develop ideas for replacing these institutions."[117] The wizards acknowledged that the structure of LambdaMOO necessarily gave the wizards some capabilities that are inherently incompatible with completely democratic institutions. At the same time, the memo insisted that the wizards did not *want* dictatorial powers and hoped that LambdaMOO participants would creatively rework existing institutions and fashion new ones that would improve the MOO.[118]

On the one hand, this memo signaled a momentous change—the explicit return of "wizardly fiat," an acknowledgment that the powerful few could take actions outside of the procedures and laws that bound the rest of the MOO population. On the other hand, the memo did no more than confirm what many MOOers had long insisted—that the MOO was not and could not ever truly be a democracy because the wizards, an appointed rather than elected body, could always have the last word.[119] The memo then was like a coup d'etat by a group that had always held the reins of power. Some saw it as a drastic and disappointing change; one player called the day of the memo's issuance "black Thursday."[120] Others, however, viewed it as a belated admission of a longstanding reality. As one participant wrote, "LTAD only removes the suspension-of-disbelief clause that had been the working condition of discourse [up until now]."[121] One could argue that it changed everything or that it changed virtually nothing at all.

The day after the wizards issued their memo, a petition was proposed to affirm the population's assent to the return of wizardly fiat as described in the memo. This petition explained, "This ballot is an attempt to determine the legal and social standing of LTAD. The passage of this ballot ... indicates: The LTAD declaration is legal. The population has shown its confidence in the Wizards. The population has shown its consent to LTAD."[122] Some viewed this petition as "silly and unnecessary."[123] They argued that speaking in the language of "consent" when the population had no choice *but* to consent to the wizardly action was disingenuous: "LTAD is the law of the land, whether we like it or not, because the wizards have the final authority here.... The idea that the players can consent to this or not is just plain silly.... it is similar to consenting to the sunrise every morning. Put me down as a 'no' vote."[124] However, a sufficient majority supported the ballot. It passed 321 to 111, with 272 abstentions.[125]

Why did so many participants willingly acquiesce to the return of wizardly fiat? Part of the answer is that many felt that they had no choice: why oppose the inevitable? (The high proportion of abstaining voters may have been the result of such a sentiment.) In addition, some residents believed that wizards *should* be allowed to intervene without going through procedural rigmarole. These players genuinely thought that an oligarchy was the best structure for governing the MOO. But another part of the explanation for LTAD's broad support by the populace lies in the widespread frustration with what had preceded it—the ceaseless bickering among the politically active segments of the population and the enduring institutional stalemate.

In the months leading up to LTAD, conflict had been plentiful. The intense disagreements between the "formalizers" and the "resisters" had led to stagnation rather than innovation or compromise. As one participant grumbled, "The problem is that we have two factions that have been fighting each other for so long that they have built up so much distrust and dislike that they probably couldn't manage to agree on what you get when you add two and two together."[126] The disagreements among the factions had led to seemingly insurmountable gridlock. Nearly everyone supported change of some sort or another, but no perspective had enough supporters to dislodge the status quo. One participant mused, "I have heard the so-called PE [power elite] members decry current conditions but act in such a way as to perpetuate them. I have heard their critics defame them and yet struggle to maintain MOO institutions such as Arbitration, just as it is." This player wondered, "If both of these 'sides' complain so much about how bad things are, how evil things have become, why do they conspire to keep the same structure in place?"[127]

Although nearly everyone criticized the current system, change seemed impossible to realize. Just about the only thing that the various sides seemed to agree on was that arbitration was not succeeding as a dispute-resolution mechanism. Whether it should be replaced with a more formal mechanism or a less formal one, whether the Lambda legal system should be more explicitly codified and elaborated or whether it should be scaled back or eliminated, remained intensely contentious. Moreover, players were engaging in nasty, personal attacks, sometimes even putting forward petitions to banish enemies from the MOO altogether. Many participants, even those who had once cared about Lambda politics, found themselves becoming disillusioned: "Once I thought we as a community had the strength and creativity to do something more interesting than settle for the unjust forms of law and enforcement we are confronted with in real life. Do we still have that?" one player asked doubtfully.[128]

Another frustrated player urged everyone to take a virtual deep breath and stop taking themselves so seriously: "Conflict is good. Without conflict there can be no compromise, without dialogue we can't come to the best decisions, and if no one *cared* about the decisions, the MOO could never evolve.... but there are limits. Now calm down and repeat after me. This is a Moo. This is a Moo. This is a place where I spend some/much/all of my time, but is not my real life. This does not exist. It will all be okay."[129]

For many of those participants—formalizers and resisters alike—who believed that institutional change was both imperative and impossible, the partial return of wizardly rule provided as much relief as disappointment. Agonism had proved exhausting.

Let us return, now, for a brief moment, to Roberto Unger. Unger envisions an intensely contentious society, in which conflict is a constant. This conflict is, indeed, a necessary corollary of antinaturalism: If nothing is to be viewed as permanently settled, if institutions and structures are to be subject to reformulation and transformation, conflict is an inevitable and necessary component of the political landscape. Unger acknowledges—and celebrates—that the social framework he advocates "must invite conflict rather than suppress it."[130] But Unger himself recognizes the dangers that ensue if a society becomes a perpetual conflict machine. He writes:

Everything ... might seem explicitly designed to reduce state and society alike to bitter strife and paralyzing confusion.... In the end, a regime of extreme instability would turn out to destabilize itself and to give way, at whatever cost, to a stabilized order. People would cry out for firm leaders and peacemaking institutions. Their freedom would seem intolerably burdensome to them if they could keep it only by accepting an uncertainty that disturbed every aspect of life and an antagonism that always stood ready to turn from programmatic disagreement to bitter quarreling and from quarreling to violence.[131]

Although in LambdaMOO the strife and confusion grew as much out of stalemate as instability, Unger accurately describes the social response to the mounting frustration. Instead of generating innovation and experimentation, perpetual conflict can produce political quiescence.

Unger speculates that the way to avoid this outcome is through the development of detailed and precise programmatic visions: "The more the conflicting partisans' visions get translated into detailed schemes of collective life ... the less likely it becomes that these visions will seem impenetrable to one another."[132] "The force of concreteness" will check instability by encouraging partisans to recognize what they share with their opponents, "for the prophetic dogmas of politics ... differ more than do the actual wants of people."[133] The experience of LambdaMOO, however, suggests that concreteness and specificity may not provide such a salve. Programmatic institutional suggestions in LambdaMOO have been extremely detailed and concrete—indeed, to be vetted by a wizard, specificity is imperative—and yet, partisans and factions have found little space for compromise. Metadisputes—disputes about the very nature of the dispute-resolution system, arguments about whether LambdaMOO should have law at all—have been especially prevalent and pointed. At least in this virtual society, it seems that the "actual wants of people" *do* differ tremendously. These repeated conflicts in LambdaMOO have been coupled with a shared recognition that social structures are up for grabs. Instead of producing creative fermentation and innovative reconceptions of political and legal mechanisms, this combination has produced factionalism, frustration, and a stalemate. Constant conflict may simply be more than a society can bear.[134]

After LTAD was pronounced, Lambda life continued and with it Lambda politics. Some insisted that LTAD "paralyzed" the existing political and legal institutions,[135] whereas others said that life in post-LTAD LambdaMOO had hardly changed at all.[136] The numbers of disputes decreased, however, and people noted that there was now a new way to deal with a situation a player found intolerable—persuade a sympathetic wizard to intervene, the virtual equivalent of running home to cry to mother.[137] A few hardy souls viewed LTAD as issuing a new challenge to the community to formulate its own, independent structures:

If we organize ourselves as a community, we may wield real power despite the wizards. The wizards may pull the plug ... on the database, they may pull the plug on any character. But they can't pull the plug on me, nor you, nor the community that has taken root here if we hold our own. None of the things the wizards control or define are paramount to our existence as a community, *if we really want it*. I guess it's a sort of maturity test. Can we organize ourselves enough to subsist as an independent community?[138]

But in the year since LTAD, no major institutional reconfigurations have emerged. The wizards' LTAD memo did provide a stark exit clause. If LambdaMOOers found the new direction "so disagreeable" that they thought that the virtual universe should come to an end, they could support a prevetted "shutdown petition." If a simple majority of MOOers supported this petition, the wizards promised that they would shut down LambdaMOO altogether. The population thus had the power to enact the virtual equivalent of nuclear meltdown by voting LambdaMOO out of existence. On March 10, 1997, this shutdown petition received enough signatures to become a ballot for consideration by the population. Many participants found the very existence of this ballot distressing, arguing that dissatisfied players had a perfectly good way of expressing their unhappiness—logging off and never returning. Why, therefore, should they have the power or the right to destroy the whole community simply because they no longer wanted to participate in it? Others felt that LambdaMOO had degenerated and should cease operation before it became even worse.[139] Some felt that the "shutdown petition" offered a good opportunity for reflection and voter mobilization. As one participant wrote,

I voted no, of course, but as one of the signers of the petition, I hope (and believe) that some good can come out of this. I think that we all tend to take things for granted, and while there are many frustrating things here, which easily come to mind, I for one hadn't thought much about what it would be like without this place.

And I don't think that caring about Lambda, the people and memories here is a sign that one has no real life; rather, in my case, I think it is one of the reasons my life is so rich. I also think that this petition will encourage a great number of people to learn a little bit about Lambda politics. Not that we need more political junkies, but enough so that people realize that it does affect their characters on Lambda.

I would be stunned if this didn't get the highest voter turnout in recent memory. And it seems completely unbelievable that this could ever pass. But if it did ... if despite the huge voter education drive that's already started, rallying the relative newbies [new players], still more than *half* of the voters wanted to shut down Lambda, then I don't know if I would want to hang out in such a bitter, angry place.[140]

Sure enough, when the polls closed on March 24, 1997, the Lambda MOO population, in the largest voter turnout in Lambda history, resoundingly defeated the shutdown ballot: 1,406 voted against, 95 in favor, and 68 abstained.

It is uncertain, however, whether the increased voter turnout spurred by the shutdown petition will have any lasting effects on Lambda politics. Whether this moment of reflection and political mobilization will create opportunities to overcome the stagnation and frustration that have hampered institutional transformation in LambdaMOO remains an open question. It is clear that virtual spaces like LambdaMOO offer—at least in theory—unparalleled opportunities "to entertain fantasies about possible forms of self-expression or association and to live them out."[141] Will the participants in virtual communities succeed in bringing this potential to life? Will they fail to take their virtual societies seriously or stay mired in factional disputes and ceaseless bickering? The lived realities of LambdaMOO suggest that all these are real possibilities. The experience of LambdaMOO further suggests that plasticity is no panacea. Unger's theoretical efforts to transcend liberalism may not, in practice, produce liberation.

Notes

I wish to thank Anne Branscomb, Joshua Dienstag, Bryant Garth, Michael Fischer, Larry Lessig, Robert Mnookin, and Stephen Robertson for helpful suggestions—and particular thanks are due to all the residents of LambdaMOO, without whom this chapter (literally) could not have existed. Thanks, also, to the American Bar Foundation for research support.

1. Robert Cover, The Supreme Court, 1982 Term—Foreword: Nomos and Narrative, 97 Harv. L. Rev 4 (1983), reprinted in Robert Cover, Narrative Violence and the Law 95, 100 (1993).

2. Roberto Unger, False Necessity, Part 1 of Politics: A Work in Constructive Social Theory 44 (1987).

3. For links to many resources about MOOs and MUDs, see The MUD Resource Collection, available at http://www.cis.upenn.edu/~lwl/mudinfo.html. The first MUD began in 1979. It was a fantasy-style adventure game, similar to a computer-based version of Dungeons and Dragons. On the history of MUDs, see generally Elizabeth Reid, Cultural Formations in Text-Based Virtual Realities, Master's thesis, University of Melbourne, 1994, p. 10, available at http://www.ee.mu.oz.au/papers/emr/index.html; see also Lauren P. Burka, A Hypertext History of Multi-User Dimensions, located in The MUD Archive, available at http://www.ccs.neu.edu/home/lpb/muddex.html.

4. *MUD* stands for "multiuser dungeon (or domain or dimension)." *MOO* stands for "MUD, object oriented." MOOs generally allow players to create and modify the virtual environment to a greater extent than do MUDs.

5. Concretely, when a guest arrives in LambdaMOO, exits the coat closet, and enters the living room, he or she will see the following description on the screen, in addition to a list of all players in the room at the time: "The Living Room: It is very bright, open, and airy here, with large plate-glass windows looking southward over the pool to the gardens beyond. On the north wall, there is a rough stonework fireplace. The east and west walls are almost completely covered with large, well-stocked bookcases. An exit in the northwest corner leads to the

kitchen and, in a more northerly direction, to the entrance hall. The door into
the coat closet is at the north end of the east wall, and at the south end is a slid-
ing glass door leading out onto a wooden deck. There are two sets of couches,
one clustered around the fireplace and one with a view out the windows. You see
README for New MOOers, Welcome Poster, a fireplace, Cockatoo, Helpful
Person Finder, lag meter, The Birthday Machine, and a map of LambdaHouse
here."

6. Pavel Curtis named LambdaMOO, and the core of the rooms in the main
house were designed to resemble his actual house. Some readers might suspect
from its name that LambdaMOO is gay-themed; this is erroneous.

7. Many, perhaps a majority of players, are college students. A study of 583 participants conducted in December 1993 revealed that the average age of players
was 23.66 years. In this same survey, 76 percent of players said that they were
male in real life and 23.4 percent said they were female (see e-mail correspondence between Pavel Curtis and Elizabeth Reid, Appendix 6 in Reid, supra note
3, at 66). Note that there is no way of confirming that survey respondents
answered honestly.

8. However, anyone who fails to log on for a certain period of time will be
"reaped" or "recycled," the virtual equivalent of death.

9. For an extensive discussion of the possibilities for virtual communities, see
Howard Rheingold, The Virtual Community (1993).

10. There have been proposals to limit guest access, so it is possible that guest
accessibility might diminish or even be eliminated.

11. As of spring 1996, reaching the top of the waiting list and receiving a
LambdaMOO character required about eight weeks.

12. This chapter focuses on the formal aspects of this order, the emergence not
of norms but of *law*. It is interesting that formal law has developed at all; many
scholars have emphasized the important role provided by informal social controls or, as Robert Ellickson puts it, of "order without law." See Robert
Ellickson, Order Without Law (1991). It would be worthwhile to ask explicitly
why informal mechanisms have not been sufficient within Lambda law, but serious discussion of this issue is beyond the scope of this chapter.

13. Roberto Unger, Social Theory: A Critical Introduction to Politics, a Work in
Constructive Social Theory 1 (1987) [henceforth Social Theory].

14. Unger, Social Theory, supra note 13, at 86.

15. Indeed, gender within LambdaMOO is not limited to the binary choice of
male and female. Characters can choose whether to be male, female, neuter, plu-
ral, or any one of several other genders.

16. "A large portion of player descriptions contain a degree of wish fulfillment;
I cannot count the number of 'mysterious but unmistakably powerful' figures I
have seen wandering around in LambdaMOO." Pavel Curtis, Mudding: Social
Phenomenon in Text-Based Virtual Realities (1993), available on the Internet at

ftp.parc.xerox.com/pub/MOO/contrib/papers. For discussion of the psychological aspects of self-presentation on MOOs, see Sherry Turkle, Life on the Screen (1995).

17. Id. at 145.

18. Id. at 154–57.

19. Unger, supra note 2, at 572–73.

20. The focus in this section is on the Lambda law/U.S. law relationship. Although LambdaMOO is certainly an international space, the majority of participants log in from U.S. sites.

21. Pavel Curtis's memo is memorialized in the history section of the LambdaMOO museum as Exhibit 11: LambdaMOO Takes a New Direction and is available at http://vesta.physics.ucla.edu/~smolin/lambda/laws_and_history/newdirection. His reintroduction of wizardly fiat is included in this book in chapter 17, appendix C. Note that in all of my quotations from text that originally appeared within LambdaMOO, I have taken the liberty of making minor grammatical and spelling corrections to increase clarity. Certain unusual aspects of Lambda speech I have left unaltered. Verbs in LambdaMOO often begin with an "at" sign (@). I have left intact certain abbreviations: *RL* stands for *real life*, *VL* stands for *virtual life*, *VR* stands for *virtual reality*, and *LM* stands for *LambdaMOO*. Also note that all references to petitions, ballots, and message numbers refer to texts that were produced in the MOO. Most of these can still be found in the MOO, but some of them have been purged from the MOO to reduce database size and have been stored in an ftp archive, located at ftp://ftp.lambda.moo.mud.org/pub/MOO/lambda/. Because what remains on the MOO and what is stored on the archive is constantly changing, I have not designated in which of the two locations any particular text that originated in LambdaMOO can currently be found.

22. As of February 1, 1996, the main criteria were that a character (1) not be a guest character or visitor and (2) be at least thirty days old, in Lambda time. *Social issues (#7233) at message 511.

23. These examples are based on several given in "help petitions" on LambdaMOO.

24. LambdaMOO has an internal e-mail system, a form of cyberspace within cyberspace. The mailing lists within LambdaMOO are extremely numerous; in early 1996, they numbered more than 175, not counting those associated with petitions, ballots, and disputes. Topics range from poetry to New York City MOOers, from discussions of the World Wide Web to gripes and complaints. Some lists—including *Group-Therapy and *Unfounded-Rumor—allow anonymous contributions. Of course, in LambdaMOO nearly everyone is anonymous—that is, a character identity in no way reveals a player's real-life identity. The existence of anonymity *within* LambdaMOO illustrates the extent to which participants take their character identities seriously and suggests that characters themselves develop social capital.

25. See notes 75–77 and accompanying text, discussing a petition that would have made the wizards accountable to a newly created Judicial Review Board.

26. For a discussion of this point within the MOO, see *Petitions-Process (#28350) at messages 317–324 and 496–502.

27. The most extreme power is, of course, the power to annihilate the MOO completely. Other important powers include the ability to remove a character from the MOO or to banish him or her for a period of time. Moreover, wizards can access information pertaining to users' real-life identities—their site information or their e-mail address. They also can enter a player's code and modify it, although they are supposed to limit this invasion to those times when it is necessary—for example, to fix a bug affecting other players.

28. The LambdaMOO population voted down a ballot called Social Ballot System, which would have allowed ballots and petitions regarding purely social matters requiring no technical implementation by the wizards. However, this distinction seems to be an artificial one. Within LambdaMOO, even changing a text is a technical change; for example, if Social Ballot System had passed, it would have required a change in "help petitions" reflecting the modification, which is itself a technical modification, albeit a minor one (see *Petition: Social_Ballot_System (#26877) and its associated mailing list for details on this proposal).

29. For the argument that real-world technological artifacts contain embedded political conceptions, see Langdon Winner, Do Artifacts Have Politics?, 109 Daedalus 121 (1980). On the importance of software as a regulatory mechanism in cyberspace, see Lawrence Lessig, Constitution and Code, 27 Cumb. L. Rev. (1996–1997).

30. This example indicates both the possibilities and the limits of "hardwiring" politics within technology. A person *can* be forced to scroll through the text of a petition but *cannot* be forced actually to read it.

31. Indeed, on most ballots only about 20 percent of the eligible population that has logged on during the voting period has actually bothered to cast a vote.

32. To require participants to vote, for example, players could be forced to stay within a voting room whenever they logged on and there were new ballots available; the only way to leave the voting room and return to "society" would be by voting. Or voting could be linked to some other aspect of MOO life; for example, those who did not vote in at least three-fourths of the last dozen ballots could be summarily denied any increase in quota. Alternatively, the system could send players notes reminding them of the current ballots and their need to vote every five minutes; the sheer annoyance would probably lead most players to vote in order to free themselves from the reminders. I am not advocating any of these systems; rather, I mean to illustrate the broad range of technological possibilities and the way that politics and technology cannot be seen as separate.

33. *Petition:TGB (#73565) at message 5.

34. See *Ballot:New-Arb (#54055); *Ballot:quota-restructuing (#25812); *Ballot:fix-ARB-elect (#42212).

35. See *Ballot:Minimal-Population-Growth (#75104); *Ballot:BirthControl (#57800).

36. See *Ballot:guest-booting (#40768); *Ballot:@Boot2 (#54631); *Ballot: FixBoot (#41859).

37. See *Ballot:@ban (#55917).

38. See *Ballot:Abuse (#68149).

39. See *Ballot:Validity (#4715).

40. See *Ballot:BurnBanHomo (#55541).

41. See *Ballot:No-Bribery (#55018).

42. Many MOOers are skeptical of this claim, although it is official policy.

43. Of course, although the mailing lists are the most public space for commentary, they are far from exclusive. A limitation of my analysis of arbitrations is that I am limited to the public record—the mailing list.

44. This language comes from *Ballot:Arbitration (#50392).

45. However, at least five votes to overturn are required for a decision to be overturned.

46. For example, if somebody refuses to participate or has not logged on within a reasonable period of time, a trial in absentia may be necessary. Id.

47. Id.

48. Note that implementing most of these punishments can be done only by a wizard. But if an arbitration decision is not overturned, the wizards are bound (or at least claim to be bound) to carry it out.

49. The etymological origin of *toading* comes from the actual toad. On some MUD's, toading is an unpleasant but far from fatal form of punishment in which the character's description is changed into that of a warty toad; he or she may also be paraded around or made to stay in some public place for the purpose of humiliation. In LambdaMOO, toading has come to mean permanent banishment.

50. *Dispute:Margeaux v. Yib (#35664) at message 7.

51. Id. at message 21.

52. *Dispute: Nosredna v. Kipp (#937865).

53. This case was brought by Nosredna, who was a wizard. Much of the discussion on the case's associated mailing list concerns the extent to which wizards can take action without going through official channels and the way to define the boundary between purely technical aspects of the MOO and social ones.

54. *Ballot:7a77 (#63854) at message 92.

55. Id. at message 41.

56. See, e.g., id. at messages 19, 26, 32.

57. *Ballot: New_Reaping (#54235).

58. See, e.g., id. at message 27.

59. See generally id.

60. As in real life, on LambdaMOO a page is a message that can be heard even if you are not in the same room; unlike real life, on LambdaMOO only the recipient of the page hears the message.

61. This is something of an overstatement; there are apparently ways to program around an @gag or @refuse command. But the commands certainly provide some degree of protection.

62. *Dispute:Abraxas v. lucifuge2 (#38613) at message 16.

63. *Dispute:Basshead v. lucifuge (#87718) at message 79.

64. *Dispute:Mickey v. Sunny (#71969) at message 27.

65. *Dispute:Abraxas v. lucifuge2 (#38613) at message 38.

66. *Dispute:Basshead v. lucifuge (#87718) at message 23.

67. *Dispute:Abraxas v. lucifuge2 (#38613) at message 50.

68. For an extensive discussion of spoofing, see Lee-Ellen Marvin, Spoof, Spam, Lurk and Lag: The Aesthetics of Text-based Virtual Realities, 1 J. Computer-Mediated Communications, Issue 2 (1995), available at http://www.usc.edu/dept/annenberg/vol1/issue2/index.html.

69. *Ballot:MooRights (#12797).

70. See the now-classic article, Julian Dibbell, A Rape in Cyberspace, Village Voice, Dec. 21, 1993, p. 36, available at http://www.levity.com/julian/cyberculture.html as well as many other locations on the World Wide Web.

71. *Ballot:AntiRape (#60535).

72. This ability to comment is much used. Dispute-associated mailing lists often have hundreds of message on them by the time the conflict is closed.

73. *Dispute:Basshead v. Lucifuge (#87718) at message 73.

74. *Dispute:Mickey v. Sunny (#71969) at message 115.

75. *Dispute:Basshead v. lucifuge (#87718) at message 20.

76. Note, however, that in *Basshead*, the arbitrator's careful, formal rulings did not prevent her initial decision from being overturned. Note also that this strategy is not limited to the arbitrators. In a libel dispute, one player invoked definitions from Black's Law Dictionary in his explanation of why the actions at issue ought to be legally cognizable. See *Dispute:Micky v. Sunny (#71969) at message 36.

77. *Ballot:Court (#54577).

78. The paragraph of "help manners" that arises in every harassment dispute is "sexual harassment (particularly involving unsolicited acts which simulate rape against unwilling participants) ... is not tolerated by the LambdaMOO community. A single incidence of such an act may, as a consequence of due process, result in permanent expulsion from LambdaMOO." Does this paragraph mean that sexual harassment is a toadable offense? Necessarily? What process is due? These and other questions arise with regularity.

79. Note that there are no provisions in the JRB ballot that prohibit people from resubmitting queries that have previously been decided. Thus, determined players could continuously try to reopen issues of law that the JRB had already settled. However, the JRB has the authority to dismiss summarily any case in which the issue of law has already been resolved.

80. See generally *Petition:Bill-of-Rights (#62261).

81. Id.

82. To a degree, then, this proposal recognized a distinction between normal law making and "higher law making," in that fundamental changes required increased involvement of the citizenry and different procedures. For a discussion of normal and higher law making, see generally, Bruce Ackerman, We the People (1991).

83. *Petition:Bill-of-Rights (#62261).

84. See *Ballot:LambdaMOO_Bill_of_Rights (#95555).

85. Unger, supra note 2, at 10.

86. See id. at 23. Unger writes that the best we can do is "invent ever more ingenious institutional instruments for our objectives. There is no escape from artifice. New artifice must cure the defects of past artifice. We pursue a mirage when we seek the pure undistorted system of free interaction."

87. Id. at 575.

88. Id. at 1 and 207.

89. See *Petition:Choosing-Justice (#12309).

90. Id. at message 2.

91. Id. at message 55.

92. See generally id.

93. See *Petition:Solve-your-differences-peacefully (#8426) and accompanying mailing list.

94. Id. at message 7 (written by petition's creator, but see also, e.g., messages 6 and 3).

95. *Petition: Beware! (#86562).

96. See *Ballot:Repeal-Arbitration (#78996).

97. See id. at message 39.

98. *Soc. at message.

99. One might argue that norms have emerged and provided sufficient regulation in other cyber locations, such as in Usenet news groups, despite the lack of face-to-face communication and the diversity of the community. However, (1) most (although not all) of the participants on Usenet have their words attached to their real-life name; (2) many of the norms are about ways of speaking—such as using emoticons (such as smiley faces) to express nuances, determining the appropriate length of posts, and so on—rather than about substantive matters like the proper balance between free speech and freedom from harassment; (3) many Usenet

groups actually have an extremely small number of regular posters, fewer than the number of LambdaMOO players who log on in an average week; and (4) these norms are insufficient to prevent frequent flame fests on many newsgroups.

100. In some cases, however, private norms might affect the standard applied by the courts—if, for example, the community's standard of care or an interpretive question were at issue.

101. Presumably, if a claim were brought in a real-life court after exhaustion within LambdaMOO, the review would be *de novo*.

102. This approach provides an illustration of how organizations can themselves generate what Robert Ellickson calls "controller-selecting rules"—the rules that determine who will resolve disputes that arise and whether the disputes enter the legal system at all. See Ellickson, supra note 12, at 131–34. For an extensive discussion of the operation of "controller-selecting" rules in cyberspace, see David G. Post, Anarchy, State, and the Internet: An Essay on Law-Making in Cyberspace, 1995 J. Online L. art. 3, available at http://www.law.cornell.edu/jol/jol.table.html. [Chapter 14 in this volume]

103. MOOs indeed have their origins in role-playing games like Dungeons and Dragons—hence, the original name of "multiuser dungeon."

104. See Turkle, supra note 16, at 177–209.

105. Id.

106. Id. at 184.

107. New State Ice Co. v. Liebmann, 285 U.S. 262, 311 (1932).

108. The notion that the protection of free speech is a protection from infringement *by the state* is entirely absent from every discussion of free speech within the MOO that I have seen. The dominant view within the MOO seems to be to view free-speech rights as inhering to individuals.

109. Turkle, supra note 16, at 192.

110. "Help dispute-process" on LambdaMOO.

111. *Petition:Bill-of-Rights (#62261) at message 95.

112. *Dispute:gru.v.SamIAm (#81090) at message 83.

113. Id.

114. *Dispute:Abraxas v. lucifuge2 (#386'13) at message 37.

115. *B:Undertakers_and_Executors_-_Elected (#80483).

116. See *News at message 300.

117. Id.

118. See id.

119. As one player put it: "But I also realize there is no real way to have self-government when the physical power here is in the hands of someone who doesn't want it. Power always flows to those who have the true physical power. The physical power here belongs to Pavel [Curtis] and his assigns. And there is

no way to wrest it from him, and since he built this place no legitimate right nor reason to" (*Arbitration at message 5183).

120. Available at http://vesta.physics.ucla.edu/~smolin/lambda/.

121. *B:LTAD(#90702) at message 23.

122. *B:LTAD(#90702).

123. Id. at message 6.

124. Id. at message 17.

125. Id. at message 32.

126. *Soc. at message 11905.

127. Id.

128. *Soc. at message 12157.

129. *Soc. at message 11951.

130. Unger, supra note 2, at 24.

131. Id. at 462.

132. Id. at 466.

133. Id. at 466–67.

134. For a similar critique of Unger, see Bernard Yack, Toward a Free Marketplace of Social Institutions: Roberto Unger's "Super-Liberal" Theory of Emancipation, 101 Harv. L. Rev. 1973–75 (1961).

135. *B:LTAD at message 19.

136. See, e.g., id. at message 26.

137. See *Arbitration at messages 5505 and 5508.

138. *Arbitration at message 5189.

139. See, e.g., *P:Shutdown (#100000) at message 235.

140. Id. at message 28.

141. Unger, supra note 2, at 579.

17

"help manners": Cyberdemocracy and Its Vicissitudes

Charles J. Stivale

What are the laws of comportment and respect in cyberspace? Assuming such "laws" (or at least, guidelines) were developed, how might they be enforced in online environments, especially those in which user anonymity is frequently the rule? These are questions that citizens of a growing number of synchronous (real-time) chat sites have addressed in a variety of ways as the popularity of Internet access has attracted more and more "cybernauts" online. The results of this "frontier" lawmaking have varied between sites, with rare successes, some notable failures, and always plenty of discussion. By drawing on my experiences and research on two so-called MOOs (multiuser dimensions, object oriented) in cyberspeak, I propose to examine issues of "frontier" legislation and self-governance that have evident analogues to experience in what "cybernauts" call RL (real life).

I also address a number of questions that an earlier version of this essay raised subsequent to its posting at LinguaMOO in January 1996. A MOO acquaintance, Susan Garfinkle, who in 1996 taught a course on Interpreting Cyberspace in the English Departent at the University of Pennsylvania, invited me to discuss the essay online with her class at PennMOO, a real-time discussion and learning site. Through advance publicity and word-of-pixel, news of this cyberseminar became known to "cybernauts" beyond the University of Pennsylvania class, and hence a

---

This chapter was originally presented at the Modern Language Association convention, December 1995. Various versions of the paper have since circulated on the Internet, and a version of the paper was published in the electronic journal *Enculturation* 1 (1997). This version appears by permission of the author.

sizable number of guests and other interested parties joined students at the event. That my reading of events on LambdaMOO, particularly those known as the SamIAm affair, did not meet with universal approval became quite evident in the contentious atmosphere that prevailed during the PennMOO seminar. Throughout this revision, I address objections raised there and since.

In order to situate my own position, let me recall the cautious attitude suggested by Constance Penley and Andrew Ross in the introduction to the *Technoculture* volume, a wariness "of the disempowering habit of demonizing technology" and a weariness with "postmodernist celebrations of the technological sublime" (xii). Since I proposed this as a talk in winter 1995, little did I realize the extent to which the demonizing tendency would galvanize the nation, indeed much of the world, focusing on issues of use and perceived potential abuse of online modes of expression. Little did I suspect, for example, that the arrest of the University of Michigan student, Jake Baker, for posting his rape/murder scenarios to a Usenet group with a woman student's real name as victim, would actually result in federal authorities manipulating postal laws to fit Baker's messages, however loathsome, into something resembling a crime. (The case was dismissed in June by a Federal judge; see Godwin 1995a). Little did I suspect that the dubious statistics in a report by University of Pittsburgh researcher Martin Rimm would be employed by a heretofore respected journalist, Philip Elmer-Dewitt, to fuel *Time* magazine's "Cyberporn" issue, which, in turn, fanned the flames of what passes for "debate" in Congress in its anticyberporn jihad.[1] Little did I suspect, therefore, that in outlining these "frontier tales" today, I would be relating analogues in text-based virtual reality not only of pressing questions, but of recent "demonizing" practices that continue to challenge us in an atmosphere that increasingly condones censorship and the limitation of our freedom of expression.

On the other hand, one has an array of choices that exemplify celebrations of the cybersublime—for example, the oft cited introduction to Michael Benedikt's *Cyberspace: First Steps* (1992). However, the source that I draw from is Mark Poster's 1996 essay "Cyberdemocracy: Internet and the Public Sphere," a surprising choice in that I do not differ at all with his analysis of the possibilities for reconceptualizing postmodern political potentialities. However, following a sophisticated analysis of the relations of text-based virtual reality to contemporary political theory, Poster offers a rather utopian view of the instantiation of these transformative political models. It is no small irony that I know this essay only thanks to the Net itself, and a further irony indicates complications that we researchers face in our speedy, digitized age. The day before presenting the first version of this paper at the Modern Language Association Convention on December 29, 1995, I attended a panel on which Mark Poster spoke (on Baudrillard), following which we chatted briefly. He thanked me for comments that I had previously sent to him about his WWW-listed essay, and I mentioned that I would be referring to it in my talk, to which he responded: "I assume you've read the latest version where I take account of your comments." For my panel presentation, the answer was, in fact, no, for I had not thought to check for an update. Forging ahead nonetheless, I stated in my introduction to the talk that the references corresponded to a heuristic, virtual Mark Poster. I subsequently consulted the "upgrade," and although Poster did make certain modifications, the original references remain intact, allowing me to frame the following tales and better to reveal clashes between cyber-theorizing and "flickering" online examples.

In particular, Poster contends, first: "The 'magic' of the Internet is that it is a technology that puts cultural acts, symbolizations in all forms, in the hands of all participants," and second, the Internet manifests an inherent "spectrum of modern versus postmodern identity construction." The "full novelty" of this displacement of ordinary speech into new forms of public spheres is most evident, says Poster, on MOOs, although he recognizes that the inhabitants "do not enjoy a democratic utopia" given the obvious hierarchies therein (notably, the elite status of site administrators, known as "wizards" or "janitors"). He maintains, though, that MOO sites do reveal "the diminution of prevailing hierarchies of race, class, and especially gender" (despite considerable research to the contrary; see Bruckman 1993 and Nakamura 1995) and that MOOs are places both "of difference from and resistance to modern society" and "of the inscription of new assemblages of self-constitution." He concludes that "because the Internet inscribes the new social figure of the cyborg and institutes a communicative practice of self-constitution, the political as we have known it is reconfigured. The wrapping of language on the Internet, its digitized, machine-mediated signifiers in a space without bodies, introduces an unprecedented novelty for political theory."

To consider some "flickering" examples, I must provide an all too brief explanation of the functioning and purposes of two sites chosen for these tales. Located on computers, respectively, at Xerox PARC (Palo Alto Research Center) in Palo Alto, California, and at the Massachusetts Institute of Technology in Cambridge, Massachusetts, LambdaMOO and MediaMOO provide virtual locations in which participants may contribute to synchronous (real-time) exchanges and programming, each site with an identified chief administrator, Pavel Curtis (Lambda) and Amy Bruckman (Media), designated as "wizards" or "janitors" (see Bruckman 1996; Curtis 1992). LambdaMOO's social function is evident in its referential paradigm, a "large" house and its grounds, with a set of main public rooms for group discussions and a vast web of individual virtual spaces created by the participants themselves (see HumbertHumbert's LambdaMOO archive). MediaMOO's paradigm is a research complex, with libraries, laboratories, class and meeting rooms, and a network of individual spaces, less extensive than on Lambda (see Bruckman and Resnick 1993). Whereas LambdaMOO's fraternity house atmosphere aptly summarizes much of the social exchange there,[2] MediaMOO presents itself as a more serious location for "media research," a difference that extends to the site administration (Bruckman 1996). That is, whereas one's LambdaMOO character registration is hindered only by a delay due to limitations on per-day admissions, MediaMOO requires the vetting of one's current research activities in media studies for admission as a registered participant. This policy helps ensure that participants will have a commonality of professional interests, thereby maximizing (in theory) research exchanges, but one result of the vetting policy, admitted or not, has been to prevent the mass influx that has slowed transmission speed and increased pandemonium on other sites, including Lambda. Moreover, whereas disclosure of real-life personal information on LambdaMOO is entirely voluntary, all registered MediaMOO citizens must accept public access to their names, e-mail addresses, and research interests through a simple, preset public command.

Once a participant has registered and chosen a character name and a gender (male, female, neuter, and half-dozen other variants) and composed a personal description, interactions within MOOsites acclimatize one quickly to a complex array of social interactions and programming possibilities (see Marvin 1996; Reid 1995). One also becomes increasingly aware of the uses, and often abuses, to which the programming language on the MOO can be put (see Cherny 1995; Stivale 1996). The term "help manners" in my title refers to the online guide that each participant (whether registered or transitory as a guest) is advised by the site administrators to consult as an orientation to the site (see appendix A).[3] This lengthy document (eight twenty-four-line screens) has evolved over the nearly six years of the online site's existence and currently states: "Like members of other communities, the inhabitants of LambdaMOO have certain expectations about the behavior of members and visitors. This article ⟨'help MANNERS'⟩ lays out a system of rules of courteous behavior, or 'manners,' which have been agreed upon by popular vote."

As appendix A shows, these "rules" are presented as a series of indications (1) against jeopardizing the site's integrity through hacking or cracking, (2) against hogging database resources, and (3) against abusing other players. Among the latter points are concise commandments against different forms of harassment—"spamming," "shouting," "spoofing," "spying," "teleporting objects that one does not own," "emoting ⟨I.E., EXPRESSING⟩ violence or obscenities"—that are all summed up by the rule to respect others players' privacy and, above all, their sensibilities. It is regarding this respect of "sensibilities" that most contention between participants arises.

In both of the sites that I consider here, despite a general desire for forms of government that do not emulate "real life," the inhabitants have discovered that some form of governing body or process is necessary in order to "enforce consensus" and to create sanctions against participants who willfully infringe on guidelines in support of that consensus. Of course, as in any documentary account, my own bias plays an important role in the selection (and exclusion) of materials, as well as in the interpretations I give to these. For example, I have met several of the individuals from the MOOs discussed and have developed friendships as well as strong enmities with certain online participants. Far from clouding my judgment, these relationships give me a healthy perspective to see through some of the cyber-democratic hyperbole often wielded by MOO-utopians. Moreover, LambdaMOO has remained and still remains the online site that I most frequent, so nothing in what follows contests the considerable efforts by programmers and administrators there or on MediaMOO for that matter. Rather, this chapter discusses the gap between best intentions in cyberspace—to enable democratic representation and to found due process—and the limitations of these intentions. In fact, in a May 16, 1996, New Direction statement (formerly item 300 on *News), the wizards at LambdaMOO have finally admitted these limitations and thereby support the main conclusions that I drew in the original version of this essay.

My account of this developing process of self-governance in cyberspace relates four broad "moments" on two sites during which these processes were transformed in significant ways. I should emphasize that participants with greater online longevity and/or different perspectives on these events may well identify not only other moments as key ones, but also place a different spin on how they unfolded. I thus recognize that this narrative is but one possible account, yet it is one that I base on extant documents as well as direct experiences within the sites (see HumbertHumbert). In appendix B I provide an outline of the successive moments as a point of reference.

I

During 1992, after several years of site development, the LambdaMOO wizards wearied of policing the rudimentary "help manners" statement on an ad hoc basis in individual disputes between participants (Curtis 1992; DIAC '94 1994). Thus, in an internal post dated December 9, 1992, entitled "On to the next stage ..." and known as "Lambda Takes a New Direction," Pavel Curtis (as archwizard Haakon) pronounced an every-participant-for-himself-or-herself policy of nonintervention by the wizards except as technicians in matters of site maintenance and development (see HumbertHumbert). He subsequently stated that the result of this was to make hassles and unfriendliness on the site not less but *more* annoying (DIAC '94 1994). In March 1993 an incident of so-called virtual rape and online abuse occurred and was described in Julian

Dibbell's December 1993 *Village Voice* essay. The offending character, Mr. Bungle, had acquired the programming capacity necessary to isolate female-presenting characters and then to "spam" to their screens (that is, transmit) sexually explicit and violent statements. Subsequent public discussion, including a "town meeting" that Mr. Bungle attended briefly, allowed many participants to express their outrage, but with no process of adjudication nor of sanctions in place, it fell to one wizard unilaterally and rather reluctantly to accede to the expression of general outrage and to "enforce consensus" by accepting responsibility for "toading" (permanently excluding) the offending character. As a result of this "germinating event" (to use Curtis's expression; DIAC '94 1994), Curtis took it upon himself to institute a petition and ballot system through which citizens could vote measures into place. Following this unilateral act (contested by a few as inherently undemocratic since accomplished by fiat) was the initial ballot that instituted a formal "dispute" process with registered mediators to hear and resolve grievances and providing possible sanctions against disputants, when appropriate.

II

Meanwhile, until fall 1993 no MediaMOO system of governance was in place other than the autocratic rule of the site's chief "janitor," Amy Bruckman. Although having initiated a "Forum on Democracy" shortly after starting the site in early 1993, Bruckman has stated that little resulted from this since no participants yet seemed invested enough at that point to pursue such a direction (DIAC '94 1994). The site's registration requirement—to have one's research activities vetted and approved as a precondition for admission—changed this attitude as a number of players contested some of Bruckman's negative decisions as arbitrary. Thus, following a public online meeting in October 1993, a MOO Council was instituted through a process by which particular players "represented" constituencies of at least fifteen MediaMOO "citizens." In practice, the Council's solely advisory role to Bruckman included deciding requests for registration, but the vagueness of the Council's broader purpose became a source of contention in itself and eventually contributed to its dissolution.

Throughout 1993, the petition, ballot, and dispute processes were developed on LambdaMOO, and all citizens were apprised of procedures and rights therein. The December 1993 Dibbell article, while bringing into very public (and print) view a number of activities of unwelcome "spam" that had occurred early in the year, also inspired a character named Dr_Jest, purported to be Mr. Bungle's latest reregistered avatar, to undertake a campaign of abuse that included homophobic comments against one MOO "citizen" who then duly availed herself of the "dispute" process. Besides massive online public debate of this dispute, the result was Dr_Jest's exclusion ("toading") despite his refusal to recognize the validity of the mediation process at all.

III

The debate on verbal abuse and, more generally, on community standards continued into 1994, inspiring an antirape ballot entitled Virtual Rape Consequences that attempted to define parameters of sexual abuse well beyond the originally slender "help manners" guidelines of "respect[ing] other players' sensibilities." While being defeated after extensive and heated discussion in the spring of 1994, the initiative spoke well of the ballot process, while also revealing the discomfort of many participants with the ongoing interpretations of appropriate behavior that discussion of the ballot had raised. As a voting MOO citizen, I opposed the *Ballot:AntiRape not because I approve of the abusive and sexually explicit behavior inflicted on all MOO participants at one time or another. Rather, like many voters, I felt that the line was not adequately delineated in the ballot proposal between what constituted abuse and what constituted playfulness, particularly in the use of certain commands designated in the proposal (cf. Stivale 1996 on levels of spam). Hence, however strictly defined some proponents felt this measure to be, others could not endorse the potential for abuse that the ballot's lack of specificity might have made possible.

The partisanship resulting from this debate created some strong divisions, and as many participants were registered on both LambdaMOO and MediaMOO (and elsewhere), discussion and debate occurring on one site had repercussions on the other.

A subsequent dispute on LambdaMOO against a player named SamIAm brought these sentiments out forcefully by overlapping from one MOO to the other and revealing the fragility of the dispute system. To this day, the exceptional procedures adopted in this dispute remain a bone of contention, particularly the recourse to a "shadow" disputant, named gru, representing unnamed disputing parties, rather than their publicly and directly evoking the dispute as established guidelines dictated.

Before continuing, however, I should point out my own stakes in this matter. I make this and other admissions both because I was accused at the PennMOO cyberseminar and subsequently of bias in favor of SamIAm and also because I wish to rectify omissions that I made in the earlier versions of this essay in a rather misguided attempt at discretion. Since open and therefore revelatory "facts" are called for, so be it.

Over several months prior to the *dispute:gru.vs.SamIAm, I had spoken online and corresponded (by internal MOOmail and regular e-mail) with SamIAm and his "typist." We discovered many common interests, and we also shared the rather intense and eventually disagreeable relationship with a character named Nancy, author of the aforementioned *Ballot:AntiRape that both SamIAm and I opposed. However, during the rancorous exchanged regarding this ballot, SamIAm seemed intent on questioning Nancy's bona fides and even honesty in arguing her pro-ballot case. Hence, the rancor between them about an internal MOO issue, laced with generous doses of personal enmity, was well established at the time of the SamIAm affair and no doubt motivated some of the efforts against him on LambdaMOO and elsewhere. Few MOO citizens, if any, have been aware of my close relationship with SamIAm's typist, and critics of this essay have adduced some sort of alliance between us from the record of comments that I have made on the MOO and from various internal political positions that I have supported. Although I would be dissembling were I to pretend not to have my own personal interests as well, I, like any other MOO citizen, have not been privileged to view any actual charges against SamIAm, and so my argument here in no way seeks to exonerate him or plead on behalf of his actions, whatever they were. Rather, I wish to call into question the procedure of the dispute against him since, presumably (if the accusers' case, maintained to this day, is to be believed) there was ample documentation available to judge him according to the formal process in place.

What makes this process so reprehensible is not merely that a citizen was deprived of the procedures afforded to all other disputants, even to Dr_Jest. It is also so because defenders of this procedure have managed to maintain the smoke screen around the events that occurred. For example, even the charges against SamIAm are contested since the secret proceedings prevented public and official statement of these, and readers of the dispute list could receive only unreliable versions of these charges posted by certain disputants themselves (cf. 54 on *dispute:gru.vs.SamIAm, posted by gru, the "shadow" disputant). These secret proceedings arose from the mediator's initial judgment that the sensitive nature of the alleged offenses required maintaining both the disputants' anonymity and nondefinition of specific charges against SamIAm. With the resultant secretive deliberation in progress, a public "trial" by unsubstantiated rumor (passing as "documented" fact posted again to the dispute list by one disputant) revealed that SamIAm had allegedly verbally abused and even threatened the offline personal or professional well-being of one or several participants on LambdaMOO.

However, following the PennMOO cyberseminar (on April 11, 1996), one student in the course, Katherine Bunt, interviewed a LambdaMOO (and PennMOO) wizard, Seth Rich, who denied that any "shadow" disputant or secretive procedures took place. In this interpretation of "facts," the disputant gru took it upon himself alone to lodge a dispute against the offending SamIAm. Yet the record of the dispute belies such distortions since, contrary to previous disputes, *no* record of specific charges from the mediator exists in any of the documents on the dispute. Whatever denials may arise from defenders of the dispute process, the bottom line remains an abuse of this process voted into place and supported in good faith by MOO citizens.[4]

Yet another factor made resolving this dispute impossible: one then anonymous disputant (later revealed by SamIAm to be none other than Nancy) retaliated preemptively against SamIAm's actual offline registrant by contacting his local system's administrator to allege commission of offenses that had yet to be adjudicated anywhere. SamIAm's typist was forced to accede to local demands to cease all MOO activities to protect an ongoing collaborative project that required access to the

Internet. Thus sanctioned in his work site without due process, he was then "sentenced" in absentia to a six-month suspension from Lambda-MOO without being able to mount a defense. Hence, from an examination of documentation on the *dispute:gru.vs.SamIAm list (see messages 197, 199, 203, 206–07, and 215 on June 6–7, 1994), the real-life personal nature of this dispute becomes evident, paralleling, if not superseding, the strictly MOO-related issues.

Meanwhile, the case had already overlapped onto MediaMOO since some SamIAm disputants on LambdaMOO were concurrently vested as MediaMOO Council members and brought forth an initiative to exclude SamIAm from this site as well. The rationale presumably was that any abuse alleged to have occurred on LambdaMOO must also have taken place on MediaMOO as well, and thus SamIAm was just as culpable on one site as on the other. Chief janitor Amy Bruckman admitted subsequently that, while the Council had no specific charge to advise on such matters, she had felt justified at the time in accepting its decision to exclude SamIAm from the site (Council discussion list). However, she also initiated a public discussion of matter (late June 1994), and once the unsubstantiated nature of the LambdaMOO charges and even a possible conflict of interest in the Council became suspected, Bruckman (as chief janitor) overturned the Council's decision and readmitted SamIAm to MediaMOO (an admission made moot in any case given the owner's agreement to refrain from all such activity). Discussion of these actions continued during the summer of 1994 among MediaMOO constituents, also addressing the role of the Council more generally. After much debate, the Council members agreed that the Council had been a noble experiment in self-governance, but with only an awkwardly defined advisory role, the Council's time spent on deliberative activities finally had become too burdensome. Thus, in late summer 1994, the Council dissolved itself, and MediaMOO returned to the autocratic governance that had existed before—that is, Bruckman assisted in technical and programming matters by a small cadre of janitors.

IV

While the MediaMOO Council experiment was instructive about the possibilities and limitations of representative self-governance on an

Internet site, the LambdaMOO experience still continues. Sunny, a vociferous proponent of what might be called MOO "civil liberties," took an increasingly unpopular stand throughout 1994 in trying to expose the nexus of self-interest that structures relationships between different participants in governance roles on the site and, indeed, between different sites on the Net. For her efforts, she was harassed with a number of disputes and even with a ballot initiative that, had it passed, would have resulted in her permanent exclusion (toading) from Lambda. In an ironic twist, however, her efforts in 1994 were recognized at the end of 1995 after she was absent from LambdaMOO for a sufficient length of time that her character was designated for recycling ("reaping"). Another ballot, opposite to the toading ballot of 1994, entitled "Save Our Sunny," would have "immortalized" her character, permanently preventing it from being reaped. Only Sunny's eleventh-hour return to thank everyone for their concern eliminated the ballot's necessity, while reminding all that, despite her extended absence, she had by no means departed definitively.

While 1994 might be considered the year of Sunny, 1995 was arguably the year of the "collective assemblage" known as Tchinek. For some LambdaMOO citizens, the SamIAm dispute was democracy in action, while for others, it brought into full view another aspect of democracy—the vulnerability of the process to be subverted by a select few. In this case, subversion was not only by one mediator's decision to block all but the most limited disclosure but also by machinations of particular disputants to manipulate real-life claims and tactics for maximum effect in the text-based virtual reality environment.

In January 1995, the appearance on LambdaMOO of a newly named character, Tchinek, claiming to serve as means of access for an authorized collective of registrants, coincided approximately with the end of SamIAm's six-month suspension and marked a new phase in political strategies.[5] On arrival, Tchinek sought a dispute, first, to test a loophole he-they had discovered and, second, to challenge the process with the claim of being above and beyond this system of arbitration. And what better way was there to offend sensibilities than to revive the SamIAm affair? Thus, in the context of a discussion on the internal *social-list about the Jake Baker case (the University of Michigan student expelled and then arrested for posting rape-murder fantasies to the Usenet), Tchinek posted publicly within LambdaMOO a copy of the letter sent in spring 1994 to the local systems' administrator of SamIAm's registrant, initially complete with name, address, and institutional affiliation of the sender (he removed the original post several hours later, replacing it with an expurgated version, without the aforementioned name, address, and affiliation). Predictably, this former disputant employed arbitration in not one but two simultaneous disputes against both Tchinek and SamIAm, but unpredictably, Tchinek then lodged a dispute against every arbitrator on LambdaMOO, which he-they then quickly withdrew. Only then, in attempting to assign an arbitrator to the dual disputes, did the arbitration programming reveal the loophole that Tchinek was exploiting: no arbitrator could adjudicate a dispute in which one of the parties had previously been involved in a dispute with that arbitrator, hence jeopardizing any dispute against Tchinek.

Undaunted, the wizards immediately patched the loophole (certain passages in the current "help manners" are a result of this effort), but although arbitrators were found for the dual disputes, they both ruled independently that "one should fix the ⟨ARBITRATION⟩ system, NOT punish Tchinek." Indeed, the arbitrator in the dispute against Tchinek stated further that "arbitration is becoming the haven for the lynch mob, and I don't like it; for this reason, I am unlikely to arbitrate any more disputes in the future, as it seems most disputants don't want arbitration, they want blood" (February 28, 95). Despite subsequent retaliation against the arbitrator (via harassment) and against Tchinek (via disputes and petitions), Tchinek succeeded not only in exposing the documentation employed against SamIAm offline based on unsubstantiated allegations but also in demonstrating the point that he-they and others critical of the dispute process had been making all along—its vulnerability to manipulation by those determined to exploit it for their own ends. Moreover, he-they ended the year with yet another dispute, this time formally contesting Pavel Curtis's unmandated initiation of the ballot and dispute process in 1993.

While these tales may strike some as an insider's view of *As the MOO Turns*, the aftermath of these allegations is quite instructive about the delicate balance between laws that regulate site administration, interstate and international communication, and the freedom of expression that sustains the very dynamic of these sites, asynchronous and synchronous alike. These tales stand, I would argue, as a sobering lesson of just how limited are the current efforts, however well intentioned, to develop online cyberdemocracy due to concomitant practices of distortion of and infringement on rights, practices imported piecemeal from real-time personal and political processes. These tales would seem to contradict any contention that "in Internet communities, [the fetishistic aura attached to authority holders] is more difficult to maintain [since] the Internet seems to discourage the endowment of individuals with inflated status" (Poster 1996). For what status could be more inflated than a site administrator's power, literally, to pull the plug on a site or, short of that, to make unilateral decisions of both programmatic and social nature with which the participants have no choice but to abide?

Moreover, in the SamIAm case, no adjudication took place offline, and in VR only the grossest subversion of the established process occurred. The result was that a researcher was required by his system's administrator to agree not to "break laws" in his workplace based solely on hearsay allegations of his already having done so or having intended to do so. Only had the researcher been subjected to some more formal punishment without due process (such as loss of contract, Internet account, or employment) could he then have tried to prove in court that a civil wrong had been committed, most likely at his own expense of time, money, and reputation. And this process would have been further complicated by discrepancies between international laws and jurisdictions.

On LambdaMOO, the petition, ballot, and dispute processes have been challenged throughout 1995 and into 1996, but most efforts to define MOO rights through various ballots (such as a Bill of Rights or a MOO Convention) have been stymied both by a mix of general cyberpolitical indifference and by gridlock among the politically committed minority on just how to cope with the complex conflicts between guarantees for freedom of expression and guarantees for virtual community standards. One exception, that confirms the general rule, is the revised version of "help manners," a stopgap measure to shore up the loopholes revealed through Tchinek's return initiatives. A subsequent twist in the saga occurred on May 16, 1996, when the LambdaMOO wizards proclaimed yet another "New Direction" (see appendix C). While maintaining the players' "voice" via petitions and ballots, the wizards finally yield *de jure* to the technocratic, top-down governmental system that has heretofore existed *de facto* by "reintroducing wizardly fiat."

More twists on this continuing saga came in early 1999. For years since the events recounted above, the character(s) Tchinek/SamIAm remained a thorn in the side of MOO citizens of Lambda. Finally, in January 1999, after a rancorous exchange about a seemingly insignificant but nonetheless annoying accusation by Tchinek of conflict of interest, one wizard simply @toaded him-them once and for all, unilaterally. In many ways, this action replicates the decision made in 1993 regarding the Mr. Bungle "rape in cyberspace," the difference being that in the interim LambdaMOO had tried and failed to institute any semblance of fair online due process. In retaliation, a Web page appeared in June 1999 entitled "Bovine Spongiform Encephalopathy" (1999). With the format of a newspaper page, this site provides a number of "articles" presumably documentating an array of abuses by members of different MOOs, notably LambdaMOO and DhalgrenMOO.[6]

The French expression, "plus ça change, plus c'est la même chose" (the more it changes, the more it stays the same) would seem to apply here, suggesting that postmodernist claims for transformation of political structures through cyberspace have yet to find practical models through which they might effectively be realized, even (or especially) on MOOs. Such a stark conclusion may strike some as self-evident, even to confirm precisely what cyberskeptics and "demonizers" have claimed all along about this application of technology. However, Poster (1996) has argued in response to such skepticism that

> the "postmodern" position need not be taken as a metaphysical assertion of a new age; that theorists are trapped within existing frameworks as much as they may be critical of them and wish not to be; that in the absence of a coherent alternative political program the best one can do is to examine phenomena such as the Internet in relation to new forms of the old democracy, while holding open the possibility that what might emerge might be something other than democracy in any shape that we may conceive it given our embeddedness in the present. Democracy, the rule by all, is surely preferable to its historic alternatives.

For those of us committed to participating in and developing online microworlds and to contributing to the concomitant community building, however fluid and even ephemeral this conception of community may be, the evidence of cyberpolitical indifference, gridlock, and lack of appropriate models should not deter us from attempting to pursue modes of governance that fall prey neither to the pitfalls of democracy nor to the traps of democracy's alternatives, particularly of the dictatorial form. This experimentation with the medium at our disposal is but one phase in a learning process that is far from complete and that might yield some unforeseen results, in some flickering virtual space-time.

Appendix A.   "help manners"

[The following excerpts from LambdaMOO were revised in 1995. The complete text is available at http://vesta.physics.ucla.edu/~smolin/lambda/laws_and_history/help_manners.]

LambdaMOO, like other MUDs, is a social community; it is populated by real people interacting through the computer network. Like Members of other communities, the inhabitants of LambdaMOO have certain expectations about the behavior of visitors. This article lays out a system of rules of courteous behavior, or "manners," which has been agreed upon by popular vote.

First of all, any action that threatens the functional integrity of the MOO, or might cause legal trouble for the MOO's supporters, will get the player responsible thrown off by the wizards. If you find a loophole or bug in the core, report it to a wizard without attempting to take advantage of it … [three paragraphs on loopholes].

Beyond that, there are two basic principles of friendly MOOing: let the MOO function and don't abuse players.

Let the MOO Function
Besides not trying to hack or break things, this means not hogging resources by taking up more memory or processing time than necessary … [three paragraphs on resources].

Don't Abuse Other Players
The MOO is a fun place to socialize, program, and play as long as people are polite to each other. Rudeness and harassment make Lambda-

MOO less pleasant for everyone. Do not harass or abuse other players, using any tactic including

• Spamming (filling their screen with unwanted text)
• Teleporting them or their objects without consent
• Emoted violence or obscenities
• Shouting (sending a message to all connect players) ... [shouting explained]
• Spoofing (causing messages to appear not attributed to your character) ...
• Spying—Don't create or use spying devices ... [Including 'silent', i.e., unannounced, "teleportation," i.e. movement, into rooms]
• Sexual harassment (particularly involving unsolicited acts which simulate rape against unwilling participants)—Such behavior is not tolerated by the LambdaMOO community. A single incidence [sic] of such an act may, as a consequence of due process, result in permanent expulsion from LambdaMOO.

In general, respect other players' privacy and their right to control their own objects, including the right to decide who may enter or remain in their rooms.

Also respect other players' sensibilities. MOO inhabitants and visitors come from a wide range of cultural backgrounds both in the U.S. and abroad and have varying ideas of what constitutes offensive speech or descriptions. Please keep text that other players can casually run across as free of potentially offensive material as you can. If you want to build objects of areas that are likely to offend some segment of the community, please give sufficient warning to casual explorers so that they can choose to avoid those objects or areas.

Self-Defense

Avoid revenge! If someone is bothering you, you have several options. The appropriate first step is usually to ask them to stop. If this fails, and avoiding the person in insufficient, useful verbs include @gag, @refuse, and @eject....

Note these following rules established by passage of *b<ALLOT>: Patch-Arbitration-Loopholes (#4223) [passed April 1995]:

• All characters are bound by some system of justice which has been voted by the people. Characters are free to suggest that this is not so, but such suggestions will [be] regarded as "mere speech" and will carry no force of law. In particular, Arbitrators will not consider such claims of exemption to be material. Characters who wish not to be subject to the lawfully created rules of this MOO are, like anyone else, free to request that their accounts be turned off.

• No character may in any way exploit the use of multiple characters to beat the system. For example, if a character is newted for punitive reasons, all characters controlled by that typist will be newted AND if that typist shows up controlling a guest during that period, he is still not welcome.

If you have a serious problem with another player, you may wish to consider invoking arbitration, in which some player decides the dispute. Since arbitration is some trouble and is binding on both parties, make sure you really want it before invoking it. See "help arbitration" for details.

Appendix B.   Chronology of Cyberdemocratic Processes at LambdaMOO and MediaMOO

Date	*LambdaMOO*	*MediaMOO*
Pre-1993	Ad hoc adjudication by wizards	—
December 1992	"LambdaMOO Takes a New Direction": intervention by wizards only on technical, not social, matters	—
Spring 1993	"A Rape in Cyberspace," the Mr. Bungle affair resolved by an ad hoc wizard intervention; discussions begin about a dispute and arbitration process	MediaMOO online: Autocratic direction by site "janitor"
Summer to fall 1993	Dispute, arbitration, petition, and ballot processes defined and activated	Site admission policy questioned; October "town meeting" leads to establishing an elected advisory Council
December 1993 Jan 1994	J. Dibbell's *Village Voice* article Dr_Jest disputed decisions by consensus	Council continues

Winter to spring 1994	Diverse ballot issues raise governance and conduct issues, including *ballot: Antirape, which fails to be passed; disputes (particularly against Sunny) take on an ad hominem/feminam tenor	Council continues
Spring to summer 1994	Dispute: gru.vs.SamIAm: due to alleged delicacy of charges, dispute procedures superseded; SamIAm "newted" (suspended) for 6 months, while "real" typist required to cease MOO activities due to allegations	Council concurs on suspending SamIAm for charges imported from LambdaMOO
Summer 1994	Sunny (and others) question the SamIAm procedures, the dispute and arbitration process	MOO citizens and Council members question the SamIAm suspension, as well as the efficacy of the Council; the Council disbands
Fall 1994	Continued questioning of the dispute and arbitration process	MediaMOO governance returns to autocratic direction by janitors
Winter 1995	Return of SamIAm (under a new character name), guerilla subversion of dispute process, redefinition of "help manners"	
1995	Attempts to define Bill of Rights and MOO Constitution as well as a new Justice process; except for revision of loopholes in "help manners" all ballots fail, both for lack of general political interest and for lack of clarity in different ballots' implications for restriction of freedom or expression.	

Appendix C.   Reintroducing Wizardly Fiat Message 300 from *News (#123):

Date: Thu May 16 11:00:54 1996 PDT
From: Haakon (#2)
To: *News (#123)
Subject: LambdaMOO Takes Another Direction

On December 9, 1992, Haakon posted "LambdaMOO Takes a New Direction" (LTAND). Its intent was to relieve the wizards of the responsibility for making social decisions and to shift that burden onto the players themselves. It indicated that the wizards would thenceforth refrain from making social decisions and serve the MOO only as technicians. Over the course of the past three and a half years, it has become obvious that this was an impossible ideal: the line between "technical" and "social" is not a clear one and never can be. The harassment that ensues each time we fail to achieve the impossible is more than we are now willing to bear.

So we now acknowledge and accept that we have unavoidably made some social decisions over the past three years and inform you that we hold ourselves free to do so henceforth.

1. We Are Reintroducing Wizardly Fiat.   In particular, we henceforth explicitly reserve the right to make decisions that will unquestionably have social impact. We also now acknowledge that any technical decision may have social implications; we will no longer attempt to justify every action we take.

Players will still have a voice, however. Your input is essential. We will keep our existing institutions for now, with the modifications described below, but we encourage you to develop ideas for replacing these institutions (as will be described in section 2).

a. Petitions   The petition system will remain in its current form, with the following change:

In cases where difficulties arise that were unanticipated by the vetting process, we reserve the right to reinterpret and/or explicitly veto any clause of any passed ballot.

We will continue to vet petitions in order to minimize the use of ballot veto, and we will continue to do so in terms of the existing vetting criteria in most cases. However, we will not rule out the possibilities of vetting being denied for other reasons or of the vetting criteria being revised by fiat.

b. Arbitration We explicitly reserve

• The right to veto any Arbitrator decision, particularly one that significantly impairs the ability of the wizards to do their jobs.
• The right to veto any Arbitration Change Proposal that is clearly not a "minor change" in the spirit of *Ballot:Arbitration (#50392) or that significantly impairs the ability of the wizards to do their jobs.

These may be temporary measures, as we hope to facilitate revision or replacement of Arbitration so that it may more adequately meet the needs of the community.

c. Wizardly Actions with Social Implications The wizards will no longer refrain from taking actions that may have social implications. In three and a half years, no adequate mechanism has been found that prevents disruptive players from creating an intolerably hostile working environment for the wizards. The LTAND ideal that we might somehow limit ourselves solely to technical decisions has proven to be untenable.

2. Alternatives to Wizards Making Social Decisions We encourage you, the players, to devise new mechanisms that will help minimize the need for the wizards to make unilateral social decisions. Several mechanisms, most notably the Arbitration system, seem less than ideal for the purpose, yet are too deeply entrenched to be changed with the petition system. We would like to try new mechanisms and to enable more radical changes than the current petition system will allow. We would like the players to propose ideas for major new institutions and ways to select among the proposals. We hope this will introduce a new dynamism to LambdaMOO that will allow us to find better solutions to some of our more fundamental problems.

Similarly, we hope to facilitate an overhaul of the current petition and ballot system if the players want it.

Do keep in mind, though, that we cannot keep LambdaMOO running without the wizards Haakon has selected. "Cyberspace" and "new social reality" rhetoric aside, so long as the MOO is located on a single RL machine at a single RL site subject to RL laws and liabilities, there will be those deemed responsible for the use of that hardware. Part of the need for administrators is also inherent in the LambdaMOO security model and the organization of LambdaCore, while some of this need is a consequence of various quirks of LambdaMOO society (e.g., the correspondence between RL identities and MOO identities needing to remain secret and yet the need for someone to maintain it). While we might consider ways to decentralize some of these tasks, the fact remains that we simply can't decentralize everything. We are still open to your suggestions for ways to decentralize what we can.

Suggestions such as

• Persons not well trusted by Haakon might be granted wizard bits as a result of popular election, or
• We might set up a "wizard machine" to run arbitrary wizardly code with NO human intervention at all

are not acceptable, however. There may be site administrators somewhere who will accept the risks involved in implementing these ideas, but we will not.

3. Rejection of the New Direction?   We realize that not everyone will agree that this is the best new direction LambdaMOO might take. We don't doubt that some of the polemics among you will be able to come up with a different slant, e.g. (just to save you some trouble)

• Wizardly blackmail
• Military coup
• Martial law
• Nuclear terrorism

Some of you may find the new direction so disagreeable that you will consider ways to force an end to the new direction or ways to make the wizards' lives miserable because of it. Instead of making the use of civil disobedience or wizard harassment be the necessary means for shutting down LambdaMOO, we will accept a simple majority decision of the following form:

Any eligible voter may author a "shutdown" petition. This will be a prevetted petition with a specific, fixed wording. Should the petition reach ballot stage (by acquiring the usual signature threshold), a vote will be held to decide whether LambdaMOO should be shut down. If the number of YES (we should shut down) votes equals or exceeds the number of NO (we should not shut down) votes received, LambdaMOO will be shut down after an 8-week grace period. (Note, only one "shutdown" petition may be active at a time.)

Shutdown petitions will be implemented at the earliest opportunity.

4. The New Direction We hope that LambdaMOO will become a more dynamic and enjoyable place for the wizards and the players. We do not want to discourage lively debate or to deprive players of a voice, and we encourage all of you to develop new ideas, mechanisms, and social policies, so as to minimize the need for direct wizardly social intervention as much as possible.

The Wizards of LambdaMOO

Notes

My thanks to Cynthia Haynes and Jan Rune Holmevik for their support. See their own collection of essays (Haynes and Holmevik 1998) for further information on MOOs. The current version is revised as of November 1999, five years after the cyberevents recounted. For an alternate perspective on the same events, see Dibbell (1998, chap. 3).

1. See, among many others, DeLoughry, Elmer-Dewitt (1995a, 1995b); Godwin (1995b, 1996); see also texts collected in Ludlow (1996).

2. Some devotees of LambdaMOO would contest this characterization, seeing it as somehow demeaning the lofty goals of site development and programming held by a certain technocratic few. See my essay on "spam" for counterdocumentation (Stivale 1996). A recent post to the LambdaMOO *social list sums up the divided sensibilities between fun and political engagement: "I always thought newbies [new characters] on Lambda Mu should be called pledges. But political cell has an appropriate ring (!) to it" (crayon, May 18, 1996).

3. The original "help manners" contained only a slim list of the basic points, almost in commandment form, that have been considerably expanded since.

4. The internal posts to LambdaMOO's dispute list as well as to the general *social list are extensive and from an array of sources: the dispute's mediator (AcidHorse), the shadow disputant (gru), one accuser (Nancy), the accused

(SamIAm, posting directly at first and then through e-mail messages forwarded to the lists by active registrants), and a number of commentators (most notably Sunny).

5. I learned of this supposed collective status only by querying Tchinek directly about his name and entity. While some have objected to my accepting this self-characterization, everyone who adopts a character name, description, and gender on a MOO must be taken at such face value (perhaps screen value is a more apt metaphor), even when the character adopts a Spivak gender or makes its home in a shopping cart.

6. In a not unrelated event, I sought to join DhalgrenMOO following the @toading in winter 1999 but was eventually refused membership by the main wizard when I continued to express my belief in the conspiracy against SamIAm, apparently excised from the cyberpopular imagination through a concerted revisionist historical process.

References

Benedikt, Michael, ed. 1992. *Cyberspace: First Steps*. Cambridge, MA: MIT Press.

"Bovine Spongiform Encephalopathy." 1999. Available at http://members. xoom.com/NonServIAm/index.html.

Bruckman, Amy. 1993. "Gender Swapping on the Internet." *Proceedings of INET*, 1993. In Ludlow, ed., *High Noon on the Electronic Frontier* (Cambridge: MIT Press, 1996), 317–325.

Bruckman, Amy. 1996. "Finding One's Own in Cyberspace." *Technology Review* (January). Available at http://www.techreview.com/articles/jan96/ Bruckman.html.

Bruckman, Amy, and Mitchel Resnick. 1993. "Virtual Professional Community: Results from the MediaMOO Project." Available at media.mit.edu/pub/asb/ papers/MediaMOO-3cyberconf.

Bunt, Katherine. 1996. "Perspectives on the Toxic Event at PennMOO: Social Norms or Socially Propagated Truth." Unpublished essay.

Cherny, Lynn. 1995. "'Objectifying' the Body in the Discourse of an Object-Oriented MUD." *Works and Days* 25–26: 151–72. Available at http:// gradeng.en.iup.edu/works&days.

Curtis, Pavel. 1992. "Mudding: Social Phenomena in Text-Based Virtual Realities." *Proceedings of DIAC '92*. In Ludlow (1996, 347–68).

Curtis, Pavel, and David Nichols. 1993. "MUDs Grow Up: Social Virtual Reality in the Real World." Available at parcftp.xerox.com/pub/MOO/papers/ MUDsGrowUp.

DeLoughry, Thomas J. 1995. "Researcher Who Studied On-Line Porn Gets Invitation from Congress, Criticism from Scholars." *Chronicle of Higher Education*, July 21, p. A19.

Dibbell, Julian. 1993. "A Rape in Cyberspace." *Village Voice*, December 21, pp. 36–42, reprinted in Mark Dery, ed., *Flame Wars: The Discourse of Cyberculture*. Durham: Duke University Press. 237–61. Also reprinted in Ludlow (1996, 375–95). Available at http://vesta.physics.ucla.edu/~smolin/lambda/laws_and_history/VillageVoice.txt.

Dibbell, Julian. 1998. *My Tiny Life: Crime and Passion in a Virtual World*. New York: Owl Books.

DIAC '94. 1994. "Democracy in Cyberspace." Amy Bruckman, Pavel Curtis, Nancy Deuel, Mitchell Resnick. Video.

Elmer-Dewitt, Philip. 1995a. "Fire Storm on the Computer Nets." *Time*, July 24, p. 57.

Elmer-Dewitt, Philip. 1995b. "On a Screen Near You: Cyberporn." *Time*, July 3, pp. 38–45.

Godwin, Mike. 1995a. "Artist or Criminal?" *Internet World* 6, no. 9 (September): 96–100.

Godwin, Mike. 1995b. "Philip's Folly." *Internet World* 6, no. 10 (October): 102–04.

Godwin, Mike. 1996. "The Wrong Spin." *Internet World* 7, no. 1 (January): 86–87.

Haynes, Cynthia, and Jan Rune Holmevik, eds. 1998. *High Wired: On the Design, Use, and Theory of Educational MOOs*. Ann Arbor: University of Michigan Press.

HumbertHumbert's LambdaMOO archive. Available at http://vesta.physics.ucla.edu/~smolin/lambda.

Ludlow, Peter, ed. 1996. *High Noon on the Electronic Frontier: Conceptual Issues in Cyberspace*. Cambridge, MA: MIT Press.

Marvin, Lee Ellen. 1996. "Spoof, Spam, Lurk, and Lag: The Aesthetics of Text-Based Virtual Realities." *Journal of Computer-Mediated Communication* 1, no. 2. Available at http://www.ascusc.org/jcmc/vol1/issue2/marvin.html.

Nakamura, Lisa. 1995. "Race in/for Cyberspace: Identity Tourism and Racial Passing on the Internet." *Works and Days* 25/26: 181–94. Available at http://gradeng.en.iup.edu/works&days.

Penley, Constance, and Andrew Ross, eds. 1991. *Technoculture*. Minneapolis: University of Minnesota Press.

Poster, Mark. 1996. "Cyberdemocracy: Internet and the Public Sphere." Available at http://www.hnet.uci.edu/mposter/writings/democ.html.

Reid, Elizabeth. 1995. "Virtual Worlds: Culture and Imagination." In Steven G. Jones, ed., *Cybersociety: Computer-Mediated Communication and Community*. Thousand Oaks, CA: Sage. 164–183.

Stivale, Charles J. 1996. "'Spam': Heteroglossia and Harassment in Cyberspace." *Readerly/Writerly Texts* 3, no. 2 (1996): 74–93. Reprinted in David Porter, ed., *Internet Culture*. New York: Routledge, 1997. 133–44.

18

Due Process and Cyberjurisdiction

David R. Johnson

Introduction

Online communication has given rise to a new global commerce in ideas, information, and services. Because electronic messages readily cross territorial borders, and many online transactions have no necessary relationship to any particular physical location, existing geographically based legal systems have difficulty regulating this new phenomenon. As users and system operators (sysops) encounter conflicts and seek to resolve disputes, they take action to establish rules and decide individual cases. This creates a new form of law—a law of cyberspace—based on private contracting on a global basis and enforced by a combination of the sysop's ultimate right to banish unruly users and the user's ultimate right to migrate to other online service providers.

Will this emerging cyberlaw provide "due process"? Will it, in other words, respect basic principles of fairness, as embodied in current legal doctrines? These take the form of procedural protections against arbitrary action by governmental authorities and substantive rights not to have life, liberty, and property taken away to serve the interests of an oppressive majority. There are some signs that the emerging cyberlaw will honor basic principles of procedural fairness and respect for individuals. However, the goal is to protect users from arbitrary actions of

This chapter originally appeared in electronic form in the *Journal of Computer-Mediated Communication* 2, no. 1 (June 1996). Reprinted by permission of the author. © 1996, David R. Johnson.

their information service providers rather than from arbitrary actions of their governments. Consequently, the methods used to achieve this goal online must differ from those available in established national legal systems.

Is Due Process Necessary in Cyberspace?

At first glance, global online communications might not seem to be in need of special protections for users or specific limitations on the prerogatives of system operators. A decision to sign up with an online commercial information service or an Internet access provider is clearly voluntary—unlike involuntary subjugation to territorial laws imposed by local sovereigns. The rules of the electronic road are set, for the most part, by private contracts—not by legislators enacting statutes, administrators making regulatory decisions, or judges interpreting the law. If a system operator adopts rules that seem oppressive, the local "netizenry" can vote with their modems and go to another, more congenial jurisdiction. Indeed, it is possible for some technologically sophisticated users to transmit messages without dealing through intermediaries who know who they are or who can enforce compliance with any established rules.

This primary reliance on action by private parties is important in establishing the relative freedom of users of computer-mediated communications from governmental intrusion. But there remain important questions raised by the potential of system operators or of majorities of communities of users to oppress individuals and minorities. While those who disagree with local rules are free to migrate, many users will have invested very substantial amounts of time and effort in establishing a particular online identity (building a reputation based on a particular e-mail address or Web page location, for example). And many seek to participate actively in particular online cybercommunities, over long periods of time. For them, separation from their cybercommunities would impose a very substantial personal loss. Thus, the check on sysop power provided by the user's right to abandon an online area is importantly mitigated by the costs imposed on the user who walks away. And the sysop's power of banishment can become the occasion for substantial injustice if it is imposed without adequate cause or without the use of procedures that give the user (and, perhaps, the cybercommunity) a chance to be heard.

Some sysops will challenge the relevance of "due process" in the Net-world, stressing that the rights assured apply only to limit powers exercised by sovereign governments. They will also protest that private commercial and associational dealings are not generally burdened with prohibitions against irrationality. What for government is prohibited censorship is, for a private electronic publisher, editing. What for government constitutes discrimination is, for an online community, the right of free association.

The arguments for some form of protection in netlaw for users' right may prove persuasive. Traditional legal authorities have difficulty regulating a global electronic network. Entrepreneurs advocate self-regulation, and the system providers may become the effective "government" of the Networld. They collectively do have a monopoly on what passes for "force" in this environment (the off-on switch). Insofar as they band together to establish standards (as they have already done, in effect, to create the Internet protocols and domain-name system and associated rules), collectively they do exercise something akin to sovereignty within their particular sphere.

Sysops may have to admit that the stakes involved in disputes about the creation or application of online rules can be high, from the perspective of a user. If they are not constrained by some basic principles of fairness and respect for individual rights that have evolved within the context of the Networld culture, then external governments may be unwilling to defer to netizen claims to a right to self-government. Moreover, a failure to protect online rights to "life, liberty and property" in the Networld would likely deter many potential participants and stifle online commerce.

What Due Process Is Now Provided to Users?

Rules online may be promulgated either by common practices developed by users or by private contract between provider and user. Most of these contractual rules are set by contracts of adhesion, with little or no opportunity for bargaining. Many commercial service providers' contracts purport to reserve to the sysop the right to deny service to anyone at any time for any reason. Sometimes users demand changes to online rules—and interactive capability online provides ample opportunity, as a practical matter, to petition their online governments and to discuss preferable changes. But there is no established procedure or practice of putting proposed changes out for comment. To the contrary, many contracts for online services provide that the user agrees in advance to abide by the system's rules however arbitrary they might be or however often they may change in the future. The user's only recourse, *in extremis*, is to quit the system if a new rule change is objectionable.

Similarly, most cases involving application of online rules to particular cases and specific users proceed on the basis of unilateral action by the sysop, who acts as prosecutor, judge, jury, and executioner. There have been exceptions—such as the famous case of the multiuser domain called LambdaMOO, whose users called for the creation of an independent judiciary after one member had his ID rendered nonfunctional by the site wizard on the basis of a public outcry against antisocial conduct by that member. Now a pilot project has been initiated to establish a Virtual Magistrate to rule on online disputes, via e-mail, that would give those with claims regarding the application of online rules a chance to have their cases heard by a neutral party. At the present justice in cyberspace is summary justice (or self-help vigilante revenge).

The current lack of meaningful protection in cyberspace is ironic, given the potential the medium offers to facilitate rational dispute resolution and public debate. Online conferences can readily marshall diverse views regarding proposed regulations. (The Nuclear Regulatory Commission is experimenting with online rule making, and Congress has discovered that e-mail is an effective means for at least some constituents to make their views known.) Moreover, focused adjudications can be conducted much more cost effectively online than in the real world. All parties can attend at their convenience. Experts and neutrals can be located and consulted quickly online. The entire proceeding can be archived as part of an electronic record. The Net can thus facilitate thoughtful discussion of new rules, rational analysis of the facts, and expeditious adjudication of online controversies.

How Will Due Process Arise in Cyberspace?

As the number of online services and users increases, the number of disputes and the magnitude of the interests affected by such disputes will also increase. Formerly it did not matter what the operator in the back room called your server. Today large companies contend aggressively to trademark "domain names" and to maintain a legally protected space to call their own. It doesn't matter much that your phone number changes when you change jobs. But some employees may face serious disruptions in their professional lives if their prior service provider declines to forward their e-mail. Many intensive users of online communication would recoil in horror at the thought that a sysop could unilaterally destroy their online identity without cause or that a committee of technical personnel who administer naming conventions in the Networld could eliminate their hard-won Web page addresses based on engineering concerns. They have come to expect a legally guaranteed entitlement to present one's case and to seek to establish individual rights against oppression. They will likely insist on proprietary rights in phone numbers, e-mail addresses, and Web page identities as well as entitlement to a reasonable presentation of their grievances.

The first stage in the development of such online due process rights will take the form of recognition that important personal (and corporate) interests are at stake. This may at first take the form of appeals to existing legal authorities for protection. But local authorities cannot easily control a global Net, may not have jurisdiction over all relevant parties, and will be inclined to defer to the terms of the contracts that users agreed to as a condition of going online. So these appeals will ultimately have to be made directly to sysops and ultimately to the group of interconnected systems that collectively control most of the traffic exchanged online. Collectively, those who control access to the interconnected systems have the power to discipline or deny interchange of messages to sites that fail to conform to a cyberspace norm.

The Internet community of long-term users has demonstrated its ability (via the Interned Engineering Task Force, for example) to come up with policies and protocols that govern the technical transmission of messages across the many networks and make the entire system work.

Those who don't go along with these rules have systems that simply don't interconnect. Similarly, rules regarding "due process" for users can be effectively adopted by consensus, so long as this higher-level type of "standard" or "protocol" is a required condition for connection or for inclusion in the groups collaborating to enhance the functionality of online communications.

Some elements of such principles may be based, in part, on technical architectures—such as the location of authority to change a domain name. Some elements may simply correspond to accepted practices for dealing with user complaints or rule violations; failure to follow those practices might make an area of the Networld suspect or less frequently pointed to by means of hypertext links supported by responsible providers.

The principles and basic rights that gain general acceptance—such as the transportability (or ownership by the user) of a domain name—are unlikely be embodied in a written constitution. The technology of global online communication is developing so rapidly that it will be difficult to deal with many potential issues by means of such written rules. The Internet community has responded to this difficulty in part by developing a loose doctrine of Netiquette that is based on group discussion and can adapt in a manner similar to the common law. Accordingly, there will likely be no definitive law library of authoritative texts from which one can determine the extent of due process protection accorded in the Networld—and even past cases, though widely reported, will need to be discussed from time to time in light of new conditions. There will be only a weak version of *stare decisis* in computer communications because the rational presumption will be that relevant circumstances (including the capabilities of technologies and the mix and interests of online participants) may well have changed since the last time an issue was considered. But there will be wisdom derived from discussion among informed and neutral parties.

For example, when spamming (sending multiple, intrusive, and off-point messages to newsgroups) became a problem in the Internet, the offended users took direct, vigilante action—flooding the offending party's mailbox with hate mail. But there turned out to be a technical means to eliminate inappropriate messages much more surgically: a cancellation message appearing to come from the originating party (a cancelbot) could be sent. Soon a discussion group was formed to spread news of new spamming episodes and also to deliberate on when and whether this cancelbot technology should be used to remove offensive messages. Some self-help justice is still present, of course, but the reaction to spamming has generated a growing sense that severe actions taken to protect the online public's interests—whether canceling messages or eliminating IDs—ought to be preceded by thoughtful discussion and implemented by a neutral decision maker. This cultural practice has the potential to become, in effect, a type of "due process" right enjoyed by all users in the Networld.

How Will Due Process on the Net Differ from Due Process in the Nonvirtual World?

"Due process" in cyberspace may arise in the form of a general consensus among most users and sysops that the ultimate enforcement tools available (banishment, cancellation of IDs, elimination of online addresses) ought not to be wielded arbitrarily. Users will avoid systems that reserve to the sysop the right to terminate a user, alter valuable identifying information, or adopt rules prohibiting legitimate and established activities, arbitrarily. Users accused of wrongdoing will demand and get a hearing—and any cavalier treatment of individual cases will be widely reported and discussed in a manner detrimental to the callous system operator. Such protection cannot readily be built directly into the laws of local sovereigns, who may not even have jurisdiction over all the interested parties. They will, however, become part of what connecting network managers expect from one another and what users in general demand. They will become, in effect, a form of private global Netlaw, probably applied by private arbitration and enforced by means of all parties' ability to decide with whom they will deal.

Under United States law, due process is guaranteed by virtue of a written constitution, covering a particular geographically defined place and its citizens. It is based on key conceptions regarding the duty of a "state" to serve the interests of its citizens in an equitable manner. In contrast, the protection of fairness for individual users in the global Networld will rely less on the law of territorially based jurisdictions and more on the actions of online communities. The efficacy of Netlaw will depend more on sysops who control the on-off buttons and the reactions of their customers, wherever they may reside, than they will on theories relating to limits of "sovereign" powers. Moreover, the nature of the beneficiaries of the online version of "due process" may differ from that of those who can invoke the established real-world doctrines. Users can do business online without necessarily disclosing the details of their identity or the other roles they play in the real world. Thus, those who formulate the doctrine of online due process will need to decide whether such rights attach to any online persona, whether the user claiming rights must disclose additional personal information as a condition of appearing in the forum that can vindicate any such right, and whether rights to life, liberty, and property online may belong to a group or "corporate" entity.

Perhaps the most important question regarding "due process" in cyberspace concerns the online equivalent of the right to life, a question presented when a sysop desires to remove an online identity against the wishes of the user. This kind of question can arise, for example, when a user violates rules applicable to a particular online space or annoys other users to the point of outrage. Is the user in question entitled to a decision based on analysis of competent evidence rather than on the whim of a sysop or the cries of an online lynch crowd? Must the decision maker be neutral? Should the penalty fit the crime? To the extent that users desire and expect such restraint by sysops to whom they give their business, limitations on sysop action may evolve as a natural evolution of the new Netlaw.

There may be specific attributes of United States–based due process that will have little or no applicability online. For example, a right to a six- or twelve-person jury (a limitation based on historical factors and the constraints on summoning people to a physical, real-time courthouse) has little application to the capacity of the Networld to allow interaction with neutral evaluators at their own convenience. U.S. due process guarantees a right to confront accusers and witnesses in person. That right may make little sense when the deeds in question took place entirely online. U.S. due process guarantees a right to cross-examine witnesses in an elaborate procedural dance. That level of formality may be unachievable or irrelevant online.

In contrast, certain features of online interaction may facilitate the growth of new forms of "due process" rights. It may be judged fair to allow an accused party to reply by e-mail or public posting to any allegations of wrongdoing. To facilitate such replies, it may be easy, and therefore fairer, to give proactive e-mail notice to any persons whose actions online are the subject of public discussion. Given the relative importance of community sentiment and the likely ability of dispersed contributors to enhance the quality of deliberations in a particular case, online tribunals may be much more open to discussion by "friends of the court"—even to the point of allowing nonparties to participate in online questioning and argument.

One important feature of the U.S. doctrine of due process offers protection to corporations and other organizations that are permitted to act as legal persons. In the Networld, the whole idea of legal personhood takes on a new dimension—because participants in online interactions cannot easily tell (and may not care) whether an online identity belongs to only one individual. The Networld offers important opportunities for online collaboration in the delivery of services and information by means of group action. Accordingly, it is only a matter of time before the Networld faces the question whether any due process rights attach to coherent groups presenting themselves via e-mail or Web pages—conferring on them additional rights and duties distinct from those of the individual participants. We already allow "real" corporations to register domain names. It's not clear why such groups need to be registered in any particular physical territory. Exactly how we go about evolving the protections afforded or denied to collective entities online may influence what kinds of electronic commerce can evolve.

One ultimate issue for the development of due process online will be the question of whether to evolve a doctrine that protects individuals against having to bear undue burdens even if the policy decisions imposing such burdens are taken for the greater good. Currently system operators enjoy an eminent-domain power unconstrained by any need to compensate the victims of a reassigned e-mail address, a canceled domain name, or the enactment of a new rule outlawing some activity that the individual user had counted on continuing as a commercial operator. Users maintain some protection against tyranny by virtue of their ability to move to another system. But a doctrine ensuring compensation for such takings would provide far greater protection against unreasonable burdens imposed by collective decisions that cannot readily be remedied by migration—an increasingly likely type of decision as the Networld welcomes increasingly valuable investment-backed expectations. (Of course, to be viable, such a doctrine would likely require something akin to the government's taxing power.) The assertion of such a claim to compensation may put to the test the question of whether limitations on the power of those charged with online governance stem only from the ability of unhappy users to desert—or, instead, derive from a joint commitment of online netizens to resolve cases rationally and prevent the imposition of unfair burdens on individual users who do not deserve their fate.

Conclusion

Due process in cyberspace will concern a different set of persons—online personas (whether individual, corporate, or group) rather than the citizens of a given nation state. It will protect a different set of values—the continuing life of an online identity, the liberty to engage in established activities free from arbitrary new rules, and the property of an established domain name or well-known Web page address. Procedural protections will likely take the form of an ensured opportunity for community discussion as distinct from physical rights (such as the confrontation of witnesses) or particular real-time dramatic processes (such as cross-examination). Indeed, the substantive protections of due process in cyberspace may well differ in content from place to place, with users free to choose their online environments on the basis of whether the local rules suit their needs. But despite these differences, the law of most areas of cyberspace will very likely embody many of the same core principles that underlie current due process doctrine—respect for the interests of individuals in the face of majority oppression, thoughtful and rational evaluation of individual cases, and appropriate opportunities to participate in creating and applying the law of the Networld.

19

Virtual Magistrate Project Press Release

For Immediate Release, March 4, 1996
Virtual Magistrate Established for the Internet
Voluntary Dispute Resolution for Network Conflicts

INTERNET—The newly established Virtual Magistrate Project will assist in the rapid, initial resolution of computer network disputes. The specialized system of online arbitration and fact-finding was announced by Timothy C. Leixner, chair of the Board of Directors of the National Center for Automated Information Research (NCAIR), which is funding the pilot project. The Fellows of the Cyberspace Law Institute helped in the development of the project.

"Millions of people around the world communicate and conduct business on computer networks," said Mr. Leixner in announcing the project. "Disputes are inevitable, and existing courts can be too slow, too cumbersome, and too local to have global effect. We need to explore new forms of dispute resolution, provide timely relief, and develop appropriate sanctions that are suitable for worldwide computer networks. That is the purpose of the Virtual Magistrate Project."

A pool of neutral arbitrators with experience in the law and in the use of computer networks will serve as the Virtual Magistrates. The magistrates (who do not have to be lawyers) will be selected jointly by the

Since this press release, the Virtual Magistrate Project has moved to Chicago-Kent College of Law, at ⟨http://www.vmag.org⟩.

American Arbitration Association and the Cyberspace Law Institute and will undergo training in arbitration techniques.

Complaints will be accepted either through electronic mail or through a form on the Virtual Magistrate's World Wide Web site. Internet users, system operators, and others affected by network messages, postings, and files may be the source of complaints. Initially, the Virtual Magistrate will decide whether it would be reasonable for a system operator to delete or otherwise restrict access to a challenged message, posting, or file.

Objections may be based on copyright or trademark infringement, misappropriation of trade secrets, defamation, fraud, deceptive trade practices, inappropriate (obscene, lewd, or otherwise violative of local system rules) materials, invasion of privacy, and other wrongful content. At a later date, the Virtual Magistrate may accept complaints about other network-related activities.

The need for a fast and accessible resolution of disputes is highlighted by ongoing litigation involving Netcom On-Line Communications Services and the Church of Scientology. The Church alleged that postings made by a Netcom user infringed on the Church's copyrights. The case is before federal district court, and a lengthy proceeding is expected. Arbitration though the Virtual Magistrate Project might have been able to offer an independent assessment of whether there was infringement. Prompt identification of reasonable responses for system operators would clearly be beneficial to all. Use of the Virtual Magistrate for immediate resolution of disputes would not preclude traditional litigation.

An impartial magistrate will be assigned to each complaint. Proceedings will normally take place through electronic mail. The goal is to reach a decision within seventy-two hours (three business days) whenever possible. Information on cases decided by the Virtual Magistrate will be publicly available at a World Wide Web site maintained by the Villanova Center for Information Law and Policy at http://vmag. law.vill.edu:8080/. Other documentation for the Project is available at the same Web site.

David Johnson, codirector of the Cyberspace Law Institute said: "The Virtual Magistrate Project is not a solution to all network problems. Some matters will inevitably end up in traditional courts. If the Virtual

Magistrate Project can contribute to the swift, inexpensive, and fair resolution of some disputes, then it will be a success."

Paul Evan Peters, executive director of the Coalition for Networked Information, a diverse partnership of over two hundred institutions and organizations promoting the scholarly and intellectually productive uses of the Internet commented: "This project promises an extremely important and much needed alternative to legislation, contract negotiation, and litigation for addressing the uncertainties that we should all face together in the rapidly evolving networked resource and service environment."

The Virtual Magistrate Project is a pilot project. Adjustments to the rules and procedures will be made based on experience. The Project will be evaluated by the participants at a conference to be convened by NCAIR and CLI in May 1996, and decisions will be made about finding a more permanent structure and funding. NCAIR has made $75,000 available for the operation of the pilot.

NCAIR is a nonprofit, educational corporation actively engaged in the study and application of technology to the legal and accounting professions since 1966.

The American Arbitration Association (AAA) is a public-service, not-for-profit organization offering a broad range of dispute-resolution services to corporations, attorneys, insurers, individuals, trade associations, unions, consumers, and all levels of government. AAA has been an international focal point for private dispute resolution since arbitration became an acceptable alternative to courts in the 1920s.

George Friedman, senior vice president of AAA, said: "Given the increasing inaccessibility of the court system and the explosive growth of online technology, it is quite appropriate that an effort would be made to develop a means of resolving disputes simply and quickly online. The American Arbitration Association is delighted to be a founding partner of the Virtual Magistrate Project, which will undoubtedly pave new ground in advancing alternative dispute resolution."

The Villanova Center for Information Law and Policy will maintain a public online repository of Virtual Magistrate complaints, decisions, and documents. The Villanova Center will also maintain electronic discussion groups for magistrates, participants, and other interested parties, and it will work jointly with AAA to prepare training materials. The Villanova Center is at Villanova University School of Law, near Philadelphia.

How Can I Find the Virtual Magistrate Project on the Internet?
Copies of the Virtual Magistrate's rules and other descriptive materials can be obtained at http://www.vmag.org.

20

Virtual Magistrate Issues Its First Decision

For Immediate Release, May 21, 1996
Recommends That AOL Remove a Subscriber Message Offering
Millions of E-mail Addresses for Sale

The Virtual Magistrate Project today released its first decision. The case involved a disputed message posted on America Online (AOL) by Email America. The decision recommended that the message offering the sale of e-mail addresses be removed by AOL because it violated the AOL service agreement as well as Internet customs.

The Virtual Magistrate Project is an Internet-based arbitration service that assists in the rapid, initial resolution of computer network disputes. The Project opened for business in March 1996. The basic decision offered by the Virtual Magistrate is whether a network message, file, or posting should be taken down or left in view.

The case name is Tierney and Email America, VM Docket No. 96-0001 (May 8, 1996). The date of the decision is May 20, 1996. The full text and related materials and correspondence are available for public inspection through the Virtual Magistrate Home Page at http://vmag.law.vill.edu:8080.

The complainant in the case is James Tierney, who is a member of America Online and is affiliated with the Virtual Magistrate Project as a adviser on consumer fraud issues. Tierney is also a former attorney general for the State of Maine. His complaint was directed against Email

Since this press release, the Virtual Magistrate Project has moved to Chicago-Kent College of Law, at ⟨http://www.vmag.org⟩.

America, which had posted a message on AOL offering to sell lists of as many as twenty million e-mail addresses. The complaint alleged that Email America's message was an invasion of privacy, against sound public policy, and deceptive. Tierney characterized Email America's offering as promoting spamming or junk e-mail. These terms describe indiscriminate, bulk, direct-mail marketing via e-mail.

America Online voluntarily participated in the case. The AOL submission pointed out that its terms of service agreement permits the removal of messages that are harmful or offensive or otherwise in violation of AOL rules. AOL also stated that it does not encourage indiscriminate, unsolicited bulk mail on its system. AOL considers such mailings inconsistent with Internet custom and practice, an impediment to service, and potentially deleterious to its system. Unsolicited bulk mail has also been the subject of numerous complaints from AOL subscribers.

The Virtual Magistrate ruled that the determination of what constitute harmful or offensive activity can take into account the limitations of the AOL system, Internet custom and practice, and customer complaints. The Magistrate determined that removal or blocking of the message in question would be permissible under the AOL Terms of Service Agreement and that AOL should remove the message from its system.

The case was decided by N. M. Norton Jr., a partner with the law firm of Wright, Lindsey & Jennings in Little Rock, Arkansas. Mr. Norton was recently a member of the U.S. National Information Infrastructure Advisory Council. He is one of eight individuals selected so far to serve as Virtual Magistrates.

The Virtual Magistrate Project is an experimental service developed by the Cyberspace Law Institute and funded by the National Center for Automated Information Research. Operational elements of the Project are provided by the American Arbitration Association and the Villanova Center for Information Law and Policy. Documents explaining the rules, procedures, and purpose of the Project are available on the Virtual Magistrate home page.

Virtual Magistrate executive director Robert Gellman said, "The Virtual Magistrate Project is off to a good start with this decision. We expect the Project to demonstrate how computer networks can police themselves. The decision supports the right of system operators to establish appropriate rules governing their services. We were disappointed that Email America did not respond to repeated requests to participate in this case. But since there was an active complaint and a participating system operator, we proceeded with the case."

William K. Slate II, president and chief executive officer of the American Arbitration Association, said, "This first decision of the Virtual Magistrate is truly the birth of online alternative dispute resolution. The case demonstrates that online technology can be used to resolve disputes with impressive speed and efficiency, while maintaining the fairness and integrity associated with ADR. The American Arbitration Association is pleased to be playing a leading role in developing this leading-edge technology."

V

Utopia, Dystopia, and Pirate Utopias

21

Utopia Redux

Karrie Jacobs

First came the fall of communism. Then there was the advertising campaign for the beverage Fruitopia. Now the pitchmen for cyberspace, the so-called digerati, are promoting this virtual place where you are now as terra incognita, where we can start life anew.

No question about it, the concept of utopia has been thoroughly degraded and commercialized.

Wired executive editor Kevin Kelly:

The reason why the hippies and people like myself got interested in [computers] is that they are model worlds, small universes. They are ways to recreate civilization. We get to ask the great questions of all time: What is life? What is human? What is civilization? And you ask it not in the way the old philosophers asked it, sitting in armchairs, but by actually trying it. Let's try and make life. Let's try and make community.

—*New York Times Magazine*

Author Douglas Rushkoff:

As computer programmers and psychedelic warriors together realize that "all is one," a common belief emerges that the evolution of humanity has been a willful progression toward the construction of Cyberia, the next dimensional home for the consciousness.

—*Cyberia*

Wired editor Louis Rossetto:

[Hot *Wired* readers] connect to us to connect to their friends, to connect to a community, to be part of a mind-set and a consciousness that transcends the

---

limits of the old media. And in the process, they start to begin to build a new society, a new culture, a new way of thinking about community.

—*New York Times*

Electronic Frontier Foundation cofounder John Perry Barlow:

All the current power relationships on the planet are currently being disassembled, it's going to be up in the air. Ultimately, centralized anything is going to be greatly deemphasized and redistributed.

—*New Perspectives Quarterly*

What redistribution of power? I can't believe Kelly, Rushkoff, Rossetto, and Barlow don't know better. I can't believe they don't understand that the electronic culture in which they operate is still largely run by white men (and written about by them; see "Scenarios: The Future of the Future," published by *Wired* in October 1995) and still dominated by big corporations such as ATT, Microsoft, and Sony.

Inside this new world, the one that begins where our fingertips touch the keyboard and ends at a Web site advertising Chrysler's newest models or in a meandering BBS discussion about the movie *Kids*, we find the old life and the old communities. When people put on their electronic masks—disguising gender, race, physical attributes—mostly they play themselves. When corporations go online and invite us to interact, they are selling the same products they sell on billboards, TV commercials, and newspaper coupons.

The world on this side of the computer screen is such a seamless continuation of the world on the other side that even the Secret Service is here. In September, they announced a bust of six "hackers" accused of trading in stolen cellular phone codes. Apparently, those arrested had no qualms about discussing their activities on a BBS dedicated to the subjects of phone and credit card fraud—that the Secret Service had set up themselves. Perhaps the "hackers" truly believed the Net was an anarchic environment in which the Feds would not venture.

I agree with one of the harshest critics of computer culture, Jerry Mander, when he says, "The only problems that will be solved by computers are the problems that corporations may face."

The cyber hucksters are part of a long tradition. They are doing what salesmen have always done. They sell us a new technology or a new piece of turf, and we invest in it all our hopes and dreams. We disengage from the world as we know it and push ourselves forward, believing it will be better. Our grandparents did it, traveling in steerage, to their next dimensional home. Our parents went to the World's Fair and came away inspired, believing in the future according to General Motors. We listen blissfully to the crackle of our modems and think that what we're hearing is the theme music of a new society.

I'm willing to grant that there is at least one truly utopian quality to the Net: standardization.

The original Utopia, as described by Sir Thomas More's Utopia in 1516, was an island secreted in the southern hemisphere of the still largely unexplored New World. The Utopians, women as well as men, worked six hours a day at their chosen trade, lived in extended families, had no money, and selected all their necessities from the sixteenth-century equivalent of Wal-Mart for free. Gold and silver were kept on hand only to cover the expenses of waging war (mostly fought by foreign mercenaries) and, when not needed, were melted down and stored in the form of chamber pots and shackles on the legs of the slaves who, conveniently, did the nation's dirty work.

What strikes me as the most oppressive—and familiar—quality of More's island state is that Utopians couldn't escape the confines of their own lives because every place on the island was the same as every other place: "There are 54 cities on the island, all spacious and magnificent, identical in language, customs, institutions, and laws," More wrote. "So far as the location permits, all of them are built on the same plan and have the same appearance."

More might have been writing about America's shopping malls or Holiday Inns. Or his description could apply to the cities built by Soviet architects 450 years after his death, with their identical apartment blocks punctuated every mile or so by a grim public square, a token shopping area, a pub, and a drab community center.

Reflections of the original Utopia—a word, by the way, that literally means "no place"—can also be seen in the way software designers have repackaged the world. You can go anywhere on the Web with Netscape, and you will still be within the familiar confines of your "navigator." Like More's Utopia, the Net is a place where "if you know one of their cities, you know them all." Whether hopping from Web site to Web site or getting money from an ATM, the electronic world is a place with a limited range of gestures.

Sure, the success of film and television is their ability to channel our fantasy lives into familiar formats. But online, all aspects of our lives—grocery shopping, religion, sex, conversation—are subject to formatting. They are parceled into rectangles of text or image. We type. We click. We answer "yes," "no," or "cancel." The Net whittles the vastness of the planet into something neat and manageable.

"Wherever they go, though they take nothing, they lack for nothing," wrote Sir Thomas More of the first Utopians, "because they are at home everywhere."

"This is my home," the globe-trotting John Perry Barlow told a conference last year in Amsterdam, holding his PowerBook aloft. He went on to say that cyberspace should grow into "a global collective consciousness smart enough to keep God company, a great eco system of mind."

Like the Utopians, we may find that there is no escape from the confines of our lives. The old Utopia was an island. The new one is a world stuffed in a box.

22

The God of the Digerati

Jedediah S. Purdy

"No ambition, however extravagant, no fantasy, however outlandish, can any longer be dismissed as crazy or impossible. This is the age when you can finally do it all.... You can become whatever you want to be." This bold invitation stretches across the first few pages of the October 1994 issue of *Wired* magazine, emblazoned over a computer-generated, Dali-esque landscape populated by transparent human forms whose brains, muscles, and entrails are tangles of silicon chips and fiber-optic cable. The phrases echo a favorite slogan of *Wired* editor Kevin Kelly: "We are as gods, and we might as well get good at it." Do these proposals amount to the same thing? Should we accept them? And if we do, what might be the consequences for our culture and politics?

These questions are not idle. *Wired* is the lifestyle magazine par excellence—the chapbook of tastes, taboos, and aspirations—for the shock troops of the information economy. More than 300,000 readers earn their average annual income of over $80,000 designing, selling, and hacking the computing systems that increasingly shape everyone's workplace, home, and civic life. More than any other group's, their job description includes designing the future. *Wired* outfits that future, announcing which ideas and products are "wired" and which "tired"; keeping up a "jargon watch" so that readers will know to say "lifestyle reboot," not "power cocooning"; pointing out the goods and manner

---

that bring "street cred," as in credibility; and holding forth on "fetishes," the supergoods of the superwired.

Prominent among the magazine's fetishes is a new brand of libertarianism, the hoary political temperament that thinks of government as serving only to iron out a few inconveniences that arise between private individuals and otherwise staying out of the way. *Wired* exchanges the gray woolens of conventional, economically minded libertarianism for the shimmering colors and romantic rhetoric of a technologically enhanced Friedrich Nietzsche. The magazine heralds a nascent political culture, a Nietzschean libertarianism.

The Nietzschean Tribe

Nietzsche, the German philosopher and iconoclast who died in 1900, has been the perennial source of twentieth-century efforts to break the chains of the past and create an entirely new intellectual and moral universe. He thought that all the old myths of religion, nation, and philosophy had failed and that people found themselves for the first time in a world without gods or magic. While desperately painful, this situation presented an opportunity. Christian morality, with its secular avatar, liberal democracy, had oppressed the most strong-willed and charismatic individuals, drawing them into its cult of meekness and sowing self-contempt with the doctrine that humanity is essentially sinful. With this burden lifted, the strongest individuals could create new myths, remake themselves as they wished, and form communities of the equally strong and likeminded. They would become, in the unfortunately popular phrase, supermen. *Wired* styles its readership a tribe of budding supermen. The magazine's first issue declared boldly, "*Wired* is about the most powerful people on the planet today—the Digital Generation." Publisher Louis Rossetto prefers the term *digerati*, a play on *literati*, for the new economic and, increasingly, cultural elite. This elite not only enjoys the usual perquisites of its position but anticipates expensive biological and electronic advances that promise people the capacity to tinker with themselves in unprecedented ways.

The quote that begins this essay comes from a leader of the Extropians, favorites of editor Kevin Kelly. The Extropians are committed to "turning humanity into something far superior" through technology, espousing "a philosophy of freedom from limitations of any kind." Those who can afford it will eventually be able to overcome mortality by "downloading" consciousness into computers, where it will survive forever as disembodied mind, perhaps helped along by robotic accessories and virtual-reality sensations. They are equally committed to pharmaceutical, surgical, and other ways of concentrating and expanding the power of the mind. They also "*hate* government" and wish to develop wholly voluntary communities governed by "spontaneous order."

Extreme as they are, the Extropians are representative lunatics. In "Birth of a Digital Nation," a piece that aspires to take a generational pulse, contributing editor Jon Katz writes that the zeitgeist honors "relying on oneself to be the captain of one's ship and charting one's own course." Nearly every issue of *Wired* includes a lionizing portrait of a trail-blazing, go-it-alone entrepreneur, delivered in tones that would make Ayn Rand blush. The magazine's governing assumption is that we make ourselves and our communities as we will.

The tone of these voluntary communities, among which the digerati are preeminent, is pungently technopagan. This is a tribal libertarianism. Just over a year ago *Wired* featured a cover story on Burning Man, a weekend gathering in the deserts of Nevada where technology and counterculture meet in a festival of body paint, drumming, and electronically enhanced mayhem, culminating in the burning of a huge human figure, a custom last practiced by Europe's ancient Celts. The following issue featured an admiring interview with Canadian media studies professor Derrick de Kerckhove, who believes that Internet users have reattained "a tribal world, [where] the cosmos has a presence. It's alive. The tribe shares in this huge, organic reality." In a sense, the magazine's Tired/Wired and Fetish features track the symbols of tribal membership, which require constant updating; this tribe is all about being on the move, and about buying.

Gods and Their Worlds

Stranger stuff yet lurks in *Wired*'s circuits. In *Out of Control*, editor Kevin Kelly proposes that the old line between "the born and the made"

has been irremediably blurred. Biotechnology, especially genetic engineering, has begun to insert technical processes into organisms. At the
same time, self-replicating computer programs that mimic evolution by
developing unplanned order and the early stages of "artificial intelligence," bring the dynamics of living things into machinery.

According to Kelly, these changes enable us to see what has always
been true but hitherto hidden. "Life" means not carbon-based organisms
but any self-ordering, self-reproducing system—what Kelly calls a *vivisystem*. We are vivisystems, but so, too, are computer networks, market
economies, and "hybrid patches of nerve and silicon." Moreover, Kelly
speculates, life has a tendency to spread itself into previously inert matter, fighting back against entropy—hence the label Extropian—and slowing the death of the universe. By passing from us into computers, "Life
has conquered carbon" and gone on, leaving humanity "a mere passing
station on hyperlife's gallop into space."

Here again, *Wired* shows Nietzsche's mark. His last work, dubiously
edited and written in the mental eclipse of creeping dementia, highlights
the idea of a "will to power" that flows through the universe, forging
order out of chaos. We are among the chief agents of that order. In this
view, *Wired* draws not only on Nietzsche but also on a tradition of
romantic vitalism that forgoes troublesome political and ethical questions in favor of celebrating "life," whatever it might do.

Only man can make a computer, so it is our task to extend life's march
by building the next vivisystem. We do this by designing computer
programs that replicate and expand themselves in unpredictable ways,
setting in motion a "post-Darwinian evolution." The best of these, in
Kelly's view, will be virtual-reality programs in which creators can
become virtual inhabitants. This is not so far-fetched as it seems. Some
people already spend considerable time in "virtual communities," multiuser versions of the computerized role-playing games that came into
prominence in the 1980s, where players interact with each other and perhaps with "bots" (programs designed to imitate people) in a landscape
described onscreen. This technology could be straightforwardly united
with the indeterminate "evolution" of self-replicating programs and with
the virtual-reality techniques that give users the impression of actually
inhabiting programmed landscapes.

A few people, mostly college students, have largely withdrawn from their embodied lives to participate in virtual communities. Kelly wants this practice to go much further, to see more people inhabiting specialized online communities, sometimes of their own making. Creating these worlds extends "life," and "every creative act is no more or less than the reenactment of the creation." By entering these realms, their programmers reproduce the "old theme" of "the god who lowered himself into his own world." Kelly identifies this theme with Jesus, but one wonders if Narcissus is not a more appropriate touchstone for his ambition.

Gods and Our World

These odd ideas shape the attitudes that *Wired* prescribes to the digerati. Take, for instance, *Wired*'s worshipful attitude to the free market. Markets are ideal in stances of "spontaneous order" and so very nearly of life itself. It is in this light that the magazine celebrates the economic dislocation that accompanies industry's replacement by the information economy. Last year, Kelly wrote in *Wired*, "In a poetic sense, the prime task of the Network Economy is to destroy—company by company, industry by industry—the industrial economy." Knowing that Kelly considers economic transition an evolutionary triumph of one vivisystem over another, in which people are only "a way-station," illuminates the rhapsodic tone of his description.

The irony of this view is that the free-for-all that *Wired* admires on the Internet is threatened less by government than by the prospect of domination by megacorporations. Less than a year ago, as *Wired*'s online publishing efforts foundered, Microsoft announced plans to devote a healthy portion of its $9 billion in cash to dominating that field. A favorite *Wired* icon for the information feedback loop, a dragon curling in a circle to swallow its own tail, could become more apt as a symbol of the timeless libertarian paradox: monopoly verging on feudalism emerges from unregulated competition to bite libertarianism in the posterior.

In the same vein, Kelly's technoromanticism guides *Wired* to a willful obtuseness before ecological concerns. Last year, UCLA's Gregory Stock, who "believes that genetic engineering is the next stage in natural evolution," told the magazine: "The planet is undergoing a massive extinction.... [W]e're at the center of it." We shouldn't be concerned, though, because "modern technology is a major evolutionary transition.... It would be astonishing if that occurred without disrupting existing life." In an earlier issue, Paul Levinson reassured readers that, now that DNA can be preserved for possible reconstruction, "extinction [no longer means] gone for good." To be sure, large-scale extinction and global warming can be considered "evolutionary transitions," triumphs of the human and industrial vivisystems, if one interprets them insistently enough. Similarly, if the existence of a species is reduced to a matter of recoverable genetic information, we may be comforted about the loss of the ecosystem that it now inhabits. Still, the reader is right to think that something—perhaps the most important thing—is lost in this view. Kelly's bizarre biological ideas underlie a giddy indifference to public policy.

Such complacency is an intrinsic temptation of this attitude. When any transformation is taken to be the fruit of life's battle against entropy, debating social and economic change appears fatuous. Trends take on an air of inevitability and of inevitable goodness. Any doctrine that celebrates the raw power of natural processes as they flow through society will end by sacrificing the rigors of democratic deliberation for the pleasures of vitalist enthusiasm.

The Technocratic Conceit

Of course, there is more to *Wired* than romantic libertarianism. The magazine now and again veers into a Panglossian picture of democracy's future on the Internet. Contributing editor Jon Katz, in particular, enjoys comparing the digerati to Jeffersonian yeomen—rugged, self-reliant individualists with their own ideas and the courage to voice them. Katz is fond of asking questions like, "Can we build a new kind of politics? Can we construct a more civil society with our powerful technologies? Are we extending the evolution of freedom among human beings?" Regrettably, he answers with tired observations and insubstantial proposals: the digerati are uninterested in and disaffected from mainstream politics and haven't contributed much to that politics except defense of their own cyberinterests; however, if they ever put their lively minds to politics, they would probably come up with something worthwhile.

The substance of that something, when made explicit, usually rests on the benefits of online conversation and the extraordinary availability of information on the Internet. Both of these are valuable, especially for citizens who are committed to particular issues and have trouble finding neighbors who share their interests and adequate resources in the local library. The more we cultivate informed, contentious citizenship, the better off we all are. However, these technologies chiefly enhance the efforts of already engaged men and women; they enrich the margins more than they affect the main current of politics. Overlooking this fact is typical of the technophiles' tendency to mistake new tools for new worlds. Katz refers in awed tones to "the unprecedented ability of individuals to speak directly to each other" on the Net, but thoughtful folk will recall that earlier eras are known, now and again, to have achieved conversation. Moreover, the picture of democracy that *Wired* honors rests not so much on shared deliberation as on "spontaneous order." Kelly offers as a parable for democracy a stadium full of people who, without express instructions, manipulate light sticks to form patterns. This sort of "hive mind," as Kelly unnervingly puts it, may be a fitting ideal for stadium performances; it is less obviously one for self-government. In fact, this is a basically vitalistic picture of democracy.

This vitalism bordering on mysticism spurs *Wired* to contempt for the banal institutions of government itself. Frequent contributor and Net guru John Perry Barlow suggests that in short order, "the U.S. Senate will seem about as relevant as the House of Lords." In the same spirit, *Wired* publisher Louis Rossetto told the *New York Times* three years ago, "In ten or twenty years, the world will be completely transformed.... [We will see] not just the change from L.B.J. to Nixon, but whether there will be a President at all." By every indication, the *Wired* crew would prefer that there not be. An admiring article on cyberspace tax dodgers who operate out of the Caribbean gleefully invited readers to imagine a future "nation state—with 20 percent of its current tax revenue." The Extropians have already imagined it.

The Poverty of Godhood

In some ways, it is best not to take all this too seriously. *Wired* is redolent of intellectual pretense and factual delusion. Some portion of the magazine is just the adolescent effusion of overgrown boys with too much money. The article on Burning Man misses no chance to show young, bare-breasted celebrants in body paint. Every few issues, a breathless piece on the future of military technology evokes video games brought down to earth. A long description of Internet entrepreneurs in Canada's near-Arctic Northwest Territories is mostly an admiring look at hard-drinking, hard-living frontiersmen recognizable from any Louis L'Amour novel. Whether Hefner or Hemingway, the young men of *Wired*—and the magazine's readers are mostly men—get their share of fantasy material.

The more ambitious moments are equally unsatisfactory. Professor Derrick de Kerckhove's claim that we are rediscovering a "living cosmos" turns on the fact that, on the Internet, language is both experienced in real time and given permanent, recorded existence. The first supposedly creates an organic immediacy, while the second secures ontological stability: permanent language becomes part of the structure of things. This "new guise of language," when parsed, means that we have verbatim records of our conversations, get our mail almost instantly, and see magazines as soon as they go online. One wonders whether, once L.B.J. and Nixon began taping their Oval Office conversations, they experienced a living cosmos. Envision the transcript: "P: Henry, I feel so [expletive deleted] tribal!"

More seriously, the future that *Wired* evokes belongs to a single population—the digerati—who are happy to tout their experience as universal. The information economy emphatically does not mean "reenacting the Creation" for most of its workers. Data-entry workers, shop clerks, and the warehouse staff at amazon.com will face the same problems as ever—depressed wages, battles over benefits, barriers to unionization, and inadequate political representation in a Congress whose resemblance to the House of Lords is for them a matter of economic class more than of anachronism. Their situations will be the less stable for the "creative destruction" of firms and industries that Kelly celebrates. Tribalism will do them little good, as is generally true of lesser tribes.

Libertarianism or Limits?

It is precisely because the digerati are not a lesser tribe that their defining cultural document demands attention. *Wired*'s unlikely ideas and improbable prognostications are less significant in the end than its temperament, the turn of mind, and set of moral—and amoral—priorities that it displays. Temperament is a theme too little appreciated in reflecting about culture and politics. Although no temperament neatly supports any particular political order, there are echoes, affinities, and latent hostilities between habits of mind and political practices.

The *Wired* temperament is contemptuous of all limits—of law, community, morality, place, even embodiment. The magazine's ideal is the unbounded individual who, when something looks good to him, will do it, buy it, invent it, or become it without delay. This temperament seeks comradeship only among its perceived equals in self-invention and world making; rather than scorn the less exalted, it is likely to forget their existence altogether. Boundless individualism, in which law, community, and every activity are radically voluntary, is an adolescent doctrine, a fantasy shopping trip without end.

In contrast, liberal democracy at its best starts from a recognition of certain limitations that we all have in common. None of us is perfectly wise, good, or fit to rule over others. All of us need help sometimes, from neighbors and from institutions. We are bound by moral obligation to our fellow citizens. We share stewardship of an irreplaceable natural world. This eminently adult temperament is alien to the digerati.

The choice of which temperament we will cultivate is timely, for it lies near the heart of our decisions about how to regard the ascendant, global, information-based economy. Will we see in it the latest set of temptations to our familiar maladies of greed, mutual indifference, and self-absorption and work to address those with the best resources of liberalism, privately and through our political institutions? Or will we pretend with *Wired* that those hazards and their accompanying obligations are finally behind us, that the millennium has come in a microchip?

The invitation to godhood inhabits a long tradition in our culture, from the original temptation in Eden to the bargain of Faust. Kelly has this tradition in mind when he asks about the prospects for creating artificial evolution: "Have we ever resisted temptation before?" Before accepting too blithely, though, we should recall that bargains in this tradition are tragic at best, destructive at worst. With this in mind, we do refuse temptation, not least when we decline the pleasures of glib libertarianism, idle romanticism, and technophilic hubris. In the face of these, refusal deserves pride of place among the liberal virtues. We should learn to recognize an infernal bargain when we see one.

23

Californian Ideology

Richard Barbrook and Andy Cameron

Not to lie about the future is impossible and one can lie about it at will.
—Naum Gabo[1]

As the Dam Bursts ...

At the end of the twentieth century, the long predicted convergence of the media, computing, and telecommunications into hypermedia is finally happening.[2] Once again, capitalism's relentless drive to diversify and intensify the creative powers of human labor is on the verge of qualitatively transforming the way in which we work, play, and live together. By integrating different technologies around common protocols, something is being created that is more than the sum of its parts. When the ability to produce and receive unlimited amounts of information in any form is combined with the reach of the global telephone networks, existing forms of work and leisure can be fundamentally transformed. New industries will be born, and current stock-market favorites will be swept away. At such moments of profound social change, anyone who can offer a simple explanation of what is happening will be listened to with great interest. At this crucial juncture, a loose alliance of writers, hackers, capitalists, and artists from the West Coast of the United States

Versions of this chapter have appeared in *Mute* 3 (1995), on the HyperMedia Research Centre's Web site, and on the *nettime* e-list, among other locations on the Internet. Reprinted by permission of the authors. © Richard Barbrook and Andy Cameron, 2001.

have succeeded in defining a heterogeneous orthodoxy for the coming information age—the Californian Ideology.

This new faith has emerged from a bizarre fusion of the cultural bohemianism of San Francisco with the high-tech industries of Silicon Valley. Promoted in magazines, books, TV programs, Web sites, newsgroups, and Net conferences, the Californian ideology promiscuously combines the free-wheeling spirit of the hippies and the entrepreneurial zeal of the yuppies. This amalgamation of opposites has been achieved through a profound faith in the emancipatory potential of the new information technologies. In the digital utopia, everybody will be both hip and rich. Not surprisingly, this optimistic vision of the future has been enthusiastically embraced by computer nerds, slacker students, innovative capitalists, social activists, trendy academics, futurist bureaucrats, and opportunistic politicians across the United States. As usual, Europeans have not been slow in copying the latest fad from America. While a recent European Union Commission report recommends following the Californian "free-market" model for building the "information superhighway," cutting-edge artists and academics eagerly imitate the "posthuman" philosophers of the West Coast's Extropian cult.[3] With no obvious rivals, the triumph of the Californian Ideology appears to be complete.

The widespread appeal of these West Coast ideologues isn't simply the result of their infectious optimism. Above all, they are passionate advocates of what appears to be an impeccably libertarian form of politics: they want information technologies to be used to create a new "Jeffersonian democracy" where all individuals will be able to express themselves freely within cyberspace.[4] However, by championing this seemingly admirable ideal, these technoboosters are at the same time reproducing some of the most atavistic features of American society, especially those derived from the bitter legacy of slavery. Their utopian vision of California depends on a willful blindness toward the other, much less positive features of life on the West Coast—racism, poverty, and environmental degradation.[5] Ironically, in the not too distant past the intellectuals and artists of the Bay Area were passionately concerned about these issues.

Ronald Reagan versus the Hippies

On May 15, 1969, Governor Ronald Reagan ordered armed police to carry out a dawn raid against hippie protesters who had occupied People's Park near the Berkeley campus of the University of California. During the subsequent battle, one man was shot dead and 128 other people needed hospital treatment.[6] On that day, the "straight" world and the counterculture appeared to be implacably opposed. On one side of the barricades, Governor Reagan and his followers advocated unfettered private enterprise and supported the invasion of Vietnam. On the other side, the hippies championed a social revolution at home and opposed imperial expansion abroad. In the year of the raid on People's Park, it seemed that the historical choice between these two opposing visions of America's future could only be settled through violent conflict. As Jerry Rubin, one of the Yippie leaders, said at the time: "Our search for adventure and heroism takes us outside America, to a life of self-creation and rebellion. In response, America is ready to destroy us."[7]

During in the 1960s, radicals from the Bay Area pioneered the political outlook and cultural style of New Left movements across the world. Breaking with the narrow politics of the postwar era, they launched campaigns against militarism, racism, sexual discrimination, homophobia, mindless consumerism, and pollution. In place of the traditional left's rigid hierarchies, they created collective and democratic structures that supposedly prefigured the libertarian society of the future. Above all, the Californian New Left combined political struggle with cultural rebellion. Unlike their parents, the hippies refused to conform to the rigid social conventions imposed on "organization men" by the military, universities, corporations, and even left-wing political parties. Instead they openly declared their rejection of the straight world through their casual dress, sexual promiscuity, loud music, and recreational drugs.[8]

The radical hippies were liberals in the social sense of the word. They championed universalist, rational, and progressive ideals, such as democracy, tolerance, self-fulfillment, and social justice. Emboldened by over twenty years of economic growth, they believed that history was on their side. In sci-fi novels, they dreamt of "ecotopia"—a future California where cars had disappeared, industrial production was ecologically viable, sexual relationships were egalitarian, and daily life was lived in community groups.[9] For some hippies, this vision could be realized only by rejecting scientific progress as a false god and returning to nature. Others, in contrast, believed that technological progress would inevitably turn their libertarian principles into social fact. Crucially, influenced by the theories of Marshall McLuhan, these technophiliacs thought that the convergence of media, computing, and telecommunications would inevitably create the *electronic agora*—a virtual place where everyone would be able to express their opinions without fear of censorship.[10] Despite being a middle-aged English professor, McLuhan preached the radical message that the power of big business and big government would be imminently overthrown by the intrinsically empowering effects of new technology on individuals:

Electronic media ... abolish the spatial dimension ... By electricity, we everywhere resume person-to-person relations as if on the smallest village scale. It is a relation in depth, and without delegation of functions or powers ... Dialogue supersedes the lecture.[11]

Encouraged by McLuhan's predictions, West Coast radicals became involved in developing new information technologies for the alternative press, community radio stations, home-brew computer clubs, and video collectives. These community media activists believed that they were in the forefront of the fight to build a new America. The creation of the electronic agora was the first step toward the implementation of direct democracy within all social institutions.[12] The struggle might be hard, but "ecotopia" was almost at hand.

The Rise of the "Virtual Class"

Who would have predicted that less than thirty years after the battle for People's Park, squares and hippies would together create the Californian Ideology? Who would have thought that such a contradictory mix of technological determinism and libertarian individualism would becoming the hybrid orthodoxy of the information age? And who would have suspected that as technology and freedom were worshipped more and more, it would become less and less possible to say anything sensible about the society in which they were applied?

The Californian Ideology derives its popularity from the very ambiguity of its precepts. Over the last few decades, the pioneering work of the community media activists has been largely recuperated by the high-tech and media industries. Although companies in these sectors can mechanize and subcontract much of their labor needs, they remain dependent on key people who can research and create original products, from software programs and computer chips to books and TV programs. Along with some high-tech entrepreneurs, these skilled workers form the so-called virtual class—"the techno-intelligentsia of cognitive scientists, engineers, computer scientists, video-game developers, and all the other communications specialists."[13] Unable to subject them to the discipline of the assemblyline or replace them by machines, managers have organized such intellectual workers through fixed-term contracts. Like the "labor aristocracy" of the last century, core personnel in the media, computing, and telecoms industries experience the rewards and insecurities of the marketplace. On the one hand, these high-tech artisans not only tend to be well paid but also have considerable autonomy over their pace of work and place of employment. As a result, the cultural divide between the hippie and the organization man has now become rather fuzzy. On the other hand, these workers are tied by the terms of their contracts and have no guarantee of continued employment. Lacking the free time of the hippies, work itself has become the main route to self-fulfillment for much of the virtual class.[14]

The Californian Ideology offers a way of understanding the lived reality of these high-tech artisans. On the one hand, these core workers are a privileged part of the labor force. On the other hand, they are the heirs of the radical ideas of the community media activists. The Californian Ideology, therefore, simultaneously reflects the disciplines of market economics and the freedoms of hippie artisanship. This bizarre hybrid is made possible only through a nearly universal belief in technological determinism. Ever since the 1960s, liberals—in the social sense of the word—have hoped that the new information technologies would realize their ideals. Responding to the challenge of the New Left, the New Right has resurrected an older form of liberalism—economic liberalism.[15] In place of the collective freedom sought by the hippie radicals, they have championed the liberty of individuals within the marketplace. Yet even these conservatives couldn't resist the romance of the new information technologies. Back in the 1960s, McLuhan's predictions were reinterpreted as an advertisement for new forms of media, computing, and telecommunications being developed by the private sector. From the 1970s onward, Toffler, de Sola Pool, and other gurus attempted to prove that the advent of hypermedia would paradoxically involve a return to the economic liberalism of the past.[16] This retro-utopia echoed the predictions of Asimov, Heinlein, and other macho sci-fi novelists whose future worlds were always filled with space traders, superslick salesmen, genius scientists, pirate captains, and other rugged individualists.[17] The path of technological progress didn't always lead to "ecotopia"—it could instead lead back to the America of the Founding Fathers.

Agora or Marketplace?

The ambiguity of the Californian Ideology is most pronounced in its contradictory visions of the digital future. The development of hypermedia is a key component of the next stage of capitalism. As Zuboff points out, the introduction of media, computing, and telecommunications technologies into the factory and the office is the culmination of a long process of separation of the workforce from direct involvement in production.[18] If only for competitive reasons, all major industrial economies will eventually be forced to wire up their populations to obtain the productivity gains of digital working. What is unknown is the social and cultural impact of allowing people to produce and exchange almost unlimited quantities of information on a global scale. Above all, will the advent of hypermedia realize the utopias of either the New Left or the New Right? As a hybrid faith, the Californian Ideology happily answers this conundrum by believing in both visions at the same time—and by not criticizing either of them.

On the one hand, the anticorporate purity of the New Left has been preserved by the advocates of the "virtual community." According to their guru, Howard Rheingold, the values of the counterculture baby boomers are shaping the development of new information technologies. As a consequence, community activists will be able to use hypermedia to replace corporate capitalism and big government with a high-tech "gift economy." Bulletin board systems, Net real-time conferences, and chat facilities already rely on the voluntary exchange of information and knowledge among their participants. In Rheingold's view, the members of the "virtual class" are still in the forefront of the struggle for social liberation. Despite the frenzied commercial and political involvement in building the "information superhighway," the electronic agora will inevitably triumph over its corporate and bureaucratic enemies.[19]

On the other hand, other West Coast ideologues have embraced the laissez-faire ideology of their erstwhile conservative enemy. For example, *Wired*—the monthly bible of the "virtual class"—has uncritically reproduced the views of Newt Gingrich, the extreme-right Republican leader of the House of Representatives, and the Tofflers, who are his close advisors.[20] Ignoring their policies for welfare cutbacks, the magazine is instead mesmerized by their enthusiasm for the libertarian possibilities offered by new information technologies. However, although they borrow McLuhan's technological determinism, Gingrich and the Tofflers aren't advocates of the electronic agora. On the contrary, they claim that the convergence of the media, computing, and telecommunications will produce an *electronic marketplace*: "In cyberspace ..., market after market is being transformed by technological progress from a 'natural monopoly' to one in which competition is the rule."[21]

In this version of the Californian Ideology, each member of the 'virtual class' is promised the opportunity to become a successful high-tech entrepreneur. Information technologies, so the argument goes, empower the individual, enhance personal freedom, and radically reduce the power of the nation state. Existing social, political, and legal power structures will wither away to be replaced by unfettered interactions between autonomous individuals and their software. These restyled McLuhanites vigorously argue that big government should stay off the backs of resourceful entrepreneurs who are the only people cool and courageous enough to take risks. In place of counterproductive regulations, visionary engineers are inventing the tools needed to create a "free market" within cyberspace, such as encryption, digital money, and verification procedures. Indeed, attempts to interfere with the emergent properties of these technological and economic forces, particularly by the government, merely rebound on those who are foolish enough to defy the primary laws of nature. According to the executive editor of *Wired*, the "invisible hand" of the marketplace and the blind forces of Darwinian evolution are actually one and the same thing.[22] As in Heinlein's and Asimov's sci-fi novels, the path forward to the future seems to lead back to the past. The twenty-first-century information age will be the realization of the eighteenth-century liberal ideals of Thomas Jefferson: "the ... creation of a new civilization, founded in the eternal truths of the American Idea."[23]

The Myth of the "Free Market"

Following the victory of Gingrich's party in the 1994 legislative elections, this right-wing version of the Californian Ideology is now in the ascendant. Yet the sacred tenets of economic liberalism are contradicted by the actual history of hypermedia. For instance, the iconic technologies of the computer and the Net could only have been invented with the aid of massive state subsidies and the enthusiastic involvement of amateurs. Private enterprise has played an important role but only as one part of a mixed economy.

For example, the first computer—the Difference Engine—was designed and built by private companies, but its development was only made possible through a British government grant of £17,470, which was a small fortune in 1834.[24] From Colossus to EDVAC, from flight simulators to virtual reality, the development of computing has depended at key moments on public research handouts or fat contracts with public agencies. The IBM Corporation built the first programable digital computer only after it was requested to do so by the U.S. Defense Department during the Korean War. Ever since, the development of successive generations of computers has been directly or indirectly subsidized by the American defense budget.[25] As well as state aid, the evolution of computing has also depended on the involvement of do-it-yourself culture. For instance, the personal computer was invented by amateur techies who wanted to construct their own cheap machines. The existence of a "gift economy" amongs hobbyists was a necessary precondition for the subsequent success of products made by Apple and Microsoft. Even now, shareware programs still play a vital role in advancing software design.

The history of the Internet also contradicts the tenets of the free-market ideologues. For the first twenty years of its existence, the Net's development was almost completely dependent on the much reviled American federal government. Whether via the U.S. military or through the universities, large amounts of taxpayers' dollars went into building the Net infrastructure and subsidizing the cost of using its services. At the same time, many of the key Net programs and applications were invented either by hobbyists or by professionals working in their spare time. For instance, the MUD program, which allows real-time Net conferencing, was invented by a group of students who wanted to play fantasy games over a computer network.[26]

One of the weirdest things about the rightward drift of the Californian Ideology is that the West Coast itself is a creation of the mixed economy. Government dollars were used to build the irrigation systems, highways, schools, universities, and other infrastructural projects that make the good life possible in California. On top of these public subsidies, the West Coast high-tech industrial complex has been feasting off the fattest pork barrel in history for decades. The U.S. government has poured billions of tax dollars into buying planes, missiles, electronics, and nuclear bombs from Californian companies. For those not blinded by free-market dogmas, it was obvious that Americans have always had state planning: they call it the defense budget.[27] At the same time, key elements of the West Coast's lifestyle come from its long tradition of cultural bohemianism. Although they were later commercialized, community media, new-age spiritualism, surfing, health food, recreational drugs, pop music, and many other forms of cultural heterodoxy all emerged from the decidedly noncommercial scenes based around university campuses, artists' communities, and rural communes. Without its d.i.y. culture, California's myths wouldn't have the global resonance that they have today.[28]

All of this public funding and community involvement has had an enormously beneficial—albeit unacknowledged and uncosted—effect on the development of Silicon Valley and other high-tech industries. Capitalist entrepreneurs often have an inflated sense of their own resourcefulness in developing new ideas and give little recognition to the contributions made by either the state, their own labor force, or the wider community. All technological progress is cumulative: it depends on the results of a collective historical process and must be counted, at least in part, as a collective achievement. Hence, as in every other industrialized country, American entrepreneurs have inevitably relied on state intervention and d.i.y. initiatives to nurture and develop their industries. When Japanese companies threatened to take over the American microchip market, the libertarian computer capitalists of California had no ideological qualms about joining a state-sponsored cartel organized to fight off the invaders from the East. Until the Net programs allowing community participation within cyberspace could be included, Bill Gates believed that Microsoft had no choice but to delay the launch of Windows '95.[29] As in other sectors of the modern economy, the question facing the emerging hypermedia industry isn't whether it will be organized as a mixed economy but what sort of mixed economy it will be.

Freedom Is Slavery

If its holy precepts are refuted by profane history, why have the myths of the free market so influenced the proponents of the Californian Ideology? Living within a contract culture, the high-tech artisans lead a schizophrenic existence. On the one hand, they cannot challenge the primacy of the marketplace over their lives. On the other hand, they resent attempts by those in authority to encroach on their individual autonomy. By mixing New Left and New Right, the Californian Ideology provides a mystical resolution of the contradictory attitudes held by members of the "virtual class." Crucially, antistatism provides the means to reconcile radical and reactionary ideas about technological progress. While the New Left resents the government for funding the military-industrial complex, the New Right attacks the state for interfering with the spontaneous dissemination of new technologies by market competition. Despite the central role played by public intervention in developing hypermedia, the Californian ideologues preach an antistatist gospel of high-tech libertarianism—a bizarre mish-mash of hippie anarchism and economic liberalism beefed up with lots of technological determinism. Rather than comprehend really existing capitalism, gurus from both New Left and New Right much prefer to advocate rival versions of a digital "Jeffersonian democracy." For instance, Howard Rheingold on the New Left believes that the electronic agora will allow individuals to exercise the sort of media freedom advocated by the Founding Fathers. Similarly, those on the New Right claim that the removal of all regulatory curbs on the private enterprise will create media freedom worthy of a "Jeffersonian democracy."[30]

The triumph of this retrofuturism is a result of the failure of renewal in the United States during the late 1960s and early 1970s. Following the confrontation at People's Park, the struggle between the American establishment and the counterculture entered into a spiral of violent confrontation. While the Vietnamese—at the cost of enormous human suffering—were able to expel the American invaders from their country, the hippies and their allies in the black civil rights movement were eventually crushed by a combination of state repression and cultural cooption.

The Californian Ideology perfectly encapsulates the consequences of this defeat for members of the "virtual class." Although they enjoy cultural freedoms won by the hippies, most of them are no longer actively involved in the struggle to build "ecotopia." Instead of openly rebelling against the system, these high-tech artisans now accept that individual freedom can be achieved only by working within the constraints of technological progress and the "free market." In many cyberpunk novels, this asocial libertarianism is personified by the central character of the hacker, who is a lone individual fighting for survival within the virtual world of information.[31]

The drift toward the right by the Californian ideologues is helped by their unquestioning acceptance of the liberal ideal of the self-sufficient individual. In American folklore, the nation was built out of a wilderness by free-booting individuals—the trappers, cowboys, preachers, and settlers of the frontier. The American revolution itself was fought to protect the freedoms and property of individuals against oppressive laws and unjust taxes imposed by a foreign monarch. For both the New Left and the New Right, the early years of the American republic provide a potent model for their rival versions of individual freedom. Yet there is a profound contradiction at the center of this primordial American dream: individuals in this period prospered only through the suffering of others. Nowhere is this clearer than in the life of Thomas Jefferson—the chief icon of the Californian ideology. Thomas Jefferson was the man who wrote the inspiring call for democracy and liberty in the American Declaration of Independence and—at the same time—owned nearly two hundred human beings as slaves. As a politician, he championed the right of American farmers and artisans to determine their own destinies without being subject to the restrictions of feudal Europe. Like other liberals of the period, he thought that political liberties could be protected from authoritarian governments only by the widespread ownership of individual private property. The rights of citizens were derived from this fundamental natural right. To encourage self-sufficiency, he proposed that all Americans should be given at least fifty acres of land to guarantee their economic independence. Yet while idealizing the small farmers and businessmen of the frontier, Jefferson was actually a Virginian plantation owner living off the labor of his slaves. Although the South's 'peculiar institution' troubled his conscience, he still believed that the natural rights of man included the right to own human beings as private property. In "Jeffersonian democracy," freedom for white folks was based on slavery for black people.[32]

Forward into the Past

Despite the eventual emancipation of the slaves and the victories of the civil rights movement, racial segregation still lies at the center of American politics—especially on the West Coast. In the 1994 election for governor in California, Republican Pete Wilson won through a vicious anti-immigrant campaign. Nationally, the triumph of Gingrich's Republican Party in the legislative elections was based on the mobilization of "angry white males" against the supposed threat from black welfare scroungers, illegal immigrants from Mexico, and other "uppity" minorities. These politicians have reaped the electoral benefits of the increasing polarization between the mainly white, affluent suburbanites (most of whom vote) and the largely nonwhite, poorer inner-city dwellers (most of whom don't vote).[33]

Although they retain some hippie ideals, many Californian ideologues have found it impossible to take a clear stand against the divisive policies of the Republicans. This is because the high-tech and media industries are a key element of the New Right electoral coalition. In part, both capitalists and well-paid workers fear that the open acknowledgment of public funding of their companies would justify tax rises to pay for desperately needed spending on health care, environmental protection, housing, public transport, and education. More important, many members of the virtual class want to be seduced by the libertarian rhetoric and technological enthusiasm of the New Right. Working for high-tech and media companies, they would like to believe that the electronic marketplace can somehow solve America's pressing social and economic problems without any sacrifices on their part. Caught in the contradictions of the Californian Ideology, Gingrich is—as one *Wired* contributor put it—both their "friend *and* foe."[34]

In the United States, a major redistribution of wealth is urgently needed in the long-term economic well-being of the majority of the population. However, this is against the short-term interests of rich white folks, including many members of the "virtual class." Rather than share with their poor black or Hispanic neighbors, the yuppies instead retreat into their affluent suburbs, protected by armed guards and secure with their private welfare services.[35] The deprived only participate in the information age by providing cheap nonunionized labor for the unhealthy factories of the Silicon Valley chip manufacturers.[36] Even the construction of cyberspace could become an integral part of the fragmentation of American society into antagonistic, racially determined classes. Already red-lined by profit-hungry telephone companies, the inhabitants of poor inner-city areas are now threatened with exclusion from the new online services through lack of money.[37] In contrast, members of the "virtual class" and other professionals can play at being cyberpunks within hyperreality without having to meet any of their impoverished neighbors. Alongside the ever-widening social divisions, another apartheid is being created between the "information-rich" and the 'information-poor'. In this high-tech "Jeffersonian democracy," the relationship between masters and slaves endures in a new form.

Cyborg Masters and Robot Slaves

The fear of the rebellious "underclass" has now corrupted the most fundamental tenet of the Californian Ideology—its belief in the emancipatory potentiality of the new information technologies. While the proponents of the electronic agora and the electronic marketplace promise to liberate individuals from the hierarchies of the state and private monopolies, the social polarization of American society is bringing forth a more oppressive vision of the digital future. The technologies of freedom are turning into the machines of dominance.

At his estate at Monticello, Jefferson invented many clever gadgets for his house, such as a dumb waiter to deliver food from the kitchen into the dining room. By mediating his contacts with his slaves through technology, this revolutionary individualist spared himself from facing the reality of his dependence on the forced labor of his fellow human beings.[38] In the late-twentieth century, technology is once again being used to reinforce the difference between the masters and the slaves.

According to some visionaries, the search for the perfection of mind, body, and spirit will inevitably lead to the emergence of the "posthuman"—a biotechnological manifestation of the social privileges of the "virtual class." While the hippies saw self-development as part of social liberation, the high-tech artisans of contemporary California are more likely to seek individual self-fulfillment through therapy, spiritualism, exercise, or other narcissistic pursuits. Their desire to escape into the gated suburb of the hyperreal is only one aspect of this deep self-obsession.[39] Emboldened by supposed advances in "Artificial Intelligence" and medical science, the Extropian cult fantasises of abandoning the "wetware" of the human state altogether to become living machines.[40] Just like Virek and the Tessier-Ashpools in Gibson's *Sprawl* novels, they believe that social privilege will eventually endow them with immortality.[41] Instead of predicting the emancipation of humanity, this form of technological determinism can only envisage a deepening of social segregation.

Despite these fantasies, white people in California remain dependent on their darker-skinned fellow humans to work in their factories, pick their crops, look after their children, and tend their gardens. Following the 1992 Los Angeler riots, they increasingly fear that this "underclass" will someday demand its liberation. If human slaves are ultimately unreliable, then mechanical ones will have to be invented. The search for the holy grail of "Artificial Intelligence" reveals this desire for the Golem— a strong and loyal slave whose skin is the color of the earth and whose innards are made of sand. As in Asimov's Robot novels, the technoutopians imagine that it is possible to obtain slavelike labor from inanimate machines.[42] Yet although technology can store or amplify labor, it can never remove the necessity for humans to invent, build, and maintain these machines in the first place. Slave labor cannot be obtained without somebody being enslaved.

Across the world, the Californian Ideology has been embraced as an optimistic and emancipatory form of technological determinism. Yet this utopian fantasy of the West Coast depends on its blindness toward—and dependence on—the social and racial polarization of the society from which it was born. Despite its radical rhetoric, the Californian Ideology is ultimately pessimistic about fundamental social change. Unlike the hippies, its advocates are not struggling to build "ecotopia" or even to help revive the New Deal. Instead, the social liberalism of New Left and the economic liberalism of New Right have converged into an ambiguous dream of a high-tech "Jeffersonian democracy." Interpreted generously, this retrofuturism could be a vision of a cybernetic frontier where high-tech artisans discover their individual self-fulfillment in either the electronic agora or the electronic marketplace. However, as the zeitgeist of the "virtual class," the Californian Ideology is at the same time an exclusive faith. If only some people have access to the new information technologies, "Jeffersonian democracy" can become a high-tech version of the plantation economy of the Old South. Reflecting its deep ambiguity, the Californian Ideology's technological determinism is not simply optimistic and emancipatory. It is simultaneously a deeply pessimistic and repressive vision of the future.

There Are Alternatives

Despite its deep contradictions, people across the world still believe that the Californian Ideology expresses the only way forward to the future. With the increasing globalization of the world economy, many members of the "virtual class" in Europe and Asia feel more affinity with their Californian peers than with other workers within their own country. Yet, in reality, debate has never been more possible or more necessary. The Californian Ideology was developed by a group of people living within one specific country with a particular mix of socioeconomic and technological choices. Its eclectic and contradictory blend of conservative economics and hippie radicalism reflects the history of the West Coast—and not the inevitable future of the rest of the world. For instance, the antistatist assumptions of the Californian ideologues are rather parochial. In Singapore, the government is not only organizing the construction of a fiber-optic network but also trying to control the ideological suitability of the information distributed over it. Given the much faster growth rates of the Asian "tigers," the digital future will not necessarily arrive first in California.[43]

Despite the neoliberal recommendations of the Bangemann Report, most European authorities are also determined to be closely involved within the development of new information technologies. Minitel—the first successful online network in the world—was the deliberate creation of the French state. Responding to an official report on the potential impact of hypermedia, the government decided to pour resources into developing "cutting-edge" technologies. In 1981, France Telecom launched the Minitel system, which provided a mix of text-based information and communications facilities. As a monopoly, this nationalized telephone company was able to build up a critical mass of users for its pioneering online system by giving away free terminals to anyone willing to forgo paper telephone directories. Once the market had been created, commercial and community providers were then able to find enough customers or participants to thrive within the system. Ever since, millions of French people from all social backgrounds have happily booked tickets, chatted each other up, and politically organized online without realizing they were breaking the libertarian precepts of the Californian Ideology.[44]

Far from demonizing the state, the overwhelming majority of the French population believes that more public intervention is needed for an efficient and healthy society.[45] In the recent presidential elections, almost every candidate had to advocate—at least rhetorically—greater state intervention to end social exclusion of the unemployed and homeless. Unlike its American equivalent, the French revolution went beyond economic liberalism to popular democracy. Following the victory of the Jacobins over their liberal opponents in 1792, the democratic republic in France became the embodiment of the general will. As such, the state was believed to defend the interests of all citizens rather than just to protect the rights of individual property owners. The discourse of French politics allows for collective action by the state to mitigate—or even remove—problems encountered by society. While the Californian ideologues try to ignore the taxpayers' dollars subsidizing the development of hypermedia, the French government can openly intervene in this sector of the economy.[46]

Although its technology is now dated, the history of Minitel clearly refutes the antistatist prejudices of the Californian ideologues—and of the Bangemann committee. The digital future will be a hybrid of state intervention, capitalist entrepreneurship, and d.i.y. culture. Crucially, if the state can foster the development of hypermedia, conscious action could also be taken to prevent the emergence of the social apartheid between the "information rich" and the "information poor." By not leaving everything up to the vagaries of market forces, the European Union and its member states could ensure that every citizen has the opportunity to be connected to a broadband fiber-optic network at the lowest possible price.

In the first instance, this would be a much needed job-creation scheme for semiskilled labor in a period of mass unemployment. As a Keynesian employment measure, nothing beats paying people to dig holes in the road and fill them in again.[47] Even more important, the construction of a fiber-optic network into homes and businesses could give everyone access to new online services and create a large vibrant community of shared expertise. The long-term gains to the economy and to society from the building of the "infobahn" would be immeasurable. It would allow industry to work more efficiently and market new products. It would ensure that education and information services were available to all. No doubt the "infobahn" will create a mass market for private companies to sell existing information commodities—films, TV programs, music, and books—across the Net. At the same time, once people can distribute as well as receive hypermedia, a flourishing of community media and special-interest groups will quickly emerge. For all this to happen, collective intervention will be needed to ensure that all citizens are included within the digital future.

The Rebirth of the Modern

Even if it is not in circumstances of their own choosing, it is now necessary for Europeans to assert their own vision of the future. There are varying ways forward toward the information society—and some paths are more desirable than others. To make an informed choice, European digital artisans need to develop a more coherent analysis of the impact of hypermedia than can be found within the ambiguities of the Californian Ideology. The members of the European "virtual class" must create their own distinctive self-identity.

This alternative understanding of the future starts from a rejection of any form of social apartheid—both inside and outside cyberspace. Any program for developing hypermedia must ensure that the whole population can have access to the new online services. In place of New Left or New Right anarchism, a European strategy for developing the new information technologies must openly acknowledge the inevitability of some form of mixed economy—the creative and antagonistic mix of state, corporate, and d.i.y. initiatives. The indeterminacy of the digital future is a result of the ubiquity of this mixed economy within the modern world. No one knows exactly what the relative strengths of each component will be, but collective action can ensure that no social group is deliberately excluded from cyberspace.

A European strategy for the information age must also celebrate the creative powers of the digital artisans. Because their labor cannot be deskilled or mechanized, members of the 'virtual class' exercise great control over their own work. Rather than succumbing to the fatalism of the Californian Ideology, we should embrace the Promethean possibilities of hypermedia. Within the limitations of the mixed economy, digital artisans are able to invent something completely new—something that has not been predicted in any sci-fi novel. These innovative forms of knowledge and communications will sample the achievements of others, including some aspects of the Californian Ideology. It is now impossible for any serious movement for social emancipation not to include demands for feminism, drug culture, gay liberation, ethnic identity, and other issues pioneered by West Coast radicals. Similarly, any attempt to develop hypermedia within Europe will need some of the entrepreneurial zeal and can-do attitude championed by the Californian New Right. Yet, at the same time, the development of hypermedia means innovation, creativity, and invention. There are no precedents for all aspects of the digital future.

As pioneers of the new, the digital artisans need to reconnect themselves with the theory and practice of productive art. They are not just employees of others—or even would-be cybernetic entrepreneurs. They are also artist-engineers—designers of the next stage of modernity. Drawing on the experience of the Saint-Simonists and constructivists, the digital artisans can create a new machine aesthetic for the information age.[48] For instance, musicians have used computers to develop purely digital forms of music, such as jungle and techno.[49] Interactive artists have explored the potential of CD-ROM technologies, as shown by the work of ANTI-rom. The HyperMedia Research Centre has constructed an experimental virtual social space called J's Joint.[50] In each instance, artist-engineers are trying to push beyond the limitations of both the technologies and their own creativity. Above all, these new forms of expression and communications are connected with the wider culture. The developers of hypermedia must reassert the possibility of rational and conscious control over the shape of the digital future. Unlike the elitism of the Californian Ideology, the European artist-engineers must construct a cyberspace that is inclusive and universal. Now is the time for the rebirth of the Modern:

Present circumstances favour making luxury national. Luxury will become useful and moral when it is enjoyed by the whole nation. The honour and advantage of employing directly, in political arrangements, the progress of exact sciences and the fine arts ... have been reserved for our century.[51]

Notes

We would like to thank Andrej Kerlep, Dick Pountain, Helen Barbrook, Les Levidow, Jeremy Quinn, Jim McLellan, John Barker, John Wyver, Rhiannon Patterson, and the members of the Hypermedia Research Centre of the University of Westminster, London, for their help in writing this article.

1. Naum Gabo and Antoine Pevsner, "The Realistic Manifesto, 1920," in John E. Bowlt, ed., *Russian Art of the Avant-Garde: Theory and Criticism* (London: Thames & Hudson, 1976), p. 214.

2. For over twenty-five years, experts have been predicting the imminent arrival of the information age. See Alain Touraine, *La Société post-industrielle* (Paris: Éditions Denoâl, 1969); Zbigniew Brzezinski, *Between Two Ages: America's Role in the Technetronic Era* (New York: Viking Press, 1970); Daniel Bell, *The Coming of the Post-Industrial Society* (New York: Basic Books Naum, 1973); Alvin Toffler, *The Third Wave* (London: Pan, 1980); Simon Nora and Alain Minc, *The Computerisation of Society* (Cambridge, MA: MIT Press, 1980); and Ithiel de Sola Pool, *Technologies of Freedom* (Cambridge, MA: Belknap Press of Harvard University Press, 1983).

3. See Martin Bangemann, *Europe and the Global Information Society* (Brussels: 1994); and the program and abstracts of Warwick University's Virtual Futures Conference.

4. See Mitch Kapor, "Where Is the Digital Highway Really Heading," *Wired* (July-August 1993).

5. See Mike Davis, *City of Quartz* (London: Verso, 1990); Richard Walker, "California Rages against the Dying of the Light," *New Left Review* (January-February 1995); and the records of Ice-T, Snoop Dog, Dr. Dre, Ice Cube, NWA, and many other West Coast rappers.

6. See George Katsiaficas, *The Imagination of the New Left: A Global Analysis of 1968* (Boston: South End Press, 1987), p. 124.

7. Jerry Rubin, "An Emergency Letter to my Brothers and Sisters in the Movement," in Peter Stansill and David Zane Mairowitz, eds., *BAMN: Outlaw Manifestos and Ephemera 1965–70* (London: Penguin, 1971), p. 244.

8. For the key role played by popular culture in the self-identity of the American New Left, see Katsiaficas, *The Imagination of the New Left*; and Charles Reich,

The Greening of America (New York: Random House, 1970). For a description of the lives of white-collar workers in 1950s America, see William Whyte, *The Organization Man* (New York: Simon & Schuster, 1956).

9. In a best-selling novel of the mid-1970s, the northern half of the West Coast has seceded from the rest of the United States to form a hippie utopia. See Ernest Callenbach, *Ecotopia* (New York: Bantam, 1975). This idealization of Californian community life can also be found in John Brunner, *The Shockwave Rider* (London: Methuen, 1975); and even in later works, such as Kim Stanley Robinson, *Pacific Edge* (London: Grafton, 1990).

10. For an analysis of attempts to create direct democracy through media technologies, see Richard Barbrook, *Media Freedom: The Contradictions of Communications in the Age of Modernity* (London: Pluto, 1995).

11. Marshall McLuhan, *Understanding Media* (London: Routledge & Kegan Paul, 1964), pp. 255–56. Also see Marshall McLuhan and Quentin Fiore, *The Medium Is the Massage* (London: Penguin, 1967); and Gerald Emanuel Stern, ed., *McLuhan: Hot and Cool* (London: Penguin, 1968).

12. See John Downing, *Radical Media* (Boston: South End Press, 1984).

13. Arthur Kroker and Michael A. Weinstein, *Data Trash: The Theory of the Virtual Class* (Montreal: New World Perspectives, 1994), p. 15. This analysis follows that of those futurologists who thought that "knowledge workers" were the embryo of a new ruling class (see Bell, *The Coming of the Post-Industrial Society*) and economists who believe that "symbolic analysts" will become the dominant section of the workforce under globalized capitalism (see Robert Reich, *The Work of Nations: A Blueprint for the Future* (London: Simon & Schuster, 1991). In contrast, back in the 1960s, some New Left theorists believed that these scientific-technical workers were leading the struggle for social liberation through factory occupations and demands for self-management. See Serge Mallet, *The New Working Class* (Nottingham: Spokesman Books, 1975).

14. See Dennis Hayes, *Behind the Silicon Curtain* (London: Free Association Books, 1989), for a description of contract work in Silicon Valley. For a fictional treatment of the same subject, see Douglas Coupland, *Microserfs* (London: Flamingo, 1995). For more theoretical examinations of post-Fordist labor organization, see Alain Lipietz, *L'audace ou l'enlisement* (Paris: Éditions La Découverte, 1984), and *Mirages and Miracles* (London: Verso, 1987); Benjamin Coriat, *L'Atelier et le robot* (Paris: Christian Bourgois Editeur, 1990); and Toni Negri, *Revolution Retrieved: Selected Writings on Marx, Keynes, Capitalist Crisis and New Social Subjects 1967–83* (London: Red Notes, 1988).

15. There is considerable political and semantic confusion about the meaning of *liberalism* on both sides of the Atlantic. For instance, Americans use *liberalism* to describe any policies that happen to be supported by the supposedly left-of-center Democratic Party. However, as Lipset points out, this narrow sense of the word hides the almost universal acceptance in the United States of *liberalism* in its classical meaning. As he puts it: "These [liberal] values were evident in the

twentieth century fact that ... the United States not only lacked a viable social-ist party, but also has never developed a British or European-style Conserva-tive or Tory party." See Seymour Martin Lipset, *American Exceptionalism: A Double-Edged Sword* (New York: Norton, 1996), pp. 31–32. The convergence of the New Left and New Right around the Californian ideology, therefore, is a specific example of the wider consensus around antistatist liberalism as a politi-cal discourse in the United States.

16. For McLuhan's success on the corporate junket circuit, see Tom Wolfe, "What If He Is Right?," *The Pump House Gang* (London: Bantam Books, 1968). For the use of his ideas by conservative thinkers, see Zbigniew Brzezinski, *Between Two Ages: America's Role in the Technetronic Era* (New York: Viking Press, 1970); Bell, *The Coming of the Post-Industrial Society*; Toffler, *The Third Wave*; and Pool, *Technologies of Freedom*.

17. Heroic males are common throughout classic sci-fi novels. See D. D. Harriman in Robert Heinlein, *The Man Who Sold the Moon* (New York: Signet, 1950), or the leading characters in Isaac Asimov, *The Foundation Trilogy* (New York: Gnome Press, 1953), *I, Robot* (London: Panther, 1968), and *The Rest of the Robots* (London: Panther, 1968). Hagbard Celine—a more psychedelic ver-sion of this male archetype—is the central character in Robert Shea and Robert Anton Wilson, *The Illuminati Trilogy* (New York: Dell, 1975). In the timechart of "future history" at the front of Robert Heinlein's novel, it predicts that, after a period of social crisis caused by rapid technological advance, stability would restored in the 1980s and 1990s through "an opening of new frontiers and a return to nineteenth-century economy"!

18. See Shoshana Zuboff, *In the Age of the Smart Machine: The Future of Work and Power* (New York: Heinemann, 1988). Of course, this analysis is derived from Karl Marx, *Grundrisse* (London: Penguin, 1973), and "Results of the Immediate Process of Production," in Albert Dragstedt, ed., *Value Studies by Marx* (London: New Park, 1976).

19. See Howard Rheingold, *Virtual Communities* (London: Secker & Warburg, 1994), and his home pages.

20. See the gushing interview with the Tofflers in Peter Schwartz, "Shock Wave (Anti) Warrior," *Wired* (November 1993); and for the magazine's characteristic ambiguity over the Speaker of the House's reactionary political program, see the aptly named interview with Newt Gingrich in Esther Dyson, "Friend and Foe," *Wired* (August 1995).

21. Progress and Freedom Foundation, "Cyberspace and the American Dream: A Magna Carta for the Knowledge Age" (1994), at ⟨http://www.pff.org/position.html⟩.

22. See Kevin Kelly, *Out of Control: The New Biology of Machines* (London: Fourth Estate, 1994). For a critique of the book, see Richard Barbrook, "The Pinocchio Theory," at ⟨http://www.hrc.wmin.ac.uk⟩.

23. Progress and Freedom Foundation, "Cyberspace and the American Dream" conference. Toffler and friends also proudly proclaim that "America ... remains

the land of individual freedom, and this freedom clearly extends to cyberspace" Also see Mitch Kapor, "Where Is the Digital Highway Really Heading?," *Wired* (July-August 1993).

24. See Simon Schaffer, "Babbage's Intelligence: Calculating Engines and the Factory System" *Critical Inquiry* 21 (1) (Autumn 1994).

25. See Jonathan Palfreman and Doron Swade, *The Dream Machine* (London: BBC, 1991), pp. 32–36, for an account of how a lack of state intervention meant that Nazi Germany lost the opportunity to build the world's first electronic computer. In 1941 the German High Command refused further funding to Konrad Zuze, who had pioneered the use of binary code, stored programs, and electronic logic gates.

26. See Howard Rheingold, *Virtual Communities* (London: Secker & Warburg, 1994).

27. As President Clinton's former Labor Secretary puts it: "Recall that through the postwar era the Pentagon has quietly been in charge of helping American corporations move ahead with technologies like jet engines, airframes, transistors, integrated circuits, new materials, lasers, and optic fibers.... The Pentagon and the 600 national laboratories which work with it and with the Department of Energy are the closest thing America has to Japan's well-known Ministry of International Trade and Industry." See Reich, *The Work of Nations*, p. 159.

28. For an account of how these cultural innovations emerged from the early LSD scene, see Tom Wolfe, *The Electric Kool-Aid Acid Test* (New York: Bantam Books, 1968). One of the drivers of the famous bus was Stewart Brand, who is now a leading contributor to *Wired*.

29. Dennis Hayes, *Behind the Silicon Curtain* (London: Free Association Books, 1989), pp. 21–22, points out that the U.S. computer industry has already been encouraged by the Pentagon to form cartels against foreign competition. Gates admits that he'd only recently realized the "massive structural change" that was being caused by the Net. See "The Bill Gates Column," *The Guardian*, 20 July 1995.

30. See Howard Rheingold's home pages, and Kapor, "Where Is the Digital Highway Really Heading?" Despite the libertarian instincts of both these writers, their infatuation with the era of the founding fathers is shared by the neofascist militia and patriot movements. See Chip Berlet, "*Armed Militias, Right Wing Populism and Scapegoating*," report, Political Research Associates, Cambridge, Mass. (1995).

31. See the hacker heroes in William Gibson, *Neuromancer* (London: Grafton, 1984), *Count Zero* (London: Grafton, 1986), and *Mona Lisa Overdrive* (London: Grafton, 1989); or in Bruce Sterling, ed., *Mirrorshades* (London: Paladin, 1988). A prototype of this sort of antihero is Deckard, the existential hunter of replicants in Ridley Scott's movie *Bladerunner*.

32. According to Miller, Thomas Jefferson believed that black people could not be members of the Lockean social contract that bound together citizens of the

American republic: "The rights of man ... while theoretically and ideally the birthright of every human being, applied in practice in the United States only to white men: the black slaves were excluded from consideration because, while admittedly human beings, they were also property, and where the rights of man conflicted with the rights of property, property took precedence." See John Miller, *The Wolf by the Ears: Thomas Jefferson and Slavery* (New York: Free Press, 1977), p. 13. Jefferson's opposition to slavery was at best rhetorical. In a letter of April 22, 1820, he disingenuously suggested that the best way to encourage the abolition of slavery would be to legalize the private ownership of human beings in all states of the Union and the frontier territories. He claimed that "their diffusion over a greater surface would make them individually happier, and proportionally facilitate the accomplishment of their emancipation, by dividing the burden on a greater number of coadjutors [slave-owners]." See Merill Peterson, ed., *The Portable Thomas Jefferson* (New York: Viking Press, 1975), p. 568. For a description of life on his plantation, also see Paul Wilstach, *Jefferson and Monticello* (London: William Heinemann, 1925).

33. For California's turn to the right, see Richard Walker, "California Rages against the Dying of the Light," *New Left Review* (January-February 1995).

34. See Esther Dyson, "Friend and Foe," *Wired* (August 1995). Esther Dyson collaborated with the Tofflers in the writing of the Peace and Progress Foundation's *Cyberspace and the American Dream*, which is a futurist manifesto designed to win votes for Gingrich from members of the virtual class.

35. For the rise of the fortified suburbs, see Mike Davis, *City of Quartz* (London: Verso, 1990), and "Blade Runner: *Urban Control, the Ecology of Fear* Open Magazine Pamphlet Series, Westfield, NJ, 1992). These "gated suburbs" provide the inspiration for the alienated background of many cyberpunk sci-fi novels, such as Neal Stephenson, *Snow Crash* (New York: Roc, 1992).

36. See Dennis Hayes, *Behind the Silicon Curtain* (London: Free Association Books, 1989).

37. See Reginald Stuart, "High-Tech Redlining," *Utne Reader* (March-April 1995).

38. See Wilstach, *Jefferson and Monticello*.

39. See Hayes, *Behind the Silicon Curtain*.

40. For an exposition of their retrofuturist program, see the Extropian FAQ, available at ⟨http://www.extropy.org/faq/faq.htm⟩.

41. See Gibson, *Neuromancer* and *Count Zero*.

42. See Asimov, *I, Robot* and *The Rest of the Robots*.

43. See William Gibson and Sandy Sandfort, "Disneyland with the Death Penalty," *Wired* (September-October 1993). Since these articles are an attack on Singapore, it is ironic that the real Disneyland is in California—whose repressive penal code includes the death penalty.

44. For the report that led to the creation of Minitel, see Simon Nora and Alain Minc, *The Computerization of Society* (Cambridge, MA: MIT Press, 1980). An

account of the early years of Minitel can be found in Michel Marchand, *The Mintel Saga: A French Success Story* (Paris: Larousse, 1988).

45. According to a poll carried out during the 1995 presidential elections, 67 percent of the French population supported the proposition that "the state must intervene more in the economic life of our country." See "Une Majorité de Français souhaitent un vrai 'chef' pour un vrai 'Etat,'" *Le Monde*, April 11, 1995, p. 6.

46. For the influence of Jacobinism on French conceptions of democratic rights, see Richard Barbrook, *Media Freedom: The Contradictions of Communications in the Age of Modernity* (London: Pluto, 1995). Some French economists believe that the very different history of Europe has created a specific—and socially superior—model of capitalism. See Michel Albert, *Capitalism v. Capitalism* (New York: Four Wall Eight Windows, 1993), and Philippe Delmas, *Le Maître des Horloges* (Paris: Éditions Odile Jacob, 1991).

47. As Keynes himself says: '"To dig holes in the ground", paid for out of savings, will increase not only employment but the real national dividend of useful goods and services." See J. M. Keynes, *The General Theory of Employment, Interest and Money* (London: Macmillan, 1964), p. 220.

48. See Keith Taylor, ed., *Henri Saint-Simon 1760–1825: Selected Writings on Science, Industry and Social Organisation* (London: Croom Helm, 1975); and John E. Bowlt, *Russian Art of the Avant-Garde: Theory and Criticism* (London: Thames & Hudson, 1976).

49. As Goldie, a jungle music maker, puts it: "We have to take it forwards and take the drums 'n' bass and push it and push it and push it. I remember when we were saying that it couldn't be pushed anymore. It's been pushed tenfold since then." See Tony Marcus, "The War Is Over," *Mixmag* (August 1995): 46.

50. For information on ANTI-rom and J's Joint, see their contributions to the HyperMedia Research Centre's Web site, available at ⟨http://www.hrc.wmin.ac.uk⟩.

51. Henri Saint-Simon, "Sketch of the New Political System," in Keith Taylor, ed., *Henri Saint-Simon 1760–1825: Selected Writings on Science, Industry and Social Organisation* (London: Croom Helm, 1975), p. 203.

24

Bit Rot[1]

Mark Dery

Few in the media have mourned his passing, but this writer, for one, laments the fact that we don't have Tricky Nick to kick around anymore. In the December 1998 *Wired*, Nicholas Negroponte—director of MIT's Media Lab and sharp-dressed retailer of broader-bandwidth tomorrows to corporate America (and to the unwashed AOL millions in his best-selling book *Being Digital*)—announced that he was vacating his bully pulpit on the magazine's endpage. After six years there, the man whose Audio-Animatronic prose is to literary style what the Parkinsonian tics of Disneyland's Mr. Lincoln are to fluid human movement had decided to step down.

Alvin Toffler or George Gilder might have been more likely choices for back-page revelators, but Negroponte ponied up $75,000 in seed money when the Old Media barons were showing *Wired* founders Louis Rossetto and Jane Metcalfe the door. For his leap of faith, he was appointed senior columnist, even though the *Wired* style, typified by the Radical Geek journalism of Bruce Sterling and Po Bronson, was never his. Allergic to contractions and impervious to irony, Negroponte wrote in a corporate memo-speak that was equal parts Lee Iacocca and Locutus of Borg. His pet device is the everything-you-know-is-wrong oracular pronouncement, delivered with the authority of Charlton Heston reading the Ten Commandments. "At a distinguished meeting of Internet founders in 1994, I suggested that the Net would have a billion users by 2000," he writes. "Vint Cerf laughed in my face. Others rolled their eyes at what seemed vintage Negroponte hyperbole."[2] Then, the other tasseled loafer drops: "Of course, no one expected the Internet to take off the way it has." What fools these newbies be!

Negroponte's sign-off is as good a sign as any that the self-styled "cyberelite," having strutted and fretted its hour upon the media stage, has at last been yanked off it, vaudeville-style. That's not the only indicator, of course: charter readers of *Wired* have mounted a death watch for the "post-cool" Condé Nast version of the magazine, and John Perry Barlow has gone from prepare-ye-the-way-of-the-Lord pronouncements about the Internet (the "most transforming technological event since the capture of fire")[3] to writing midlife-crisis Odes to His Unit (the most imposing monument to manhood, we're given to assume, until the capture of Viagra).[4]

"Face it—the Digital Revolution is over," writes Negroponte, in his final column, by which he means that the titanic changes wrought by the computerization of seemingly everything have ceased to be a thing of wonder and are now a matter of fact.[5] But the subtext in his sign-off is that, while computerization and globalization have indeed caused cultural upheavals of plate-tectonic magnitude, the Revolution—in the capital *R*, countercultural sense that Rossetto always used it—has fizzled like a soggy squib. The Third-Wave fantasies of New Age neoliberals and Gingrichian "conservative futurists"—government decentralized right out of existence, social ills remedied by computers in the schools and laptops for the poor, a benevolent "Long Boom" whose rising tide lifts all boats—are washed up. Their epitaph is written in Newt Gingrich's unceremonious exit from the national stage by the seat of his pants and, more profoundly, by the social polarization and economic inequity wrought by the laissez-faire gospel preached from *Wired*'s pulpit. "Everyone on the planet believes in the free market now, like they believe in gravity," crowed the magazine's then-managing editor John Battelle, in the heady days of 1995.[6] A mere four years later, as Asian economies plummeted in financial freefall and the wreckage of the former Soviet Union slid into the abyss of gangster capitalism, Battelle's words dripped with unintended irony.

Negroponte's departure marks the end of an era when Magna Cartas for the Knowledge Age and Declarations of the Independence of Cyberspace were taken seriously, at least by the self-anointed "digital elite."

Oddly, Negroponte himself seems not to have noticed how "retro" his Jetsonian visions of digital butlers and supercomputing cufflinks seem in the politically turbulent, economically anxious '00s. At the end of a century that witnessed acid rain and global warming, Bhopal and Chernobyl, he beckoned us toward a future where technology never fails, corporations are always benign, and there's a high-tech magic bullet for every social malady.

In Negroponte's future, the employers who track us through "active badges" woven into our work clothes have only a smarter workplace in mind ("When you have a call, the phone you're nearest rings"); heaven forfend they should spy on us or monitor our bathroom breaks in the name of Taylorist efficiency.[7] Likewise, it's unthinkable that Negroponte's electronic cottages, controlled by ubiquitous, networked computing, would go haywire like the smart house from hell in *The Demon Seed*, where Julie Christie ends up held hostage by the "Enviromod" system that runs her "luxurious, totally automated home staffed by electronic housekeepers and security guards."

And speaking of security guards, criminals are conspicuously absent from Negroponte's visions of things to come. The "intelligent doorknobs" of his smart houses, which "let the Federal Express man in and Fido out," never open to the technosavvy psychopath.[8] Troubling thoughts of social ills such as crime and unemployment and homelessness rarely crease the Negroponte brow. In fact, he's strangely uninterested in social *anything*, from neighborhood life to national politics. Despite his insistence that the Digital Revolution™ is about communication, not computers, there's no real civic life or public sphere to speak of in his future.

There, most of the communicating takes place between you and talkative doorknobs or "interface agents" such as the "eight-inch-high holographic assistants walking across your desk."[9] In the next millennium, predicts Negroponte, "we will find that we are talking as much or more with machines than we are with humans."[10] Thus, the Information Age autism of his wistful "dream for the interface"—that "computers will be more like people."[11] Appliances and household fixtures enjoy a rich social life in Negroponte's future, exchanging electronic "handshakes" and "mating calls." "If your refrigerator notices that you are out of milk," he writes, "it can 'ask' your car to remind you to pick some up on your way home."[12] Human community, meanwhile, consists of "digital neighborhoods in which physical space will be irrelevant"—knowledge workers dialing in from their electronic cocoons, squeezing their social lives through phone lines.[13]

It's no accident that the personalized electronic newspaper that Negroponte's infotopians read is titled, with unwitting irony, *The Daily Me.* The individual, in Negroponte's future, is the self-interested social atom familiar from eighteenth-century laissez-faire capitalism. Years spent hosting dog-and-pony shows for corporate investors at the Media Lab have shaped Negroponte's concept of the body politic. In his laissez-faire Tomorrowland, the citizen has been redefined as the consumer. Purchasing power equals empowerment: "In the digital world, consumers hold almost all the power, which is a nice change."[14] Grassroots activism means organizing "by church group to buy Barbies directly from Mattel."[15] Negroponte's future is a commodity future inhabited by inexhaustible producers and insatiable consumers, a candy store for Sharper Image shoppers crammed full of Dick Tracy wristwatches, talking toasters, and wearable laptops. There's no room on this Carousel of Progress for those unhappy campers who want more out of life than "a Larry King personality" for their newspaper interface or a computer-TV that allows them to transform the weather report into "an animated cartoon with your favorite Disney character."[16]

Negroponte would probably argue that his job description is limited to technological extrapolation, not social responsibility. "The Media Lab isn't a social-science organization," he told the technology journalist David Bennahum, in a *New York* magazine profile of the Lab. "We don't study. We're inventors. And then we try things."[17] Like McLuhan's protestations that he was merely a clinical observer of the electronic revolution, Negroponte's attempt to wrap his laissez-faire futurism in the lab coat of the disinterested tinkerer doesn't quite convince.

The "Dammit, Jim, I'm-an-Inventor, Not-a-Social Scientist" defense died at Hiroshima, where Robert Oppenheimer's blithe dismissal of the moral implications of his invention—"When you see something that is technically sweet, you go ahead and do it"—came back to haunt the world in nightmare images of walking corpses. Obviously, the Media

Lab is playing with Flubber, not fire; the road to Armageddon isn't paved with propeller-head inventions like the technology that enables two Media Labbers to exchange business cards with a handshake, transmitting data through a minute electrical charge conducted across their skin. But Media Labbers like Bruce Blumberg and Neil Gershenfeld sound like members of a (post)human potential cult, babbling about "creating a collective consciousness" and editing the human genome so that Homo Cyber can grow computer chips out of his body.[18] If ever there were technically sweet dreams with profound social consequences, these are them.

Moreover, the corporate "We" in "We're inventors" fudges the fact that the Media Lab's poster boy *isn't* an inventor. He is, by all accounts, a world-class salesman. His clients are the power elite—captains of industry, heads of state—and the product he's pitching, a corporate-friendly future where global capitalism has consigned the nation state and its meddlesome regulations to the desktop Recycle Bin of history, is elitist to the core.

In his final *Wired* column, Negroponte blithely asserts that "any store that is not open twenty-four hours will be noncompetitive"—a prediction calculated to gladden the hearts of minimum-wage workers everywhere—and that "retirement will disappear as a concept," a prophecy that is already a grim reality for cash-strapped retirees forced to return to the workforce in an America where real wages for working stiffs fell by 19 percent from 1972 to 1994.[19]

In *Being Digital*, a funny thing happens on the way to the Rapture. Five pages from the end, an unhappy little cloud momentarily darkens Negroponte's digital visions of nothing but blue skies. "Every technology or gift of science has a dark side," he concedes, on page 227 (!) of a 231-page hymn to the Deus ex Machina. "As we move toward such a digital world, an entire sector of the population will be or feel disenfranchised. When a fifty-year-old steelworker loses his job, unlike his twenty-five-year-old son he may have no digital resilience at all."[20]

But the nutty professor who is a bottomless font of solutions to bandwidth bottlenecks and power sources for wearable computers is surprisingly silent when it comes to what he calls the "worst of all" the social consequences of the computer revolution: job loss due to automation.

A minute of silence for the downsized; then Negroponte banishes the specter of defeatist thinking with one of those today-is-the-first-day-of-the-rest-of-your-life bromides he always seems to have up his pinstriped sleeve: "But being digital, nevertheless, does give much cause for optimism. Like a force of nature, the digital age cannot be denied or stopped. It has four very powerful qualities that will result in its ultimate triumph: decentralizing, globalizing, harmonizing, and empowering."[21]

Naturally, there will be a little roadkill on the Road Ahead, like that fifty-year-old steelworker. But steelworkers are Tired, not Wired, anyway; they're manual laborers, not Way Cool Brain Lords like the digerati, and they make actual *things* out of clunky, uncool atoms. The sooner they and other Second-Wave throwbacks make way for the electric youth in whom Negroponte places his faith, the better. The kids know that the solution to the income gap, the worrisome fact that "a quarter of us have acceptable standards of living and three-quarters don't," is—what else?—digital technology. Electronic interconnectedness "can be a natural force drawing people into greater world harmony," even, presumably, if some live in the cyberbaronial splendor of Bill Gates and others live in abject poverty.[22] (Memo to my Interface Agent: Palmtops for the homeless!)

Those of us who like our paeans to progress with a little history on the side, as a corrective, will recall similarly dizzy responses to the invention of telegraphy in the middle of the last century. "It is impossible that old prejudices and hostilities should longer exist, while such an instrument has been created for an exchange of thought between all the nations of the earth," wrote Charles Briggs and Augustus Maverick, in 1858.[23] But Negroponte, who likes to scandalize the Sven Birkertses of the world with the unapologetic admission that he doesn't like to read, writes utopian philosophy for the Age of Amnesia. History is, like, so *over*.

So, too, is serious thought about the social and economic fallout of postindustrialization and globalization for America's working poor, Mexican maquiladora workers, Indonesian sweatshop laborers, and others whose daily worries are a little more pressing than the inelegance of fax technology. The everyday reality of underclass life has never much concerned the man who breezily redefined the "needy" and the "have-nots," in a *New York Times* editorial, as the technologically illiterate—

the "digitally homeless," a phrase that wins the Newt Gingrich Let-Them-Eat-Laptops Award for cloud-dwelling detachment from the lives of the little people.[24]

The son of a shipping magnate, Negroponte grew up in "the stylish circles" of New York and London, according to Stewart Brand, and went to Choate Academy and Le Rosey, an elite boarding school in Switzerland.[25] Now he sells the future to prospective corporate investors in a Media Lab that eats up $25 million a year. His future is the future of a man who hobnobs with French cabinet members, Japanese prime ministers, and OPEC sheiks, a man who buys a lot of white wine, and owns a BMW and a house in France and another in Greece. A frequent flyer who travels 300,000 miles a year, he glides through the stratosphere both socially and literally, aloof from Second-Wave concerns like geography and time zones, health care and child care, social justice and economic equity. (He can, however, work himself into a lather over "jaggies," the staircase effect that makes certain letters look funny on computer screens, or succumb to weltschmerz over the design flaws of the RJ-11 phone connector.) In his evocations of interactive systems that are "as stern and disciplinarian as a Bavarian nanny" and intelligent toasters that brand your morning toast with the closing price of your favorite stock (you *do* have a favorite stock, don't you?), he speaks the language of the corporate ruling class.[26] His dearest dream is a digital butler and a smart house that will return us to the age of domestic servants without the simmering resentment of the underclasses.

"I get the sense that the problems you're trying to fix here [at the Media Lab] are those of people like yourself: relatively well-off," said Bennahum. Negroponte conceded that "yes, we will do things that look privileged and exclusive and sort of 'toys for the rich.' But in truth these are very much the tools to think with for the world at large, and I hope that these kinds of things get extended to the developing world."[27] The trickle-down theory of imagineering.

One question often goes unasked in Sunday-supplement puff pieces about the Lab: what, precisely, are these "tools to think with"? According to Negroponte, the Lab is the birthplace of computer-programmable LEGO/Logo toys and QuickTime, a video technology for computers.[28] But as Bennahum points out in his *New York* article, "None of the computer applications that capture the imagination of our day—the Internet, World Wide Web, hypertext, e-mail—were invented at the Lab. It cannot lay claim to much that went on to change the world. And the Lab's best work, in three-dimensional holography, is hardly the stuff of popular inspiration."[29]

What *is* the stuff of popular inspiration are Negroponte's conjurations of a technotopia just around the bend, where "computer displays may be sold by the gallon and painted on, CD-ROMs may be edible, and parallel processors may be applied like suntan lotion."[30] Recalling General Electric's 1950s catchphrase, "Progress is our most important product," the Lab's best-known invention is its vision of the future. "The Media Lab's product is not a 'product' but a seat on an expedition across the technological frontiers," writes Fred Hapgood, in a swoony *Wired* article about the Lab.[31] In other words, it offers a corporate-sponsored theme-park ride into the technological sublime.

The track record of corporate futurism isn't a chronicle of things foretold; it's an ectoplasmic manifestation of the wish-fulfillment fantasies of anxious managers. It hardly matters that Negroponte's future never seems to work as advertised when it arrives, if it arrives at all. "This guy has left a far more concrete legacy of predictive folly and clouded thinking than should be ignored," writes a source who prefers to remain anonymous. "His 'digital butler' is today's infuriating Portico/Wildfire. His online video rental business is today's Divx failure. And so on. What people revile Negroponte for is being a high-tech version of Michael Keaton's character in *Night Shift* ("Idea for better tuna salad: feed the fish mayonnaise"; "Cure for pollution: edible garbage") except better-paid and infinitely more self-serious. He's a nonpracticing Master of His Own Domain who confused himself with a Master of the Universe and succeeded, for a time, in confusing the world around him in exactly the same way."

More charitably, he and the Media Lab he heads are the manufacturing plant of the future—an assembly line for vaporware, technologies that exist only as consensual hallucinations in the mass mind. The quintessential piece of vaporware is virtual reality, a technology that was obsolete before it ever really existed. Collapsing under the weight of the impossible expectations shoveled on top of it by cyberhypesters, VR was a victim of overexposure in the Age of Attention Deficit Disorder.

Obviously, VR exists in literal fact, but the crude, polygonal state of the art falls far short of the disembodied ecstasies evoked by Jaron Lanier and William Gibson. Like VR in its early 1990s, mass-media incarnation, commodities of the future will be consumed as concepts only, living out their fifteen-minute life cycles in the vivarium of the mass media.

Strangely, Negroponte's gadget-happy evocations of self-cleaning shirts, transmitting neckties, and driverless cars have always seemed, at least to this reader, decidedly retro. For example, his "intelligent environments," with their talking toasters and digital domestics, recall Buckminster Fuller's Dymaxion House of 1927, complete with automatic hair clipper, vacuum toothbrush, and self-activating laundry unit that would deliver clean, dry clothes in three minutes. His "electronic window in my living room" is reminiscent of the wall-sized videoscreens that have been a sci-f: fixture from *1984* to the Arnold Schwarzenegger vehicle, *Total Recall*. Even the people who flit through *Being Digital*'s pages seem as if they've stepped out of cryogenic deep-freeze: does anyone really talk like the receptionist who tells Negroponte, "Oh, that cannot be, sir?"[32] They and the world they inhabit is a memory of futures past—the top-down technocracies of the 1939 World's Fair or Disney's Tomorrowland, socially engineered utopias presumably overseen by the visionary elites who "basically drive civilization," as Stewart Brand famously informed the *Los Angeles Times*.[33]

Negroponte seems to live in the semiotic mirage glimpsed by the protagonist of "The Gernsback Continuum," William Gibson's short story about a Machine-Age tomorrow that never was, governed by "a dream logic that knew nothing of pollution, the finite bounds of fossil fuel."[34] Like Gibson's hallucinatory technopolis, a streamlined fantasy straight out of Fritz Lang's *Metropolis* populated by blond, blue-eyed Aryans clad in spotless white, Negroponte's future is corporate, elitist, and whiter than white. Vexing questions about the future of race and gender politics never intrude in *Being Digital* for the simple reason that the stratosphere of power where Negroponte spends much of his time, like the penthouse redoubt of *Blade Runner*'s Tyrell corporate pyramid, seems to be the exclusive province of white guys. (To the best of my knowledge, the sole allusion to racial tensions in Negroponte's book is the author's lament that regulations force NYNEX to "put telephone booths in the *darkest* corners [my italics] of Brooklyn (where they last all of forty-eight hours),'' an unfortunate turn of phrase that probably seemed clever at the time.)³⁵

Like Gibson's bright-eyed technophiles, "smug, happy, and utterly content with themselves and their world," Negroponte exudes the managerial class's nonchalant air of superiority, untroubled by intellectual ambivalence or the merest shadow of self-doubt. We've met his like before: they're the technocratic elites of pulp myth—the hyperrational rulers of H. G. Wells's *Men Like Gods*, the cloud-dwelling ruling class in the old *Star Trek* episode "The Cloudminders." Those who remember the future, it seems, are doomed to repeat it.

Notes

1. *Bit rot*, according to *The New Hacker's Dictionary*, is a "hypothetical disease, the existence of which has been deduced from the observation that unused programs or features will often stop working after insufficient time has passed, even if 'nothing has changed.' The theory explains that bits decay as if they were radioactive. As time passes, the contents of a file or the code in a program will become increasingly garbled" (p. 65). I use the term punningly, in light of Negroponte's obsession with digital bits, which he exalts as almost morally superior to lowly atoms. "Digital technology can be a natural force drawing people into greater harmony," he writes, in *Being Digital* (New York: Knopf, 1995), p. 230. The Digital Age, he assures, is by its very nature "globalizing, harmonizing, and empowering" (p. 229). New age cyberblather of this sort, typical of Negroponte, adequately earns the term *bit rot*.

2. Nicholas Negroponte, "The Third Shall Be First: The Net Leverages Latecomers in the Developing World," *Wired* (January 1998): 96.

3. "What Are We Doing On-Line?," *Harper's Magazine* (August 1995): 35.

4. John Perry Barlow, "A Ladies' Man and Shameless," available at http://www.nervemag.com/Barlow/shameless.

5. Nicholas Negroponte, "Beyond Digital," *Wired* (December 1998): 288.

6. From an online statement "crafted, at its core, by [founder and publisher] Louis Rossetto" and posted by then-managing editor John Battelle (jbat) in Topic 129 [wired]: New Republic Slams *Wired!*, on the WELL, January 14, 1995.

7. Negroponte, *Being Digital*, p. 209.

8. Negroponte, "Beyond Digital," ibid.

9. Negroponte, *Being Digital*, p. 148.

10. Ibid., p. 145.

11. Ibid., p. 101.

12. Ibid., p. 213.

13. Ibid., p. 7.

14. Negroponte, "The Future of Retail," *Wired* (July 1998), p. 184.

15. Ibid.

16. Negroponte, *Being Digital*, pp. 218, 55.

17. David S. Bennahum, "Mr. Big Idea," *New York*, November 13, 1995, p. 76.

18. Ibid., p. 73.

19. David Corn, "Tribes and Tariffs," *The Nation*, May 25, 1998, p. 25.

20. Negroponte, *Being Digital*, p. 227.

21. Ibid., p. 229.

22. Ibid., p. 230.

23. Quoted in Edwin Diamond and Stephen Bates, "VR, MUD, ROM, BOM-FOG!," *The Nation*, February 5, 1996, p. 31.

24. Nicholas Negroponte, "Homeless@info.hwy.net," *New York Times*, February 11, 1995, Op-Ed section, p. 19.

25. Stewart Brand, *The Media Lab: Inventing the Future at MIT* (New York: Penguin, 1988), p. 6.

26. Negroponte, *Being Digital*, p. 218.

27. David S. Bennahum, "Meme 1.07," 1995, available at www.reach.com/matrix/welcome.html.

28. Negroponte takes credit for midwifing the birth of multimedia, whose arrival he dates from the Aspen Movie Map, an interactive simulator he and his MIT colleagues created in 1978. It used videodiscs to take users on a navigable, interactive trip through the streets and buildings of Aspen, Colorado. But the Map was developed by Negroponte's Architecture Machine Group, the Lab's precursor. As well, Stewart Brand claims that the desktop metaphor in personal computing is descended, "via Xerox PARC and Apple Computer," from Arch Mac's research into "spatial data management," but that, too, precedes the Lab.

29. Bennahum, "Mr. Big Idea," p. 72.

30. Negroponte, *Being Digital*, p. 211.

31. Fred Hapgood, "The Lab at 10," *Wired* (November 1995): 143.

32. Negroponte, *Being Digital*, p. 12.

33. Paul Keegan, "The Digerati," *New York Times Magazine*, May 21, 1995, p. 42.

34. William Gibson, "The Gernsback Continuum," in Bruce Sterling, ed., *Mirrorshades: The Cyberpunk Anthology* (New York: Ace, 1988), p. 9.

35. Negroponte, *Being Digital*, p. 77.

25

The Temporary Autonomous Zone

Hakim Bey

"... this time however I come as the victorious Dionysus, who will turn the world into a holiday.... Not that I have much time ..."
—Nietzsche (from his last "insane" letter to Cosima Wagner)

Pirate Utopias

The sea rovers and corsairs of the 18th century created an "information network" that spanned the globe: primitive and devoted primarily to grim business, the net nevertheless functioned admirably. Scattered throughout the net were islands, remote hideouts where ships could be watered and provisioned, booty traded for luxuries and necessities. Some of these islands supported "intentional communities," whole mini-societies living consciously outside the law and determined to keep it up, even if only for a short but merry life.

Some years ago I looked through a lot of secondary material on piracy hoping to find a study of these enclaves—but it appeared as if no historian has yet found them worthy of analysis. (William Burroughs has mentioned the subject, as did the late British anarchist Larry Law—but no systematic research has been carried out.) I retreated to primary sources and constructed my own theory, some aspects of which will be discussed in this essay. I called the settlements "Pirate Utopias."

Recently Bruce Sterling, one of the leading exponents of Cyberpunk science fiction, published a near-future romance based on the assumption

that the decay of political systems will lead to a decentralized proliferation of experiments in living: giant worker-owned corporations, independent enclaves devoted to "data piracy," Green-Social-Democrat
enclaves, Zerowork enclaves, anarchist liberated zones, etc. The information economy which supports this diversity is called the Net; the
enclaves (and the book's title) are Islands in the Net.

The medieval Assassins founded a "State" which consisted of a network of remote mountain valleys and castles, separated by thousands of
miles, strategically invulnerable to invasion, connected by the information flow of secret agents, at war with all governments, and devoted only
to knowledge. Modern technology, culminating in the spy satellite,
makes this kind of autonomy a romantic dream. No more pirate islands!
In the future the same technology—freed from all political control—
could make possible an entire world of autonomous zones. But for now
the concept remains precisely science fiction—pure speculation.

Are we who live in the present doomed never to experience autonomy,
never to stand for one moment on a bit of land ruled only by freedom?
Are we reduced either to nostalgia for the past or nostalgia for the
future? Must we wait until the entire world is freed of political control
before even one of us can claim to know freedom? Logic and emotion
unite to condemn such a supposition. Reason demands that one cannot
struggle for what one does not know; and the heart revolts at a universe
so cruel as to visit such injustices on our generation alone of humankind.

To say that "I will not be free till all humans (or all sentient creatures)
are free" is simply to cave in to a kind of nirvana-stupor, to abdicate our
humanity, to define ourselves as losers.

I believe that by extrapolating from past and future stories about
"islands in the net" we may collect evidence to suggest that a certain
kind of "free enclave" is not only possible in our time but also existent.
All my research and speculation has crystallized around the concept of
the TEMPORARY AUTONOMOUS ZONE (hereafter abbreviated
TAZ). Despite its synthesizing force for my own thinking, however, I
don't intend the TAZ to be taken as more than an essay ("attempt"),
a suggestion, almost a poetic fancy. Despite the occasional Ranterish
enthusiasm of my language I am not trying to construct political dogma.
In fact I have deliberately refrained from defining the TAZ—I circle
around the subject, firing off exploratory beams. In the end the TAZ is

almost self-explanatory. If the phrase became current, it would be understood without difficulty ... understood in action.

Waiting for the Revolution

How is it that "the world turned upside-down" always manages to Right itself? Why does reaction always follow revolution, like seasons in Hell?

Uprising, and the Latin form, *insurrection*, are words used by historians to label failed revolutions—movements which do not match the expected curve, the consensus-approved trajectory: revolution, reaction, betrayal, the founding of a stronger and even more oppressive State—the turning of the wheel, the return of history again and again to its highest form: jackboot on the face of humanity forever.

By failing to follow this curve, the up-rising suggests the possibility of a movement outside and beyond the Hegelian spiral of that "progress" which is secretly nothing more than a vicious circle. *Surgo*—rise up, surge. *Insurgo*—rise up, raise oneself up. A bootstrap operation. A goodbye to that wretched parody of the karmic round, historical revolutionary futility. The slogan "Revolution!" has mutated from tocsin to toxin, a malign pseudo-Gnostic fate-trap, a nightmare where no matter how we struggle we never escape that evil Aeon, that incubus the State, one State after another, every "heaven" ruled by yet one more evil angel.

If History IS "Time," as it claims to be, then the uprising is a moment that springs up and out of Time, violates the "law" of History. If the State IS History, as it claims to be, then the insurrection is the forbidden moment, an unforgivable denial of the dialectic—shimmying up the pole and out of the smokehole, a shaman's maneuver carried out at an "impossible angle" to the universe. History says the Revolution attains "permanence," or at least duration, while the uprising is "temporary." In this sense an uprising is like a "peak experience" as opposed to the standard of "ordinary" consciousness and experience. Like festivals, uprisings cannot happen every day—otherwise they would not be "nonordinary." But such moments of intensity give shape and meaning to the entirety of a life. The shaman returns—you can't stay up on the roof forever—but things have changed, shifts and integrations have occurred —a difference is made.

You will argue that this is a counsel of despair. What of the anarchist dream, the Stateless state, the Commune, the autonomous zone with duration, a free society, a free culture? Are we to abandon that hope in return for some existentialist *acte gratuit*? The point is not to change consciousness but to change the world.

I accept this as a fair criticism. I'd make two rejoinders nevertheless; first, revolution has never yet resulted in achieving this dream. The vision comes to life in the moment of uprising—but as soon as "the Revolution" triumphs and the State returns, the dream and the ideal are already betrayed. I have not given up hope or even expectation of change—but I distrust the word *Revolution*. Second, even if we replace the revolutionary approach with a concept of insurrection blossoming spontaneously into anarchist culture, our own particular historical situation is not propitious for such a vast undertaking. Absolutely nothing but a futile martyrdom could possibly result now from a head-on collision with the terminal State, the megacorporate information State, the empire of Spectacle and Simulation. Its guns are all pointed at us, while our meager weaponry finds nothing to aim at but a hysteresis, a rigid vacuity, a Spook capable of smothering every spark in an ectoplasm of information, a society of capitulation ruled by the image of the Cop and the absorbant eye of the TV screen.

In short, we're not touting the TAZ as an exclusive end in itself, replacing all other forms of organization, tactics, and goals. We recommend it because it can provide the quality of enhancement associated with the uprising without necessarily leading to violence and martyrdom. The TAZ is like an uprising which does not engage directly with the State, a guerilla operation which liberates an area (of land, of time, of imagination) and then dissolves itself to re-form elsewhere/elsewhen, before the State can crush it. Because the State is concerned primarily with Simulation rather than substance, the TAZ can "occupy" these areas clandestinely and carry on its festal purposes for quite a while in relative peace. Perhaps certain small TAZs have lasted whole lifetimes because they went unnoticed, like hillbilly enclaves—because they never intersected with the Spectacle, never appeared outside that real life which is invisible to the agents of Simulation.

Babylon takes its abstractions for realities; precisely within this margin of error the TAZ can come into existence. Getting the TAZ started may involve tactics of violence and defense, but its greatest strength lies in its invisibility—the State cannot recognize it because History has no definition of it. As soon as the TAZ is named (represented, mediated), it must vanish, it will vanish, leaving behind it an empty husk, only to spring up again somewhere else, once again invisible because undefinable in terms of the Spectacle. The TAZ is thus a perfect tactic for an era in which the State is omnipresent and all-powerful and yet simultaneously riddled with cracks and vacancies. And because the TAZ is a microcosm of that "anarchist dream" of a free culture, I can think of no better tactic by which to work toward that goal while at the same time experiencing some of its benefits here and now.

In sum, realism demands not only that we give up waiting for "the Revolution" but also that we give up wanting it. "Uprising," yes—as often as possible and even at the risk of violence. The spasming of the Simulated State will be "spectacular," but in most cases the best and most radical tactic will be to refuse to engage in spectacular violence, to withdraw from the area of simulation, to disappear.

The TAZ is an encampment of guerilla ontologists: strike and run away. Keep moving the entire tribe, even if it's only data in the Web. The TAZ must be capable of defense; but both the "strike" and the "defense" should, if possible, evade the violence of the State, which is no longer a meaningful violence. The strike is made at structures of control, essentially at ideas; the defense is "invisibility," a martial art, and "invulnerability"—an "occult" art within the martial arts. The "nomadic war machine" conquers without being noticed and moves on before the map can be adjusted. As to the future—Only the autonomous can plan autonomy, organize for it, create it. It's a bootstrap operation. The first step is somewhat akin to satori—the realization that the TAZ begins with a simple act of realization....

The Psychotopology of Everyday Life

The concept of the TAZ arises first out of a critique of Revolution and an appreciation of the Insurrection. The former labels the latter a failure; but for us uprising represents a far more interesting possibility, from the standard of a psychology of liberation, than all the "successful" revolutions of bourgeoisie, communists, fascists, etc.

The second generating force behind the TAZ springs from the historical development I call "the closure of the map." The last bit of Earth unclaimed by any nation-state was eaten up in 1899. Ours is the first century without terra incognita, without a frontier. Nationality is the highest principle of world governance—not one speck of rock in the South Seas can be left open, not one remote valley, not even the Moon and planets. This is the apotheosis of "territorial gangsterism." Not one square inch of Earth goes unpoliced or untaxed ... in theory.

The "map" is a political abstract grid, a gigantic con enforced by the carrot/stick conditioning of the "Expert" State, until for most of us the map becomes the territory—no longer "Turtle Island," but "the USA." And yet because the map is an abstraction, it cannot cover Earth with 1:1 accuracy. Within the fractal complexities of actual geography the map can see only dimensional grids. Hidden enfolded immensities escape the measuring rod. The map is not accurate; the map cannot be accurate.

So—Revolution is closed, but insurgency is open. For the time being we concentrate our force on temporary "power surges," avoiding all entanglements with "permanent solutions."

And—the map is closed, but the autonomous zone is open. Metaphorically it unfolds within the fractal dimensions invisible to the cartography of Control. And here we should introduce the concept of psychotopology (and -topography) as an alternative "science" to that of the State's surveying and mapmaking and "psychic imperialism." Only psychotopography can draw 1:1 maps of reality because only the human mind provides sufficient complexity to model the real. But a 1:1 map cannot "control" its territory because it is virtually identical with its territory. It can only be used to suggest, in a sense gesture towards, certain features. We are looking for "spaces" (geographic, social, cultural, imaginal) with potential to flower as autonomous zones—and we are looking for times in which these spaces are relatively open, either through neglect on the part of the State or because they have somehow escaped notice by the mapmakers, or for whatever reason. Psychotopology is the art of dowsing for potential TAZs.

The closures of Revolution and of the map, however, are only the negative sources of the TAZ; much remains to be said of its positive inspirations. Reaction alone cannot provide the energy needed to "manifest" a TAZ. An uprising must be for something as well.

1

First, we can speak of a natural anthropology of the TAZ. The nuclear family is the base unit of consensus society but not of the TAZ. ("Families!—how I hate them! the misers of love!"—Gide.) The nuclear family, with its attendant "oedipal miseries," appears to have been a Neolithic invention, a response to the "agricultural revolution" with its imposed scarcity and its imposed hierarchy. The Paleolithic model is at once more primal and more radical: the band. The typical hunter/ gatherer nomadic or semi-nomadic band consists of about 50 people. Within larger tribal societies the band-structure is fulfilled by clans within the tribe or by sodalities such as initiatic or secret societies, hunt or war societies, gender societies, "children's republics," and so on. If the nuclear family is produced by scarcity (and results in miserliness), the band is produced by abundance—and results in prodigality. The family is closed, by genetics, by the male's possession of women and children, by the hierarchic totality of agricultural/industrial society. The band is open—not to everyone, of course, but to the affinity group, the initiates sworn to a bond of love. The band is not part of a larger hierarchy but rather part of a horizontal pattern of custom, extended kinship, contract and alliance, spiritual affinities, etc. (American Indian society preserves certain aspects of this structure even now.)

In our own post-Spectacular Society of Simulation many forces are working—largely invisibly—to phase out the nuclear family and bring back the band. Breakdowns in the structure of Work resonate in the shattered "stability" of the unit-home and unit-family. One's "band" nowadays includes friends, ex-spouses and -lovers, people met at different jobs and pow-wows, affinity groups, special-interest networks, mail networks, etc. The nuclear family becomes more and more obviously a trap, a cultural sinkhole, a neurotic secret implosion of split atoms—and the obvious counter-strategy emerges spontaneously in the almost unconscious rediscovery of the more archaic and yet more post-industrial possibility of the band.

2

The TAZ as festival. Stephen Pearl Andrews once offered, as an image of anarchist society, the dinner party, in which all structure of authority dissolves in conviviality and celebration.... Here we might also invoke

Fourier and his concept of the senses as the basis of social becoming—
"touch-rut" and "gastrosophy," and his paean to the neglected implications of smell and taste. The ancient concepts of jubilee and saturnalia
originate in an intuition that certain events lie outside the scope of "profane time," the measuring-rod of the State and of History. These holidays literally occupied gaps in the calendar—intercalary intervals. By the
Middle Ages, nearly a third of the year was given over to holidays.
Perhaps the riots against calendar reform had less to do with the "eleven
lost days" than with a sense that imperial science was conspiring to
close up these gaps in the calendar where the people's freedoms had
accumulated—a coup d'etat, a mapping of the year, a seizure of time
itself, turning the organic cosmos into a clockwork universe. The death
of the festival.

Participants in insurrection invariably note its festive aspects, even in
the midst of armed struggle, danger, and risk. The uprising is like a saturnalia which has slipped loose (or been forced to vanish) from its intercalary interval and is now at liberty to pop up anywhere or when. Freed
of time and place, it nevertheless possesses a nose for the ripeness of
events and an affinity for the genius loci; the science of psychotopology
indicates "flows of forces" and "spots of power" (to borrow occultist
metaphors) which localize the TAZ spatiotemporally or at least help to
define its relation to moment and locale.

The media invite us to "come celebrate the moments of your life" with
the spurious unification of commodity and spectacle, the famous non-
event of pure representation. In response to this obscenity we have, on
the one hand, the spectrum of refusal (chronicled by the Situationists,
John Zerzan, Bob Black, et al.)—and on the other hand, the emergence
of a festal culture removed and even hidden from the would-be managers
of our leisure. "Fight for the right to party" is in fact not a parody of the
radical struggle but a new manifestation of it, appropriate to an age
which offers TVs and telephones as ways to "reach out and touch" other
human beings, ways to "Be There!"

Pearl Andrews was right: the dinner party is already "the seed of the
new society taking shape within the shell of the old" (IWW Preamble).
The sixties-style "tribal gathering," the forest conclave of eco-saboteurs,

the idyllic Beltane of the neo-pagans, anarchist conferences, gay faery circles ... Harlem rent parties of the twenties, nightclubs, banquets, old-time libertarian picnics—we should realize that all these are already "liberated zones" of a sort or at least potential TAZs. Whether open only to a few friends, like a dinner party, or to thousands of celebrants, like a Be-In, the party is always "open" because it is not "ordered"; it may be planned, but unless it "happens," it's a failure. The element of spontaneity is crucial.

The essence of the party: face-to-face, a group of humans synergize their efforts to realize mutual desires, whether for good food and cheer, dance, conversation, the arts of life; perhaps even for erotic pleasure, or to create a communal artwork, or to attain the very transport of bliss— in short, a "union of egoists" (as Stirner put it) in its simplest form— or else, in Kropotkin's terms, a basic biological drive to "mutual aid." (Here we should also mention Bataille's "economy of excess" and his theory of potlatch culture.)

3

Vital in shaping TAZ reality is the concept of psychic nomadism (or as we jokingly call it, "rootless cosmopolitanism"). Aspects of this phenomenon have been discussed by Deleuze and Guattari in *Nomadology: The War Machine*, by Lyotard [and Van Den Abbeele] in *Driftworks*, and by various authors in the "Oasis" issue of *Semiotext(e)*. We use the term "psychic nomadism" here rather than "urban nomadism," "nomadology," "driftwork," etc., simply in order to garner all these concepts into a single loose complex, to be studied in light of the coming-into-being of the TAZ. "The death of God," in some ways a de-centering of the entire "European" project, opened a multi-perspective post-ideological worldview able to move "rootlessly" from philosophy to tribal myth, from natural science to Taoism—able to see for the first time through eyes like some golden insect's, each facet giving a view of an entirely other world.

But this vision was attained at the expense of inhabiting an epoch where speed and "commodity fetishism" have created a tyrannical false unity which tends to blur all cultural diversity and individuality, so that "one place is as good as another." This paradox creates "gypsies," psy-

chic travelers driven by desire or curiosity, wanderers with shallow loy-
alties (in fact disloyal to the "European Project," which has lost all its
charm and vitality), not tied down to any particular time and place, in
search of diversity and adventure.... This description covers not only the
X-class artists and intellectuals but also migrant laborers, refugees, the
"homeless," tourists, the RV and mobile-home culture—also people who
"travel" via the Net but may never leave their own rooms (or those
like Thoreau, who "have travelled much—in Concord"); and finally it
includes "everybody," all of us, living through our automobiles, our
vacations, our TVs, books, movies, telephones, changing jobs, changing
"lifestyles," religions, diets, etc., etc.

Psychic nomadism as a tactic, what Deleuze and Guattari metaphorically call "the war machine," shifts the paradox from a passive to
an active and perhaps even "violent" mode. "God"'s last throes and
deathbed rattles have been going on for such a long time—in the form of
Capitalism, Fascism, and Communism, for example—that there's still a
lot of "creative destruction" to be carried out by post-Bakuninist post-
Nietzschean commandos or apaches (literally "enemies") of the old Consensus. These nomads practice the razzia, they are corsairs, they are
viruses; they have both need and desire for TAZs, camps of black tents
under the desert stars, interzones, hidden fortified oases along secret caravan routes, "liberated" bits of jungle and bad-land, no-go areas, black
markets, and underground bazaars.

These nomads chart their courses by strange stars, which might be
luminous clusters of data in cyberspace or perhaps hallucinations. Lay
down a map of the land; over that, set a map of political change; over
that, a map of the Net, especially the counter-Net with its emphasis on
clandestine information-flow and logistics—and finally, over all, the 1:1
map of the creative imagination, aesthetics, values. The resultant grid
comes to life, animated by unexpected eddies and surges of energy, co-
agulations of light, secret tunnels, surprises.

The Net and the Web

The next factor contributing to the TAZ is so vast and ambiguous that
it needs a section unto itself.

We've spoken of the Net, which can be defined as the totality of all information and communication transfer. Some of these transfers are privileged and limited to various elites, which gives the Net a hierarchic aspect. Other transactions are open to all—so the Net has a horizontal or non-hierarchic aspect as well. Military and Intelligence data are restricted, as are banking and currency information and the like. But for the most part the telephone, the postal system, public data banks, etc. are accessible to everyone and anyone. Thus within the Net there has begun to emerge a shadowy sort of counter-Net, which we will call the Web (as if the Net were a fishing-net and the Web were spider-webs woven through the interstices and broken sections of the Net). Generally we'll use the term *Web* to refer to the alternate horizontal open structure of info-exchange, the non-hierarchic network, and reserve the term *counter-Net* to indicate clandestine illegal and rebellious use of the Web, including actual data piracy and other forms of leeching off the Net itself. Net, Web, and counter-Net are all parts of the same whole pattern complex—they blur into each other at innumerable points. The terms are not meant to define areas but to suggest tendencies.

(Digression: Before you condemn the Web or counter-Net for its "parasitism," which can never be a truly revolutionary force, ask yourself what "production" consists of in the Age of Simulation. What is the "productive class"? Perhaps you'll be forced to admit that these terms seem to have lost their meaning. In any case the answers to such questions are so complex that the TAZ tends to ignore them altogether and simply picks up what it can use. "Culture is our Nature"—and we are the thieving magpies, or the hunter/gatherers of the world of CommTech.)

The present forms of the unofficial Web are, one must suppose, still rather primitive: the marginal zine network, the BBS networks, pirated software, hacking, phone-phreaking, some influence in print and radio, almost none in the other big media—no TV stations, no satellites, no fiber-optics, no cable, etc., etc. However the Net itself presents a pattern of changing/evolving relations between subjects ("users") and objects ("data"). The nature of these relations has been exhaustively explored, from McLuhan to Virilio. It would take pages and pages to "prove" what by now "everyone knows." Rather than rehash it all, I am interested in asking how these evolving relations suggest modes of implementation for the TAZ.

The TAZ has a temporary but actual location in time and a temporary but actual location in space. But clearly it must also have "location" in the Web, and this location is of a different sort, not actual but virtual, not immediate but instantaneous. The Web not only provides logistical support for the TAZ; it also helps to bring it into being; crudely speaking one might say that the TAZ "exists" in information-space as well as in the "real world." The Web can compact a great deal of time, as data, into an infinitesimal "space." We have noted that the TAZ, because it is temporary, must necessarily lack some of the advantages of a freedom which experiences duration and a more-or-less fixed locale. But the Web can provide a kind of substitute for some of this duration and locale—it can inform the TAZ, from its inception, with vast amounts of compacted time and space which have been "subtilized" as data.

At this moment in the evolution of the Web, and considering our demands for the "face-to-face" and the sensual, we must consider the Web primarily as a support system, capable of carrying information from one TAZ to another, of defending the TAZ, rendering it "invisible" or giving it teeth, as the situation might demand. But more than that: If the TAZ is a nomad camp, then the Web helps provide the epics, songs, genealogies, and legends of the tribe; it provides the secret caravan routes and raiding trails which make up the flowlines of tribal economy; it even contains some of the very roads they will follow, some of the very dreams they will experience as signs and portents.

The Web does not depend for its existence on any computer technology. Word-of-mouth, mail, the marginal zine network, "phone trees," and the like already suffice to construct an information webwork. The key is not the brand or level of tech involved but the openness and horizontality of the structure. Nevertheless, the whole concept of the Net implies the use of computers. In the SciFi imagination the Net is headed for the condition of Cyberspace (as in Tron or Neuromancer) and the pseudo-telepathy of "virtual reality." As a Cyberpunk fan I can't help but envision "reality hacking" playing a major role in the creation of TAZs. Like Gibson and Sterling I am assuming that the official Net will never succeed in shutting down the Web or the counter-Net—that data-piracy, unauthorized transmissions, and the free flow of information can never be frozen. (In fact, as I understand it, chaos theory predicts that any universal Control-system is impossible.)

However, leaving aside all mere speculation about the future, we must face a very serious question about the Web and the tech it involves. The TAZ desires above all to avoid mediation, to experience its existence as immediate. The very essence of the affair is "breast-to-breast" as the sufis say, or face-to-face. But, BUT: the very essence of the Web is mediation. Machines here are our ambassadors—the flesh is irrelevant except as a terminal, with all the sinister connotations of the term.

The TAZ may perhaps best find its own space by wrapping its head around two seemingly contradictory attitudes toward Hi-Tech and its apotheosis the Net: (1) what we might call the Fifth Estate/Neo-Paleolithic Post-Situ Ultra-Green position, which construes itself as a luddite argument against mediation and against the Net; and (2) the Cyberpunk utopianists, futuro-libertarians, Reality Hackers, and their allies who see the Net as a step forward in evolution and who assume that any possible ill effects of mediation can be overcome—at least, once we've liberated the means of production.

The TAZ agrees with the hackers because it wants to come into being—in part—through the Net, even through the mediation of the Net. But it also agrees with the greens because it retains intense awareness of itself as body and feels only revulsion for CyberGnosis, the attempt to transcend the body through instantaneity and simulation. The TAZ tends to view the Tech/anti-Tech dichotomy as misleading, like most dichotomies, in which apparent opposites turn out to be falsifications or even hallucinations caused by semantics. This is a way of saying that the TAZ wants to live in this world, not in the idea of another world, some visionary world born of false unification (all green OR all metal), which can only be more pie in the sky by-&-by (or as Alice put it, "Jam yesterday or jam tomorrow, but never jam today").

The TAZ is "utopian" in the sense that it envisions an intensification of everyday life, or as the Surrealists might have said, life's penetration by the Marvelous. But it cannot be utopian in the actual meaning of the word, nowhere, or NoPlace Place. The TAZ is somewhere. It lies at the intersection of many forces, like some pagan power-spot at the junction of mysterious ley-lines, visible to the adept in seemingly unrelated bits of terrain, landscape, flows of air, water, animals. But now the lines are not all etched in time and space. Some of them exist only "within" the Web, even though they also intersect with real times and places. Perhaps some of the lines are "non-ordinary" in the sense that no convention for quantifying them exists. These lines might better be studied in the light of chaos science than of sociology, statistics, economics, etc. The patterns of force which bring the TAZ into being have something in common with those chaotic "Strange Attractors" which exist, so to speak, between the dimensions.

The TAZ by its very nature seizes every available means to realize itself—it will come to life whether in a cave or an L-5 Space City—but above all it will live, now, or as soon as possible, in however suspect or ramshackle a form, spontaneously, without regard for ideology or even anti-ideology. It will use the computer because the computer exists, but it will also use powers which are so completely unrelated to alienation or simulation that they guarantee a certain psychic paleolithism to the TAZ, a primordial-shamanic spirit which will "infect" even the Net itself (the true meaning of Cyberpunk as I read it). Because the TAZ is an intensification, a surplus, an excess, a potlatch, life spending itself in living rather than merely surviving (that snivelling shibboleth of the eighties), it cannot be defined either by Tech or anti-Tech. It contradicts itself like a true despiser of hobgoblins because it wills itself to be, at any cost in damage to "perfection," to the immobility of the final.

In the Mandelbrot Set and its computer-graphic realization we watch —in a fractal universe—maps which are embedded and in fact hidden within maps within maps, etc., to the limits of computational power. What is it for, this map which in a sense bears a 1:1 relation with a fractal dimension? What can one do with it, other than admire its psychedelic elegance?

If we were to imagine an information map—a cartographic projection of the Net in its entirety—we would have to include in it the features of chaos, which have already begun to appear, for example, in the operations of complex parallel processing, telecommunications, transfers of electronic "money," viruses, guerilla hacking, and so on.

Each of these "areas" of chaos could be represented by topographs similar to the Mandelbrot Set, such that the "peninsulas" are embedded or hidden within the map—such that they seem to "disappear." This "writing"—parts of which vanish, parts of which efface themselves—represents the very process by which the Net is already compromised, incomplete to its own view, ultimately un-Controllable. In other words, the M Set, or something like it, might prove to be useful in "plotting" (in all senses of the word) the emergence of the counterNet as a chaotic process, a "creative evolution" in Prigogine's term. If nothing else the M Set serves as a metaphor for a "mapping" of the TAZ's interface with the Net as a disappearance of information. Every "catastrophe" in the Net is a node of power for the Web, the counter-Net. The Net will be damaged by chaos, while the Web may thrive on it.

Whether through simple data piracy, or else by a more complex development of actual rapport with chaos, the Web-hacker, the cybernetician of the TAZ, will find ways to take advantage of perturbations, crashes, and breakdowns in the Net (ways to make information out of "entropy"). As a bricoleur, a scavenger of information shards, smuggler, blackmailer, perhaps even cyberterrorist, the TAZ-hacker will work for the evolution of clandestine fractal connections. These connections, and the different information that flows among and between them, will form "power outlets" for the coming-into-being of the TAZ itself—as if one were to steal electricity from the energy-monopoly to light an abandoned house for squatters.

Thus the Web, in order to produce situations conducive to the TAZ, will parasitize the Net—but we can also conceive of this strategy as an attempt to build toward the construction of an alternative and autonomous Net, "free" and no longer parasitic, which will serve as the basis for a "new society emerging from the shell of the old." The counter-Net and the TAZ can be considered, practically speaking, as ends in themselves—but theoretically they can also be viewed as forms of struggle toward a different reality.

Having said this we must still admit to some qualms about computers, some still unanswered questions, especially about the Personal Computer.

The story of computer networks, BBSs, and various other experiments in electro-democracy has so far been one of hobbyism for the most part. Many anarchists and libertarians have deep faith in the PC as a weapon of liberation and self-liberation—but no real gains to show, no palpable liberty.

I have little interest in some hypothetical emergent entrepreneurial class of self-employed data/word processors who will soon be able to carry on a vast cottage industry or piecemeal shitwork for various corporations and bureaucracies. Moreover, it takes no ESP to foresee that this "class" will develop its underclass—a sort of lumpen yuppetariat: housewives, for example, who will provide their families with "second incomes" by turning their own homes into electro-sweatshops, little Work-tyrannies where the "boss" is a computer network.

Also I am not impressed by the sort of information and services proffered by contemporary "radical" networks. Somewhere—one is told—there exists an "information economy." Maybe so; but the info being traded over the "alternative" BBSs seems to consist entirely of chitchat and techie-talk. Is this an economy? or merely a pastime for enthusiasts? OK, PCs have created yet another "print revolution"—OK, marginal webworks are evolving—OK, I can now carry on six phone conversations at once. But what difference has this made in my ordinary life?

Frankly, I already had plenty of data to enrich my perceptions, what with books, movies, TV, theater, telephones, the U.S. Postal Service, altered states of consciousness, and so on. Do I really need a PC in order to obtain yet more such data? You offer me secret information? Well . . . perhaps I'm tempted—but still I demand marvelous secrets, not just unlisted telephone numbers or the trivia of cops and politicians. Most of all I want computers to provide me with information linked to real goods—"the good things in life," as the IWW Preamble puts it. And here, since I'm accusing the hackers and BBSers of irritating intellectual vagueness, I must myself descend from the baroque clouds of Theory & Critique and explain what I mean by "real goods."

Let's say that for both political and personal reasons I desire good food, better than I can obtain from Capitalism—unpolluted food still blessed with strong and natural flavors. To complicate the game imagine that the food I crave is illegal—raw milk perhaps, or the exquisite Cuban fruit mamey, which cannot be imported fresh into the U.S. because its seed is hallucinogenic (or so I'm told). I am not a farmer. Let's pretend I'm an importer of rare perfumes and aphrodisiacs and sharpen the play by assuming most of my stock is also illegal. Or maybe I only want to trade word processing services for organic turnips but refuse to report the transaction to the IRS (as required by law, believe it or not). Or maybe I want to meet other humans for consensual but illegal acts of mutual pleasure (this has actually been tried, but all the hard-sex BBSs have been busted—and what use is an underground with lousy security?). In short, assume that I'm fed up with mere information, the ghost in the machine. According to you, computers should already be quite capable of facilitating my desires for food, drugs, sex, tax evasion. So what's the matter? Why isn't it happening?

The TAZ has occurred, is occurring, and will occur with or without the computer. But for the TAZ to reach its full potential it must become less a matter of spontaneous combustion and more a matter of "islands in the Net." The Net, or rather the counter-Net, assumes the promise of an integral aspect of the TAZ, an addition that will multiply its potential, a "quantum jump" (odd how this expression has come to mean a big leap) in complexity and significance. The TAZ must now exist within a world of pure space, the world of the senses. Liminal, even evanescent, the TAZ must combine information and desire in order to fulfill its adventure (its "happening"), in order to fill itself to the borders of its destiny, to saturate itself with its own becoming.

Perhaps the Neo-Paleolithic School are correct when they assert that all forms of alienation and mediation must be destroyed or abandoned before our goals can be realized—or perhaps true anarchy will be realized only in Outer Space, as some futuro-libertarians assert. But the TAZ does not concern itself very much with "was" or "will be." The TAZ is interested in results, successful raids on consensus reality, breakthroughs into more intense and more abundant life. If the computer cannot be used in this project, then the computer will have to be overcome. My intuition however suggests that the counter-Net is already coming into being, perhaps already exists—but I cannot prove it. I've based the theory of the TAZ in large part on this intuition. Of course the Web also involves non-computerized networks of exchange such as samizdat, the black market, etc.—but the full potential of non-hierarchic information networking logically leads to the computer as the tool par excellence. Now I'm waiting for the hackers to prove I'm right, that my intuition is valid. Where are my turnips?

"Gone to Croatan"

We have no desire to define the TAZ or to elaborate dogmas about how it must be created. Our contention is rather that it has been created, will be created, and is being created. Therefore, it would prove more valuable and interesting to look at some TAZs past and present and to speculate about future manifestations; by evoking a few prototypes we may be able to gauge the potential scope of the complex and perhaps even get a glimpse of an "archetype." Rather than attempt any sort of ency-clopaedism we'll adopt a scatter-shot technique, a mosaic of glimpses, beginning quite arbitrarily with the 16th and 17th centuries and the settlement of the New World.

The opening of the "new" world was conceived from the start as an occultist operation. The magus John Dee, spiritual advisor to Elizabeth I, seems to have invented the concept of "magical imperialism" and infected an entire generation with it. Halkyut and Raleigh fell under his spell, and Raleigh used his connections with the "School of Night"—a cabal of advanced thinkers, aristocrats, and adepts—to further the causes of exploration, colonization, and mapmaking. The Tempest was a propaganda-piece for the new ideology, and the Roanoke Colony was its first showcase experiment.

The alchemical view of the New World associated it with materia prima or hyle, the "state of Nature," innocence and all-possibility ("Virgin-ia"), a chaos or inchoateness which the adept would transmute into "gold"—that is, into spiritual perfection as well as material abundance. But this alchemical vision is also informed in part by an actual fascination with the inchoate, a sneaking sympathy for it, a feeling of yearning for its formless form which took the symbol of the "Indian" for its focus: "Man" in the state of nature, uncorrupted by "government." Caliban, the Wild Man, is lodged like a virus in the very machine of Occult Imperialism; the forest/animal/humans are invested from the very start with the magic power of the marginal, despised, and outcaste. On the one hand, Caliban is ugly, and Nature a "howling wilderness"— on the other, Caliban is noble and unchained, and Nature an Eden. This split in European consciousness predates the Romantic/Classical dichotomy; it's rooted in Renaissance High Magic. The discovery of America (Eldorado, the Fountain of Youth) crystallized it; and it precipitated in actual schemes for colonization.

We were taught in elementary school that the first settlements in Roanoke failed; the colonists disappeared, leaving behind them only the cryptic message "Gone to Croatan." Later reports of "grey-eyed Indians" were dismissed as legend. What really happened, the textbook implied, was that the Indians massacred the defenseless settlers. However, "Croatan" was not some Eldorado; it was the name of a neighboring tribe of friendly Indians. Apparently the settlement was simply moved back from the coast into the Great Dismal Swamp and absorbed into the tribe. And the grey-eyed Indians were real—they're still there, and they still call themselves Croatans.

So—the very first colony in the New World chose to renounce its contract with Prospero (Dee/Raleigh/Empire) and go over to the Wild Men with Caliban. They dropped out. They became "Indians," "went native," opted for chaos over the appalling miseries of serfing for the plutocrats and intellectuals of London.

As America came into being where once there had been "Turtle Island," Croatan remained embedded in its collective psyche. Out beyond the frontier, the state of Nature (i.e., no State) still prevailed— and within the consciousness of the settlers the option of wildness always lurked, the temptation to give up on Church, farmwork, literacy, taxes— all the burdens of civilization—and "go to Croatan" in some way or another. Moreover, as the Revolution in England was betrayed, first by Cromwell and then by Restoration, waves of Protestant radicals fled or were transported to the New World (which had now become a prison, a place of exile). Antinomians, Familists, rogue Quakers, Levellers, Diggers, and Ranters were now introduced to the occult shadow of wildness and rushed to embrace it.

Anne Hutchinson and her friends were only the best known (i.e., the most upper-class) of the Antinomians—having had the bad luck to be caught up in Bay Colony politics—but a much more radical wing of the movement clearly existed. The incidents Hawthorne relates in "The Maypole of Merry Mount" are thoroughly historical; apparently the extremists had decided to renounce Christianity altogether and revert to paganism. If they had succeeded in uniting with their Indian allies the result might have been an Antinomian/Celtic/Algonquin syncretic religion, a sort of 17th-century North American Santeria.

Sectarians were able to thrive better under the looser and more corrupt administrations in the Caribbean, where rival European interests had left many islands deserted or even unclaimed. Barbados and Jamaica in particular must have been settled by many extremists, and I believe that Levellerish and Ranterish influences contributed to the Buccaneer "utopia" on Tortuga. Here for the first time, thanks to Esquemelin, we can study a successful New World proto-TAZ in some depth. Fleeing from hideous "benefits" of Imperialism such as slavery, serfdom, racism, and intolerance, from the tortures of impressment and the living death of the plantations, the Buccaneers adopted Indian ways, intermarried with Caribs, accepted blacks and Spaniards as equals, rejected all nationality, elected their captains democratically, and reverted to the "state of Nature." Having declared themselves "at war with all the world," they sailed forth to plunder under mutual contracts called "Articles" which were so egalitarian that every member received a full share and the Captain usually only $1\frac{1}{4}$ or $1\frac{1}{2}$ shares. Flogging and punishments were forbidden—quarrels were settled by vote or by the code duello.

It is simply wrong to brand the pirates as mere sea-going highwaymen or even proto-capitalists, as some historians have done. In a sense they were "social bandits," although their base communities were not traditional peasant societies but "utopias" created almost ex nihilo in terra incognita, enclaves of total liberty occupying empty spaces on the map. After the fall of Tortuga, the Buccaneer ideal remained alive all through the "Golden Age" of Piracy (ca. 1660–1720) and resulted in land-settlements in Belize, for example, which was founded by Buccaneers. Then, as the scene shifted to Madagascar—an island still unclaimed by any imperial power and ruled only by a patchwork of native kings (chiefs) eager for pirate allies—the Pirate Utopia reached its highest form.

Defoe's account of Captain Mission and the founding of Libertatia may be, as some historians claim, a literary hoax meant to propagandize for radical Whig theory—but it was embedded in *The General History of the Pyrates* (1724–28), most of which is still accepted as true and accurate. Moreover the story of Capt. Mission was not criticized when the book appeared, and many old Madagascar hands still survived. They seem to have believed it, no doubt because they had experienced pirate enclaves very much like Libertatia. Once again, rescued slaves, natives, and even traditional enemies such as the Portuguese were all invited to join as equals. (Liberating slave ships was a major preoccupation.) Land was held in common, representatives elected for short terms, booty shared; doctrines of liberty were preached far more radical than even those of *Common Sense.*

Libertatia hoped to endure, and Mission died in its defense. But most of the pirate utopias were meant to be temporary; in fact, the corsairs' true "republics" were their ships, which sailed under Articles. The shore enclaves usually had no law at all. The last classic example, Nassau in the Bahamas, a beachfront resort of shacks and tents devoted to wine, women (and probably boys too, to judge by Birge's *Sodomy and Piracy*), song (the pirates were inordinately fond of music and used to hire on bands for entire cruises), and wretched excess, vanished overnight when the British fleet appeared in the Bay. Blackbeard and "Calico Jack" Rackham and his crew of pirate women moved on to wilder shores and nastier fates, while others meekly accepted the Pardon and reformed. But the Buccaneer tradition lasted, both in Madagascar where the mixed-blood children of the pirates began to carve out kingdoms of their own, and in the Caribbean, where escaped slaves as well as mixed black/white/red groups were able to thrive in the mountains and backlands as "Maroons." The Maroon community in Jamaica still retained a degree of autonomy and many of the old folkways when Zora Neale Hurston visited there in the 1920s (see *Tell My Horse*). The Maroons of Suriname still practice African "paganism."

Throughout the 18th century, North America also produced a number of drop-out "tri-racial isolate communities." (This clinical-sounding term was invented by the Eugenics Movement, which produced the first scientific studies of these communities. Unfortunately the "science" merely served as an excuse for hatred of racial "mongrels" and the poor, and the "solution to the problem" was usually forced sterilization.) The nuclei invariably consisted of runaway slaves and serfs, "criminals" (i.e., the very poor), "prostitutes" (i.e., white women who married non-whites), and members of various native tribes. In some cases, such as the Seminole and Cherokee, the traditional tribal structure absorbed the newcomers; in other cases, new tribes were formed. Thus we have the Maroons of the Great Dismal Swamp, who persisted through the 18th and 19th centuries, adopting runaway slaves, functioning as a way station on the Underground Railway, and serving as a religious and ideological center for slave rebellions. The religion was HooDoo, a mixture of African, native, and Christian elements, and according to the historian H. Leaming-Bey the elders of the faith and the leaders of the Great Dismal Maroons were known as "the Seven Finger High Glister."

The Ramapaughs of northern New Jersey (incorrectly known as the "Jackson Whites") present another romantic and archetypal genealogy: freed slaves of the Dutch poltroons, various Delaware and Algonquin clans, the usual "prostitutes," the "Hessians" (a catch-phrase for lost British mercenaries, drop-out Loyalists, etc.), and local bands of social bandits such as Claudius Smith's.

An African-Islamic origin is claimed by some of the groups, such as the Moors of Delaware and the Ben Ishmaels, who migrated from Kentucky to Ohio in the mid-18th century. The Ishmaels practiced polygamy, never drank alcohol, made their living as minstrels, intermarried with Indians and adopted their customs, and were so devoted to nomadism that they built their houses on wheels. Their annual migration triangulated on frontier towns with names like Mecca and Medina. In the 19th century some of them espoused anarchist ideals, and they were targeted by the Eugenicists for a particularly vicious pogrom of salvation-by-extermination. Some of the earliest Eugenics laws were passed in their honor. As a tribe they "disappeared" in the 1920s but probably swelled the ranks of early "Black Islamic" sects such as the Moorish Science Temple. I myself grew up on legends of the "Kallikaks" of the nearby New Jersey Pine Barrens (and of course on Lovecraft, a rabid racist who was fascinated by the isolate communities). The legends turned out to be folk-memories of the slanders of the Eugenicists, whose U.S. headquarters were in Vineland, New Jersey, and who undertook the usual "reforms" against "miscegenation" and "feeblemindedness" in the Barrens (including the publication of photographs of the Kallikaks, crudely and obviously retouched to make them look like monsters of misbreeding).

The "isolate communities"—at least, those which have retained their identity into the 20th century—consistently refuse to be absorbed into either mainstream culture or the black "subculture" into which modern sociologists prefer to categorize them. In the 1970s, inspired by the Native American renaissance, a number of groups—including the Moors and the Ramapaughs—applied to the B.I.A. for recognition as Indian tribes. They received support from native activists but were refused official status. If they'd won, after all, it might have set a dangerous precedent for drop-outs of all sorts, from "white Peyotists" and hippies to black nationalists, aryans, anarchists and libertarians—a "reservation" for anyone and everyone! The "European Project" cannot recognize the existence of the Wild Man—green chaos is still too much of a threat to the imperial dream of order.

Essentially the Moors and Ramapaughs rejected the "diachronic" or historical explanation of their origins in favor of a "synchronic" self-identity based on a "myth" of Indian adoption. Or to put it another way, they named themselves "Indians." If everyone who wished "to be an Indian" could accomplish this by an act of self-naming, imagine what a departure to Croatan would take place. That old occult shadow still haunts the remnants of our forests (which, by the way, have greatly increased in the Northeast since the 18th or 19th century as vast tracts of farmland return to scrub. Thoreau on his deathbed dreamed of the return of "... Indians ... forests ...": the return of the repressed).

The Moors and Ramapaughs of course have good materialist reasons to think of themselves as Indians—after all, they have Indian ancestors—but if we view their self-naming in "mythic" as well as historical terms, we'll learn more of relevance to our quest for the TAZ. Within tribal societies there exist what some anthropologists call *mannenbunden*: totemic societies devoted to an identity with "Nature" in the act of shapeshifting, of becoming the totem-animal (werewolves, jaguar shamans, leopard men, cat-witches, etc.). In the context of an entire colonial society (as Taussig points out in Shamanism, Colonialism, and the Wild Man) the shapeshifting power is seen as inhering in the native culture as a whole—thus the most repressed sector of the society acquires a paradoxical power through the myth of its occult knowledge, which is feared and desired by the colonist. Of course the natives really do have certain occult knowledge; but in response to Imperial perception of native culture as a kind of "spiritual wild(er)ness," the natives come to see themselves more and more consciously in that role. Even as they are marginalized, the Margin takes on an aura of magic. Before the whiteman, they were simply tribes of people—now, they are "guardians of Nature," inhabitants of the "state of Nature." Finally the colonist himself is seduced by this "myth." Whenever an American wants to drop out or back into Nature, invariably he "becomes an Indian." The Massachusetts radical democrats (spiritual descendents of the radical Protestants) who organized the Tea Party and who literally believed that governments could be abolished (the whole Berkshire region declared itself in a "state of Nature"!), disguised themselves as "Mohawks." Thus the colonists, who suddenly saw themselves marginalized vis-à-vis the motherland, adopted the role of the marginalized natives, thereby (in a sense) seeking to participate in their occult power, their mythic radiance. From the Mountain Men to the Boy Scouts, the dream of "becoming an Indian" flows beneath myriad strands of American history, culture, and consciousness.

The sexual imagery connected to "tri-racial" groups also bears out this hypothesis. "Natives" of course are always immoral, but racial renegades and drop-outs must be downright polymorphous perverse. The Buccaneers were buggers, the Maroons and Mountain Men were miscegenists, the "Jukes and Kallikaks" indulged in fornication and incest (leading to mutations such as polydactyly), the children ran around naked and masturbated openly, etc., etc. Reverting to a "state of Nature" paradoxically seems to allow for the practice of every "unnatural" act; or so it would appear if we believe the Puritans and Eugenicists. And since many people in repressed moralistic racist societies secretly desire exactly these licentious acts, they project them outwards onto the marginalized and thereby convince themselves that they themselves remain civilized and pure. And in fact some marginalized communities do really reject consensus morality—the pirates certainly did!—and no doubt actually act out some of civilization's repressed desires. (Wouldn't you?) Becoming "wild" is always an erotic act, an act of nakedness.

Before leaving the subject of the "tri-racial isolates," I'd like to recall Nietzsche's enthusiasm for "race mixing." Impressed by the vigor and beauty of hybrid cultures, he offered miscegenation not only as a solution to the problem of race but also as the principle for a new humanity freed of ethnic and national chauvinism—a precursor to the "psychic nomad," perhaps. Nietzsche's dream still seems as remote now as it did to him. Chauvinism still rules OK. Mixed cultures remain submerged. But the autonomous zones of the Buccaneers and Maroons, Ishmaels and Moors, Ramapaughs and "Kallikaks" remain, or their stories remain, as indications of what Nietzsche might have called "the Will to Power as Disappearance." We must return to this theme.

Music as an Organizational Principle

Meanwhile, however, we turn to the history of classical anarchism in the light of the TAZ concept.

Before the "closure of the map," a good deal of anti-authoritarian energy went into "escapist" communes such as Modern Times, the various Phalansteries, and so on. Interestingly, some of them were not intended to last "forever" but only as long as the project proved fulfilling. By Socialist/Utopian standards these experiments were "failures," and therefore we know little about them.

When escape beyond the frontier proved impossible, the era of revolutionary urban Communes began in Europe. The Communes of Paris, Lyons, and Marseilles did not survive long enough to take on any characteristics of permanence, and one wonders if they were meant to. From our point of view the chief matter of fascination is the spirit of the Communes. During and after these years anarchists took up the practice of revolutionary nomadism, drifting from uprising to uprising, looking to keep alive in themselves the intensity of spirit they experienced in the moment of insurrection. In fact, certain anarchists of the Stirnerite/Nietzschean strain came to look on this activity as an end in itself, a way of always occupying an autonomous zone, the interzone which opens up in the midst or wake of war and revolution (cf. Pynchon's "zone" in *Gravity's Rainbow*). They declared that if any socialist revolution succeeded, they'd be the first to turn against it. Short of universal anarchy they had no intention of ever stopping. In Russia in 1917 they greeted the free Soviets with joy: this was their goal. But as soon as the Bolsheviks betrayed the Revolution, the individualist anarchists were the first to go back on the warpath. After Kronstadt, of course, all anarchists condemned the "Soviet Union" (a contradiction in terms) and moved on in search of new insurrections.

Makhno's Ukraine and anarchist Spain were meant to have duration, and despite the exigencies of continual war both succeeded to a certain extent: not that they lasted a "long time," but they were successfully organized and could have persisted if not for outside aggression. Therefore, from among the experiments of the inter-War period I'll concentrate instead on the madcap Republic of Fiume, which is much less well known and was not meant to endure. Gabriele D'Annunzio, Decadent poet, artist, musician, aesthete, womanizer, pioneer daredevil aeronautist, black magician, genius, and cad, emerged from World War I as a hero with a small army at his beck and command: the "Arditi." At a loss for adventure, he decided to capture the city of Fiume from Yugoslavia and give it to Italy. After a necromantic ceremony with his mistress in a cemetery in Venice he set out to conquer Fiume and succeeded without any trouble to speak of. But Italy turned down his generous offer; the Prime Minister called him a fool.

In a huff, D'Annunzio decided to declare independence and see how long he could get away with it. He and one of his anarchist friends wrote the Constitution, which declared music to be the central principle of the State. The Navy (made up of deserters and Milanese anarchist maritime unionists) named themselves the Uscochi, after the long-vanished pirates who once lived on local offshore islands and preyed on Venetian and Ottoman shipping. The modern Uscochi succeeded in some wild coups: several rich Italian merchant vessels suddenly gave the Republic a future: money in the coffers! Artists, bohemians, adventurers, anarchists (D'Annunzio corresponded with Malatesta), fugitives and Stateless refugees, homosexuals, military dandies (the uniform was black with pirate skull-&-crossbones—later stolen by the SS), and crank reformers of every stripe (including Buddhists, Theosophists, and Vedantists) began to show up at Fiume in droves. The party never stopped. Every morning D'Annunzio read poetry and manifestos from his balcony; every evening a concert, then fireworks. This made up the entire activity of the government. Eighteen months later, when the wine and money had run out and the Italian fleet finally showed up and lobbed a few shells at the Municipal Palace, no one had the energy to resist.

D'Annunzio, like many Italian anarchists, later veered toward fascism —in fact, Mussolini (the ex-Syndicalist) himself seduced the poet along that route. By the time D'Annunzio realized his error, it was too late: he was too old and sick. But Il Duce had him killed anyway—pushed off a balcony—and turned him into a "martyr." As for Fiume, though it lacked the seriousness of the free Ukraine or Barcelona, it can probably teach us more about certain aspects of our quest. It was in some ways the last of the pirate utopias (or the only modern example)—in other ways, perhaps, it was very nearly the first modern TAZ.

I believe that if we compare Fiume with the Paris uprising of 1968 (also the Italian urban insurrections of the early seventies), as well as with the American countercultural communes and their anarcho– New Left influences, we should notice certain similarities, such as the importance of aesthetic theory (cf. the Situationists)—also, what might be called "pirate economics," living high off the surplus of social overproduction—even the popularity of colorful military uniforms—and the concept of music as revolutionary social change—and finally their shared air of impermanence, of being ready to move on, shape-shift, re-locate to other universities, mountaintops, ghettos, factories, safe houses, abandoned farms—or even other planes of reality. No one was trying to impose yet another Revolutionary Dictatorship, either at Fiume, Paris, or Millbrook. Either the world would change, or it wouldn't. Meanwhile keep on the move and live intensely.

The Munich Soviet (or "Council Republic") of 1919 exhibited certain features of the TAZ, even though—like most revolutions—its stated goals were not exactly "temporary." Gustav Landauer's participation as Minister of Culture along with Silvio Gesell as Minister of Economics and other anti-authoritarian and extreme libertarian socialists, such as the poet/playwrights Erich Mahsam and Ernst Toller, and Ret Marut (the novelist B. Traven), gave the Soviet a distinct anarchist flavor. Landauer, who had spent years of isolation working on his grand synthesis of Nietzsche, Proudhon, Kropotkin, Stirner, Meister Eckhardt, the radical mystics, and the Romantic volk-philosophers, knew from the start that the Soviet was doomed; he hoped only that it would last long enough to be understood. Kurt Eisner, the martyred founder of the Soviet, believed quite literally that poets and poetry should form the basis of the revolution. Plans were launched to devote a large piece of Bavaria to an experiment in anarcho-socialist economy and community. Landauer drew up proposals for a Free School system and a People's Theater. Support for the Soviet was more or less confined to the poorest working-class and bohemian neighborhoods of Munich and to groups like the Wandervogel (the neo-Romantic youth movement), Jewish radicals (like Buber), the Expressionists, and other marginals. Thus historians dismiss it as the "Coffeehouse Republic" and belittle its significance in comparison with Marxist and Spartacist participation in Germany's post-War revolution(s). Outmaneuvered by the Communists and eventually murdered by soldiers under the influence of the occult/fascist Thule Society, Landauer deserves to be remembered as a saint. Yet even anarchists nowadays tend to misunderstand and condemn him for "selling out" to a "socialist government." If the Soviet had lasted even a year, we would weep at the mention of its beauty—but before even the first flowers of that Spring had wilted, the geist and the spirit of poetry were crushed, and we have forgotten. Imagine what it must have been to breathe the air of a city in which the Minister of Culture has just predicted that schoolchildren will soon be memorizing the works of Walt Whitman. Ah, for a time machine ...

The Will to Power as Disappearance

Foucault, Baudrillard, et al. have discussed various modes of "disappearance" at great length. Here I wish to suggest that the TAZ is in some sense a tactic of disappearance. When the Theorists speak of the disappearance of the Social they mean in part the impossibility of the "Social Revolution" and in part the impossibility of "the State"—the abyss of power, the end of the discourse of power. The anarchist question in this case should then be: Why bother to confront a "power" which has lost all meaning and become sheer Simulation? Such confrontations will only result in dangerous and ugly spasms of violence by the emptyheaded shit-for-brains who've inherited the keys to all the armories and prisons. (Perhaps this is a crude American misunderstanding of sublime and subtle Franco-Germanic Theory. If so, fine; whoever said understanding was needed to make use of an idea?)

As I read it, disappearance seems to be a very logical radical option for our time, not at all a disaster or death for the radical project. Unlike the morbid deathfreak nihilistic interpretation of Theory, mine intends to mine it for useful strategies in the always ongoing "revolution of everyday life": the struggle that cannot cease even with the last failure of political or social revolution because nothing except the end of the world can bring an end to everyday life or to our aspirations for the good things, for the Marvelous. And as Nietzsche said, if the world could come to an end, logically it would have done so; it has not, so it does not. And so, as one of the sufis said, no matter how many draughts of forbidden wine we drink, we will carry this raging thirst into eternity.

Zerzan and Black have independently noted certain "elements of Refusal" (Zerzan's term) which perhaps can be seen as somehow symptomatic of a radical culture of disappearance, partly unconscious but partly conscious, which influences far more people than any leftist or anarchist idea. These gestures are made against institutions and in that sense are "negative"—but each negative gesture also suggests a "positive" tactic to replace rather than merely refuse the despised institution.

For example, the negative gesture against schooling is "voluntary illiteracy." Since I do not share the liberal worship of literacy for the sake of social ameliorization, I cannot quite share the gasps of dismay heard everywhere at this phenomenon: I sympathize with children who refuse books along with the garbage in the books. There are however positive alternatives which make use of the same energy of disappearance. Homeschooling and craft-apprenticeship, like truancy, result in an absence from the prison of school. Hacking is another form of "education" with certain features of "invisibility."

A mass-scale negative gesture against politics consists simply of not voting. "Apathy" (i.e., a healthy boredom with the weary Spectacle) keeps over half the nation from the polls; anarchism never accomplished as much! (Nor did anarchism have anything to do with the failure of the recent Census.) Again, there are positive parallels: "networking" as an alternative to politics is practiced at many levels of society, and non-hierarchic organization has attained popularity even outside the anarchist movement, simply because it works. (ACT UP and Earth First! are two examples. Alcoholics Anonymous, oddly enough, is another.)

Refusal of Work can take the forms of absenteeism, on-job drunkenness, sabotage, and sheer inattention—but it can also give rise to new modes of rebellion: more self-employment, participation in the "black" economy and "lavoro nero," welfare scams and other criminal options, pot farming, etc.—all more or less "invisible" activities compared to traditional leftist confrontational tactics such as the general strike.

Refusal of the Church? Well, the "negative gesture" here probably consists of ... watching television. But the positive alternatives include all sorts of non-authoritarian forms of spirituality, from "unchurched" Christianity to neo-paganism. The "Free Religions" as I like to call them —small, self-created, half-serious/half-fun cults influenced by such currents as Discordianism and anarcho-Taoism—are to be found all over marginal America and provide a growing "fourth way" outside the mainstream churches, the televangelical bigots, and New Age vapidity and consumerism. It might also be said that the chief refusal of orthodoxy consists of the construction of "private moralities" in the Nietzschean sense: the spirituality of "free spirits."

The negative refusal of Home is "homelessness," which most consider a form of victimization, not wishing to be forced into nomadology. But "homelessness" can in a sense be a virtue, an adventure—so it appears, at least, to the huge international movement of the squatters, our modern hobos.

The negative refusal of the Family is clearly divorce or some other symptom of "breakdown." The positive alternative springs from the realization that life can be happier without the nuclear family, whereupon a hundred flowers bloom—from single parentage to group marriage to erotic affinity group. The "European Project" fights a major rearguard action in defense of "Family"—oedipal misery lies at the heart of Control. Alternatives exist—but they must remain in hiding, especially since the War against Sex of the 1980s and 1990s.

What is the refusal of Art? The "negative gesture" is not to be found in the silly nihilism of an "Art Strike" or the defacing of some famous painting—it is to be seen in the almost universal glassy-eyed boredom that creeps over most people at the very mention of the word. But what would the "positive gesture" consist of? Is it possible to imagine an aesthetics that does not engage, that removes itself from History and even from the Market? or at least tends to do so? which wants to replace representation with presence? How does presence make itself felt even in (or through) representation?

"Chaos Linguistics" traces a presence which is continually disappearing from all orderings of language and meaning systems; an elusive presence, evanescent, *latif* ("subtle," a term in sufi alchemy)—the Strange Attractor around which memes accrue, chaotically forming new and spontaneous orders. Here we have an aesthetics of the borderland between chaos and order, the margin, the area of "catastrophe" where the breakdown of the system can equal enlightenment. . . .

The disappearance of the artist IS "the suppression and realization of art," in Situationist terms. But from where do we vanish? And are we ever seen or heard of again? We go to Croatan—what's our fate? All our art consists of a goodbye note to history—"Gone To Croatan"—but where is it, and what will we do there?

First: We're not talking here about literally vanishing from the world and its future:—no escape backward in time to paleolithic "original leisure society"—no forever utopia, no backmountain hideaway, no island; also, no post-Revolutionary utopia—most likely no Revolution at all!—also, no VONU, no anarchist Space Stations—nor do we accept a "Baudrillardian disappearance" into the silence of an ironic hyperconformity. I have no quarrel with any Rimbauds who escape Art for whatever Abyssinia they can find. But we can't build an aesthetics, even an aesthetics of disappearance, on the simple act of never coming back. By saying we're not an avant-garde and that there is no avant-garde, we've written our "Gone to Croatan"—the question then becomes, how to envision "everyday life" in Croatan? particularly if we cannot say that Croatan exists in Time (Stone Age or Post-Revolution) or Space, either as utopia or as some forgotten midwestern town or as Abyssinia? Where and when is the world of unmediated creativity? If it can exist, it does exist—but perhaps only as a sort of alternate reality which we so far have not learned to perceive. Where would we look for the seeds—the weeds cracking through our sidewalks—from this other world into our world? the clues, the right directions for searching? a finger pointing at the moon?

I believe, or would at least like to propose, that the only solution to the "suppression and realization" of Art lies in the emergence of the TAZ. I would strongly reject the criticism that the TAZ itself is "nothing but" a work of art, although it may have some of the trappings. I do suggest that the TAZ is the only possible "time" and "place" for art to happen for the sheer pleasure of creative play and as an actual contribution to the forces which allow the TAZ to cohere and manifest.

Art in the World of Art has become a commodity; but deeper than that lies the problem of re-presentation itself, and the refusal of all mediation. In the TAZ art as a commodity will simply become impossible; it will instead be a condition of life. Mediation is harder to overcome, but the removal of all barriers between artists and "users" of art will tend toward a condition in which (as A. K. Coomaraswamy described it) "the artist is not a special sort of person, but every person is a special sort of artist."

In sum: disappearance is not necessarily a "catastrophe"— except in the mathematical sense of "a sudden topological change." All the positive gestures sketched here seem to involve various degrees of invisibility rather than traditional revolutionary confrontation. The "New Left" never really believed in its own existence till it saw itself on the Evening News. The New Autonomy, by contrast, will either infiltrate the media and subvert "it" from within—or else never be "seen" at all. The TAZ exists not only beyond Control but also beyond definition, beyond gazing and naming as acts of enslaving, beyond the understanding of the State, beyond the State's ability to see.

Ratholes in the Babylon of Information

The TAZ as a conscious radical tactic will emerge under certain conditions:

1. *Psychological liberation.* That is, we must realize (make real) the moments and spaces in which freedom is not only possible but actual.

We must know in what ways we are genuinely oppressed and also in what ways we are self-repressed or ensnared in a fantasy in which ideas oppress us. WORK, for example, is a far more actual source of misery for most of us than legislative politics. Alienation is far more dangerous for us than toothless outdated dying ideologies. Mental addiction to "ideals"—which in fact turn out to be mere projections of our resentment and sensations of victimization—will never further our project. The TAZ is not a harbinger of some pie-in-the-sky Social Utopia to which we must sacrifice our lives that our children's children may breathe a bit of free air. The TAZ must be the scene of our present autonomy, but it can only exist on the condition that we already know ourselves as free beings.

2. *The counter-Net must expand.*   At present it reflects more abstraction than actuality. Zines and BBSs exchange information, which is part of the necessary groundwork of the TAZ, but very little of this information relates to concrete goods and services necessary for the autonomous life. We do not live in CyberSpace; to dream that we do is to fall into CyberGnosis, the false transcendence of the body. The TAZ is a physical place and we are either in it or not. All the senses must be involved. The Web is like a new sense in some ways, but it must be added to the others—the others must not be subtracted from it, as in some horrible parody of the mystic trance. Without the Web, the full realization of the TAZ-complex would be impossible. But the Web is not the end in itself. It's a weapon.

3. *The apparatus of Control—the "State"—must (or so we must assume) continue to deliquesce and petrify simultaneously,* must progress on its present course in which hysterical rigidity comes more and more to mask a vacuity, an abyss of power. As power "disappears," our will to power must be disappearance.

We've already dealt with the question of whether the TAZ can be viewed "merely" as a work of art. But you will also demand to know whether it is more than a poor rat-hole in the Babylon of Information or rather a maze of tunnels, more and more connected, but devoted only to the economic dead-end of piratical parasitism? I'll answer that I'd rather be a rat in the wall than a rat in the cage—but I'll also insist that the TAZ transcends these categories.

A world in which the TAZ succeeded in putting down roots might resemble the world envisioned by "P.M." in his fantasy novel *bolo'bolo*. Perhaps the TAZ is a "proto-bolo." But inasmuch as the TAZ exists now, it stands for much more than the mundanity of negativity or countercultural drop-out-ism. We've mentioned the festal aspect of the moment which is unControlled, and which adheres in spontaneous self-ordering, however brief. It is "epiphanic"—a peak experience on the social as well as individual scale.

Liberation is realized struggle—this is the essence of Nietzsche's "self-overcoming." The present thesis might also take for a sign Nietzsche's wandering. It is the precursor of the drift, in the Situ sense of the derive and Lyotard's definition of driftwork. We can foresee a whole new geography, a kind of pilgrimage-map in which holy sites are replaced by peak experiences and TAZs: a real science of psychotopography, perhaps to be called "geo-autonomy" or "anarchomancy."

The TAZ involves a kind of ferality, a growth from tameness to wild(er)ness, a "return" which is also a step forward. It also demands a "yoga" of chaos, a project of "higher" orderings (of consciousness or simply of life) which are approached by "surfing the wave-front of chaos," of complex dynamism. The TAZ is an art of life in continual rising up, wild but gentle—a seducer not a rapist, a smuggler rather than a bloody pirate, a dancer not an eschatologist.

Let us admit that we have attended parties where for one brief night a republic of gratified desires was attained. Shall we not confess that the politics of that night have more reality and force for us than those of, say, the entire U.S. Government? Some of the "parties" we've mentioned lasted for two or three years. Is this something worth imagining, worth fighting for? Let us study invisibility, webworking, psychic nomadism—and who knows what we might attain?

Spring Equinox, 1990

Appendix: Interview with Noam Chomsky on Anarchism, Marxism, and Hope for the Future

Kevin Doyle

Noam Chomsky is widely known for his critique of U.S foreign policy and for his work as a linguist. Less well known is his ongoing support for libertarian socialist objectives. In a special interview done for *Red and Black Revolution*, Chomsky gives his views on anarchism and Marxism and the prospects for socialism now. The interview was conducted in May 1995 by Kevin Doyle.

RBR: First off, Noam, for quite a time now you've been an advocate for the anarchist idea. Many people are familiar with the introduction you wrote in 1970 to Daniel Gurin's *Anarchism*, but more recently—for instance, in the film *Manufacturing Consent*—you took the opportunity to highlight again the potential of anarchism and the anarchist idea. What is it that attracts you to anarchism?

Chomsky: I was attracted to anarchism as a young teenager, as soon as I began to think about the world beyond a pretty narrow range, and haven't seen much reason to revise those early attitudes since. I think it only makes sense to seek out and identify structures of authority, hierarchy, and domination in every aspect of life and to challenge them. Unless a justification for them can be given, they are illegitimate and should be dismantled to increase the scope of human freedom. That includes political power, ownership and management, relations among men and women, parents and children, our control over the fate of future

This interview first appeared in *Red and Black Revolution*, available at ⟨http://flag.blackened.net/revolt/wsm.html⟩. Reprinted by permission of Noam Chomsky and Red and Black Revolution. © Red and Black Revolution, 1996.

generations (the basic moral imperative behind the environmental movement, in my view), and much else. Naturally this means a challenge to the huge institutions of coercion and control: the state, the unaccountable private tyrannies that control most of the domestic and international economy, and so on. But not only these. That is what I have always understood to be the essence of anarchism: the conviction that the burden of proof has to be placed on authority and that it should be dismantled if that burden cannot be met. Sometimes the burden can be met. If I'm taking a walk with my grandchildren and they dart out into a busy street, I will use not only authority but also physical coercion to stop them. The act should be challenged, but I think it can readily meet the challenge. And there are other cases. Life is a complex affair, we understand very little about humans and society, and grand pronouncements are generally more a source of harm than of benefit. But the perspective is a valid one, I think, and can lead us quite a long way. Beyond such generalities, we begin to look at cases, which is where the questions of human interest and concern arise.

RBR: It's true to say that your ideas and critique are now more widely known than ever before. It should also be said that your views are widely respected. How do you think your support for anarchism is received in this context? In particular, I'm interested in the response you receive from people who are getting interested in politics for the first time and who may, perhaps, have come across your views. Are such people surprised by your support for anarchism? Are they interested?

Chomsky: The general intellectual culture, as you know, associates anarchism with chaos, violence, bombs, disruption, and so on. So people are often surprised when I speak positively of anarchism and identify myself with leading traditions within it. But my impression is that among the general public, the basic ideas seem reasonable when the clouds are cleared away. Of course, when we turn to specific matters—say, the nature of families or how an economy would work in a society that is more free and just—questions and controversy arise. But that is as it should be. Physics can't really explain how water flows from the tap in your sink. When we turn to vastly more complex questions of human significance, understanding is very thin, and there is plenty of room for disagreement, experimentation, both intellectual and real-life exploration of possibilities, to help us learn more.

RBR: Perhaps, more than any other idea, anarchism has suffered from the problem of misrepresentation. Anarchism can mean many things to many people. Do you often find yourself having to explain what it is that you mean by anarchism? Does the misrepresentation of anarchism bother you?

Chomsky: All misrepresentation is a nuisance. Much of it can be traced back to structures of power that have an interest in preventing understanding, for pretty obvious reasons. It's well to recall David Hume's *Principles of Government*. He expressed surprise that people ever submitted to their rulers. He concluded that since "Force is always on the side of the governed, the governors have nothing to support them but opinion. 'Tis therefore, on opinion only that government is founded; and this maxim extends to the most despotic and most military governments, as well as to the most free and most popular." Hume was very astute— and incidentally, hardly a libertarian by the standards of the day. He surely underestimates the efficacy of force, but his observation seems to me basically correct and important, particularly in the more free societies, where the art of controlling opinion is therefore far more refined. Misrepresentation and other forms of befuddlement are a natural concomitant.

So does misrepresentation bother me? Sure, but so does rotten weather. It will exist as long as concentrations of power engender a kind of commissar class to defend them. Since they are usually not very bright or are bright enough to know that they'd better avoid the arena of fact and argument, they'll turn to misrepresentation, vilification, and other devices that are available to those who know that they'll be protected by the various means available to the powerful. We should understand why all this occurs and unravel it as best we can. That's part of the project of liberation—of ourselves and others or, more reasonably, of people working together to achieve these aims.

Sounds simple-minded, and it is. But I have yet to find much commentary on human life and society that is not simple-minded, when absurdity and self-serving posturing are cleared away.

RBR: How about in more established left-wing circles, where one might expect to find greater familiarity with what anarchism actually stands for? Do you encounter any surprise here at your views and support for anarchism?

Chomsky: If I understand what you mean by "established left-wing circles," there is not too much surprise about my views on anarchism because very little is known about my views on anything. These are not the circles I deal with. You'll rarely find a reference to anything I say or write. That's not completely true of course. Thus in the U.S. (but less commonly in the U.K. or elsewhere), you'd find some familiarity with what I do in certain of the more critical and independent sectors of what might be called "established left-wing circles," and I have personal friends and associates scattered here and there. But have a look at the books and journals, and you'll see what I mean. I don't expect what I write and say to be any more welcome in these circles than in the faculty club or editorial board room—again, with exceptions. The question arises only marginally, so much so that it's hard to answer.

RBR: A number of people have noted that you use the term *libertarian socialist* in the same context as you use the word *anarchism*. Do you see these terms as essentially similar? Is anarchism a type of socialism to you? The description has been used before that "anarchism is equivalent to socialism with freedom." Would you agree with this basic equation?

Chomsky: The introduction to Guerin's book that you mentioned opens with a quote from an anarchist sympathizer a century ago, who says that "anarchism has a broad back" and "endures anything." One major element has been what has traditionally been called *libertarian socialism*. I've tried to explain there and elsewhere what I mean by that, stressing that it's hardly original. I'm taking the ideas from leading figures in the anarchist movement whom I quote and who rather consistently describe themselves as socialists, while harshly condemning the new class of radical intellectuals who seek to attain state power in the course of popular struggle and to become the vicious Red bureaucracy of which Bakunin warned; what's often called *socialism*. I rather agree with Rudolf Rocker's perception that these (quite central) tendencies in anarchism draw from the best of Enlightenment and classical liberal thought, well beyond what he described. In fact, as I've tried to show they contrast sharply with Marxist-Leninist doctrine and practice, the libertarian doctrines that are fashionable in the U.S. and U.K. particularly, and other contemporary ideologies, all of which seem to me to reduce to advocacy of one or another form of illegitimate authority, quite often real tyranny.

The Spanish Revolution

RBR: In the past, when you have spoken about anarchism, you have often emphasized the example of the Spanish Revolution. For you there would seem to be two aspects to this example. On the one hand, the experience of the Spanish Revolution is, you say, a good example of anarchism in action. On the other, you have also stressed that the Spanish revolution is a good example of what workers can achieve through their own efforts using participatory democracy. Are these two aspects —anarchism in action and participatory democracy—one and the same thing for you? Is anarchism a philosophy for people's power?

Chomsky: I'm reluctant to use fancy polysyllables like *philosophy* to refer to what seems ordinary common sense. And I'm also uncomfortable with slogans. The achievements of Spanish workers and peasants, before the revolution was crushed, were impressive in many ways. The term *participatory democracy* is a more recent one, which developed in a different context, but there surely are points of similarity. I'm sorry if this seems evasive. It is, but that's because I don't think either the concept of anarchism or of participatory democracy is clear enough to be able to answer the question whether they are the same.

RBR: One of the main achievements of the Spanish Revolution was the degree of grassroots democracy established. In terms of people, it is estimated that over three million were involved. Rural and urban production was managed by workers themselves. Is it a coincidence to your mind that anarchists, known for their advocacy of individual freedom, succeeded in this area of collective administration?

Chomsky: No coincidence at all. The tendencies in anarchism that I've always found most persuasive seek a highly organized society, integrating many different kinds of structures (workplace, community, and manifold other forms of voluntary association) but controlled by participants, not by those in a position to give orders (except, again, when authority can be justified, as is sometimes the case, in specific contingencies).

Democracy

RBR: Anarchists often expend a great deal of effort at building up grassroots democracy. Indeed they are often accused of taking democracy to extremes. Yet despite this, many anarchists would not readily identify democracy as a central component of anarchist philosophy. Anarchists often describe their politics as being about socialism or being about the individual—they are less likely to say that anarchism is about democracy. Would you agree that democratic ideas are a central feature of anarchism?

Chomsky: Criticism of democracy among anarchists has often been criticism of parliamentary democracy, as it has arisen within societies with deeply repressive features. Take the U.S., which has been as free as any, since its origins. American democracy was founded on the principle, stressed by James Madison in the Constitutional Convention in 1787, that the primary function of government is "to protect the minority of the opulent from the majority." Thus he warned that in England, the only quasi-democratic model of the day, if the general population were allowed a say in public affairs, they would implement agrarian reform or other atrocities and that the American system must be carefully crafted to avoid such crimes against "the rights of property," which must be defended (in fact, must prevail). Parliamentary democracy within this framework does merit sharp criticism by genuine libertarians, and I've left out many other features that are hardly subtle—slavery, to mention just one, or the wage slavery that was bitterly condemned by working people who had never heard of anarchism or communism right through the nineteenth century and beyond.

Leninism

RBR: The importance of grassroots democracy to any meaningful change in society would seem to be self-evident. Yet the left has been ambiguous about this in the past. I'm speaking generally, of social democracy, but also of Bolshevism—traditions on the left that would seem to have more in common with elitist thinking than with strict democratic practice. Lenin, to use a well-known example, was skeptical that workers could develop anything more than "trade union consciousness" —by which, I assume, he meant that workers could not see far beyond their immediate predicament. Similarly, the Fabian socialist, Beatrice Webb, who was very influential in the Labour Party in England, had the view that workers were only interested in "horse racing odds"! Where does this elitism originate, and what is it doing on the left?

Chomsky: I'm afraid it's hard for me to answer this. If the left is understood to include Bolshevism, then I would flatly dissociate myself from the left. Lenin was one of the greatest enemies of socialism, in my opinion, for reasons I've discussed. The idea that workers are only interested in horse-racing is an absurdity that cannot withstand even a superficial look at labor history or the lively and independent working-class press that flourished in many places, including the manufacturing towns of New England not many miles from where I'm writing—not to speak of the inspiring record of the courageous struggles of persecuted and oppressed people throughout history, until this very moment. Take the most miserable corner of this hemisphere, Haiti, regarded by the European conquerors as a paradise and the source of no small part of Europe's wealth, now devastated, perhaps beyond recovery. In the past few years, under conditions so miserable that few people in the rich countries can imagine them, peasants and slum-dwellers constructed a popular democratic movement based on grassroots organizations that surpasses just about anything I know of elsewhere. Only deeply committed commissars could fail to collapse with ridicule when they hear the solemn pronouncements of American intellectuals and political leaders about how the U.S. has to teach Haitians the lessons of democracy. Their achievements were so substantial and frightening to the powerful that they had to be subjected to yet another dose of vicious terror, with considerably more U.S. support than is publicly acknowledged, and they still have not surrendered. Are they interested only in horse-racing?

I'd suggest some lines I've occasionally quoted from Rousseau: "when I see multitudes of entirely naked savages scorn European voluptuousness and endure hunger, fire, the sword, and death to preserve only their independence, I feel that it does not behoove slaves to reason about freedom."

RBR: Speaking generally again, your own work—*Deterring Democracy* [1992], *Necessary Illusions* [1989], etc.—has dealt consistently with the role and prevalence of elitist ideas in societies such as our own. You have argued that within Western (or parliamentary) democracy there is a deep antagonism to any real role or input from the mass of people, lest it threaten the uneven distribution in wealth, which favors the rich. Your work is quite convincing here, but, this aside, some have been shocked by your assertions. For instance, you compare the politics of President John F. Kennedy with Lenin, more or less equating the two. This, I might add, has shocked supporters of both camps! Can you elaborate a little on the validity of the comparison?

Chomsky: I haven't actually "equated" the doctrines of the liberal intellectuals of the Kennedy administration with Leninists, but I have noted striking points of similarity—rather as predicted by Bakunin a century earlier in his perceptive commentary on the "new class." For example, I quoted passages from McNamara on the need to enhance managerial control if we are to be truly "free" and about how the "undermanagement" that is "the real threat to democracy" is an assault against reason itself. Change a few words in these passages, and we have standard Leninist doctrine. I've argued that the roots are rather deep, in both cases. Without further clarification about what people find "shocking," I can't comment further. The comparisons are specific, and I think both proper and properly qualified. If not, that's an error, and I'd be interested to be enlightened about it.

Marxism

RBR: Specifically, *Leninism* refers to a form of Marxism that developed with V. I. Lenin. Are you implicitly distinguishing the works of Marx from the particular criticism you have of Lenin when you use the term *Leninism?* Do you see a continuity between Marx's views and Lenin's later practices?

Chomsky: Bakunin's warnings about the "Red bureaucracy" that would institute "the worst of all despotic governments" were long before Lenin, and were directed against the followers of Mr. Marx. There were, in fact, followers of many different kinds; Pannekoek, Luxembourg, Mattick, and others are very far from Lenin, and their views often converge with elements of anarcho-syndicalism. Korsch and others wrote sympathetically of the anarchist revolution in Spain, in fact. There are continuities from Marx to Lenin, but there are also continuities to Marxists who were harshly critical of Lenin and Bolshevism. Teodor Shanin's work in the past years on Marx's later attitudes toward peasant revolution is also relevant here. I'm far from being a Marx scholar and wouldn't venture any serious judgment on which of these continuities reflects the real Marx, if there even can be an answer to that question.

RBR: Recently, we obtained a copy of your own *Notes on Anarchism* (republished last year by Discussion Bulletin in the U.S.). In this you mention the views of the "early Marx," in particular his development of the idea of alienation under capitalism. Do you generally agree with this division in Marx's life and work—a young, more libertarian socialist but, in later years, a firm authoritarian?

Chomsky: The early Marx draws extensively from the milieu in which he lived, and one finds many similarities to the thinking that animated classical liberalism, aspects of the Enlightenment and French and German Romanticism. Again, I'm not enough of a Marx scholar to pretend to an authoritative judgment. My impression, for what it is worth, is that the early Marx was very much a figure of the late Enlightenment, and the later Marx was a highly authoritarian activist, and a critical analyst of capitalism, who had little to say about socialist alternatives. But those are impressions.

RBR: From my understanding, the core part of your overall view is informed by your concept of human nature. In the past the idea of human nature was seen, perhaps, as something regressive, even limiting. For instance, the unchanging aspect of human nature is often used as an argument for why things can't be changed fundamentally in the direction of anarchism. You take a different view? Why?

Chomsky: The core part of anyone's point of view is some concept of human nature, however it may be remote from awareness or lack articulation. At least, that is true of people who consider themselves moral agents, not monsters. Monsters aside, whether a person who advocates reform or revolution, or stability or return to earlier stages, or simply cultivating one's own garden, takes stand on the grounds that it is good for people. But that judgment is based on some conception of human nature, which a reasonable person will try to make as clear as possible, if only so that it can be evaluated. So in this respect I'm no different from anyone else.

You're right that human nature has been seen as something regressive, but that must be the result of profound confusion. Is my granddaughter no different from a rock, a salamander, a chicken, a monkey? A person who dismisses this absurdity as absurd recognizes that there is a distinctive human nature. We are left only with the question of what it is— a highly nontrivial and fascinating question, with enormous scientific interest and human significance. We know a fair amount about certain aspects of it—not those of major human significance. Beyond that, we are left with our hopes and wishes, intuitions and speculations.

There is nothing regressive about the fact that a human embryo is so constrained that it does not grow wings, or that its visual system cannot function in the manner of an insect, or that it lacks the homing instinct of pigeons. The same factors that constrain the organism's development also enable it to attain a rich, complex, and highly articulated structure, similar in fundamental ways to conspecifics, with rich and remarkable capacities. An organism that lacked such determinative intrinsic structure, which of course radically limits the paths of development, would be some kind of amoeboid creature, to be pitied (even if it could survive somehow). The scope and limits of development are logically related.

Take language, one of the few distinctive human capacities about which much is known. We have very strong reasons to believe that all possible human languages are very similar; a Martian scientist observing humans might conclude that there is just a single language, with minor variants. The reason is that the particular aspect of human nature that underlies the growth of language allows very restricted options. Is this limiting? Of course. Is it liberating? Also of course. It is these very restrictions that make it possible for a rich and intricate system of expression of thought to develop in similar ways on the basis of very rudimentary, scattered, and varied experience.

What about the matter of biologically determined human differences? That these exist is surely true and a cause for joy, not fear or regret. Life among clones would not be worth living, and a sane person will only rejoice that others have abilities that they do not share. That should be elementary. What is commonly believed about these matters is strange indeed, in my opinion.

Is human nature, whatever it is, conducive to the development of anarchist forms of life or a barrier to them? We do not know enough to answer, one way or the other. These are matters for experimentation and discovery, not empty pronouncements.

The Future

RBR: To begin finishing off, I'd like to ask you briefly about some current issues on the left. I don't know if the situation is similar in the U.S., but here, with the fall of the Soviet Union, a certain demoralization has set in on the left. It isn't so much that people were dear supporters of what existed in the Soviet Union, but rather it's a general feeling that with the demise of the Soviet Union the idea of socialism has also been dragged down. Have you come across this type of demoralization? What's your response to it?

Chomsky: My response to the end of Soviet tyranny was similar to my reaction to the defeat of Hitler and Mussolini. In all cases, it is a victory

for the human spirit. It should have been particularly welcome to socialists, since a great enemy of socialism had at last collapsed. Like you, I
was intrigued to see how people—including people who had considered
themselves anti-Stalinist and anti-Leninist—were demoralized by the collapse of the tyranny. What it reveals is that they were more deeply committed to Leninism than they believed.

There are, however, other reasons to be concerned about the elimination of this brutal and tyrannical system, which was as much socialist as
it was democratic (recall that it claimed to be both and that the latter
claim was ridiculed in the West, while the former was eagerly accepted,
as a weapon against socialism—one of the many examples of the service
of Western intellectuals to power). One reason has to do with the nature
of the cold war. In my view, it was in significant measure a special case
of the North-South conflict, to use the current euphemism for Europe's
conquest of much of the world. Eastern Europe had been the original
third world, and the cold war from 1917 had no slight resemblance
to the reaction of attempts by other parts of the third world to pursue
an independent course, though in this case differences of scale gave the
conflict a life of its own. For this reason, it was only reasonable to expect the region to return pretty much to its earlier status: parts of the
West, like the Czech Republic or Western Poland, could be expected
to rejoin it, while others revert to the traditional service role, the
ex-Nomenklatura becoming the standard third-world elite (with the
approval of Western state-corporate power, which generally prefers
them to alternatives). That was not a pretty prospect, and it has led to
immense suffering.

Another reason for concern has to do with the matter of deterrence
and nonalignment. Grotesque as the Soviet empire was, its very existence
offered a certain space for nonalignment, and for perfectly cynical reasons, it sometimes provided assistance to victims of Western attack.
Those options are gone, and the South is suffering the consequences.

A third reason has to do with what the business press calls "the pam-
pered Western workers" with their "luxurious lifestyles." With much of
Eastern Europe returning to the fold, owners and managers have powerful new weapons against the working classes and the poor at home. GM
and VW can transfer production not only to Mexico and Brazil (or at

least threaten to, which often amounts to the same thing) but also to Poland and Hungary, where they can find skilled and trained workers at a fraction of the cost. They are gloating about it, understandably, given the guiding values.

We can learn a lot about what the cold war (or any other conflict) was about by looking at who is cheering and who is unhappy after it ends. By that criterion, the victors in the cold war include Western elites and the ex-Nomenklatura, now rich beyond their wildest dreams, and the losers include a substantial part of the population of the East along with working people and the poor in the West, as well as popular sectors in the South that have sought an independent path.

Such ideas tend to arouse near hysteria among Western intellectuals, when they can even perceive them, which is rare. That's easy to show. It's also understandable. The observations are correct and subversive of power and privilege—hence, hysteria.

In general, the reactions of an honest person to the end of the cold war will be more complex than just pleasure over the collapse of a brutal tyranny, and prevailing reactions are suffused with extreme hypocrisy, in my opinion.

Capitalism

RBR: In many ways the left today finds itself back at its original starting point in the last century. Like then, it now faces a form of capitalism that is in the ascendancy. There would seem to be greater consensus today, more than at any other time in history, that capitalism is the only valid form of economic organization possible, this despite the fact that wealth inequality is widening. Against this backdrop, one could argue that the left is unsure of how to go forward. How do you look at the current period? Is it a question of back to basics? Should the effort now be toward bringing out the libertarian tradition in socialism and toward stressing democratic ideas?

Chomsky: This is mostly propaganda, in my opinion. What is called capitalism is basically a system of corporate mercantilism, with huge and largely unaccountable private tyrannies exercising vast control over the economy, political systems, and social and cultural life, operating in close cooperation with powerful states that intervene massively in the domestic economy and international society. That is dramatically true of the United States, contrary to much illusion. The rich and privileged are no more willing to face market discipline than they have been in the past, though they consider it just fine for the general population. Merely to cite a few illustrations, the Reagan administration, which reveled in free-market rhetoric, also boasted to the business community that it was the most protectionist in postwar U.S. history—actually more than all others combined. Newt Gingrich, who leads the current crusade, represents a superrich district that receives more federal subsidies than any other suburban region in the country, outside of the federal system itself. The conservatives who are calling for an end to school lunches for hungry children are also demanding an increase in the budget for the Pentagon, which was established in the late 1940s in its current form because—as the business press was kind enough to tell us—high-tech industry cannot survive in a "pure, competitive, unsubsidized, 'free enterprise' economy," and the government must be its "savior." Without the savior, Gingrich's constituents would be poor working people (if they were lucky). There would be no computers, electronics generally, aviation industry, metallurgy, automation, etc., etc., right down the list. Anarchists, of all people, should not be taken in by these traditional frauds.

More than ever, libertarian socialist ideas are relevant, and the population is very much open to them. Despite a huge mass of corporate propaganda, outside of educated circles, people still maintain pretty much their traditional attitudes. In the U.S., for example, more than 80 percent of the population regard the economic system as "inherently unfair" and the political system as a fraud, which serves the "special interests," not "the people." Overwhelming majorities think working people have too little voice in public affairs (the same is true in England), that the government has the responsibility of assisting people in need, that spending for education and health should take precedence over budget cutting and tax cuts, that the current Republican proposals that are sailing through Congress benefit the rich and harm the general population, and so on. Intellectuals may tell a different story, but it's not all that difficult to find out the facts.

RBR: To a point anarchist ideas have been vindicated by the collapse of the Soviet Union—the predictions of Bakunin have proven to be correct. Do you think that anarchists should take heart from this general development and from the perceptiveness of Bakunin's analysis? Should anarchists look to the period ahead with greater confidence in their ideas and history?

Chomsky: I think—at least hope—that the answer is implicit in the above. I think the current era has ominous portent and signs of great hope. Which result ensues depends on what we make of the opportunities.

Name Index

Index of Corporations, Organizations, Agencies, and Other Groups

Subject Index

Trade union consciousness, 441
Trades, 154
Trademark, 156, 162, 163, 166, 340
 in cyberspace, 157
 dilution, 153
 infringement, 153
 rights, 152
 on Web page, 153
Transactions
 illegal, 5
 territorially based, 164
Transborder Data Flow (TDF), 149
Transparency of nodes, 68
Transportability, 334
Trials, 257
Tribal world, 355
Tribalism, 361
Tri-racial isolate communities, 421,
 425
True names, 70

UnControlled, 434
Underclass, 375, 376, 395
Underground Railway, 422
Undermanagement, 442
Unemployment, 391
Uniform Resource Locator (URL),
 174
Union of egoists, 409
Unionization, 360
Unions, 232
United States Constitution, 2, 87
 Commerce Clause of, 222
United States Customs, 150
United States foreign policy, 435
United States judiciary, 39
United States military, 370
United States Supreme Court, 165
Untraceability of electronic payments,
 89
Uprising, 403–405, 408
Urban infrastructure, 231
URL. *See* Uniform Resource Locator
Use of force, on citizens, 147
Use tax, 226

Usenet news, 44, 71
 discussion groups, 151
 newsgroups, 152, 169
 no centralized location, 151
Utopia(s), 16–23, 397, 420, 431
 community based, 21
 digital, 364
 as fantasy, 377
 hippie, 50
 LambdaMOO as, 285
 More's, 351, 352
 New Left, 368
 New Right, 368
 as party, 23
 pirate, 22, 401, 420, 421, 427
 as possibility, 286
 retro-, 368
 rural, 52
 short-lived, 21
 standards of, 425
 visions of, 20, 364

V-chip, 31
Vaporware, 396
Verb abuse, 261
Verbal abuse, 310, 312
Verification, 62
Vetting, 253, 254, 270
 of research activities, 309
Video conferencing, 44
Vietnam, 365
Vigilante action, 334
Violence, 405, 436
Virtual Class, 19, 50, 366–369, 372,
 373, 375–377, 380
Virtual communities. *See* Community,
 virtual
Virtual environment, plasticity of,
 268
Virtual Magistrate, 16
Virtual play space, LambdaMOO as,
 247–248
Virtual rape, 283, 308, 310
Virtual rapists, 263
Virtual reality (VR), 396, 397, 412